British Genealogical Books in Print

Stuart A. Raymond

Published by the
Federation of Family History Societies (Publications) Ltd.,
2-4 Killer Street, Ramsbottom, Bury
Lancashire BL0 9BZ

Copies also obtainable from:
S.A. & M.J.Raymond, P.O.Box 35, Exeter, EX1 3YZ, U.K.
E mail: stuart@samjraymond.softnet.co.uk
http://www.soft.net.uk/samjraymond/igb.htm

Copyright © S. A. Raymond

First published 1999

ISBN: 1-86006-095-1

ISSN: 1033-2065

Printed and bound at The Alden Press, Oxford and Northampton

Contents

Introduction	4
1. Commercial and Private Publishers	7
2. Societies	51
3. Libraries and Record Offices	100
Subject Index	119
Family Name Index	139
Author Index	141
Place Name Index	150

Introduction

The genealogist today is faced with a bewildering array of publications which may be of use in tracing family trees. These include basic introductory guides, guides to specific sources such as the census, transcripts of original sources such as parish registers, completed family histories, *etc., etc.* Genealogical books are published by a wide range of organizations: commercial and private publishers, libraries, record offices, institutions, societies, *etc.*. Keeping track of what is currently available is not easy, especially since many current titles are not listed in the bibliographic tools used by booksellers, such as *Books in Print.*

This book is an attempt to remedy this situation, and to list all titles likely to be of interest to the British genealogist which are currently in print. Guides to sources, transcripts and indexes of sources, and family histories, are all included. In general, local histories have been excluded; however, there is a great deal in this volume which will be of interest to the local historian. It was originally intended to list microfiche and microfilm in this volume; however, such are their numbers that they will be the subject of another volume, *British Genealogical Microfiche.* A few CD-Roms that have come to my notice have been listed here, but there are probably many more to be identified. Geographically, the listing is confined to books published anywhere in the world relating to England, Scotland and Wales; Ireland is excluded. The publications of member societies of the Federation of Family History Societies have been excluded, since they are fully listed already in:

PERKINS, JOHN. *Current publications from member societies.* 9th ed. Federation of Family History Societies, 1997.

Scottish family history societies are not F.F.H.S. members, so their publications have been listed here.

The inclusion of a publishers' listing in this volume does not indicate that everything published by that publisher is included. Many record societies, in particular, publish material of interest to local historians which does not fit the criteria for inclusion here.

Arrangement of this listing is by publisher; however, there are also extensive indexes of authors, surnames, placenames, and subjects. The latter in particular provides the means to identify the titles being sought.

This volume has been compiled by means of a questionnaire sent to publishers — and therefore suffers from the faults of inconsistency common to such volumes. My ideal has been to provide accurate bibliographic citations; however, publishers have not always provided sufficent detail to enable me to do so. Titles have not always been properly cited; pagination and ISBN's are frequently missing, and some relevant books have not been reported by their publishers. Consequently, complete accuracy cannot be guaranteed. In some cases I have been able to check details from other sources; however, this has not been possible in many other cases. A few publishers have not responded to inquiries, and I am aware of a number of titles that I have not been able to include due to lack of sufficient information. The prices quoted are as reported by publishers; where possible I have also indicated the cost of postage within or to the U.K. Genealogists should be aware that the prices quoted are liable to change, and that neither I nor the Federation of Family History Societies are to be held responsible for such changes.

This volume may be kept up to date by reference to the new book listings in journals such as *Family tree magazine, Family history news and digest*, and the *Genealogists' Magazine,* backruns of which were consulted to identify relevant publishers. Many publishers now have web sites; addresses of these have been given where known, and may also be checked for new titles. An invaluable site is provided at: http://www.hmc.gov.uk/socs/list.htm This site lists the publications of numerous record societies issued since 1982. It is worth noting that many record society publications are also available on microfiche; see my *British Genealogical Microfiche* for details.

Books listed here may be obtained from a variety of sources. The publications of commercial publishers may in general be obtained from any High Street bookseller. Most family history societies maintain bookstalls relevant to their particular interests. A wider range of genealogical books are stocked by the Society of Genealogists, the Federation of Family History Societies, and Family Tree Magazine. There are also a handful of specialist genealogical booksellers — including the present author — whose expertise in locating books may be drawn upon. And, of course, it may be easiest to purchase direct from the publisher. When ordering, please mention that you identified books in *British Genealogical Books in Print.*

This book has been typed by Mark Gant, Mary Raymond, Paul Raymond, and Cynthia Hanson; my thanks to them, and to Bob Boyd, who has seen it through the press.

Stuart Raymond

PART 1

Commercial and Private Publishers

Mrs J.S. Ackers
Thimble Hall, Snowhill, Scorton, Preston, Lancashire, PR3 1AY

ACKERS, J.S.,& ACKERS, C. *Surname index: return of Papists, 1767, Diocese of Chester.* £2.00 (inc. p&p).

ACKERS, J.S., & ACKERS, C. *Surname index: Bishop Leyburn's confirmation register, 1687.* £2.50 (inc. p&p).

ACKERS, J.S., & ACKERS, C. *Index of people mentioned in 17th and 18th century wills of Lancashire Roman Catholics.* Looseleaf. £5.00 (inc. p&p). Price will increase as the index expands.

Alba Publishing
20, Dounhill Court, Jedburgh, Roxburghshire, TD8 6LJ.
Phone (01835) 863455.

MCLEISH, PETER. *Hamilton Academical Who's Who.* 1-899468-80-3. 1997. £7.99.

MCLEISH, NORRIE. *Ancestral voices: story of the McLeish name.* 1-87370801-7. 1991. £18.50.

Colin E. Allen
128 Bush Road, Cuxton, Rochester, ME2 1HA

ALLEN, COLIN E., ed. *A transcript with index of the 1821 Militia Ballot list for the parish of St. Margaret, Rochester, Kent.* 1995. £2.20.

Allen & Todd
9 Square Street, Ramsbottom, Bury, BLO 9JD

TODD, ANDREW. *Nuts and bolts: family history problem solving through family reconstitution techniques.* 0-948781-14-9. 1998. £3.00.

TODD, ANDREW. *Shadows of ancestors.* 1996. £2.50 + p&p (on surname study).

Ancestral Publications
P.O. Box 463, Yarra Glen, Vic., 3775, Australia

LESLIE, IAN. *Family threads: recollections and research.* 1875961054. 1995. Leslie, Walter and Vining families of England, Scotland, Australia.

Ancestry, Inc.
P.O. Box 476, Salt Lake City, UT., 84110-0476, U.S.A.

IRVINE, SHERRY. *Your English ancestry: a guide for North Americans.* 244pp. Rev. ed. 0-916489-53-1. $US17.95.

IRVINE, SHERRY. *Your Scottish ancestry: a guide for North Americans.* 253pp. 0-916489-65-5. $US17.95.

Arden Enterprises
Ashton Lodge, Church Road, Lyminge, Folkestone, CT18 8JA
Phone: (01303) 862368

HYDE, PATRICIA, & HARINGTON, DUNCAN. *Faversham Hundred records vol. 2. Hearth tax returns for Faversham Hundred 1662-1674, with supporting documents.* 0-9530998-0-6. £25.00 + p&p £2.50.

Australia's Immigration and Family History Centre
P.O. Box 937, Harvey Bay, Queensland 4655, Australia
email: jreakes@aia.net.au
http://www.peg.apc.org/nfrasertravel/hervey/family/family.htm

REAKES, JANET. *Census and musters: Australia and the British Isles.* 0-9590093-8-8. $A13.00.

REAKES, JANET. *How to use the IGI and wills.* 1-875314-12-4. $A14.00.

REAKES, JANET. *How to use the parish registers: Australia and the British Isles.* 0-875314-05-9. $A16.00.

REAKES, JANET. *How to trace your English ancestors (inc. Wales).* 08606-281-2. $A18.00.

Avero Publications Ltd.
20 Great North Road, Newcastle on Tyne, NE2 4PS

Biography database 1680-1830. CD-Rom. £75.00 + VAT.

Clive Ayton
P.O. Box 19, West P.D.O., Nottingham, NG8 5JE

AYTON, CLIVE. *1871 London census surname index.*
Regents Park, St. Pancras, Part 1. RG10/199-203. £4.95.
Haggerstone West, Shoreditch. RG10/461-467. £4.95.
Green, Bethnal Green, part 1. RG10/481-485. £4.95.
Green, Bethnal Green, Part 2. RG10/486-490. £4.95.
St. James, Bermondsey, Part 1. RG10/633-636. Forthcoming.

Wendy Baker
103 Rattray Road, Montmorency, Vic., 3094, Australia

BAKER, WENDY. *The international genealogical index on CD-Rom: an introduction.* 0-9586624-1-X. 1996.

Barrie & Jenkins
20 Vauxhall Bridge Road, London, SW1V 2SA

LOOMES, BRIAN. *The concise guide to tracing your ancestors.* 192pp. 0-7126-9877-9. 1993. £9.99.

B.T. Batsford
583 Fulham Road, London, SW6 5BY

FRIAR, STEPHEN. *Batsford companion to local history.* 432pp. 0-7134-6181-0. £14.99.
EDWARDS, PETER. *Rural life: guide to local records.* 176pp. 0-7134-67886. £15.99.

Peter Bell
68 West Port, Edinburgh, EH1 2LD
Phone: (0131)5562198

BELL, PETER. *Victorian biography: a checklist of contemporary biographies of British men and women dying between 1851 and 1901.* 200pp. 1-871538-11-4. 1993. £20.00 + p&p.
Ministers of the Church of Scotland from 1560 to 1929: an index to Fasti Ecclesiæ Scoticanæ. First draft. Volume 1: A-D. c.166pp. 1-871538-25-4. 1997. £30.00 + p&p.

A. & C. Black (Publishers) Ltd.
35 Bedford Row, London, WC1R 4JH
Phone: (0171) 2420946
email: enquiries@acblack.co.uk

FITZHUGH, TERRICK, V.H. *The dictionary of genealogy,* rev. Susan Lumas. 5th ed. 0-7136-4859-7. 1998.

Mrs Susan Bourne
26 Brookside Road, Istead Rise, Northfleet, Kent. DA13 9JJ

BOURNE, SUSAN. *Early census returns for Kent, 1801-1831.* 1996. £5.00 (inc. p&p).
BOURNE, SUSAN. *Indexes for the Kent family historian.* 4th ed. 1-89789617-4. 1997. £1.50 (inc. p&p).
BOURNE, SUSAN. *Indexes for the Suffolk family historian.* 2nd ed. 1997. Forthcoming.
BOURNE, SUSAN. *Six Kent repositories.* 2nd ed. 1997. £3.00.

Robert Boyd Publications
260 Colwell Drive, Witney, Oxfordshire, OX8 7LW

POLS, ROBERT. *Understanding old photographs.* 86pp. 1-899536-01-9. 1995. £4.95.

Boydell & Brewer
P.O. Box 9, Woodbridge, Suffolk, IP12 3DF
Phone: (01394) 411320

BRAULT, GEORGE J. *Rolls of arms of Edward I, 1272-1307.* 2 vols. 1104pp. 0-85115-669-X. £150.00 / $US270.00.
BRAULT, GEORGE J. *Early blazon: heraldic terminology in the twelfth and thirteenth centuries with special reference to Arthurian heraldry.* 321pp. 0-85115-711-4. £45.00 / $US71.00.
BULLOCK-DAVIES, CONSTANCE. *Register of royal and baronial domestic minstrels, 1272-1327.* 243pp. 0-85115-431-X. 1986. £40.00.
KEATS-ROHAN, K.S.B. *Domesday people.* A register of persons occurring in English documents 1066-1166, 1. c.352pp. 0-85115-722-X. 1998 (forthcoming). £50.00 / $US90.00.
KEATS-ROHAN, K.S.B., & THORNTON, DAVID E. *Domesday names: an index of Latin personal and place names in Domesday Book.* 544pp. 0-85115-429-8. £60.00 / $US108.00.

OESTMAN, CORD. *Lordship and community: the L'Estrange family in Hunstanton in the first half of the sixteenth century.* 301pp. 0-85115-3518. 1994. £35.00.

RANSFORD, ROSALIND, ed. *The early charters of the Augustinian canons of Waltham Abbey, Essex, 1062-1230.* 0-85115-516-2. 1989. £55.00.

Titles published on behalf of the Suffolk Records Society and the Lincolnshire Record Society are listed under those societies, below, part 2.

Mrs. Joan Browning
5, Vernon's Close, Henham, Bishop's Stortford, Herts., CM22 6AE

BROWNING, DOUGLAS, et al, eds. *Oakham marriages 1754-1837; and the Rutland militia rolls 1779-1783.* 1979. £3.00 (inc. p&p).

C.H.B. Cole
Upcott Barton, Poughill, Crediton, Devon. EX17 4LF

COLE, CHARLES. *The Cole family of Ashreigney.* 4 vols. 1997. £77.00.

Brewin Books
Doric House, 56 Alcester Road, Studley, Warwickshire, B80 7LG
Phone: (01527) 854228

AUSTIN, JOHN D. *Merevale church and abbey: the stained glass, monuments and history of the church of Our Lady and Merevale Abbey.* 160pp. 1-85858114-1 (pb); 1-85858-115-X(hb). 1998. £11.95 (pb); £35.00 (hb).

FREEMAN, GWENDOLEN. *United family record: some late Victorians.* 0-947731-57-1. £6.95. Freeman family history.

HUMPHRIES, VANADIA. *Men of great renown.* 184pp. 1-85858-092-7. 1997. £16.95. Passey family of Benson, Oxfordshire, 19-20th c.

MIMMS, PETER. *Only for life: a labouring family from Civil War to Second World War.* 1-85858-065-X. £19.95. Mimms family history.

PERRY, TONY. *The Fowler legacy.* 64pp. 1-85858-094-3. 1997. £5.95. Of Wolverhampton, 19-20th c.

PRICE, VICTOR J. *Tracing your family tree.* 0-947731-50-4. £2.95.

PRICE, VICTOR J. *Register offices of births, deaths, marriages in England, Scotland, Wales and Ireland.* 1-85858-021-8. £2.95.

WHITE, ALAN. *A Worcestershire dynasty: Dixons of Tardebigge. The history of a North Worcestershire family farming and business empire.* 96pp. 185858-110-9. 1997. £8.95.

British Agencies for Adoption and Fostering
Skyline House, 200 Union Street, London, SE1 OLX

STAFFORD, G. *Where to find adoption records, a guide for counsellors.* 124pp. 1-873868-09-X. 1993. £12.00.

Bucks Publications
Varneys, Rudds Lane, Haddenham, Bucks., HP17 8JP
email: eve@varneys.demon.co.uk

KIDD, R., & MCLAUGHLIN, EVE, ed. *Princes Risborough Baptist Chapel births 1797-1837; members list 1797-1840's.* £3.50 + p&p 35p.

MCLAUGHLIN, EVE. *Bucks insurance directory 1715-30.* £4.00 + p&p 45p.

MCLAUGHLIN, EVE, ed. *Marlow marriages 1787-94.* £2.50 + p&p 35p.

MCLAUGHLIN, EVE, ed. *Marlow residents 1851.* £3.00 + p&p 35p.

MCLAUGHLIN, EVE, ed. *Princes Risborough 1821 + 1831.* £3.00 + p&p 35p.

MCLAUGHLIN, EVE, ed. *Swanbourne chapel registers to 1837.* £2.00 + p&p 30p.

MCLAUGHLIN, EVE. *Tracing your Bucks ancestors.* £3.00 + p&p 50p.

MCLAUGHLIN, EVE, ed. *Wycombe chairmakers, 1798, 1851.* £3.00 + p&p 35p. Covers High Wycombe and West Wycombe.

QUICK, BARBARA, & QUICK, KEVIN, eds. *Bledlow charity books.* 6 vols.
1. *1720-1830.* £3.25.
2. *1831-35.* £3.75.
3. *1780-1830.* £3.25.
4. *Beneficiaries 1800-16.* £3.25.
5. *1815-36.* £3.00.
6. *1824-29.* £3.50.
6A. *Bledlow school accounts 1826-31.* £1.50 + p&p 30p.

QUICK, PETER. *War memorials series.*
1. *Newport Hundred.* £4.00 + p&p 45p.
2. *Cottesloe Hundred.* £3.50 + p&p 45p.
3. *Aylesbury Hundred (pt).* £4.00 + p&p 45p.
4. *North Central.* £4.00 + p&p 45p.
5. *West Central.* £4.00 + p&p 45p.
6. *Milton Keynes area.* £3.50 + p&p 45p.
7. *Buckingham Hundred.* £3.50 + p&p 45p.
8. *Aylesbury town and pt. hundred.* £3.50 + p&p 45p.
9. *Princes Risborough; Missendens area.* £3.50 + p&p 45p.
10. *Amersham, Chesham area.* £3.50 + p&p 45p.
11. *Wycombe area.* £4.00 + p&p 45p.
12. *Marlow, Beaconsfield, Chalfonts.* £3.50 + p&p 45p.

QUICK, K. *Map of Bucks.* A4. 75p. A3. £1.50 + p&p 30p.

TYRWHITT-DRAKE, BARNEY. *Universal directory for Bucks., 1796.* £4.50 + p&p 50p.

Amersham area war memorials: Amersham, Chalfonts, Chenies, Chesham, Latimer. £3.50 + p&p 35p.

Amersham. Napoleon v. Amersham: list of men 1798 from posse comitatus. £1.50 + p&p 30p

Aylesbury Hundred war memorials. £3.00 + p&p 40p.

Aylesbury town war memorials. £3.50 + p&p 40p.

Aylesbury census 1851. £10.50 + p&p £1.00.

Aylesbury v. Napoleon. 1798, all men 16-60. £2.00 + p&p 30p.

Beaconsfield census 1851. £4.50 + p&p 45p.

Buckingham settlement papers. £4.00 + p&p 45p.

Bucks insurance directory 1775-84. £4.50 + p&p 45p.

Bucks convicts. £5.50 + p&p 50p. Lists persons transported to Australia.

Bucks gazetteer. £2.00 + p&p 35p.

Chalfont St. Peter settlement papers. £3.00 + p&p 30p.

Chalfonts v. Napoleon 1798: all men, 16-60. £1.80 + p&p 30p.

Great Hampden census 1851. £1.50 + p&p 30p.

Haddenham census 1851. £5.00 + p&p 30p.

Horwoods, Whaddon, Shenley v. Napoleon, 1798. £2.00 + p&p 30p.

Iver settlement papers. £3.00 + p&p 30p.

Marlow Independent Chapel, C., B. 1777-1906; M. 1864-1906. £2.50 + p&p 35p.

Marlow Independent Chapel: C., B. 1777-1906; M. 1864-1906. £2.50 + p&p 35p.

Milton Keynes area war memorials. £4.00 + p&p 40p.

Missenden area war memorials. £4.00 + p&p 40p.

Missendens v. Napoleon 1798. £1.80 + p&p 30p.

Newport Pagnell settlement papers. £3.00 + p&p 35p.

Posse comitatus for Buckinghamshire 1798. 5 computer disks. £17.00.

Princes Risborough 1851 census. £3.00.

Quainton settlement papers Say & Sele apprenticeship charity. £3.25 + p+p 35p.

Stoke Poges settlement papers. £3.00 + p&p 35p.

Stony Stratford settlement papers. £3.50 + p&p 35p.

Thornborough in George I's time. M. 1654-1725; pewholders 1720; voters 1722. £2.00 + p&p 35p.

Whaddon village map c1800. £3.00 + p&p 45p. Occupiers named; also includes 1798 listing.

Workhouse census 1841. £3.50 + p&p 50p. Covers all Buckinghamshire workhouses.

D.M. Burch
4 Tynedale Close, Oadby, Leicestershire, LE2 4TS

BURCH, DOROTHY. *Hurlocks of London, 17th to 20th centuries.* 86p. 0-9525641-0-6. 1995. £6.50 (inc. p&p).

Cambridge University Press
Publishing Division, The Edinburgh Building, Cambridge, CB2 2RU.
Email: information@cup.cam.ac.uk.
Phone: (01223) 312393

The history of Parliament on CD-ROM. 0-521-62907-1. 1998. £425.00 + VAT. (until 31.3.1999)

FINNEGAN, RUTH, ed. *From family tree to family history.* 208pp. Studying family and community history **1**. 0-521-46001-8(hb); 0-521-46577-X(pb). 1994. £35.00(hb); £12.95(pb).

PRYCE, W.T.R. *From family history to community history.* 256pp. Studying family and community history **2**. 0-521-46578-8(pb); 0-521-46002-6(hb). 1994. £12.95(pb); £35.00(hb).

GOLBY, J. *Communities and families.* Studying family and community history 3.. 256pp. 0-521-46003-4(hb); 0521-46579-6(pb). 1994. £35.00(hb); £12.95(pb).

FINNEGAN, RUTH, DRAKE, MICHAEL, & EUSTACE, JACQUELINE. *Sources and methods for family and community historians: a handbook.* 2nd ed. 336pp. Studying family and community history **4**. 0521-59992-X. 1997. £12.95.

Campden Record Series
c/o Miss R. J. Wilson, Hart Croft, 14, Pear Tree Close, Chipping Campden, Gloucestershire, GL55 6DB.

BISHOP, LEIGHTON, ed. *The general accounts of the churchwardens of Chipping Campden, 1626-1907.* 864pp. 0-9518745-1-9. 1992. £20.00 (inc. p&p).

CART Publications
66c, Fortress Road, Kentish Town, London, NW5 2HG
Cheques to C.E. Allen.

Anglesey & Caernarfonshire contiguous parishes. 1-901824-49-7. Forthcoming. £1.00 + p&p 30p.
Bedfordshire contiguous parishes. 1-901824-09-8. £1.00 + p&p 30p.
Berkshire contiguous parishes. 1-901824-00-4. £1.00 + p&p 30p.
Brecon & Radnorshire contiguous parishes. 1-901824-44-6. Forthcoming. £1.00 + p&p 30p.
Buckinghamshire contiguous parishes. 1-901824-01-2. £1.00 + p&p 30p.
Cardigan & Pembrokeshire contiguous parishes. 1-901824-46-2. Forthcoming. £1.00 + p&p 30p.
Carmarthen & Glamorgan contiguous parishes. 1-901824-47-x. Forthcoming. £1.00 + p&p 30p.
Cheshire contiguous parishes. 1-901824-14-4. £1.00 + p&p 30p.
Cornwall contiguous parishes. 1-901824-10-1. £1.00 + p&p 30p.
Cumberland contiguous parishes. 1-901824-17-9. £1.00 + p&p 30p.
Derbyshire contiguous parishes. 1-901824-38-1. Forthcoming. £1.00 + p&p 30p.
Devon contiguous parishes. 1-901824-29-2. £1.00 + p&p 30p.
Dorset contiguous parishes. 1-901824-30-6. £1.00 + p&p 30p.
Durham contiguous parishes. 1-901824-27-6. £1.00 + p&p 30p.
Essex contiguous parishes. 1-901824-07-1. £1.00 + p&p 30p.
Flint & Denbighshire contiguous parishes. 1-901824-48-9. £1.00 + p&p 30p.
Gloucestershire contiguous parishes. 1-901824-32-2. Forthcoming. £1.00 + p&p 30p.
Hampshire contiguous parishes. 1-901824-13-6. £1.00 + p&p 30p.
Herefordshire contiguous parishes. 1-901824-37-3. Forthcoming. £1.00 + p&p 30p.
Hertfordshire contiguous parishes. 1-901824-19-5. £1.00 + p&p 30p.
Huntingdonshire contiguous parishes. 1-901824-21-7. £1.00 + p&p 30p.
Kent contiguous parishes. 1-901824-02-X. £1.00 + p&p 30p.
Lancashire contiguous parishes. 1-901824-22-5. £1.00 + p&p 30p.
Leicestershire contiguous parishes. 1-901824-34-9. Forthcoming. £1.00 + p&p 30p.
Lincolnshire contiguous parishes. 1-901824-41-1. Forthcoming. £2.00.
Merioneth & Montgomeryshire contiguous parishes. 1-901824-45-4. Forthcoming. £1.00 + p&p 30p.
Monmouthshire contiguous parishes. 1-901824-36-5. £1.00 + p&p 30p.
Norfolk contiguous parishes. 1-901824-20-9. Forthcoming. £2.00.
Northamptonshire contiguous parishes. 1-901824-43-8. Forthcoming. £1.00 + p&p 30p.
Northumberland contiguous parishes. 1-901824-16-x. £1.00 + p&p 30p.
Nottinghamshire contiguous parishes. 1-901824-23-3. £1.00 + p&p 30p.
Oxfordshire contiguous parishes. 1-901824 15 2. £1.00 + p&p 30p.
Shropshire contiguous parishes. 1-901824-40-3. Forthcoming. £1.00 + p&p 30p.
Somerset contiguous parishes. 1-901824-28-4. Forthcoming. £1.00 + p&p 30p.
Staffordshire contiguous parishes. 1-901824-35-7. Forthcoming. £1.00 + p&p 30p.
Suffolk contiguous parishes. 1-901824-31-4. Forthcoming. £2.00.

Surrey contiguous parishes. 1-901824-04-7. £1.00 + p&p 30p.
Sussex contiguous parishes. 1-901824-12-8. £1.00 + p&p 30p.
Warwickshire contiguous parishes. 1-901824-33-x. Forthcoming. £1.00 + p&p 30p.
Westmorland contiguous parishes. 1-901824-18-7. £1.00 + p&p 30p.
Wiltshire contiguous parishes. 1-901824-24-1. £1.00 + p&p 30p.
Worcestershire contiguous parishes. 1-901824-26-8. £1.00 + p&p 30p.
East Riding contiguous parishes. 1-901824-03-9. £1.00 + p&p 30p.
North Riding contiguous parishes. 1-901824-05-5. £1.00 + p&p 30p.
West Riding contiguous parishes. 1-901824-06-3. £1.00 + p&p 30p.

Casmic Services
56 Stoneleigh Road, Solihull B91 1DQ
Phone: (0121) 6821818
PAIN, JOHN G. *1861 census surname index and address index for ...*
RG9/497. *Hurton, Nettlestead, Teston, West Farleigh & Yalding.* 1997. £2.75.
RG9/498. *Barming, Linton, Maidstone Union Workhouse, Marden and Staplehurst.* 1997. £2.75.
RG9/499. *Bearstead, Boughton Monchelsea, East Farleigh, Loose & Otham.* £2.75.
RG9/500 and RG9/501 combined. *Maidstone (part).* Forthcoming.
RG9/502 and RG9/503 combined. *Maidstone (part).* Forthcoming.
RG9/505. *Boughton Malherbe, Harrietsham, Lenham, Otterden and Wychling.* Forthcoming.
RG9/506. *Broomfield, Chart Sutton, East Sutton, Headcorn, Langley, Leeds, Sutton Valence and Ulcomb.* Forthcoming.
RG9/511. *Charing, Egerton, Little Chart, Pluckley, Smarden & Westwell.* £2.50.
RG9/512. *Ashford.* £2.50.
RG9/513. *Bethersden, Great Chart, Hothfield, Kingsnorth & Shadoxhurst.* £2.00.
RG9/514. *Aldington, Bilsington, Bonnington, Hurst, Orlestone, Ruckinge, & Warehorne.* £2.50.
RG9/515. *Bircholt, Brabourne, Hinxhill, Mersham, Sevington, Smeeth, & Willesborough.* £2.50.
RG9/516. *Boughton Aluph, Brook, Challock, Chilham, Crundale, Eastwell, Godmersham, Hastingleigh, Kennington, Molash, Wye.* £2.75.
PAIN, JOHN G. *1861 census: Kent foreigners.* Forthcoming.
PAIN, JOHN G. *Parish Records: Kennington, Kent, 1761-1850.* £5.00. Baptisms, marriages and burials.
PAIN, JOHN G. *Parish records: Kingsnorth, Kent: baptisms 1737-1850; marriages 1755-1850; and burials, 1772-1850.* £4.00.

Centre for Metropolitan History
Institute of Historical Research, Senate House, Malet Street, London, WC1E 7HU
Phone: (0171) 6360272, ext. 240.
CARLIN, MARTHA, ed. *London and Southwark inventories, 1316-1650: a handlist of extents for debts.* xxvii, 103pp. 1-871348-41-2. 1997. £6.99.
GALLOWAY, JAMES A., & MURPHY, MARGARET, & MYHILL, OLWEN. *Kentish demesne accounts: a catalogue (with a summary of accounts 1350-1500).* xi, 55pp. 1-871348-17-X. 1993. £5.50.

Centre of East Anglian Studies
University of East Anglia, Norwich, NR4 7TJ
TAYLOR, BARRY. *Bibliography of Norfolk history, 1974-1988.* 215pp. 0906219-30-2. 1991. £12.00.
WILSON, J.H. *Wymondham inventories, 1591-1641.* iv, 46pp. 1983. £2.25.
SMITH, A HASSELL, & BAKER, C.M., eds. *Papers of Nathaniel Bacon of Stiffkey.* 3 vols. 1979-90.
v.1. 0-906219-04-3. £15.00.
v.2. 0-906219-16-7. £18.00.
v.3. 0-906219-27-2. £18.00.

Barbara J. Chambers
39 Chatterton, Letchworth Garden City, Hertfordshire, SG6 2JY
CHAMBERS, BARBARA J. *Do I have any army ancestors?* 0-9528045-3-0. 1998. £1.90 (inc. p&p)
CHAMBERS, BARBARA J. *1st Foot Guards (from 1815 1st or Grenadier Foot Guards) 1803 to 1823.* 2 vols. 0-9528045-2-2(v.1) 0-9528045-1-4(v.2). 1997. v.1. £12.00. v.2. £13.30 (prices include p&p).

CHAMBERS, BARBARA J. *Regimental service returns for 1806: PRO WO25/8711120.* 3 vols. Fiche or booklet. 1998- .
v.1 *1st & 3rd & 4th battallions 1st (Royal) Regiment of Foot.* 1998. £4.00.
v.2 *1st batallion 2nd (Queens) Regiment of Foot; 1st and 2nd batallions 3rd (Buffs) Regiment of Foot; 1st & 2nd batallions 4th (Kings) Regiment of Foot.* 1998. £3.00.
v.3. *1st & 2nd Life Guards; Royal Horse Guards; 1st, 2nd & 3rd Dragoon Guards.* Forthcoming.

Jill Chambers
4 Quills, Letchworth, Hertfordshire, SG6 2RG
Email: jchambers@sprynet.co.uk

CHAMBERS, JILL. *The story of the 1830 Swing riots.* 300pp. 1995. £11.00. Includes biographical information on men transported to New South Wales.
CHAMBERS, JILL. *Wiltshire machine breakers.* 2 vols. 1993. v.1. The riots and trials. 329pp. £10.00. v.2. The rioters. 271pp. 1993. £8.50. The set £16.00
CHAMBERS, JILL. *Hampshire machine breakers.* 2nd ed. 521pp. 1996. £16.50.
CHAMBERS, JILL. *Buckinghamshire machine breakers.* 2nd ed. 338pp. £12.00.
CHAMBERS, JILL. *Criminal petitions index.* Pt.1. HO17/40-49. 80pp. 1997. £3.40. Also available on fiche. Pt.2. HO17/50-59. Forthcoming.
Machine breakers news. 3 issues p.a. Subcription £3.00.

Clearfield Company
200 East Eager Street, Baltimore, Maryland 21202, U.S.A.

ADAM, FRANK. *The clans, septs and regiments of the Scottish Highlands.* 8th ed. 624pp. Reprint 1998 (originally published 1970). $US45.00.
BARBER, HENRY. *British family names: their origin and meaning.* 286pp. Reprint 1997 (originally published 1903). $US25.00.
BARING-GOULD, SABINE. *Family names and their story.* 432pp. Reprint 1996 (originally published 1910). $US32.50.
BRIDGER, CHARLES. *An index to printed pedigrees and arms contained in county and local histories, the Heralds' visitations, and in the more important genealogical collections.* 384pp. Reprint 1997 (originally published 1867). $US35.00.
BURKE, ARTHUR M. *Key to the ancient parish registers of England and Wales.* 163pp. Reprint 1996 (originally published 1908) $US18.00.
BURKE, JOHN. *A genealogical and heraldic history of the commoners of Great Britain and Ireland.* 4 vols. 3,133pp. Reprint 1988 (originally published 1834-8 & 1907). $US200.00.
CAMERON, VIOLA R. *Emigrants from Scotland to America, 1774-1775.* 117pp. Reprint 1990 (originally published 1930). $US15.00.
CHILD, HEATHER. *Heraldic design: a handbook for students.* 180pp. Reprint 1998 (originally published 1966). $US22.50.
COLDHAM, PETER WILSON. *English adventurers and emigrants, 1609-1660: abstracts of examinations in the High Court of Admiralty with reference to colonial America.* 219pp. Reprint 1981 (originally published 1984). $US22.50.
COLDHAM, PETER WILSON. *English estates of American colonists: American wills and administrations in the Prerogative Court of Canterbury, 1700-1799.* 151pp. Reprint 1991 (originally published 1980). $US15.00.
CROZIER, WILLIAM ARMSTRONG. *Crozier's general armory.* 2nd ed. 155pp. Reprint 1996 (originally published 1904). $US17.00.
DOBSON, DAVID. *American data from the 'Aberdeen Journal', 1748-1783.* 102pp. 0-8063-4766-X. 1988. $US14.00.
DOBSON, DAVID. *Scottish maritime records.* 32pp. 0-8063-4717-1. 1996. $US8.50.
DOBSON, DAVID. *Scottish Quakers and early America 1650-1700.* 52pp. 08063-4765-1. 1998. $US10.95.
DOBSON, DAVID. *Jacobites of Angus, 1689-1746.* 0-8063-4716-3. 49pp. 1997. $US10.00.
DOBSON, DAVID. *Scottish soldiers in colonial America.* 2 vols in 1. 63pp. 0-8063-4718-X. 1997. $US11.00.
EWEN, CECIL HENRY L'ESTRANGE. *A history of surnames of the British Isles: a concise account of their origin, evolution, etymology and legal status.* 539pp. Reprint 1995 (originally published 1931). $US41.50.
FOSTER, JOSEPH. *Some feudal coats of arms from heraldic rolls, 1298-1418.* 296pp. Reprint 1994 (originally published 1902). $US26.00.

GRAHAM, IAN CHARLES CARGILL. *Colonists from Scotland: emigration from Scotland to North America 1707-1783.* 213pp. Reprint 1997 (originally published 1956). $US23.00.

GRANT, FRANCIS J., SIR. *The manual of heraldry: a concise description of the several terms used, and containing a dictionary of every designation in the sciences.* 142pp. Reprint 1997 (originally published 1914). $US16.50.

HARGREAVES-MAWDESLEY, R. *Bristol and America: a record of the first settlers in the colonies of North America, 1654-1685.* 198pp. Reprint 1997 (originally published 1929-31) $US20.00.

HARRISON, HENRY. *Surnames of the United Kingdom: a concise etymological dictionary.* 2 vols. in 1. 622pp. Reprinted 1996 (originally published 1912-18). $US45.00.

HITCHING, FRANK, K., & HITCHING, S. *References to English surnames in 1601 and 1602.* 2 vols in 1. 70 + 95pp. Reprint 1998 (originally published 1910-1911). Index to names in printed parish registers.

JOHNSTONE, C.L. *The historical families of Dumfriesshire and the border wars.* 213pp. Reprint 1998 (originally published 1889) $US24.00.

LART, CHARLES EDMUND. *Huguenot pedigrees.* 2 vols. in 1. 258pp. Reprint 1997 (originally published 1924-5). $US27.50.

MCDONNELL, FRANCIS. *Jacobites of 1715 and 1745: North East Scotland.* 2 vols in 1. 96pp. 1996. $US12.50.

MACLEAN, JOHN P. *An historical account of the settlements of Scotch Highlanders in America prior to the peace of 1783.* 455pp. Reprint 1997 (originally published 1900). $US36.50.

MARSHALL, GEORGE W. *The genealogists guide.* 4th ed. 880pp. Reprint 1998 (originally published 1903). $US65.00. Bibliography of English pedigrees. Authoritative.

MARTIN, CHARLES TRICE. *The record interpreter: a collection of abbreviations, Latin words and names used in English historical manuscripts and records.* 2nd ed. 464pp. Reprint 1997 (originally published 1910). $US35.00.

MILLETT, STEPHEN M. *The Scottish settlers of America: the 17th and 18th centuries.* 234pp. 1992-5. $US25.00. Historical study.

NICHOLSON, GREGOE D.P. *Some early emigrants to America [and] Early emigrants to America from Liverpool.* 110p. Reprint 1996 (originally published 1965). $US12.50.

ROBERTS, T.R. *Eminent Welshmen: a short biographical dictionary of Welshmen who have obtained distinction from the earliest times to the present.* 613pp. Reprint 1995 (originally published 1908). $US45.00.

ROUND, J. HORACE. *Studies in peerage and family history.* 496pp. Reprint. 1996 (originally published 1901) $US39.95.

SHAW, WILLIAM A. *The knights of England: a complete record from the earliest time to the present day of the knights of all the orders of chivalry in England, Scotland and Ireland.* 2 vols. 1,316pp. Reprint 1995 (originally published 1906). US95.00.

SIMS, RICHARD. *An index to the pedigrees and arms contained in the Heralds' visitations and other genealogical manuscripts in the British Museum.* 330pp. Reprint 1997 (originally published 1867) $US31.50.

WATERS, HENRY F. *Genealogical gleanings in England: abstracts of wills relating to early American families.* 2 vols. 1,811pp. 0-8063-0371-9. Reprint 1997 (originally published 1901). $US115.00.

WHYTE, DONALD. *A dictionary of Scottish emigrants to the U.S.A.* Vol. 1. 517pp. Originally published 1972. Reprint forthcoming.

C.H.B. Cole

Upcott Barton, Poughill, Crediton, Devon, EX17 4LF

COLE, CHARLES. *The Cole family of Ashreigney, Devonshire.* 4 vols. 2,200pp. 1997. £78.00.

COLE, CHARLES. *The Cole families of North Molton, Coleridge, Bishop's Nympton and South Molton.* 300pp. 1997. £25.00.

COLE, CHARLES, ed. *Ashreigney parish registers, Devonshire, 1607-1981.* 1981. Price by arrangement.

COLE, CHARLES. *The Wright family of Haweside, Southport, Lancashire.* 53pp. 1998. £12.00.

COLE, CHARLES. *The Moor family of Burnley and Southport, Lancashire.* 46pp. 1998. £11.00.

COLE, CHARLES. *The Woolway family of Burrington, Devonshire.* 169pp. 1996. £20.00.
COLE, CHARLES. *The Brockell family of the North Riding, Yorkshire.* 46pp. 1998. £11.00.
COLE, CHARLES. *The Clapp family of the Tiverton area, Devonshire.* 112pp. 1996. £17.00.
COLE, CHARLES. *The Spedding family of Batley and Dewsbury, West Yorkshire.* 177pp. 1998. £20.00.
COLE, CHARLES. *The Dore family of Charlbury and Hailey, Oxfordshire.* 70pp. 1997. £14.00.
COLE, CHARLES. *The Tooms family of Market Harborough, Leics.* 41pp. 1994. £5.00.
COLE, CHARLES. *Sandford St. Martin, Oxfordshire: land tax, 1760-1831.* 26pp. 1994. £5.00.
COLE, CHARLES. *The history of Sandford St. Martin, Oxfordshire.* 452pp. 1996. £27.50. Traces occupants of every house.

Computing for Genealogists
3 Hollywood Road, Bolton, Lancashire, BL1 6HL
Phone: (01204) 847080
E-mail: JOE.HOUGHTON@ZEN.CO.UK

HOUGHTON, JOE. *Computers & the family historian: making more of Brothers Keeper for Windows.* 3rd. ed. 1998. £5.00 + 70p s.a.e. (A4 size).
HOUGHTON, JOE. *Computers & the family historian: genealogy on the Internet.* 4th ed. 1998. £5.00 + 70p s.a.e. (A4 size).
HOUGHTON, JOE. *Computers & the family historian: getting started: a guide for the terrified.* 3rd ed. 1997. £4.00 + 70p s.a.e. (A4 size).

Countryside Books
2 Highfield Avenue, Newbury, Berks., RG14 5DS Phone: (01635) 43816

BRECKON, BILL, & PARKER, JEFFREY. *Tracing the history of houses.* 192pp. 1-85306-128-X. £7.95 + p&p 75p.
COLE, JEAN, & TITFORD, JOHN. *Tracing your family tree.* 224pp. New ed. 1-85306-448-3. 1997. £9.95 + p&p 75p.
GANDY, MICHAEL. *Short cuts in family history.* 96pp. 1-85306-316-9. £7.95 + p&p 75p. Also published by the Federation of Family History Societies.

MCLAUGHLIN, EVE. *First steps in family history.* 112pp. 4th ed. 1-85306548-X. 1998. £7.95 + p&p 75p.
MCLAUGHLIN, EVE. *Further steps in family history.* 176pp. 1995. 1-85306062-3. £8.95 + p&p 75p.
SAUL, PAULINE. *Tracing your ancestors: the A-Z guide.* 288pp. 6th ed. 1-85306-379-7. £9.95 + p&p 75p.
PELLING, GEORGE. *Beginning your family history.* New ed. 96p. 1-85306383-5. 1998. £7.95 + p&p 75p. Also published by the Federation of Family History Societies.
POLS, ROBERT. *Dating old photographs.* 96pp. 1-85306-231-6. £7.95 + p&p 75p. Also published by the Federation of Family History Societies.
TITFORD, JOHN. *Writing and publishing your family history.* 128pp. 185306-384-3. 1996. £7.95 + p&p 75p. Also published by the Federation of Family History Societies.

M.L.K. Curtis
The Stock House, Berkeley, Gloucestershire, GL13 9BY

CURTIS, M.L.K. *Arlingham: index of marriages in the nineteenth century.* 0-9520185-9-4. 1996.
CURTIS, M.L.K. *Arlingham: index of baptisms in the nineteenth century.* 0-9528015-0-7. 1996.
CURTIS, M.L.K. *Arlingham: index of burials in the nineteenth century.* 0-9528015-1-5. 1996.

Dartmoor Press
P.O. Box 132, Plymouth PL4 7YL

BROWN, MIKE. *Guide to churchwardens' accounts.* 64pp. £3.00.
BROWN, MIKE. *Guide to nineteenth century vestry minutes from rural parishes.* 39pp. £2.50.
BROWN, MIKE. *Handy guide to acts and statutes.* 30pp. £2.35.
BROWN, MIKE. *An introduction to tracing your house history from manorial records.* 39pp. 1998. £2.50.
BROWN, MIKE. *Manorial records for genealogists.* 20pp. 1998. £1.75.
BROWN, MIKE. *Understanding three life leases & other post-medieval deeds - a practical guide for family historians.* 68pp. 1998. £3.50.

BROWN, MIKE. *Buckland in the Moor registers & BTs transcripts.* Rev. ed. 1998.

BROWN, MIKE. *Dartmoor region MI indexes.* 23 vols.
1. *Horrabridge Chapel, Horrabridge, Sampford.* 1998. £2.25.
2. *Meavy, Hooe, Meavy Chapel, Bickleigh.* 1998. £2.25.
3. *Buckland Monachorum.* 1998.
4. *Walkhampton.* 1998. £2.25.
5. *Whitchurch Pt.1. A-K* 1998. £2.25.
6. *Whitchurch Pt.2. L-Z* 1998. £2.25.
7. *Sheepstor, Princetown, Postbridge.* 1998. £2.25.
8. *Lydford, Brentor.* 1998. £2.25.
9. *Mary Tavy, Zoar Down Chapel.* 1998. £2.25.
10. *Peter Tavy.* 1998. £2.25.
11. *Shaugh Prior.* 1998. £2.25.
12. *Cornwood Pt.1; A-H.* 1998. £2.25.
13. *Cornwood Pt.2; I-R.* 1998. £2.25.
14. *Cornwood Pt.3; S-Z, Ivybridge.* 1998. £2.25.
15. *Harford, Dean Prior.* 1998. £2.25.
16. *South Brent.* 1998. £2.25.
17. *Ugborough.* 1998. £2.25.
18. *Buckfastleigh, Holne, Scoritton Chapel.* 1998. £2.25.
19. *Widecombe, Leusdon, Buckland.* 1998. £2.25.
20. *Lustleigh, Manaton, North Bovey, Ilsington Chapel.* 1998. £2.25.
21. *Ilsington.* 1998. £2.25.
22. *Moretonhampstead, Cross Street Chapel, Gidleigh, Chagford.* 1998. £2.25.
23. *Providence, Throwleigh, South Tawton, Drewsteignton, Belstone.* 1998. £2.25.

BROWN, MIKE. *Essential mini-guide to Dartmoor region MI's, surname distributions & parish registers.* 28pp. £1.00.

BROWN, MIKE. *Guide notes to monuments in Devon churches & graveyards.*
1. *Buckland Monachorum.* 1998.
2. *Dunsford, Moretonhampstead.* 1998. £1.50.
3. *Plympton St. Mary, Plympton St. Maurice.* 1998. £1.50.
4. *Tavistock (St. Eustacious).* 1998. £1.50.
6. *St. Budeaux, Plymouth St. Andrews.* 1998. £1.50.
12. *Kelly, Lamerton.* 1998. £1.50.
13. *Beer Ferrers, Sydenham Damerel.* 1998. £1.50.
14. *Widecombe, Buckland in the Moor.* 1998. £1.50.

BROWN, MIKE. *Heraldic & genealogical notes from Dartmoor churches.* 4 vols.
1. *Bickleigh, Buckland Monachorum, Meavy, Walkhampton, Sampford.* 1997. £3.00.
2. *Gidleigh, Lustleigh, Manaton, North Bovey.* 1997. £3.00.
3. *Buckland in the Moor, Leusdon, Sheepstor, Widecombe.* 1998. £3.50.
4. *Ugborough, Harford, Ivybridge, Shaugh Prior.* 1998. £4.00.

BROWN, MIKE. *Full transcripts of all personal war memorials in the Dartmoor region.* 1998. £3.00.

BROWN, MIKE. *A short collection of epitaphs from selected Dartmoor graves.* 1997. £1.00.

BROWN, MIKE. *A short collection of epitaphs from selected West Devon graveyards.* 1997. £1.00.

BROWN, MIKE. *A short collection of epitaphs from Stoke Damerel & other Plymouth churches.* 1997. £1.00.

BROWN, MIKE. *Notes on some Dartmoor wills.* 1997. £2.50.

BROWN, MIKE. *Dartmoor region tithe apportionments indexes.*
1. *Lydford, Mary Tavy, Peter Tavy, Whitchurch.* 16pp. 1996. £1.50.
2. *Sampford, Walkhampton, Sheepstor, Meavy, Shaugh Prior.* 16pp. 1996. £1.50.
3. *Cornwood, Harford, Ugborough, South Brent, Dean Prior.* 16pp. 1996. £1.50.
4. *Ashburton, Buckland in the Moor.* 16pp. 1996. £1.50.
5. *Buckfastleigh, Holne, Widecombe, Ilsington, Manaton.* 16pp. 1996. £1.50.
6. *Lustleigh, North Bovey, Chagford, Moretonhampstead, Gidleigh.* 16pp. 1996. £1.50.
7. *Throwleigh, Drewsteignton, South Tawton, Belstone, Sourton.* 16pp. 1996. £1.50.
8. *A-Z Dartmoor wide property namelist.* 1998. £1.50.

BROWN, MIKE. *Buckland in the Moor who's who 1600-1900 vol. 1. Smerdon.* 1996. £4.50.

BROWN, MIKE. *Buckland in the Moor who's who 1600-1900 vol.2. Burnell, Hext, Leaman, Lear, Mann.* 1997. £3.00.

BROWN, MIKE. *Buckland in the Moor who's who, 1600-1900, vol.3. Andrews, Bennet, Baker, Chrispin, Ellis, Fisher, Hamlyn, Mead, Norrish, Parsons, Tapper, Windeat, Woodleigh.* 1997. £4.50.

BROWN, MIKE. *Buckland in the Moor property owners & occupiers 1600-1900.* 1997. £1.80.

BROWN, MIKE. *Buckland in the Moor returns of occupiers 1600-1900.* 1998. £4.00. Transcripts of selected tax rolls, rate lists, census, manor rentals & surveys etc.

BROWN, MIKE. *A guide to the heraldry at Kitley House.* 40pp. £2.50.

BROWN, MIKE. *Devon manor surveys. Vol.1. Maristow, 1765.* 24pp. £2.00.

BROWN, MIKE. *Sheepstor property owners and occupiers 1718-1914.* 1998. £4.50.

BROWN, MIKE. *Walkhampton Survey ... Extracts from Walkhampton registers.* 2 vols. 1998.
  1. *Baptisms 1676-1837.* 1998. £1.50.
  2. *Marriages and burials 1676-1837.* 1998. £1.50.

BROWN, MIKE. *Walkhampton survey vol. 7. Churchwardens' accounts, parish apprentices.* 1998. £1.50. Includes full list of parish apprentices 1740-1838.

BROWN, MIKE. *Towards a fuller pedigree of the Bastards of Kitley.* 1998. £4.50.

BROWN, MIKE. *Pedigree of the Bourchier Wreys of Tawstock.* Forthcoming.

BROWN, MIKE. *The Pollexfen pedigree re-examined.* 32pp. £2.35.

BROWN, MIKE. *Smerdon vol.2: register transcripts from Buckland, Ashburton, Widecombe, Ilsington; 81 census entries from Dartmoor parishes.* 1997. £3.50.

BROWN, MIKE. *Smerdon vol.3: register transcripts from Dartmoor parishes, Dartmoor-wide MI list.* 1997. £1.80. Registers not covered in vol. 2.

BROWN, MIKE. *The Toops, monumental masons of Western Dartmoor.* 1998. £4.50.

Devon & Cornwall notes & queries
c/o N. Annett, 3 Johnson Drive, Broomhill, Devon

GRAY, TODD, ed. *Devon documents.* 228pp. 0-95283-620-3. 1996. £9.50.

Devon Books
Halsgrove House, Lower Moor Way, Tiverton, EX16 6SS
Phone: (01884) 243242

MAXTED, IAN. *In pursuit of Devon's history.* 120pp. 0-86114-917-3. 1997. £6.95.

Diamond Publishing Group
45 St. Mary's Road, Ealing, London, W5 5RG
Family history monthly. £25.00 per annum.

Ms. J. Dobb
17 MacRobertson Street, Mawson, A.C.T., 2607, Australia

DOBB, JAN. *The Brumbys from Lincolnshire.* 120pp. 0-646-27108-3. 1996. $A10.00 + p&p.

David Dobson
8, Lawhead Road West, St. Andrews, Fife, Scotland, KY16 9NE
Phone: (01334) 476544
Email: ddobson@zetnet.co.uk
http://www.users.zetnet.co.uk/dobson/genealogy/

DOBSON, DAVID. *Scots-Irish links [Pt.1].* 1-899686-95-9. £3.50.

DOBSON, DAVID. *Scots-Irish links [Pt.2].* 1-880686-16-9. £3.00.

DOBSON, DAVID. *Fife burgess rolls [Pt.1].* 1-889686-90-8. £3.00.

DOBSON, DAVID. *Fife burgess rolls [Pt.2].* 1-889686-07-X. £3.50.

DOBSON, DAVID. *St. Andrews burgess rolls [Pt.1].* 1-899686-85-1. £3.50.

DOBSON, DAVID. *St. Andrews burgess rolls [Pt.2].* 1-899686-21-5. £3.00.

DOBSON, DAVID. *Scots schoolmasters, c17.* 1-899686-26-6. £3.50.

DOBSON, DAVID. *Scots soldiers in colonial America [Pt.1].* 1-889686-140. £3.00.

DOBSON, DAVID. *Scots soldiers in colonial America [Pt.2].* £3.00.

DOBSON, DAVID. *Scots soldiers in colonial America [Pt.3].* £3.00

DOBSON, DAVID. *Scots soldiers in continental Europe. [Pt.1.]* £3.00

DOBSON, DAVID. *Scottish soldiers, 1600-1800 [Pt.1].* £4.00.

DOBSON, DAVID. *Jacobites of Angus 1689-1746 [Pt.1].* £3.00.

DOBSON, DAVID. *Jacobites of Angus 1689-1746 [Pt.2].* £3.00.

DOBSON, DAVID. *Scottish goldsmiths 1600-1800.* £4.50.

Scottish mariners series
Aberdeen 1600-1700. 1-899686-15-0. £3.00.
Aberdeen 1700-1800 [Pt.1] 1-899686-20-7. £3.00.
Aberdeen 1700-1800 [Pt.2] £3.00.
Angus 1600-1700. 1-899686-05-3. £3.50.
Angus 1700-1800 [Pt.1]. 1-899686-10-X. £3.00.
Angus 1700-1800 [Pt.2].
The Clyde, 1600-1700. 1-899686-50-9. £3.00.
The Clyde, 1700-1800. 1-899686-55-X. £3.50.
Fife 1700-1800. 1-899686-35-5. £3.00.
Kirkcaldy 1600-1700. 1-899686-30-4. £3.50.
Lothians 1600-1700 [Pt.1]. 1-899686-40-4. £3.00.
Lothians 1600-1700 [Pt.2]. 1-899686-45-2. £2.50.
Lothians 1700-1800. 1-899686-31-2. £3.00.
St. Andrews, 1600-1700. 1-899686-25-8. £2.50.
Scots whalers pre 1800 [Pt.1]. 1-899686-36-3. £3.00.
Dundee whalers, 1750-1850 [Pt.2] 1-899686-56-8. £3.00.
Scottish maritime records. 1-899686-86-X. £2.50.
Scottish seafarers, 1800-1830. £3.00.

Scottish emigrants series
Aberdeen / North-East [Pt.1]. 1-899668-60-6. £3.50.
Aberdeen / North-East [Pt.2]. 1-899668-65-7. £3.00.
Argyll / N. Highlands. 1-899668-70-3. £3.00.
Fife. 1-899668-75-4. £3.00.
Glasgow / West. 1-899668-80-0. £3.00.
Lothian. 1-899668-41-X. £3.00.
Orkney and Shetland. 1-899686-76-2. £2.50.
Southern Scotland. 1-899686-01-0. £3.00.
Moray & Banff. 1-899686-61-4. £3.00.
Angus & Perth. 1-899686-81-9. £2.50.
Scots in Canada & U.S.A. 1825-1900. £5.00.
Scots in the West Indies. £4.50.
Scots in Australasia [Pt.1]. 1-899686-00-2. £4.50.
Scots in Australasia [Pt.2]. 1-899686-91-6. £4.00.
Scots in Australasia [Pt.3]. 1-899686-22-3. £4.50.

Mary Dudley-Higham
c/o Genesis Publications, 5272 Williams Road, Suison, CA., 94585, U.S.A.
DUDLEY-HIGHAM, MARY. *The Bellamys and Cornish cousins of North Cornwall, England.* 200pp. 0-9662010-0-0. 1994. $US29.95 ($40.00 overseas). Originally of Penhallym, Jacobstow.

Paul Duncan
1 Langham Gardens, Wilson, W.A. 6107, Australia
DUNCAN, PAUL. *In service: the story of the Duncan family of Woodbury in Devon, with some distaff-sides and Australian off-shoots.* 0-6462683-1-7. 1995. $A15.95 + p&p (airmail) $A3.00.

Andrew Dunsire
2 College Road, Copmanthorpe, York, YO2 3US
DUNSIRE, ANDREW. *The Dunsire families of Fife 1660-1875: a surname history.* viii, 149pp. 0-9531443-0-5. 1997. £5.00 + 70p p&p. Published by Fife Family History Society.

EPB Marketing
Dep. T., 15 Pentlands, Fuller Slade, Milton Keynes, MK11 2AF
CHADWICK, R.M. *The key to your ancestors.* 0-9523584-1-7. 1995. £5.45 (inc. p&p).

Marie de G. Eedle
5 Champions Gardens, Beaminster, Dorset, DT8 3AL
EEDLE, MARIE D.G. *The Daniels and Knowle.* 0-9512205-1-9. 1993. £2.50.
EEDLE, MARIE D.G. *The Hines of Beaminster.* 0-9512205-3-5. 1995. £2.50.
EEDLE, MARIE D.G. *Horn Hill tunnel.* 0-9512205-2-7. 1994. £2.00. Includes list of subscribers to building a tunnel, 1832.

Egon Publishers
Royston Road, Baldock, Herts., SG7 6NW
CRELLIN, VIVIAN. *Baldock's middle ages, as recorded in the surviving parish records.* 0-905858-97-2. 1995. £15.95. Many documents.
CRELLIN, VIVIAN. *A market town in Tudor times: from the parish records of Baldock.* 0-899998-09-8. Many facsimiles.

Elliot Right Way Books
Kingswood Buildings, Brighton Road, Lower Kingswood, Tadworth, Surrey, KT20 6TD
Phone (01737) 832202
CATLETT, ESTELLE. *Track down your ancestors: draw up your family tree.* Rev. ed. 0-7160-2082-3. 1997. £3.99 + p&p 50p.

Everton Publishers Inc.
P.O. Box 368, Logan, UT., 84323-0368, U.S.A.
SMITH, FRANK. *Immigrants to America appearing in English records.* $US11.50.
PREECE, PHYLLIS PASTORE, & PREECE, FLOREN STOCKS. *Handy guide to English genealogical research.* $US7.50.
SMITH, FRANK. *A genealogical gazetteer of Scotland.* $US14.00.

Fairmount Press
10 Kincarrathie Crescent, Perth, PH2 7HH
DUNCAN, JEREMY. *Tracing your royal ancestors: a guide for those of Scottish or English descent.* 0-947749-0-4. £4.95.

Family History Library
Salt Lake City Distribution Center, 1999 West 1700 South, Salt Lake City, UT., 84104-4233, U.S.A.
Available in the U.K. from: 399 Garretts Green Lane, Garretts Green, nr. Birmingham, B33 0UH
Research outline: England. 75 cents.
1851 British census. CD-Rom. $US5.00. For Devon, Norfolk and Warwick counties only.
Various free leaflets are also available.

Family Tree Magazine
61 Great Whyte, Ramsey, Huntingdon, Cambridgeshire, PE17 1HL
Phone: (01487) 814050
Family tree magazine. 12 issues. £22.00 p.a.
Practical family tree. 6 issues. £10.00 p.a.
COLE, JEAN, & CHURCH, ROSEMARY. *In and around record repositories in Great Britain and Ireland.* 4th ed. 1998. £5.95.

Pam Fisher
9 Slatebrook Close, Groby, Leicester, LE6 0EE
East Midlands ancestor. ISSN 1363-2760. Quarterly. £7.50 per annum.
FISHER, PAM. *Finding East Midlands ancestors.* 1998. £6.50 + p&p £1.10. Covers Derbyshire, Leicestershire, Lincolnshire, Northamptonshire, Nottinghamshire and Rutland.

Miss P. Franklin
Flat 21, Chiswick House, Bell Barn Road, Edgbaston, Birmingham, B15 2AA
FRANKLIN, PAULINE. *The L'Oste family of Lincolnshire.* 186pp. 0-9525917-0-7. 1994. £5.00 + £1.50 p&p.

Frontier Press
P.O. Box 3715, Suite 3, Galveston, TX., 77552, U.S.A.
e-mail: kgfrontier@aol.com
ERIKSON, CHARLOTTE. *Leaving England: essays on British emigration in the nineteenth century.* 1994. $US39.95. Studies on ships passenger lists.

Gale
P.O. Box 45, Reading RG1 8HF
Phone: (0118) 9577218
Email: sales@psmedia.co.uk
Biography and genealogy master index 1998. 1222pp. 0-7876-0110-1. 1997. £257.00. Also available on CD-Rom (0-7876-0251-5; £433.00). Indexes 450,000 biographical articles. Previous editions and cumulations also available.
Abridged biography and genealogy master index. 2nd ed. 3 vols., 4,511pp. 0-8103-6878-1. £331.00.
Passenger and immigration lists index. 1998 supplement.
Pt.1. 577pp. 0-7676-1203-0. 1997. £173.00.
Pt.2. 575pp. 0-7876-1879-9. 1998. £173.00.
Previous cumulations and supplements also available.
Author biographies master index. 5th ed. 2 vols. 1,813pp. 0-7876-2143-9. 1997. £207.00.
Concise dictionary of British literary biography. 8 vols. 3911pp. 0-81037980-5. £383.00.

Harry Galloway Publishers and Booksellers
Orders: The Cottage, Manor Terrace, Paignton, Devon, TQ3 3RQ
Email: bernard__welchman__ familyhistorian@compuserve.com
Correspondence: "Staverton", 19 Kirke Grove, Taunton, Somerset, TA2 8SB
Phone: (01823) 282267
This publisher also has many reprints etc. on microfiche; see *British Genealogical Microfiche.*
DWELLY, E., ed. *XVII century directory of Somerset.* 324pp. 1-873931-263. Originally published 1932. £25.00 + p&p. £1.00. Subsidy returns.
DWELLY, E., ed. *Exchequer depositions by commission 1565-1610 for Somerset.* 40pp. 1-873931-04-2. 1992. £3.00 + p&p. £1.00.

HAWKINGS, DAVID T., ed. *Index to Somerset Estate Duty Office wills and letters of administration, 1805-1811.* 98pp. 1-873931-50-6. £12.50 + p&p. £1.00.

HAWKINGS, DAVID T., ed. *Index to Somerset Estate Duty Office wills, 1812-1857.* 322pp. 1-873931-51-4. 1995. £25.00 + p&p. £1.00. An index to 13,005 wills.

HOLWORTHY, R., ed. *Hearth tax for Somerset.* 248pp. 1-873931-37-9. Originally published 1916. £25.00 + p&p. £1.00.

KNOX, GEORGE, ed. *Surname index for the 1891 census of North Somerset.* 8 vols. £35.00 + p&p. £1.00.
v.1. *Axbridge, Cheddar, Compton Bishop, Loxton & Christon, Nyland Cum Batcombe, Rowberrow, Shipham, Winscombe and Sidcot School.* 56pp. 1-873931-31-x. £4.00 + p&p. £1.00.
v.2. *Blagdon, Burrington, Butcombe, Charterhouse, Churchill, Congresbury, Hewish, Puxton and Wrington.* 52pp. 1-873931-30-1. £4.00 + p&p. £1.00.
v.3. *Berrow, Bleadon, Brean, East Brent, Brent Knoll, Burnham, Highbridge, Lympsham and 13 ships.* 73pp. 1-873931-33-6. £4.00 + p&p. £1.00.
v.4-5. *Banwell, Hutton, Kewstoke, Locking, Uphill, Weston-SuperMare, Wick St. Lawrence and Worle.* Pt.1. (surnames A-J). 102pp. 1-87393115-8. £5.00. Pt.2. (surnames K-Z). 99pp. 1-873931-16-6. £5.00 + p&p. £1.00.
v.6. *Dundry, Backwell, Barrow Gurney, Failand, Flax Bourton, Long Ashton, Long Ashton Workhouse, Ridgehill, Winford and Wraxall.* 66pp. 1-873931-32-8. £4.00 + p&p. £1.00.
v.7. *Abbots Leigh, Clapton in Gordano, Easton in Gordano, Portbury, Portishead and Walton in Gordano.* 71pp. 1-873931-34-4. £4.00 + p&p. £1.00.
v.8. *Brockley, Clevedon, Kenn, Kingston Seymour, Nailsea, Tickenham, Yatton.* 103pp. 1-873931-14-X. £5.00 + p&p. £1.00.

LILLY, DEREK B., & LILLY, JANE, ed. *St. Andrew's, Clevedon churchwardens' accounts 1730-1801.* 54pp. 1-873931-22-0. 1994. £5.00 + p&p. £1.00.

MEDLYCOTT, MERVYN, SIR. *Somerset wills index: printed and manuscript copies.* 191pp. 1-873931-17-4. 1993. £25.00 + p&p. £1.00.

MUNCKTON, T., ed. *Chancellors farm accounts 1766-1767.* 53pp. 1-873931-43-3. £4.50 + p&p. £1.00.

SOMERSET COUNTY LIBRARY SERVICE, & ALLEN, N.V. *Somerset and Exmoor gazetteer.* 210pp. 1-873931-70-X. 1996. £18.00 + £2.55 p&p.

SIRAUT, M. *Index to Kirby's quest for Somerset, volume III of the Somerset Record Society's publications, being the texts of Kirby's quest of 1284-5, the nomina villarum of 1316, the exchequer lay subsidy of 1327, the county rate for 1742 and the hundreds and parishes from the 1841 census.* 56pp. 1-873931-77-8. 1996. £7.50 + p&p £2.00.

STOATE, G. *Lord of the manor: an investigation into the ownership of Wootton Courtenay, 1066-1920.* 97pp. 1-873931-79-4. 1996. £10.95 + p&p. £1.00.

TAMBLIN, S. *Criminal register indexes 1805-1816, volume I: Somerset and Dorset.* 169pp. 1-873931-76-X. £17.95 + p&p. £1.00.

WEBB, A.J., & PARRISH, P., eds. *Wilton gaol description register 1806-1818.* 48pp. 1-873931-48-4. £4.95 + p&p. £1.00. Gives details of the surname, forename, date of committal, age, place of birth and last place of residence.

WEBB, A.J. *An index to Somerset settlement & removal cases in quarter sessions 1607-1700.* 82pp. 1-873931-44-1. £4.95 + p&p. £1.00.

WEBB, ADRIAN J., ed. *Eastern Battalion muster roll of the East Somerset regiment of volunteer infantry, 1805.* 24pp. 1-873931-05-0. 2nd ed. rev. 1992. £2.00 + p&p. £1.00.

WEBB, ADRIAN J, & SKEGGS, JAMES, eds. *The roll of the 1st and 2nd Battalions of the Somerset Militia, 1758.* 47pp. 1-873931-06-9. 1993. £4.00 + p&p. £1.00.

WEBB, ADRIAN J., ed. *The 1649 assessment of the Hundred of North Petherton & the Borough of Bridgwater.* 53pp. 1-873931-18-2. 1993. £4.00 + p&p. £1.00.

WEBB, ADRIAN J., ed. *Somerset jurors list, 1748.* 2nd ed. 77pp. 1-873931-45-X. 1994. £9.00 + p&p. £1.00.

WEBB, A., ed. *The 1601 & 1628 subsidies for South Somerset.* 53pp. 1-873931-20-4. 1993. £4.50 + p&p. £1.00.

WEBB, ADRIAN J., ed. *Exchequer special commissions of inquiry: Somerset & Dorset 1560-1846.* 44pp. 1-873931-25-5. 1993. £2.00 + p&p. £1.00.

WEBB, ADRIAN J., & PARRISH, PETER. *The Wilton gaol description register, 1818-1825.* 60pp. 1-873931-19-0. 1994. £5.00 + p&p. £1.00.

WEBB, ADRIAN J., & SKEGGS, JAMES, eds. *List of the officers of the Somerset local militia, 1808-1811.* 37pp. 1-873931-21-2. 1993. £3.00 + p&p. £1.00.

WEBB, ADRIAN J., ed. *Index of Somerset probate inventories.* 123pp. 1-873931-41-7. 1995. £12.50 + p&p. £1.00.

WEBB, A.J. *A surname index to parties mentioned in abstracts of Bath & Wells diocesan records: marriage licences & allegations 1583-1681.* 75pp. 1-873931-47-6. 1995. £9.00 + p&p. £1.00.

Parish Registers

Aisholt
HURLEY, MICHAEL C., ed. *All Saints, Aisholt parish register and bishops' transcripts baptisms and burials 1598-1949, marriages 1598-1958 and monumental inscriptions 1620-1995.* Somerset Parish Register Project 10. 1-873931-60-3. 1997. £9.95 + p&p. £1.00.

Carhampton
Carhampton parish registers and civil papers. v, 147pp. 1-873931-53-0. £14.00 + p&p. £1.00.

Charlinch
HURLEY, M.C., ed. *Charlinch parish registers.* 71pp. 1-873931-80-8. 1996. £9.00 + p&p. £1.00

Creech St. Michael
WEBB, A.J., ed. *Creech St. Michael parish registers and bishops' transcripts 1606-1837.* ix, 90pp. 1997. £9.95 + p&p. £1.00.

Cutcombe
STOATE, THOMAS LAITY, ed. *Cutcombe parish registers.* 86pp. Somerset parish register project 13. 1-86241-002-X. 1998. £8.95 + p&p. £1.00.

Enmore
HURLEY, MICHAEL C., ed.*St. Michael, Enmore parish register and bishops' transcripts: baptisms 1578-1948, burials 1578-1958 and marriages 1602-1948.* 1-873931-89-1. Somerset Parish Register Project 11. 1998. £11.95 + p&p. £1.00.

Exford
STOATE, THOMAS LAITY, ed. *Parish registers of Exford, Culbone and Oare.* 97pp. Somerset parish register project 14. 1-86241-003-8. 1998. £9.95 + p&p. £1.00.

Luccombe
Luccombe parish registers and poor rates & Stoke Pero parish registers. v, 85pp. 1-873931-55-7. £9.00 + p&p. £1.00.

Luxborough
STOATE, THOMAS LAITY, ed. *Luxborough parish registers and churchwardens accounts.* 80pp. 1-86241-004-6. Somerset parish register project 15. 1998. £7.95 + p&p. £1.00.

Oake
HAWKINGS, D.T., & WEBB, ADRIAN J., eds. *Oake parish registers and bishops' transcripts, 1594-1837.* 1-873931-49-2. Somerset Parish Register Project 9. 1997. £5.95 + £1.00.

Porlock
STOATE, THOMAS LAITY, ed. *Porlock parish registers.* 153pp. 1-86241-001-1. Somerset parish register project 11. 1998. £14.95 + p&p. £1.00.

Selworthy
Selworthy parish registers and civil papers. v, 158pp. 1-873931-52-2. £14.00 + p&p. £1.00.

Timberscombe
Timberscombe parish registers. v, 65pp. 1-873931-54-9. £9.00 + p&p. £1.00.

Treborough
STOATE, T.L., ed. *Treborough and Withycombe parish registers.* 82pp. 1-873931-74-3. 1996. £9.00 + p&p. £1.00.

Wooton Courtenay
Wootton Courtenay parish registers. v, 75pp. 1-873931-56-5. £9.00 + p&p. £1.00.

Michael Gandy
3, Church Crescent, Whetstone, London, N20 OJR

GANDY, MICHAEL. *Catholic family history: a bibliography of general sources.* 151pp. 0-9520535-8-6. 1996. £8.00 + p&p 80p.

GANDY, MICHAEL. *Catholic family history: a bibliography of local sources.* 125pp. 0-9520535-9-4. 1996. £8.00 + p&p 80p.

GANDY, MICHAEL. *Catholic family history: a bibliography for Scotland.* 0-9528879-1-6. 1996. £4.50 + p&p 60p.

GANDY, MICHAEL. *Catholic family history: a bibliography for Wales.* 0-9528879-0-8. 1996. £4.50 + p&p 60p.

GANDY, MICHAEL. *Catholic missions and registers. 1700-1880.* 6 vols. 1993. The set £30.00 + p&p £2.50.
- **v.1.** *London and the Home Counties.* £6.00 + p&p 70p.
- **v.2.** *The Midlands and East Anglia.* £6.00 + p&p 70p.
- **v.3.** *Wales and the West of England.* £6.00 + p&p 70p.
- **v.4.** *North East England.* £6.00 + p&p 70p.
- **v.5.** *North West England.* £6.00 + p&p 70p.
- **v.6.** *Scotland.* £6.00 + p&p 70p.

Catholic parishes in England, Wales and Scotland: an atlas. 1993. £2.00 + p&p 50p. Reprints maps from the *Catholic directory* of the 1950s.

KELLY, B.W. *Historical notes on English Catholic missions.* 1996. Reprint, originally published 1907. £7.00.

H. Garratt
Lower Batter Farm, South Crosland, Huddersfield, HD4 7BY

GARRATT, J.H., ed. *Eckington: the court rolls, vol. V. 1694-1804.* 0-9528130-0-9. 1997. £17.00.

Genealogical Publishing Company, Inc.
1001, North Calvert Street, Baltimore, Maryland 21202, USA

BANKS, CHARLES E. *The English ancestry and homes of the Pilgrim Fathers who came to Plymouth on the Mayflower in 1620, the Fortune in 1621, and the Anne and the Little James in 1623.* 187pp. Reprint 1997 (originally published 1920). $US18.50.

BANKS, CHARLES E. *The planters of the Commonwealth: a study of the emigrants and emigration in colonial times, to which are added lists of passengers to Boston and the Bay colony, the ships which brought them, their English homes, and the places of their settlement in Massachusetts, 1620-1640.* xiii, 231pp. Reprint 1977 (originally published 1930). $US20.00.

BANKS, CHARLES EDWARD. *Topographical dictionary of 2,285 English emigrants to New England 1620-1650.* 333pp. Reprint 1992 (originally published 1937). $US25.00.

BRANDOW, JAMES C. *Omitted chapters from Hotten's original lists of persons of quality ... and others who went from Great Britain to the American plantations, 1600-1700.* 245pp. 1983. $US20.00.

BURKE, JOHN BERNARD. *Burke's dormant and extinct peerages of the British Empire.* 642pp. Reprint 1996 (originally published 1883). $US40.00.

CAMP, ANTHONY J. *My ancestor came with the Conqueror: those who did, and some of those who probably did not.* 89pp. 1998. $US9.50. Published in the U.K. by the Society of Genealogists.

CHAPMAN, COLIN. *Pre-1841 censuses and population listings in the British Isles.* 4th ed. 82pp. 1996. $US15.00. Published in the U.K. by Lochin.

CHAPMAN, COLIN. *Tracing your British ancestors.* 108pp. 1996. $US15.00. Published in the U.K. by Lochin.

COLDHAM, PETER W. *American wills and administrations in the Prerogative Court of Canterbury, 1610-1857.* xii, 416pp. 1989. $US30.00.

COLDHAM, PETER WILSON. *American wills proved in London, 1611-1775.* 350pp. 1992. $US30.00.

COLDHAM, PETER W. *The Bristol registers of servants sent to foreign plantations, 1654-1686.* 491pp. 1988. $US30.00.

COLDHAM, PETER W. *Child apprentices in America from Christ's Hospital, London. 1617-1778.* 164pp. 1990. $US21.50.

COLDHAM, PETER W. *The complete book of emigrants 1607-1660.* 600pp. 1988. $US34.95.

COLDHAM, PETER W. *The complete book of emigrants in bondage, 1614-1775.* 920pp. 1988. $US60.00.

COLDHAM, PETER W. *Emigrants from England to the American colonies, 1773-1776.* 182pp. 1988. $US22.50.

COLDHAM, PETER W. *Emigrants in chains: a social history of forced emigration to the Americas of felons, destitute children, political and religious non-conformists, vagabonds, beggars and other undesirables, 1607-1776.* 188pp. 1994. $US21.95.

COLDHAM, PETER W. *Supplement to the complete book of emigrants in bondage, 1614-1775.* 60pp. 1992. $US9.00.

CORY, KATHLEEN B. *Tracing your Scottish ancestry.* 2nd ed. 228pp. 1998. $US16.95.

CRISPIN, M. JACKSON, & MACARY, LEONCE. *Falaise roll, recording prominent companions of William, Duke of Normandy, at the conquest of England.* 258pp. Reprint 1994 (originally published 1938-9.) $US30.00.

CROWDER, NORMAN K.A. *British army pensioners abroad 1772-1899.* 351pp. 1995. $US26.50.

DOBSON, DAVID. *Directory of Scottish settlers in North America, 1625-1825.* 7 vols. 1984-93. v.1. 267pp. 1984. $US20.00; v.2. 216pp. 1984. $US20.00; v.4. 161pp. 1985. $US17.50; v.6. 126pp. 1986. $US15.00. v.7. 121pp. 1993. $US17.50.

DOBSON, DAVID. *The original Scots colonists of early America, 1612-1783.* 370pp. 1995. $US28.50.

DOBSON, DAVID. *The original Scots colonists of early America. Supplement, 1607-1707.]* 211pp. 1998.

DOBSON, DAVID. *Scots in the Carolinas, 1680-1830.* 322pp. 1994. $US25.00.

DOBSON, DAVID. *Scots on the Chesapeake, 1607-1830.* 169pp. 1992. $US20.00. In Virginia and Maryland.

DOBSON, DAVID. *Scottish-American court records, 1733-1783.* 105pp. 1991. $US18.00.

DOBSON, DAVID. *Scottish-American heirs 1683-1883.* 165pp. 1990. $US21.50.

DOBSON, DAVID. *Scottish-American wills 1650-1900.* 134pp. 1991. $US20.00.

DOBSON, DAVID. *Ships from Scotland to America, 1628-1828.* 127pp. 1998. $US20.00.

FAIRBAIRN, JAMES. *Fairbairns book of crests of the families of Great Britain and Ireland.* 2 vols in 1. 1073pp. Reprint 1993 (originally published 1905). $US60.00.

FARIS, DAVID. *Plantagenet ancestry of seventeenth-century colonists.* 337pp. 1996. $US30.00.

FRENCH, ELIZABETH. *List of emigrants to America from Liverpool, 1697-1707.* Reprint 1983 (originally published 1913). $US5.00.

GIBSON, J.S.W. *A simplified guide to bishops transcripts and marriage licenses, their location and indexes in England, Wales and Ireland.* 3rd ed. 40pp. $US6.00. Published in U.K. by the Federation of Family History Societies.

GIBSON, J.S.W. *The hearth tax, other late Stuart tax lists, and the Association oath rolls.* 60pp. 1990. $US7.50. Published in the U.K. by the Federation of Family History Societies.

GIBSON, J.S.W. *Marriage, census and other indexes in Great Britain.* 4th ed. 1992. $US7.50. Published in the U.K. by the Federation of Family History Societies.

GIBSON, J.S.W. *Quarter sessions records in England and Wales.* 3rd ed. 47pp. 1992. $US6.50. Published in the U.K. by the Federation of Family History Societies.

GIBSON, J.S.W., & MEDLYCOTT, MERVYN. *Militia lists and musters 1757-1876: a directory of holdings in the British Isles.* 2nd ed. 42pp. 1990. $US6.50. Published in the U.K. by the Federation of Family History Societies.

GIBSON, J.S.W., & ROGERS, COLIN. *Electoral registers since 1832, and burgess rolls.* 2nd ed. 60pp. 1990. $US7.50. Published in the U.K. by the Federation of Family History Societies.

GIBSON, J.S.W., & ROGERS, COLIN. *Poll books c.1696-1872.* 2nd ed. 1990. Published in the U.K. by the Federation of Family History Societies.

HERBER, MARK D. *Ancestral trails: the complete guide to British genealogy and family history.* 688pp. 1998. $US34.95. Authoritative. Published in U.K. by Sutton Publishing.

HOFFMAN, MARIAN R. *Genealogical & local history books in print: general reference and world resources volume.* 5th ed. 375pp. 1997. $US25.00. Includes some U.K. publications.

HOWELLS, CYNDI. *Netting your ancestors: genealogical research on the Internet.* 182pp. 1998. $US19.95.

LEESON, FRANCIS L. *A directory of British peerages.* 174pp. 1986. $US12.50.

LEWIS, SAMUEL. *A topographical dictionary of England.* 4 vols in 2. Reprint 1996 (originally published 1831). $US150.00.

MOODY, DAVID. *Scottish family history.* 219pp. 1994. $US18.95.

MOODY, DAVID. *Scottish local history.* 178pp. 1994. $US18.95.

REID, JUDITH PROWSE. *Genealogical research in England's Public Record Office: a guide for North Americans.* 163pp. 1997. $US22.50.

ROWLANDS, JOHN, et al, eds. *Welsh family history.* 316pp. 1997. $US19.95. Published in the U.K. by the Association of Welsh Family History Societies.

ROWLANDS, JOHN, & ROWLANDS, SHEILA. *The surnames of Wales.* 229pp. 1996. $US19.95.

RUVIGNY & RAINEVAL, MARQUIS OF. *The blood royal of Britain (Tudor roll) and the Plantagenet roll of the blood royal.* 5 vols. 3550pp. Reprint 1994 (originally published 1903-11. The set $US235.00.

SMITH, FRANK. *Genealogical gazetteer of England: an alphabetical dictionary of places with their location, ecclesiastical jurisdiction, population, and the date of the earliest entry in the registers of every ancient parish in England.* 599pp. Reprint 1995 (originally published 1968). $US35.00.

STUART, MARGARET. *Scottish family history: a guide to works of reference on the history and genealogy of Scottish families.* 386pp. Reprint 1994 (originally published 1930). $US25.00.

STUART, RODERICK. *Royalty for commoners: the complete known lineage of John of Gaunt, son of Edward III, King of England.* 3rd ed. 342pp. 1998. $US35.00.

TAYLOR, JAMES. *The great historic families of Scotland.* 2nd ed. 2 vols in 1. 410 + 431pp. Reprint 1995 (originally published 1889). $US55.00.

TEPPER, MICHAEL. *New World immigrants: a consolidation of ship passenger lists and associated data from periodical literature.* 2 vols. 568, 602pp. 1988. $US60.00.

TEPPER, MICHAEL. *Passengers to America: a consolidation of ship passenger lists from the New England historical and genealogical register.* 554pp. 1988. $US25.00.

TURTON, W.H. *The Plantagenet ancestry, being tables showing over 7,000 of the ancestors of Elizabeth (daughter of Edward IV and wife of Henry VII), the heiress of the Plantagenets.* Reprint 1993 (originally published 1928). $US50.00.

Burke's American families with British ancestry: the lineages of 1,600 families of British origin now in the United States of America. Reprint 1996 (originally published 1939). $US47.50.

English origins of American colonists. 287pp. 1991. $US28.50. Reprint of articles from the *New York Genealogical and Biographical Record.*

The complete book of emigrants 1607-1776. CD-Rom. $US29.99.

English origins of New England families. CD-Rom. $US39.99.

Genealogical Research Directory

c/o Mrs. Elizabeth Simpson, 2 Stella Grove, Tollerton, Nottinghamshire, NG12 4EY

Genealogical Research Directory 1990. £4.00 + p&p £3.50.

Genealogical Research Directory 1991. £4.00 + p&p £3.50.

Genealogical Research Directory 1992. £4.00 + p&p £3.50.

Genealogical Research Directory 1993. £4.50 + p&p £3.50.

Genealogical Research Directory 1994. £9.50 + p&p £3.50.

Genealogical Research Directory 1995. £9.50 + p&p £3.50.

Genealogical Research Directory 1996. £9.50 + p&p £3.50.

Genealogical Research Directory 1997. £11.50 + p&p £3.50.

Genealogical Research Directory 1998. £14.50 + p&p £3.50.

Genealogical Research Directory 1990-1996 on CD-ROM. £22.95 + p&p £3.50.

Gleniel Press

Whittingehame Mains, Haddington, East Lothian, EH41 4QA

BRANDER, MICHAEL. *The clan Gleniel: cross me who dares!* 0-9525330-2-2. 1996. £14.99+ p&p £2.00.

Mr. David Gore

The Red House, Lower Basildon, Berkshire, RG8 9NG

GORE, DAVID. *A Cornish inheritance: the Harveys of Chasewater.* 0-9530912-0-1. 1997. £5.95 + p&p £1.30.

Greenway Publishing
199, Victoria Avenue, Borrowash, Derby DE72 3HG

JOHNSON, MARION. *Lords of the manor of Ockbrook: archives 1583 to 1605.* Ockbrook and Borrowash record series. 1-873064-06-3. 1994. £4.00.

JOHNSON, MARION. *Yeomen of Elizabethan Ockbrook: archives of the sixteenth century.* Ockbrook & Borrowash record series. 1-873064-05-5. 1994. £4.00.

Greenwood Press
3 Henrietta Street, London, WC2E 8LU

WILSON, EUNICE. *Dangerous sky: a resource guide to the Battle of Britain.* 0-313-28216-1. 1995. £58.50.

Bernard Griffiths
12 Linnets Road, Alresford, Hampshire, SO24 9LP

GRIFFITHS, BERNARD. *In search of my ancestors.* 0-9525606-0-7. 1995. £3.50. Family history of Griffiths, Stockman, Tellick (Tallick) and Smith, of Cornwall, Devon, Hampshire, Isle of Wight, Surrey and Sussex.

J.T. Grinter
8, Gillespie Street, Kyabram, Vic., 3620, Australia

GRINTER, J.T. *Charles Grinter of Somerset (1837-1903): his ancestors and descendants.* 0-646-35614-3. 1998.

Hambledon Press
102 Gloucester Avenue, London, NW1 8HX
Phone: (0171) 5860817
Email: hambledon@cityscape.co.uk

BARRON, CAROLINE M, & SUTTON, ANNE F., ed. *Medieval London widows, 1300-1500.* 288pp. 1-85285-085-X. 1994. £38.00.

FLETCHER, SHEILA. *Lord Lyttelton's daughters.* 288pp. 1-85285-150-3. 1997. £25.00.

GARNETT, EMMELINE. *John Marsden's will: the Hornby Castle dispute, 1780-1840.* 224pp. 1-85285-158-9. 1998. £25.00.

OUTHWAITE, R.B. *Clandestine marriage in England, 1500-1850.* 1-85285-130-9. 1995. £25.00.

Hampton House
P.O. Box 21534, Columbus, Ohio 43221, U.S.A.

MOULTON, JOY W. *Genealogical resources in English repositories.* 648pp. 0-944485-00-6. 1988. $US32.00.

MOULTON, JOY W. *Supplement to genealogical resources in English repositories.* 0-944485-01-4. 1992. $US4.75.

Harper Collins Distribution Services
P.O. Box, Glasgow, G4 0NB
Phone: (0141) 7723200

WAY, GEORGE, & SQUIRE, ROMILLY. *Collins Scottish clan & family encyclopedia.* 0-00-470547-5. 1994. £30.00.

DORWARD, D. *Scottish surnames.* 0-00-470463-0. £5.99.

Clans map of Scotland. 0-7028-1710-4. £3.25.

Collins gem clans and tartans. 0-00-458958-0. £3.99.

David Hawgood
c/o Family Tree Magazine, 61, Great Whyte, Ramsey, Huntingdon, Cambridgeshire PE17 1HL

CHRISTIAN, PETER. *Web publishing for genealogy.* 52pp. 0-948151-15-3. 1997. £4.00 + p&p 35p.

HAWGOOD, DAVID. *Computers for genealogy: an introduction.* 5th ed. 60pp. 0-948151-08-0. £3.50 + p&p 33p.

HAWGOOD, DAVID. *Computer genealogy update.* 32pp. 0-948151-14-5. 1997. £2.65 + p&p. 35p.

HAWGOOD, PETER. *Genealogy computer packages.* 48pp. 0-948151-07-2. 1993. £3.00 + p&p 35p.

HAWGOOD, DAVID. *Internet for genealogy.* 24pp. 0-948151-12-9. 1996. £1.60.

HAWGOOD, DAVID. *GEDCOM data transfer: moving your family tree.* 2nd ed. 44pp. 0-948151-09-9. £2.50 + p&p 30p.

HAWGOOD, DAVID. *I.G.I. on computer: the International Genealogical Index on CD-ROM.* 48pp. 0-948151-16-1. 1998. £2.40 + p&p 34p.

LAWTON, GUY. *Spreadsheet family trees.* 32pp. 0-948151-10-2. 1994. £3.00 + p&p 25p.

TIPPEY, DAVID. *Genealogy on the Macintosh.* 48pp. 0-948151-13-7. 1996. £3.50 + p&p 35p.

Headline Book Publishing Ltd.
338 Euston Road, London, NW1 3BH
CURRER-BRIGGS, NOEL, & GAMBIER, ROYSTON. *Debretts guide to tracing your family tree.* Rev. ed. Forthcoming.

Heart of Albion Press
2 Cross Hill Close, Wymeswold, Loughborough, Leicestershire, LE12 6UJ
Phone: (01509) 880725
Email: bobtrubs@gmtnet.co.uk
http://www.gmtnet.co.uk/indigo/albion/hoaphome.htm
BENNETT, J.D. *Members of Parliament for Leicester, 1832-1983.* 16pp. 1984. 95p.
HOSKINS, W.G. *Leicestershire yeoman families and their pedigrees.* 28pp. 1974. 45p. Discussion of the origin of surnames.
WADE-MATTHEWS, MAX. *The monuments of the church of St. Mary de Castro, Leicester.* 50pp. 1-872883-22-2. 1993. £2.95.
WADE-MATTHEWS, MAX. *The monuments of St. Martins church, Leicester.* 76pp. 1-872883-30-3. 1994. £3.95.
WADE-MATTHEWS, MAX. *The monuments of St. Nicholas church and All Saints church, Leicester.* 38pp. 1-872883-29-X. 1994. £2.50.
WADE-MATTHEWS, MAX. *The monuments of the church of St. Margaret, Leicester.* 56pp. 1-872883-37-0. 1995. £3.50.
WILSHERE, JONATHAN. *Leicester portrait photographers pre-1900.* 20pp. 1988. £2.95.
WILSHERE, JONATHAN. *Family history from local sources.* 6pp. 1971. 40p.
WILSHERE, JONATHAN, ed. *Evington parish registers 1601-1817.* 22pp. 1986. £1.50.
WILSHERE, JONATHAN. *Evington probate inventories 1557-1819.* 63pp. 1985. £1.50.
WILSHERE, JONATHAN, ed. *Allexton parish registers 1636-1836.* 21pp. 1984. £1.50.
WILSHERE, JONATHAN, ed. *Ratby probate inventories, 1621-1844.* 50pp. 1986. £1.50.

Ms. J. Henderson
76 Winyard Drive, Mooroolbark, Vic., 3138, Australia
HENDERSON, JOY. *The Curdys from Cornwall, 1737-1995.* 0-646267-79-5. 1995. $A20.00 + p&p $A5.00.

Ian Henry Publications
20 Park Drive, Romford, Essex, RM1 4LH
WILKES, IAN. *Resting places in East Anglia.* 1997. £7.25. 350 brief biographies.

Heraldry Today
Parliament Piece, Ramsbury, Marlborough, Wiltshire, SN8 2QH
PINE, L.G. *New extinct peerage.* £48.00.

Heritage Books
1540 E.Pointer Ridge Place, Suite 300, Bowie, MD., 20716, U.S.A.
http://www.hb_archives.com/bookorder.htm
ANDERSON, WILLIAM. *The Scottish nation, or, the surnames, families, literature, honours and biographical history of the people of Scotland.* 7 vols. Reprint (originally published 1876). $US274.00 + p&p (airmail) $16.00, or each vol. available separately.
BAGSHAW, SAMUEL. *History, gazetteer and directory of Shropshire, England.* 2 vols. 715pp. Reprint (originally published 1851). $US47.00 + p&p (airmail) $US10.00.
BURKE, BERNARD, SIR. *The general armory of England, Scotland, Ireland and Wales, comprising a registry of armorial bearings from the earliest to the present time.* 3 vols. 1185pp. $US72.50 + p&p (airmail) $10.00.
CRISP, FREDERICK ARTHUR. *Fragmenta genealogica.* Reprint (originally published 1894-1921). 21 vols + 14 vols of notes. Vols 2-4 $US20.00 + p&p (airmail) $10.00 per vol, vols 5-21 $US22.00 + p&p (airmail) $10.00 per vol. Notes $US27-$39.00 + p&p (airmail) $10.00 per vol. An extensive and invaluable collection of extracts from original sources, *etc.,* especially in Suffolk and Norfolk.
CRISP, FREDERICK ARTHUR. *List of parish registers and other genealogical works.* 5 vols in 1. 393pp. Reprint (originally published 1897-1902). $US27.00 + p&p (airmail) $10.00.
CROSSLEY, E.W., ed. *The parish registers of Halifax, co. York, England. Vol. II. Marriages and burials 1538-1593.* 423pp. Reprint (originally published 1914). $US31.50 + p&p (airmail) $10.00.

GARRETT-PEGGE, J.W., ed. *A transcript of the first volume, 1538-1636, of the parish register of Chesham, in the County of Buckingham.* 420pp. Reprint (originally published 1904). $US28.00 + p&p (airmail) $10.00.

GOLDIE, DOUGLAS BRUCE. *In search of Hamish McBagpipes: a concise guide to Scottish genealogy.* 116pp. 1992 (reprint). $US16.00 + p&p (airmail) $10.00.

HOWARD, JOSEPH JACKSON, & CRISP, FREDERICK ARTHUR, eds. *Visitation of England and Wales.* 21 vols + 14 vols of notes. Reprint (originally published 1891-1921), vols 1 & 3 out of print. $US27.00-$42.00 + p&p (airmail) $10.00 per vol.

JOHNSTONE, C.L. *The historical families of Dumfriesshire and the border wars.* 2nd ed. 213pp. Reprint (originally published 1889). $US21.00 + p&p (airmail) $10.00.

KINGSBURY, SUSAN MYRA, ed. *The records of the Virginia Company of London: the Court book, vol. 2. 1622-1624.* 611pp. Reprint (originally published 1906). $US39.00 + p&p (airmail) $10.00.

LEESE, T. ANNA. *Blood royal: issue of the kings and queens of medieval England 1066-1399: the Normans and Plantagenets.* 468pp. 1996. $US37.00 + p&p (airmail) $10.00.

LEWIS, ROBERT J.C.K. *Welsh family coats of arms.* 100pp. 1995. $US24.00 + p&p (airmail) $10.00.

LOWER, MARK ANTONY. *Patronymica Britannica: a dictionary of the family names of the United Kingdom.* 443pp. Reprint (originally published 1860). $US34.50 + p&p (airmail) $10.00.

MCLAREN, MIKE. *The book of Crests of Scottish-American clans.* 272pp. 1990. $US24.00 + p&p (airmail) $US10.00.

MILLETT, GEORGE BROWN, & BOLITHO, WILLIAM, eds. *The parish registers of Gulval (alias Lanisley) in the County of Cornwall, 1598-1812.* Reprint (originally published 1893). $US25.50 + p&p (airmail) $10.00.

ROGERS, CHARLES. *Scottish monuments and tombstones.* 2 vols. 534pp + 439pp. Reprint (originally published 1871-2).
Vol. 1. $US38.50 + p&p (airmail) $10.00.
Vol. 2. $US33.00 + p&pp (airmail) $10.00.

The story of the Stewarts. 194pp. Reprint (originally published 1901). $US19.00 + p&p (airmail) $10.00.

The greening peerage of Scotland: a genealogical and historical account... 339pp. Reprint (originally published 1767). $US28.50 + p&p (airmail) $10.00.

Heritage Publications

c/o Louise St. Denis, 30, Wellington St. East, Suite 2002, Toronto, Ontario, M5E 1S3, Canada

CHRISTENSEN, PENNY. *Tips for your genealogical trip abroad.* 36pp. 1-894018-10-9. 1997. $C6.00.

CHRISTENSEN, PENNY. *Genealogy on the Internet.* 1-894018-22-2. 1998. $C10.00.

CHRISTENSEN, PENNY. *Finding your Scottish ancestors.* 45pp. 1-894018-05-2. 1996. $C7.00.

CHRISTENSEN, PENNY. *Finding your English and Welsh ancestors, including Isle of Man & Channel Islands.* 137pp. 1-894018-07-9. 1998. $C16.00. In civil registration, census, parish register and probate records.

CHRISTENSEN, PENNY. *Using register offices for English and Welsh certificates.* Rev. ed. 78pp. 1-894018-09-5. 1997. $C12.00.

Heritage Quest

P.O. Box 329, 560, West 100 North, Bountiful, Utah 84011-0329, U.S.A.

DOLLARHIDE, WILLIAM. *British origins of American colonists, 1629-1775.* 59pp. 1877677698. 1997. $US12.95 + p&p.

Higginson Book Company

148-BP Washington Street, P.O. Box 778, Salem, MA., 01970, U.S.A.

This company also publishes innumerable reprints of family histories, which cannot be listed here.

FERGUSON, J.P.S. *Scottish family histories held in Scottish libraries.* 1987 (reprint of 1960 ed.). $US25.00.

GIBBONS, A., ed. *Lincoln marriage licences: an abstract of the allegation books preserved by the Registry of the Bishop of Lincoln, 1598-1628.* 1996 (reprint of 1888 edition). $US19.50.

GROOME, FRANCIS H., ed. *Ordnance gazetteer of Scotland: a graphic and accurate description of every place in Scotland.* 3 vols. 1995 (reprint of 1902 ed.) $US150.00 ($55.00 per vol).

Historical Publications
32 Ellington Street, London, N7 8PL
RICHARDSON, JOHN. *Local historian's encyclopedia*. 2nd ed. 0-9503656-7-X. 1986. £15.95.

Hodder & Stoughton
338 Euston Road, London, NW1 3BH
COLWELL, STELLA. *Teach yourself tracing your family tree*. 0-340-59825-5. £7.99.

Norman Hurst
25 Byron Avenue, Coulsdon, Surrey, CR5 2JS
HURST, NORMAN. *An alphabetical index to the Royal Military Calendar, 1820 edition*. 1996. £4.50 (inc. p&p).
HURST, NORMAN. *Naval chronicle 1799-1818: index to births, marriages and deaths*. 1-872497-00-4. 1989. £8.70 (inc. p&p).

Hutton Press Ltd.
130, Canada Drive, Cherry Burton, Beverley, E. Yorkshire, HU17 7SB
Phone: (01964) 550573
LAMMING, DOUGLAS. *An English football internationalists who's who, 1872-1988*. £9.50. Picture biographies of 1003 players.
IMRIE, MARGARET. *The manor houses of Burton Agnes and their owners*. 1993. £7.50.
CLARKE, A.A. *The policemen of Hull*. £7.95. Names all members of the force.
LAMMING, DOUGLAS. *A who's who of Hull City A.F.C., 1904-1984*. £2.95.

Iberian Publishing Co.
548 Cedar Creek Drive, Athens, GA., 30605-3408, U.S.A.
SHARPE, REGINALD R., ed. *Calendar of coroner's rolls of the City of London, A.D. 1300-1378*. $US29.00.

Mrs. G. Jennings
4 Chapel Lane, Branton, Doncaster, DN3 3NG
BOWERS, GWENDOLINE ROSE. *The lives and times of my ancestors*. 1996. £2.95 + p&p 35p. Bowers family of Great Waldingfield, Suffolk.

Brian Jones
32 Myers Avenue, Bradford, W. Yorkshire, BD2 4ET
Phone: (01274) 638792

An account of the numbers of families, communicants and souls in Wakefield town and parish 1723. £2.50.
Bradford population listings. 2 vols. £1.80 per volume. Includes various listings, 1685-1894.
Bradford tithe returns 1638. £2.30.
Bradford censuses 1780 and 1804. £2.00.
Bradford parish church burials, vol. 1. 1596-1605. Vol. 2. 1606-1615. £2.60 per vol.
Bradford parish church burials 1616-1680. Forthcoming.
Great Horton Primitive Methodist chapel, Bradford. Baptisms 1824-1837; burials 1825-1837. £2.20.
Great Horton Wesleyan Chapel, Bradford: baptisms 1816-1837. £2.50.
Index of indexers. 4 pts. Pt.1. £2.75; pt. 2. £2.20; pt. 3. £2.75; pt. 4. £2.75. pt. 5. Forthcoming.
Index of surnames in the 1841 census of ...
  Ilkley Township, Baildon and Bramhope. £1.50 (inc. p&p).
  Burley and Pool. £1.40 (inc. p&p).
  Otley Township, Esholt, Hawksworth and Menston. £1.60 (inc. p&p).
  Calverley cum Farsley with part of Stanningley. £1.40 (inc. p&p).
  Tong and Hunsworth. £1.40 (inc. p&p).
  Clayton. £1.40 (inc. p&p).
  Clifton cum Hartshead. £1.40 (inc. p&p).
  Heckmondwike. £1.40 (inc. p&p).
  Eccleshill. £1.40 (inc. p&p).
  Wetherby. £1.40 (inc. p&p).
  Harewood, Weardley, Wigton and Alwoodley. £1.60 (inc. p&p).
  Dunkeswick, East Keswick, Weeton and Wike. £1.60 (inc. p&p).
Keighley paupers 1843. £2.40.
Kilburn, South Otterington and Middleton (N.R.Y.) censuses 1811; Leeming Bar (N.R.Y.) population listing October 1877. £1.60.
Kirkgate Chapel, Bradford, baptisms, 1820-1837. Forthcoming.
Leeds census 1801. 2 vols. £5.60 (inc. p&p).
Local population listings.
  Bracewell 1801. £1.60 (inc. p&p).
  Calverley and Farsley, 1811. £1.70 (inc. p&p).
  Carlton in Craven 1811. £1.60 (inc. p&p).
  Elland cum Greetland, 1811. £2.30 (inc. p&p).
  Spofforth 1801. £1.60 (inc. p&p).
  Spofforth 1821. £1.70 (inc. p&p).
  Spofforth 1831. £1.80 (inc. p&p).
  Swillington 1852. Forthcoming.
  Thrybergh 1801. £1.60 (inc. p&p).
  Todmorden & Walsden 1811. £1.90 (inc. p&p).

Tong 1801. £1.60 (inc. p&p).
Tong 1811. £1.60 (inc. p&p).
Tong 1821. £2.20 (inc. p&p).
Wetherby 1776. £2.20 (inc. p&p).
Yeadon 1811. £1.80 (inc. p&p).
Yeadon 1821. £2.30 (inc. p&p).
Yeadon 1831. £1.60 (inc. p&p).
York 1723. Forthcoming.
Oswaldkirk (N.R.Y.) census 1821; Castle Bolton population listing c. 1880. £1.60.
Sion Chapel, Bridge Street, Bradford: transcription and surname index to the register book of births and supplementary book (1814-1837). £2.20.
Stansfield census 1821. 2 vols. £4.50.
Thirsk census 1811. £2.40.
Thirsk census 1821. £2.40.
Thornton Wesleyan Methodist Chapel, Bradford: baptisms 1817-1837. £2.50.
Toad Lane Chapel, Bradford: baptisms 1730-1756. £1.80.
Tong. St. James marriages. 4 vols. £8.73 the set, or:
  v.1. 1728-1753. £2.20.
  v.2. 1754-1781. £2.50.
  v.3. 1782-1801. £2.50.
  v.4. 1802-1814. £2.50.
Wednesbury, Staffordshire census 1801. £2.40.
Wetherby population listing 1776. £2.20.
York poll book, 1741. Forthcoming.
York oath of allegiance 1723. £3.60.
York: parish of St. Maurice census 1811. £1.60 (inc. p&p).
York: parish of St. Giles census 1821. £2.00 (inc. p&p).
York: parish of St. Giles census 1801/1811. £1.60 (inc. p&p).
Yorkshire pupils ... extracted from the censuses of the West Riding of Yorkshire. 3 vols. £2.00 per vol.

Gareth Jones
8 Deansfield Road, Brewood, Staffordshire, ST19 9EQ

Surveys of M.I.'s in S.W. Brecs and N.E. Carms.
  Aberyscir parish church. 28pp. £3.00.
  Bethel Baptist, Llandefailog Fach. £1.90.
  Llandeilo'rfan parish church. 38pp. £4.00.
  Llanfihangel Fechan parish church. £2.00.
  Llanfihangelnantbran parish church. 23pp. £2.50.
  Pontestyll Baptist, Llanpyddid. £2.00.
  Soar Baptist, Llanfihangelnantbran. 13pp. £1.70.
  Zoar C.M., Llywel. 22pp. £2.50.

Dr. A.P. Joseph
25, Westbourne Rd, Edgebaston, Birmingham, B15 3TX

Proceedings of the Second International Seminar of Jewish genealogy, 5-10th July 1987. 0-9513497-0-8. 1987. £15.00 + p&p £1.50.

George Kelsall
22 Church Street, Littleborough, Lancs., OL15 9AA

LAW, BRIAN. *Fieldens of Todmorden: a nineteenth century business dynasty.* 0-946571-27-9. 1995. £13.50.

Kingpin
21 Meldon Way, Hanover Estate, Winlaton, Tyne and Wear, NE21 6HJ. Cheques payable to M. Southwick please.

The North-Easterner magazine. Quarterly. ISSN: 1357-0315. £7.50 per annum.
SOUTHWICK, M. *North-East repositories, II.* 0-9524750-6-5. £5.00 (inc. p&p).
SOUTHWICK, M., ed. *Ancestral anomalies.* 1996. £5.50 (inc. p&p). A collection of amusing, sad, erroneous and unusual items culled from the archives.
SOUTHWICK, M., ed. *Northern yarns.* 2 vols. 0-9524750-4-9 (v.1); 0-9524750-5-7. 1996-7. £4.00 (inc. p&p) per vol.

Kingsmead Press
4 Woodspring Avenue, Worlebury, Weston Super Mare, BS2 9RJ.

GRAVES, ALGERNON. *Dictionary of artists who have exhibited works in the principal London exhibitions 1760-1893.* 0-901571-13-X. 1984. Reprint; originally published 1901. £32.50.
GRAVES, ALGERNON. *British Institution 1806-67: a complete dictionary of contributors and their work.* 0-901571-11-3. 1969. Reprint; original published 1908. £25.00.

Mrs. D. Laws
10 Ripon Road, Plumstead, London, SE18 3PS

LAWS, D. *Greenwich memorial book of World War Two losses.* Pt.1. 1996. £5.00.

Leopards Head Press
7, Murray Court, Banbury Road, Oxford, OX2 6LQ

EMMISON, F.G., & STEPHENS, ROY, eds. *Tribute to an antiquary: essays presented to Marc Fitch.* 332pp. 0-904920-00-3. 1976. £15.00.

EMMISON, F.G., ed. *Feet of fines for Essex, vol.V. 1547-1580.* 308pp. 0-904920-18-6. 1991. £8.50.

EMMISON, F.G., ed. *Feet of fines for Essex, vol.VI: 1581-1603.* 0-904920-26-7. 1993. £8.50.

MCKINLEY, RICHARD. *The surnames of Oxfordshire.* 312pp. 0-904920-01-1. 1977. £8.00.

MCKINLEY, RICHARD. *The surnames of Sussex.* 483pp. 0-904920-14-3. 1988. £19.00.

MCKINLEY, RICHARD. *The surnames of Lancashire.* 501pp. 0-904920-05-4. 1981. £12.00.

POSTLES, DAVID. *The surnames of Devon.* 332pp. 0-904920-25-9. 1995. £19.00.

STEER, FRANCIS W. *The archives of New College Oxford.* 581pp. 0-614-21820-9. 1974. $US25.00.

Lillydown Technology
Sherborne St. John, Basingstoke, RG24 9LH

TEARLE, JOHN L. *Tearle: a Bedfordshire surname.* 1996. £11.50.

Liris Interactive
5th Floor, Esley House, 24-30 Great Titchfield Street, London, W1P 7AD
Phone: (0181) 3245677

Chambers biographies CD-Rom. £49.99.

Lobb Genealogical Records
Truro Vean Terrace, Truro, Cornwall, TR1 1HA
Phone: (01872) 222209
E-mail: dlobb@cornwall.net

LOBB, D.H.V. *Lobbery.* 3 vols. 0-9520019-0-X. 1993-8. Vol.1. £12.00. Vol.2. £20.00. Vol.3. £20.00 (includes p&p.)

LOBB, D.H.V. *20,000 Lobbs around the world.* 12 chapters. 1988- . Chapter 1 now incorporated in *Lobbery*. Otherwise £12.00 per chapter (except Ch. 7, £10.00). Contact publisher for full details.

Lochin Publishing Society
6 Holywell Road, Dursley, Gloucestershire, GL11 5RS.
Phone: (01453) 547531

CHAPMAN, COLIN R. *Tracing your British ancestors.* 2nd ed. iv, 92pp. 1-873686-13-7. 1996. £3.99 + p&p 75p.

CHAPMAN, COLIN R. *Marriage laws, rites, records and customs.* iv, 116pp. 1-873686-02-1. £5.50 + p&p 75p.

CHAPMAN, COLIN R. *Pre-1841 censuses and population listings in the British Isles.* 5th ed. vi, 82pp. 1-873686-18-8. 1998. £5.00 + p&p 75p.

CHAPMAN, COLIN R. *The growth of British education and its records.* 2nd ed. iv, 84pp. 1-873686-05-6. 1996. £5.00 + p&p 75p.

CHAPMAN, COLIN R. *Ecclesiastical courts, officials and records: sin, sex and probate.* 2nd ed. iv, 80pp. 1-873686-15-3. 1997. £5.00 + p&p 75p.

CHAPMAN, COLIN R. *Tracing ancestors in Northamptonshire.* vi, 54pp. 1-873686-11-0. 1995. £4.50 + p&p 50p.

CHAPMAN, COLIN R. *Tracing ancestors in Bedfordshire.* 2nd ed. iv, 60pp. 1-873686-12-9. 1998. £4.50 + p&p 50p.

CHAPMAN, COLIN R. *Tracing ancestors in Rutland.* iv, 60pp. 1-873686-17-X. 1997. £4.50 + p&p 50p.

Lyfrow Trelyspen
Roseland Institute, Gorran, St Austell, Cornwall.
Phone: (01726) 843501

WHETTER, JAMES. *The Bodrugans: a study of a Cornish medieval knightly family.* 0-9514510-5-7. £20.00 inc. p&p.

Roy Maber
12 Fairfield, Martock, Somerset, TA12 6DY.

MABER, ROY. *The Martock geneologist: a handbook of family history, Book 1.* 1996. £8.50 + £1.00 p&p.

Macbeth Genealogical Services
43, Mills Street, Hampton, Vic. 3188, Australia.

BAKER, WENDY. *Ancestral file on CD-Rom: an introduction.* 0-9586624-2-8. 1996. $A8.00. Published by Genie Books.

BAKER, WENDY. *The International Genealogical Index on CD-Rom: an introduction.* 0-9586624-1-X. 1996. $A10.00. Published by Genie Books.
BAKER, WENDY. *A brief guide to the I.G.I.* 0-947158-21-9. 1991. Price on application.
CAIRNS-SMITH-BARTH, JOHN LAWRENCE. *Scottish family history: research & source guide vol. 1.* 189pp. 0-86252-314-2. 1986. $A18.95.
CARTER, JENNY. *England & Wales: birth, death, marriage from 1837.* 0-947158-31-6. 1992. Price on application.
MCBETH, S., ed. *Information for people leaving Great Britain 1854.* 0-947158-17-0. 1991. Price on application.
STYLES, LAURIE. *How to use the census returns to find your London family: a guide to the London census returns for 1841-1891.* 0-947158-451-X. 1994. Price on application.

Frances McDonnell Publications

8, Lawhead Road West, St.Andrews, KY16 9NE
e-mail f.mcdonnel@zetnet.co.uk

Aberdeen obituaries.
1748-1770. £3.50.
1771-1799. £4.50.
1800-1822. £4.20.
1823-1839. £4.20.
1840-1854. £4.20.
Alumni & Graduates in arts of the Aberdeen Colleges.
1810-1860. £4.00.
1840-1849. £3.50.
Birth briefs of Aberdeen 1637-1705 £3.00.
The burgess roll of Banff £2.50.
The burgess roll of Elgin £2.50.
Burgh of Paisley poll tax roll 1695.
Part 1. £2.50.
Part 2. £2.50.
General register of Sasines:
County of Aberdeen *1701-1720.* £2.75
Counties of Banff, Elgin, Forres, Nairn & Kincardine *1701-20.* £3.00.
Jacobites of 1715, north east Scotland. £3.50.
Jacobites of 1745, north east Scotland. £5.00.
Register of merchant and trade burgesses of Aberdeen.
Pt.1. *1600-1620.* £3.00.
Pt.2. *1621-1639.* £3.00.
Pt.3. *1640-1659.* £3.00.
Pt.4. *1660-1679.* £3.00.
Pt.5. *1680-1700.* £3.00.
Register of merchant and trade burgesses of old Aberdeen.
Pt.1. *1622-1699.* £3.00.
Pt.2. *1726-1885.* £2.50.
Roll of apprentices, burgh of Aberdeen
Pt.1. *1622-1699.* £3.00.
Pt.2. *1726-1885.* £2.50.
Register of testaments, Aberdeen.
1760-1800. £4.50.
1735-1759. £4.00.
1715-1734. £2.50.

Mrs E. McLaughlin

Varneys, Rudd Lane, Haddenham, Aylesbury, Buckinghamshire HP17 8JP.
Email: eve@varneys.demon.co.uk
MCLAUGHLIN, EVE. *No time for family history.* £2.00 + p&p 40p.
MCLAUGHLIN, EVE. *Parish registers.* £2.00 + p&p 40p.
MCLAUGHLIN, EVE. *Nonconformist ancestors.* £2.00 + p&p 40p.
MCLAUGHLIN, EVE. *Censuses 1841-91.* £2.00 + p&p 40p.
MCLAUGHLIN, EVE. *Annals of the poor.* £2.00 + p&p 40p.
MCLAUGHLIN, EVE. *The poor are always with us.* £2.00 + p&p 40p.
MCLAUGHLIN, EVE. *Illegitimacy.* £2.00 + p&p 40p.
MCLAUGHLIN, EVE. *Quarter sessions.* £2.00 + p&p 40p.
MCLAUGHLIN, EVE. *Manorial records.* £2.00 + p&p 40p.
MCLAUGHLIN, EVE. *Starting your family history.* £2.00 + p&p 40p.
MCLAUGHLIN, EVE. *Interviewing elderly relatives.* £1.50 + p&p 40p.
MCLAUGHLIN, EVE. *General Register Office records.* £1.50 + p&p 40p.
MCLAUGHLIN, EVE. *Reading old handwriting.* £1.50 + p&p 40p.
MCLAUGHLIN, EVE. *Simple Latin for family historians.* £1.50 + p&p 40p.
MCLAUGHLIN, EVE. *Somerset House wills.* £1.50 + p&p 40p.
MCLAUGHLIN, EVE. *Wills before 1858.* £1.50 + p&p 40p.
MCLAUGHLIN, EVE. *Family history from newspapers.* £1.50 + p&p 40p.
MCLAUGHLIN, EVE. *Making the most of the I.G.I.* £1.50 + p&p 40p.
MCLAUGHLIN, EVE. *Laying out a pedigree.* £2.50 + p&p 45p.
MCLAUGHLIN, EVE. *Surnames: their origin and meaning.* Price on application.

Macmillan Press Ltd
Houndsmill, Basingstoke, Hampshire, RG21 6XS.
Http://www.macmillan-press.co.uk
FOSTER, JANET, & SHEPPARD, JULIA. *British archives.* 704pp. 0-333-53255-4. £85.00.

Michael MacSorley
112, Holbein Close, Basingstoke, Hampshire, RG21 3EX.
The placename index of the 1891 census.
v.1. *London.* £2.50 inc. p&p
v.2. *S.E.England.* £2.50 inc. p&p
v.3. *Southern England.* £2.50 inc. p&p.
v.4. *South West England.* £2.50 inc. p&p.
v.5. *East Anglia.* £2.50 inc. p&p.
v.6. *East Midlands.* £2.50 inc. p&p.
v.7. *West Midlands.* £2.50 inc. p&p.
v.8. *Wales.* £2.50 inc. p&p.
v.9. *N.W.England.* £2.50 inc. p&p.
v.10. *N.E.England.* £2.50 inc. p&p.
v.11. *Northern England.* £2.50 inc. p&p.

McGraw-Hill Publishing Co.
McGraw-Hill House, Shoppenhangers Road, Maidenhead, Berkshire, SL6 2QL.
CROWE, ELIZABETH P. *Genealogy online: researching your roots.* 2nd ed. 0-07-014754-X 1996. £18.00.

Mainstream Publishing Co Ltd
7, Albany Street, Edinburgh, EH1 3UG.
Phone: (0131) 5572959
MARTINE, RODDY. *Scottish clan and family names.* 224pp. 1-85158-418-8. 1996. £9.99.

Manchester University Press
Oxford Road, Manchester, M13 9NR.
Phone: (0161) 2735539
Email: mup@man.ac.uk
ROGERS, COLIN D. *Tracing missing persons.* 0-7190-1901-X. 1986. £15.99.
ROGERS, COLIN D. *The family tree detective: tracing your ancestors in England and Wales.* 3rd ed. 0-7190-5213-0. 1997. £10.99.
ROGERS, COLIN. *The surname detective: investigating surname distribution in England since 1086.* 288pp. 0-7190-4047-7 (hb); 0-7190-4048-5 (pb). 1995. £45.00(hb), £12.99 (pb).
ROGERS, COLIN D., & SMITH, JOHN. *Local family history in England.* 217pp. 0-7190-3201-6. 1991. £12.99.

Mantis Consulting
P.O. Box 55322
Northlands, South Africa, 2116.
EMERY, ASHTON. *A-Z of British genealogical research.* 0-620-19603-3. 1996. £3.50 (inc. airmail)

Peter Marcan Publications
P.O.Box 3158, London, SE1 4RA.
Phone: (0171) 3570368
MARCAN, PETER, PAYNE, DAVID, & BAKER, LESLEY. *London's local history: an annotated catalogue of publications and resources issued by Greater London local authorities, local historical and archaeological societies, amenity societies and community publishing projects during the 1960s, 1970s and early 1980s.* 64pp. 0-9504211-6-2. 1983. £9.50 + p&p 85p.
MARCAN, PETER. *Greater London local history directory and bibliography: a borough by borough guide to local history organisations, their activities and publications, 1983-1987.* 1st ed. 83pp. 0-9510289-8-7. 1988. £15.00 + p&p 85p.
MARCAN, PETER. *Greater London local history directory: a borough by borough guide to local history organisations, their activities, and publications, 1988-92* 2nd ed. 117pp. 0-871811-108-2. 1993. £15.00 + p&p 85p.

Marwood Publications
Ford Farm, Wilmington, Honiton, Devon, EX14 9JU.
HAYDON, EDWIN, & HARROT, JOHN, eds. *Widworthy manorial court rolls, 1453-1617.* 0-9529149-0-5. 1997. £15.00 + p&p £2.00.

J. Maxted
10, Leighdene Close, Exeter, EX2 47N.
Exeter working papers in British book trade history
1. MAXTED, IAN. *The London book trades 1775-1800: a preliminary checklist of members.* xxxv, 257pp. 0-7129-1696-7. 1977. £9.60. Originally published by Wm. Dawson.
2. MAXTED, IAN. *The London book trades: a topographical guide.* 16pp. + 5 fiche. 0-9507306-0-2. 1980. £6.00. Indexes the previous work topographically.

2. MAXTED, IAN. *The British book trades 1710-1777: an index of masters and apprentices recorded in the Inland Revenue registers at the Public Record Office, Kew.* xii, 141pp. 0-95070306-1-0. 1983. £10.00.
3. MAXTED, IAN. *The London book trades 1735-1775: a checklist of members in trade directories and in Musgrave's obituary'.* iii, 37pp. 0-95070306-2-9. £3.00.
4. MAXTED, IAN. *The British book trades 1731-1806: a checklist of bankrupts.* viii, 36pp. 0-95070306-3-7.1985. £3.00.
7. MAXTED, IAN. *The Devon book trades: a biographical directory.* viii, 286pp. 0-95070306-6-1. 1991. £18.00.
8. MAXTED, IAN. *The British book trades 1775-1787: an index to insurance policies.* xiii, 152pp. 0-9512752-2-4. [199-?] £12.00.
9. MAXTED, IAN. *Newspaper readership in South West England: an analysis of the Flindell's Western Luminary' subscription list of 1815.* xii, 92pp. 0-9512752-33-2. 1996. £12.00.

Special series
2. MAXTED, IAN. *The British national directories 1781-1819: an index to places in the British Isles included in trade directories with general provincial coverage.* viii, 34pp. 0-95122752-1-6. 1989. £6.00.

Edwin Mellen Press
415, Ridge St./ P.O.Box 450, Lewiston, New York 14092-0450, U.S.A.
PRICE, MICHAEL. *The account book for the borough of Swansea, Wales, 1640-1660: a study in local administration during the Civil War and Interregnum.* 340pp. 0-88946-480-4. 1990.

Merton Priory Press
Whitchurch Books, 67, Merthyr Road, Whitchurch, Cardiff, CF4 1DD.
Phone: (01222) 521956
CROUCH, DAVID, ed. *Llandaff episcopal acta, 1140-1287.* xlv, 114pp. 0-9508676-4-0. 1988. £20.00.
EVANS, CHRIS, ed. *The letterbook of Richard Crawshay, 1788-1797.* xxv, 206pp. 0-9508676-5-9. 1990. £18.95. Ironmaster of Merthyr Tydfil.

GRANT, RAYMOND K.J., ed. *On the parish: an illustrated source book on the care of the poor under the old poor law.* xiv, 94pp. 0-905243-13-7.
GUY, JOHN R., ed. *The Diocese of Llandaff in 1763.* 212pp. 0-9508676-6-7. 1991. £18.95. Visitation returns.
HOPKINS, ANTHONY D.G., ed. *Medieval Neath: ministers accounts, 1262-1316.* x, 102pp. 0-9513954-0-8. 1988. £6.95.
INCE, LAURENCE. *The Knight family and the British iron industry, 1695-1902.* viii, 132pp. 0-9518065-0-0. 1991. £9.95.
LLEWELLYN, HOWARD. *A bibliography of Cardiff directories, 1795-1978.* 48pp. 0-9513886-0-6. 1989. £2.00.
RIDEN, PHILIP, ed. *George Sitwell's letterbook, 1662-66.* liv, 301pp. 0-946324-06-9. 1985. £20.00. Of Renishaw, Derbyshire; ironmaster.
RIDEN, PHILIP. *Cowbridge trades and tradesmen, 1660-1750.* vi, 47pp. 0-946045-14-3. 1981. £2.00.
THOMAS, HILARY M. ed. *The diaries of John Bird, 1790-1803.* 189pp. 0-9508676-3-2. 1987. £12.00.
THOMAS, HILARY. *A catalogue of Glamorgan estate maps.* x, 134pp. 0-905243-25-0. 1992. £25.00.

Richard Milward
159 Coombe Lane, London, SW20 OQX
MILWARD, RICHARD. *The Spencers in Wimbledon, 1744-1944.* 0-9501068-44. £11.00.

Mrs Linda Moorhouse
Elsinore House, 76, Scotforth Road, Lancaster, LA1 4SF.
The following titles consist of extracts from local newspapers, including births, marriages and deaths.
The gude auld towne of Lancaster in 1803. 104p. [199-?] £7.00 (inc. p&p).
The assize town of Lancaster in 1821. 150p. [199-?] £11.00 (inc. p&p).
The ancient Borough of Lancaster in 1831. 108p. [199-?] £7.00 (inc. p&p).
The good old town of Lancaster in 1841. 100p. 1995. £7.00 (inc. p&p).

Marion and Joe Murray
22, Cheviot Avenue, Barrhead, Renfrewshire, G78 2DR.
MURRAY, MARION, & MURRAY, JOE. *Lair owners of the Laigh Kirk: from the burgess books of Paisley, 1740-1781.* 1997. £3.00 + p&p. 35p.

MURRAY, JOE. *A register of poor: Abbey Parochial Board, 1856-1863.* 0-9529888-1-X. 1997. £15.45.

MURRAY, MARION. *Paisley papers: Renfrewshire records devolved to local areas, 1617-1978.* 0-9529888-0-1. 1996. £3.50.

Donovan J.Murrells
428, Bedonwell Road, Abbey Wood, London, SE2 0SE.

Registration districts of Norfolk in 1836. 1-898134-00-6. 1993. £3.30 (inc. p&p).
Registration districts of Suffolk in 1836. 1-898134-02-2. 1993. £3.30 (inc. p&p).
Registration districts of Essex in 1836. 1-898134-03-0. 1994. £3.30 (inc. p&p).
Registration districts of Sussex in 1836. 1-898134-04-9. 1994. £3.30 (inc. p&p).
Registration districts of Kent in 1836. 1-898134-05-7. 1996. £3.30 (inc. p&p).
Registration districts of Surrey in 1836. 1-898134-06-5. 1997. £3.30 (inc. p&p).
Registration districts of Hampshire in 1836. 1-898134-07-5. 1998. £3.30 (inc. p&p).

Naval & Military Press
Order Dept., P.O. Box 61, Dallington, Heathfield, East Sussex, TN21 9ZS. Phone: (01435) 830111. Email: order.dept@naval-military-press.co.uk http://www.great-war-casualties.com

Soldiers died in the Great War, 1914-1919. CD-ROM. 1998. £150.00 + VAT £26.25 + p&p £2.50.

Nazeing History Workshop
c/o Mrs Valerie Day, Newlands, Middle Street, Nazeing, Waltham Abbey, Essex, EN9 2LH

PRACY, DAVID. *Not a better set in the county: the story of Nazeing Wood or Park, 1778-1950.* 0-9526048-1-7. 1995. £6.00 (inc. p&p.) Includes tithe apportionment, 1847, with various lists of owners and tenants, etc., 18-20th c.

GERVIS, JOHN. *All Saints church, Nazeing: an index to parish records 1559-1840.* 0-9527794-0-4. 1996. £10.00. Published by Nazeing Parochial Church Council. An index for 1840 onwards is in course of preparation, as is an index of monumental inscriptions.

Norma C.Neill
Colywell, Commonside, Westwoodside, Doncaster, DN9 2AR

NEILL, NORMA C. *The Elam family: Quaker merchants of England and America.* 0-9522495-3-7. [1995?] £6.95 + p&p 55p.

Ngaio Press
Level 7, Wool House, 10, Brandon Street, P.O. Box 29-010, Wellington, New Zealand.
Email: ngaio@infomedia.co.nz
Http://wwww/actrix.gen.nz/users/ngaiopress.

MACGIBBON, JOHN. *Going abroad.* 0-473-04752-7. 1997. $NZ39.95 + p&p. $NZ16.00 (inc. p&p to U.K.) Study of the MacGibbon family, and of mid-19th c. emigration from Scotland to New Zealand.

Nicholson Family Library
The Rectory, Cranleigh, Surrey, GU6 8AS

NICHOLSON, NIGEL. *Nicholson: being a compilation of family trees of Nicolson and Nicholson and variants of the same name.* 1996. £25.00.

North Carolina Division of Archives and History
Historical Publications Section, Department of Cultural Resources, 109, East Jones Street, Raleigh, NC 27601-2807, U.S.A,

NEWSOME, A.R., ed. *Records of emigrants from England and Scotland to North Carolina 1777-1775.* 30pp. 0-86526-134-2. 1989. $US3.00.

NORCAP
112, Church Road, Wheatley, Oxford, OX33 1LU
Phone: (01865) 875000

Searching for family connections. 0-9509901-5-9. 1997. £10.00. For adoptees.

Northern Writers Advisory Services
77, Marford Crescent, Sale, Cheshire, M33 4DN.
Phone: (0161) 9691573

GROVES, JILL, ed. *Bowdon wills: wills and probate inventories from a Cheshire township.*
Pt.1. *1600-1650.* 80pp. 1997. £4.50.
Pt.2. *1651-1689.* Forthcoming.

GROVES, JILL. *Piggins, husslements and desperate debts: a social and economic history of North-east Cheshire, 1600-1760 through wills and probate inventories.* 80pp. 1994. £4.50.

Old Tricorn Press Ltd.
P.O.Box 60, London, SW19 1XH.
Family researcher. 6 issues p.a. Annual subscription £10.00.

Oryx Press
4041, North Central Avenue, Suite 700, Pheonix, AZ 85012-3397, U.S.A.
JOHNSON, ANNE E. *A students guide to British American genealogy.* 1995. $US24.95.

Oxbow Books
Park End Place, Oxford, OX1 1HN
Phone: (01865) 241249
Email: oxbow@patrol.i-way.co.uk
http://www.oxbowbooks.com
HANSEN, ANN NATALIE. *Oxford goldsmiths before 1800.* 162pp. 1-961-34913-1. 1996. £30.00.
For Royal Historical Society publications sold by this publisher, see under the Society in pt.2.

Oxford University Press
Great Clarendon Street, Oxford, OX2 6DP.
Phone: (01865) 556767
HANKS, PATRICK, & HODGES, FLAVIA. *A dictionary of surnames.* 880pp. 0-19-211592-8. £70.00.
HEY, DAVID, ed. *Oxford companion to local and family history.* 528pp. 0-19-211688-6(hb); 1996. £25.00. 0-19-860215-4(pb). 1998. £12.99.
HEY, DAVID. *The Oxford guide to family history.* 256pp. 0-19-869177-7(hb) 1996. £19.99. 0-19-285305 (pb). 1998. £9.99.
HEY, DAVID. *The Oxford dictionary of local & family history.* 304pp. 0-19-860080-1. 1997. £5.99.
REANEY, P.H., & WILSON, R.M. *A dictionary of English surnames.* 3rd ed. 590pp. 0-19-860092-5. 1997. £9.99.
WOODCOCK, THOMAS, & ROBINSON, JOHN MARTIN. *The Oxford guide to heraldry.* 246pp. 0-19-285224-8. 1998. £15.00.
For publications issued on behalf of the British Academy, see part 2 below.

P.B.N. Publications
22, Abbey Road, Eastbourne, E.Sussex, BN20 8TE.
WEBB, P., & WEIR, N., eds. *Early census returns in Sussex.*
1801 Ticehurst. £1.70.
1831 Ticehurst. £2.05.
1821 Hartfield. £2.35.
1821 Chiddingley. £2.80.
1821 Hailsham. £1.90.
1831 Hailsham. £1.90.
1831 St. Clement, Hastings. £2.05.
1831 East Dean and Friston. £1.30.
1831 St. John sub Castro, Lewes. £1.65.
1831 Uckfield. £1.90.
1821 & 1831 St.Mary in the Castle, Hastings. ££2.50.
1811 St.Michael, Lewes (also jury/voters 1832). £2.00.
WEBB, P., & WEIR, N., eds. *Crew members of ships trading from Newhaven between 1864-1889.* £4.25.
WEBB, P., & WEIR, N., eds. *Ewhurst householders in 1863.* £2.90.
WEBB, P., & WEIR, N., eds. *Withyham inhabitants in 1838.* £3.75.
WEBB, P., & WEIR, N., eds. *Sussex militia lists.*
Southern Division of Pevensey Rape (1803). £3.80.
Northern Division of Pevensey Rape (1803). £4.55.
Burwash (1831), Pevensey (1810) & Rottingdean (1797) £2.15.
WEBB, P., & WEIR, N., eds. *Sussex enrolments under the Navy Acts (1795-1797).* £2.50.
WEBB, P., & WEIR, N., eds. *Eastbourne war memorial 1914-1918.* £2.15.
WEBB, P., & WEIR, N., eds. *Eastbourne marriages (St.Mary's church) 1558-1753.* £3.90.
WEBB, P., & WEIR, N., eds. *Eastbourne marriages (St.Mary's church) 1754-1837.* £5.00.
WEBB, P., & WEIR, N., eds. *Eastbourne baptisms (St.Mary's church) 1558-1837.* **Pt.1.** *A to D.* £4.75. **Pt.2.** *E to K.* £4.75. **Pt.3.** *R to S.* £3.65. **Pt.5.** *T to Z.* £3.90.
WEBB, P., & WEIR, N., eds. *Hastings gaol records.*
Commitments to prison 1832-1841. £4.25.
Keepers commitment book 1842-1849 + food costs. £4.75.
Keepers commitment book 1850-53 + food costs. £4.15.

WEBB, P., & WEIR, N., eds. *Hastings registered electors 1836-7.* £2.65.
WEBB, P., & WEIR, N., eds. *Hastings and St.Leonards directory 1834.* £1.55
WEBB, P., & WEIR, N., eds. *Sussex electors 1832.* £6.10.

Peter B. Park
25, Harvey Road, Walton on Thames, Surrey, KT12 2PZ.
PARK, PETER B. *A guide to West Derby's enumeration districts in the 1851 census.* 0-9524437-0-8. 1994. £4.50 + 50p p&p.

Pennard Hill Publications
8B Sweeney Street, Ballarat, Vic., 3350, Australia.
CHUK, FLORENCE. *An index of passengers who sailed on vessels which left the Port of Bristol for Victoria, 1841-1863.* 1996.

Pentland Press Ltd.
3, Regal Lane, Soham, Ely, Cambridgeshire, CB7 5BA.
Phone: (01353) 723359
DICKER, GEOFFREY. *The family face: a history of the Dicker family.* xxx, 252pp. 1-85821-596-X. 1998. £20.00.
STANLEY, PETER EDMUND. *The house of Stanley from the 12th century.* 912pp. 1-85821-578-1. 1998. £25.00 + p&p £3.50.

Periodicals Service Company
11, Main Street, Germantown, N.Y., 112526, U.S.A
Email: psc@pix.net
European orders to: Schmidt Periodicals GmbH, Ortsteil Dettendorf, D-83075, Bad Feilnbaach, Germany.
Email: 101565.3131@compuserve.com
See also entries for the British Academy and the British Record Society.
MACRAY, WILLIAM DUNN. *A register of the members of St. Mary Magdalen College, Oxford, from the foundation of the College.* 8 vols. Reprint. Originally published Oxford University Press, 1894. $US175.00.
MADAN, FALCONER. *A summary catalogue of western manuscripts in the Bodleian Library at Oxford.* 7 vols. in 8. Reprint. Originally published Oxford: Clarendon Press, 1895-1953. $US700.00.

Public Record Office calendars
Calendar of various Chancery rolls, supplementary close rolls, Welsh rolls, scutage rolls, preserved in the Public Record Office ... 1277-1326. Reprint. Originally published H.M.S.O., 1912. $US110.00.
Calendar of charter rolls preserved in the Public Record Office. 6 vols. Reprint. Originally published 1903-27. Set $US570.00. Contents:
v.1. *Henry III, A.D. 1226-1257.*
v.2. *Henry III-Edward I, A.D. 1257-1300.*
v.3. *Edward I, Edward II, A.D. 1300-1326.*
v.4. *1-14 Edward III, A.D. 1327-1341.*
v.5. *15 Edward III-5 Henry V, A.D. 1341-1417.*
v.6. *5 Henry VI-8 Henry VIII, A.D. 1427-1516, with an appendix, A.D. 1215-1288.*
Calendar of close rolls, Edward II, A.D. 1307-[1327]. 4 vols. Reprint. Originally published H.M.S.O., 1892-8. $US345.00.
Calendar of the close rolls preserved in the Public Record Office ... Edward II, A.D. 1327-[1377]. 14 vols. Reprint. Originally published H.M.S.O., 1896-1913. $US1450.00.
Calendar of the close rolls preserved in the Public Record Office ... Richard II, A.D. 1377-[1399]. 6 vols. Reprint. Originally published H.M.S.O., 1914-27. $US550.00.
Calendar of the close rolls preserved in the Public Record Office ... Henry V, A.D. 1413-[1422]. 2 vols. Reprint. Originally published H.M.S.O., 1929-32. $US170.00.
Calendar of the close rolls preserved in the Public Record Office ... Edward IV, Edward V and Richard III, A.D. 1476-1485. Reprint. Originally published H.M.S.O., 1954. $US85.00.
Calendar of the fine rolls preserved in the Public Record Office ... Edward I-[Henry IV], A.D. 1272-[1413]. 13 vols. Reprint. Originally published H.M.S.O., 1911-33. $US1230.00. A number of further volumes have not been reprinted.
Calendar of inquisitions miscellaneous (Chancery) preserved in the Public Record Office. 3 vols. Reprint. Originally published H.M.S.O., 1916-37. $US300.00. A number of further volumes have not been reprinted.

[Calendar of] patent rolls of the reign of Henry III preserved in the Public Record Office ... A.D. 1216-[1272]. 6 vols. Reprint. Originally published H.M.S.O. 1901-13. $US550.00.

Calendar of the patent rolls preserved in the Public Record Office ... Edward I, A.D. 1272-[1307]. 4 vols. Reprint. Originally published H.M.S.O., 1893-1901. $US345.00.

Calendar of the patent rolls preserved in the Public Record Office ... Richard II, A.D. 1377-1381. 6 vols. Reprint. Originally published H.M.S.O., 1895-1909. $US585.00.

Calendar of the patent rolls preserved in the Public Record Office ... Henry IV, A.D. 1399-[1413]. 4 vols. Originally published H.M.S.O., 1903-9. $US210.00.

Calendar of the patent rolls preserved in the Public Record Office ... Henry IV, A.D. 1413-[1422]. 4 vols. Originally published H.M.S.O., 1903-9. $US300.00.

Calendar of the patent rolls preserved in the Public Record Office ... Henry VI, A.D. 1422-[1461]. 6 vols. Originally published H.M.S.O., 1901-11. $US620.00.

Calendar of the patent rolls ... Edward IV, A.D. 1461-1467. Originally publshed H.M.S.O., 1897. $US75.00.

Calendar of the patent rolls preserved in the Public Record Office ... Edward IV, Edward V, Richard III, A.D. 1476-1485. Reprint. Originally published H.M.S.O., 1901. $US140.00.

Calendar of the patent rolls ... Edward VI, 1547-[1553]. 6 vols. Reprint. Originally published H.M.S.O., 1924-29. $US345.00.

Calendar of the patent rolls ... Elizabeth, 1558-[1572]. 5 vols. Reprint. Originally published HMSO., 1898-1955. $US350.00. Covers 1485-1505. Further volumes have not been reprinted.

Calendar of inquisitions post mortem and other analagous documents preserved in the Public Record Office. 14 vols. Reprint. Originally published H.M.S.O., 1904-54. $US1350.00. Covers 1235-1377. Further vols. have not been reprinted.

Calendar of inquisitions post mortem preserved in the Public Record Office ... Henry VII. 3 vols. Reprint. Originally published H.M.S.O., 1898-1955. $US350.00. Covers 1485-1505.

Liber feodorum: the book of fees, commonly called Testa de Nevill. 3 vols. Reprint; originally published H.M.S.O., 1921-31. $US295.00. Covers 1198-1293.

Inquisitions and assessments relating to feudal aids, with other analagous documents preserved in the Public Record Office, A.D. 1284-1431. 6 vols. Reprint. Originally published H.M.S.O., 1899-1921. $US550.00.

Curia regis rolls ... preserved in the Public Record Office. 10 vols. Reprint. Originally published H.M.S.O. 1922-49. $US630.00. Covers 1189-1222. Further volumes have not been reprinted.

Phillimore & Co. Ltd.

Shopwyke Manor Barn, Chichester, West Sussex, PO20 6BG.
Email: bookshop@phillimore.co.uk
http://www.phillimore.co.uk

ADAMS, R.H. *The parish clerks of London.* 168pp. 0-900592-18-4. 1971. £30.00.

ADDISON, WILLIAM, SIR, ed. *Essex worthies: a biographical companion to the county.* 200pp. 0-85033-080-7. £9.99.

ALCOCK, N.W. *Old title deeds: a guide for local and family historians.* 112pp. 0-85033-593-0. 1994. £13.95.

ALCOCK, N.W. *People at home: living in a Warwickshire village, 1500-1800.* 256pp. 0-85033-863-8. 1993. £19.95. Study of Stoneleigh.

BIRD, CLIFFORD, & BIRD, YVONNE, *Norfolk and Norwich clocks and clockmakers.* 248pp. 0-86077-028-2. 1996. £39.95.

CURRER-BRIGGS, NOEL. *English adventurers and Virginian settlers.* 3 vols. 0-900592-32-X. £30.00. A vast quarry of edited source material — especially wills.

CURRER-BRIGGS, NOEL, & GAMBIER, ROYSTON. *Huguenot ancestry.* 160pp. 0-85033-564-7. 1985. £13.95.

DANBURY, ELIZABETH. *Palaeography for historians.* 1-86077-072-X. Forthcoming; approx. £15.99.

DARLINGTON, IDA. *The London Commissioners of Sewers and their records.* 0-900592-09-5. 1970. £3.00.

DOWLER, GRAHAM. *Gloucestershire clock and watchmakers.* 254pp. 0-85033-554-X. 1985. £25.00.

DRENNAN, B. *Keble College register.* 432pp. 0-85033-048-3. 1970. £25.00.

DUNNING, ROBERT. *Local history for beginners.* 128pp. 0-85033-377-6. 1980. £7.99.

EDWARDS, F. *Elizabethan Jesuits.* 414pp. 0-85033-375-X. 1981. £17.99.

ELLIOTT, DOUGLAS J. *Shropshire clock and watchmakers.* 192pp. 0-85033-328-8. 1979. £11.95.

EMMISON, F.G. *Introduction to archives.* 52pp. 0-85033-063-7. 1977. £1.50.

HAMILTON-EDWARDS, G. *In search of ancestry.* 224pp. 0-85033-494-2. 1983. £11.99.

HAMILTON-EDWARDS, G. *In search of Scottish ancestry.* 2nd ed. 272pp. 0-85033-513-2. 1983. £11.99.

HARVEY, JOHN. *Early nurserymen.* 290pp. 0-85033-192-7. 1975. £30.00.

HOMER, RONALD F., & HALL, DAVID W. *Provincial pewterers.* 176pp. 0-85033-572-8. 1986. £19.95. Identifies 700+ pewterers in the West Midlands, Severn Valley and Wales.

HOSKINS, W.G., ed. *Exeter militia list, 1803.* 158pp. 0-900592-54-0. 1972. £9.95.

HUMPHERY-SMITH, CECIL R. *The Phillimore atlas and index of parish registers.* 320pp. 2nd ed. 0-85033-950-2. 1995. £50.00.

IREDALE, DAVID. *Enjoying archives.* 224pp. 0-85033-561-2. 1985. £12.99.

JONES, JOHN. *The archives of Balliol College, Oxford.* 96pp. 0-85033-533-7. 1984. £14.99.

KITCHING, CHRISTOPHER. *Archives: the very essence of our heritage.* 80pp. 1-86077-018-5. 1996. £14.95.

LYNSKEY, MARIE. *Family trees: a manual for their design, production, and display.* 112pp. 0-85033-980-4. 1996. £15.95.

MARTIN, C. TRICE. *The record interpreter.* 512pp. 0-85033-465-9. 1994. £20.00. Latin glossary.

MORRIS, JOHN, general ed. *Domesday book.* 38 vols. Set: library ed. 0-85033-771-2. £800.00; limp ed. 0-85033-772-0. £530.00.

	Library	Limp
v.1. Kent	£16.00.	£10.00.
v.2. Sussex	£15.00.	£8.75.
v.3. Surrey	£12.00.	£7.00.
v.4. Hampshire	£18.00.	£11.25.
v.5. Berkshire	£14.00.	£8.25.
v.6. Wiltshire	£16.00.	£10.00.
v.7. Dorset	£18.00.	£11.25.
v.8. Somerset	£22.00.	£13.00.
v.9. Devon (2 vols.)	£44.00.	£24.50.
v.10. Cornwall	£14.00.	£8.25.
v.11. Middlesex	£12.00.	£7.00.
v.12. Hertfordshire	£15.00.	£8.75.
v.13. Buckinghamshire	£15.00.	£8.75.
v.14. Oxfordshire	£14.00.	£8.25.
v.15. Gloucestershire	£16.00.	£10.00.
v.16. Worcestershire	£16.00.	£10.00.
v.17. Herefordshire	£18.00.	£11.25.
v.18. Cambridgeshire	£16.00.	£10.00.
v.19. Huntingdonshire	£12.00.	£7.00.
v.20. Bedfordshire	£14.00.	£8.25.
v.21. Northamptonshire	£16.00.	£10.00.
v.22. Leicestershire	£14.00.	£8.25.
v.23. Warwickshire	£14.00.	£8.25.
v.24. Staffordshire	£12.00.	£7.00.
v.25. Shropshire	£20.00.	£12.50.
v.26. Cheshire	£15.00.	£8.75.
v.27. Derbyshire	£12.00.	£7.00.
v.28. Nottinghamshire	£14.00.	£8.25.
v.29. Rutland	£12.00.	£7.00.
v.30. Yorkshire (2 vols.)	£44.00.	£24.50.
v.31. Lincolnshire (2 vols.)	£38.00.	£20.00.
v.32. Essex	£24.00.	£13.50.
v.33. Norfolk (2 vols.)	£44.00.	£24.50.
v.34. Suffolk (2 vols.)	£48.00.	£27.00.
v.35. Boldon Book	£12.00.	£7.00.
v.36. Index of Places	£50.00.	N/A.
v.37. Index of Persons	£50.00.	N/A.
v.38. Index of Subjects	£50.00.	N/A.

PRICE, F.D., ed. *The Wigginton constables' book, 1691-1836.* 176pp. 0-900592-55-9. 1971. £14.95.

RICHARDSON, JOHN. *The local historians encyclopedia.* 2nd ed. 264pp. 1986. 0-950365-67-X. £15.95.

SOMERVILLE, ROBERT, SIR. *Office holders in the Duchy of Lancaster.* 298pp. 0-85033-079-3. 1972. £14.95.

STEPHENS, W.B. *Sources for English local history.* 360pp. 0-85033-911-1. 1994. £16.95.

STUART, DENIS. *Latin for local and family historians.* 144pp. 0-85033-984-7. 1995. £13.95.

STUART, DENIS. *Manorial records.* 128pp. 0-85033-821-2. 1992. £12.95.

SUMMERS, PETER, & TITTERTON, JOHN E. *Hatchments in Britain.* 10 vols.
  v.1. *Northamptonshire, Warwickshire, Worcestershire.* 0-85033-085-8. 1975. £13.95.
  v.2. *Norfolk and Suffolk.* 0-85033-230-3. 1976. £13.95.
  v.3. *Cumbria, Northumberland, Durham, Lancashire, Yorkshire.* 0-85033-329-6. 1985. £13.95.

v.4. *Oxfordshire, Berkshire, Wiltshire, Buckinghamshire, Bedfordshire.* 0-85033-451-9. 1982. £13.95.
v.5. *Kent, Surrey, Sussex.* 0-85033-535-3. £13.95.
v.6. *Essex, Middlesex, Hertfordshire, Cambridgeshire, Hunts.* 0-85033-536-1. £13.95.
v.7. *Cornwall, Devon, Dorset, Somerset, Hampshire, Isle of Wight, Gloucestershire.* 0-85033-651-1. 1988. £13.95.
v.8. *Lincolnshire, Nottinghamshire, Cheshire, Staffordshire, Derbyshire, Leicestershire, Rutland.* 0-85033-652-X. 1988. £13.95.
v.9. *Herefordshire, Shropshire, Wales, Scotland, Monmouthshire, Ireland, and hatchments in former British colonies.* 0-85033-912-X. £13.95.
v.10. *The development and use of hatchments.* 0-85033-913-8. £13.95.
TARVER, ANNE. *Church court records.* 160pp. 0-85033-927-8. 1994. £12.95.
TATE, W.E. *The parish chest.* 400pp. 0-85033-507-8. 1983. £20.00.
TRINDER, BARRIE, & COX, JEFF. *Yeomen and colliers in Telford.* 496pp. 0-85033-382-2. 1980. £20.00. Extensive transcript of probate inventories for Dawley, Lilleshall, Wellington and Wrockwardine, Shropshire, 1660-1750.
WAGNER, ANTHONY, SIR. *English genealogy.* 496pp. 0-85033-473-X. 1983. £20.00.
WEST, JOHN. *Town records.* 384pp. 0-85033-472-1. 1983. £30.00.
WEST, JOHN. *Village records.* 3rd ed. 320pp. 1-86077-040-1. 1997. £30.00.
WILLIS, ARTHUR J., & PROUDFOOT, KARIN. *Genealogy for beginners.* 208pp. 1-86077-041-X. 1996. £7.99.
WILLIS, A.J. *Canterbury licences (general), 1568-1648.* 0-900592-72-9. 1972. £30.00.
WILLIS, A.J. *Church life in Kent: church court records of the Canterbury Diocese, 1559-65.* 110pp. 0-85033-202-8. 1975. £9.95.
WILLIS, A.J. *Hampshire marriage licences, 1669-1680.* 0-85033-047-5. 1963. £10.00.
WILLIS, A.J. *Winchester ordinations 1660-1829.* 2 pts.
Pt.1. *Ordinands papers 1734-1827.* £20.00.
Pt.2. *Bishops registers etc.* £20.00.
WILLIS, A.J. *A Hampshire miscellany.* 4 vols. 1963-7.
v.1. *Metropolitical visitation.* 0-85033-050-5. £5.00.
v.2. *Laymens licences.* 0-85033-050-5. £5.00.
v.3. *Dissenters certificates.* 0-85033-041-6. £5.00.
v.4. *Exhibit books, terriers, etc.* 0-85033-044-0. £5.00.
WILLIS, A.J. *Canterbury marriage licences.* 3 vols. 1967-71.
v.1. 1751-1780. 0-85033-039-4. 1967. £30.00.
v.2. 1781-1809. 0-85033-040-8. 1970. £30.00.
v.3. 1810-1837. 0-900592-56-7. 1971. £30.00.

FAMILY HISTORIES

Anderson
ANDERSON, M.A. *Anderson families.* 192pp. 0-85033-555-8. 1984. £20.00.

Bosanquet
LEE, GRACE LAWLESS. *The story of the Bosanquets.* 178pp. 0-900592-88-5. 1996. £13.95.

Bowes
WILLS, MARGARET. *Gibside and the Bowes family.* 128pp. 0-85033-998-7. 1995. £14.95.

Carter
CURRER-BRIGGS, NOEL. *The Carters of Virginia: their English ancestry.* 128pp. 0-85033-307-5. 1979. £14.95.

Child
CHILD, K. *Some account of the Child family, 1550-1861.* 56pp. 0-85033-099-8. 1973. £1.50.

Clifford
CLIFFORD, HUGH. *The house of Clifford.* 336pp. 0-85033-634-1. 1987. £30.00.

Darby
TRINDER, BARRIE. *The Darbys of Coalbrookdale.* 88pp. 0-85033-791-7. 1992. £4.95.

Dewar
DEWAR, PETER BEAUCLERK. *The house of Dewar, 1296-1991.* 144pp. 0-951742-80-9. 1991. £16.00.

Eldred
ELDRED, NELSON B., & ELDRID, J.T. *The Saxon house of Eldred.* 176pp. 0-85033-822-0. 1992. £20.00.

Grant
STRATHSPEY, LORD. *A history of Clan Grant.* 128pp. 0-85033-442-X. 1983. £17.50.

Grimston
KING, NORAH. *The Grimstons of Gorhambury.* 192pp. 0-85033-474-8. 1984. £17.99.

Howard
ROBINSON, JOHN MARTIN. *The Dukes of Norfolk.* 296pp. 0-85033-973-1. 1995. £10.95.

Keynes
BROWN, NEVILLE. *Dissenting forebears: the maternal ancestors of J.M. Keynes.* 224pp. 0-85033-670-8. 1989. £17.99.

Kirbye
CURRER-BRIGGS, NOEL. *The search for Mr. Thomas Kirbye, gentleman.* 256pp. 0-85033-532-9. 1986. £13.99.

Leslie
KLIEFORTH, ALEXANDER LESLIE. *Grip fast: the Leslies in history.* 304pp. 0-85033-859-X. 1993. £40.00.

Mallory
MALLORY-SMITH, SHEILA. *A history of the Mallory family.* 192pp. 0-85033-576-0. 1984. £25.00.

Moffat
MOFFAT, FRANCIS. *The Moffats.* 144pp. 0-85033-645-7. 1987. £25.00.

Murray
RUTHVEN-MURRAY, PETER. *The Murrays of Rulewater.* 264pp. 0-900592-69-9. 1986. £20.00.

Nisbit
NESBITT, ROBERT CHANCELLOR. *Nisbit of that ilk.* 364pp. 0-85033-929-4. 1994. £35.00.

Pedler
PEDLER, FREDERICK, SIR. *A Pedler family history.* 144pp. 0-85033-547-7. 1984. £17.99.

PEDLER, FREDERICK, SIR. *A wider Pedler family history.* 144pp. 0-85033-706-2. 1989. £17.99.

Prideaux
PRIDEAUX, R.M. *Prideaux: a West Country clan.* 304pp. 0-85033-674-0. 1989. £25.00.

Raikes
RAIKES, R.D. *Pedigree of Raikes.* 96pp. 0-900592-73-7. 1980. £20.00.

Ridge
RIDGE, D. *A Sussex family: the family of Ridge.* 104pp. 0-85033-076-9. 1975. £9.95.

St. Leger
ST. LEGER, MOYA F. *St. Leger: the family and the race.* 176pp. 0-85033-588-4. 1986. £13.95.

Salkeld
MOORE, J. GRANGE. *Salkelds through seven centuries.* 208pp. 0-85033-644-9. 1988. £25.00.

Titford
TITFORD, JOHN. *The Titford family.* 272pp. 0-85033-681-3. 1989. £25.00.

Tyrell
BROWN, OLIVER F. *Tyrells of England.* 288pp. 0-85033-358-x. 1982. £25.00.

Wagner
WAGNER, ANTHONY, & DALE, ANTONY. *The Wagners of Brighton.* 192pp. 0-85033-445-4. 1983. £17.99.

Wigg
KIRBY, J.L. *The Wigg family.* 220pp. 0-85033-632-5. 1988. £20.00.

Wilton
WILTON, ROBERT. *The Wiltons of Cornwall.* 192pp. 0-85033-722-4. £17.99.

Worthington
WORTHINGTON, JAN. *Coopers and customs cutters: the Worthingtons of Dover.* 360pp. 1-86077-011-8. 1997. £25.00.

Photoresearch
ALLM Systems and Marketing, 21,Beechcroft Road, Bushey, Hertfordshire, WD2 2JU.

PRITCHARD, MICHAEL. *A directory of London photographers, 1841-1908.* 2nd ed. 140pp. 0-9523011-0-5. 1997. £14.95 + £1.50 p&p.

Pinhorns
94, Carisbrooke High Street, Newport, Isle of Wight, PO30 1NU.

GERHOLD, DORIAN. *Courts of equity: a guide to Chancery and other legal records for local and family historians.* iv, 30pp. 0-901262-25-0. £7.50.

HARVEY, W.J., ed. *List of the principal inhabitants of the City of London, 1640.* Offprint from *Blackmansbury.* £5.50.

LEESON, FRANCIS. *Tontines and annuities.* 20pp. 0-901262-03-X. 1968. £2.50. Guide to records, 17-18th.

MILLARD, A.M., ed. *Records of the Worshipful Company of Carpenters, volume VII. Wardens' account book 1592-1614.* 0-901262-05-6. £25.00.

SQUIBB, G.D. *Visitation pedigrees and the genealogist.* iv, 47pp. 0-901262-19-6. 1978. £7.50.

STAINES, E.W. *A guide to the monumental brasses and incised slabs on the Isle of Wight.* 0-901262-11-0. £2.50.

Local history studies libraries in Great Britain: a list. vi, 31pp. 0-901262-27-7. 1997. £7.50.

Sally Pocock

2, Fairmantle Street, Truro, Cornwall, TR1 2EG.

POCOCK, SALLY J. *Family historians guide.* 5th ed. 0-9533034-0-4. 1998. £4.50 + 75p p&p. Dictionary telling you where to look for information.

POCOCK, SALLY J. *Behind bars: a chronicle of Bodmin gaol.* 0-9533034-0-3. 1998. £4.25 + p&p.

Miss M. Purcell

128, Red Bank Road, Bispham, Blackpool, FY2 9DZ.
Phone: (01253) 353909
Cheques payable to J.Henderson please.

DUNN, JOSEPH. *Census of the Catholic congregation of Preston, 1810 and 1820,* ed. Margaret Purcell. 1-89847-00-6. 1993. £5.00 + p&p £1.00.

M. & T. Purkiss

P.O.Box 19, New Farm, Queensland, 4005, Australia.

PURKISS, MERV, & PURKISS, TREVOR. *The Purkiss family album from Suffolk, England: a profile of our earliest pioneers and their families in Australia.* 0-646-23838-8. 1995. $A52.00 + p&p.

Random House New Zealand Ltd

PB102950, NSMC Delivery, 18, Poland Road, Glenfield, Auckland 10, New Zealand

BROMELL, ANNE. *Tracing family history overseas from New Zealand.* 0-908877-42-0. $NZ39.95.

S.A.& M.J.Raymond

P.O. Box 35, Exeter, EX1 3YZ
Phone: (01392) 252193
Email: stuart@samjraymond.softnet.co.uk

Raymonds original pollbooks series

The London poll book 1768. iv, [iv], 116pp. 1-899668-00-4. Facsimile reprint. [1996.] £14.50 (inc. p&p).

The Westminster poll book 1774. iv, 152pp. 1-899668-05-5. Facsimile reprint. [1996.] £19.00 (inc. p&p).

The Westminster poll book 1818. iv, xii, 235pp. 1-899668-06-3. Facsimile reprint. 1996. £23.50 (inc. p&p).

The Westminster poll book 1841. iv, [iv], 132pp. 1-899668-09-8. Facsimile reprint. 1996. £19.00 (inc. p&p).

The Norfolk poll book 1768. iv, [iv], 256, xxxviiipp. (reprinted 2 pages on 1). 1-899668-04-7. Facsimile reprint. 1996. £18.50 (inc. p&p).

The Norfolk poll book 1806. iv, 200, viii pp (reprinted 2 pages on 1). 1-899668-03-9. Facsimile reprint. 1996. £17.50. (inc. p&p)

The Norfolk poll book 1817. iv, iv, 204pp (reprinted 2 pages on 1). 1-899668-02-0. Facsimile reprint. 1996. £18.00 (inc. p&p).

The Somerset electoral register. Eastern Division 1832. iv, 179pp. 1-899668-08-X. Facsimile reprint. 1996. £19.00 (inc. p&p).

The Somerset electoral register. Western Dvsion 1832. iv, 174pp. 1-899668-07-1. Facsimile reprint. 1996. £19.00 (inc. p&p).

The Suffolk poll book 1710. iv, 95pp. 0-9588144-8-1. Facsimile reprint. 1995. £14.25 (inc. p&p).

The Suffolk poll book 1790. iv, 133pp. £14.50 (inc. p&p).

The Yorkshire poll book 1741. [iv], [ii], 168, 174pp (reprinted 2 pages on 1). 1-899668-10-1. Facsimile reprint. 1997. £24.00. (inc. p&p).

The Yorkshire West Riding poll book 1835. [iv], 464pp (reprinted 2 pages on 1). 1-899668-01-2. Facsimile reprint. 1996. £24.50 (inc. p&p).

The Hull poll book 1835. iv, 31pp. 1-899668-11-X. Facsimile reprint. 1997. £6.50 (inc. p&p).

British genealogical library guides

(formerly British genealogical bibliographies). Published in association with the Federation of Family History Societies. See back cover.

George Redmonds
5, Knotty Lane, Lepton, Huddersfield, HD8 0ND

REDMONDS, GEORGE. *Surnames and genealogy: a new approach.* 1997. £12.95 + £1.55 p&p.

Gillian Rickard
99 Strangers Lane, Canterbury, Kent, CT1 3XN

RICKARD, GILLIAN. *Kent census surname indexes.* 9pp. 1998. £1.00 + s.a.e.

RICKARD, GILLIAN. *Kent settlement (poor law) records: a guide and catalogue.* 2 pts + supplement. The set, £8.60 + p&p 75p.
  Pt.1. *East Kent (Diocese of Canterbury).* 64pp. 0-9521828-0-7. 1993. £3.95 + p&p 55p. Supplement (to pt.1) 1997. 65p + s.a.e.
  Pt.2. *West Kent (Diocese of Rochester).* 68pp. 0-9521828-1-5. 1994. £4.50 + p&p 55p.

RICKARD, GILLIAN. *Vagrants, gypsies and travellers in Kent, 1572-1948.* 80pp. 0-9521828-2-3. 1995. £5.00 + p&p 55p.

RICKARD, GILLIAN. *Kent dissenting ministers declarations 1689-1836.* 32pp. 0-9521828-3-1. 1995. £3.50 + p&p 45p.

RICKARD, GILLIAN. *Canterbury Blackfriars Baptist Chapel births and burials 1780-1836.* 33pp. 0-9521828-4-x. £3.50 + p&p 45p.

RICKARD, GILLIAN. *Quakers in Kent: some birth, marriage, burial and other records, 1648-1806.* 64pp. 0-9521828-6-6. 1996. £5.00 + p&p 55p.

RICKARD, GILLIAN. *Kent enrolments under the Navy Act 1796.* 57pp. 0-9521828-7-4. 1996. £4.75 + p&p 55p. Lists sailors.

RICKARD, GILLIAN. *Kent inventories in the Prerogative Court of Canterbury.* 4 pts. 0-9521828-5-8. 1998-. List of 3000 Kent probate inventories.
  Pt.1. *Surnames A-C.* 1998. £5.00 + p&p 55p.
  Pt.2. *Surnames D-I.* 1998. £5.00 + p&p 55p.
  Pt.3. *Surnames J-Q.* Forthcoming.
  Pt.4. *Surnames R-Z.* Forthcoming.

RICKARD, GILLIAN. *Staplehurst Congregational Chapel baptisms 1746-1793, 1797-1837; marriages 1788-1792; deaths 1787-1792; burials 1842-1912.* Forthcoming; approx £4.00.

RICKARD, GILLIAN. *Tenterden 1831 census index.* Forthcoming; approx £4.00.

RICKARD, GILLIAN. *Black people in Kent: a list and short history.* Forthcoming.

RICKARD, GILLIAN. *Emigrants and transportees from Kent.* Forthcoming. Catalogue of records.

RICKARD, GILLIAN. *Gamekeepers and gun licences in Kent, 1786.* Forthcoming. List of gamekeepers and sponsors.

RICKARD, GILLIAN. *List of surnames in Canterbury baptisms index 1790-1840.* Forthcoming. Lists surnames and years, but no other details.

RICKARD, GILLIAN. *Kent Poor Law Union settlement records 1827-1930: abstracts and indexes.* Forthcoming.

Riverlea Publishing
1/130, Shackleton Circuit, Mawson, A.C.T., 2607, Australia

WELLS, RONALD. *Ancient ancestors with modern descendants: a companion for studies in European history and genealogy.* 620pp. 1998. $A70.00. Royal genealogies.

Robson Books
Bolsover House, 5-6, Chipstone Street, London, W1P 8LE

BROOKE-LITTLE, J.P. *An heraldic alphabet.* New ed. 234pp. 1-86105-077-1. 1997. £8.99.

Alan Ruston
41, Hampermill Lane, Oxhey, Watford, Hertfordshire, WD1 4NS

RUSTON, ALAN. *Obituaries and marriages of dissenting ministers in the Gentleman's Magazine in the 18th century.* 0-9513527-2-5. 1997. £2.50 + 35p p&p.

S&N Genealogy Supplies
Greenacres, Salisbury Road, Chilmark, Salisbury, SP3 5AH.

BAYLEY, NIGEL. *CAGe: guide to using computer software for family history.* 1-86150-000-9. £4.95.

WATKINSON, J.A. *How to research your family history.* £3.95.

WATKINSON, J.A. *Young persons guide to genealogy.* £1.95.

Savannah Publications
90, Dartmouth Road, Forest Hill, London SE23 3HZ
This publisher is now responsible for titles formerly published by J.B. Hayward & Son.

ABBOTT, P.E. *Recipients of the Distinguished Conduct Medal, 1855-1909.* 2nd ed. 127pp. 0-903754-37-1. 1987. £25.00 + p&p £3.00.

ABBOTT, P.E., & TAMPLIN, J.M.A. *British gallantry awards.* 2nd ed. 316pp. 0-903754-25-8. 1981. £30.00 + p&p £3.00.

ANDERSON, T.C. *Ubique: war services of the Bengal army.* 742pp. 0-903754-23-1. 1985. Originally published 1861. £40.00.

CARTER, NICK, & CARTER, CAROL. *The Distinguished Flying Cross and how it was won, 1918-1995.* 2 vols. 1974pp. 0-902366-00-X. 1998. £140.00 + p&p £4.50.

COOK, F., & COOK, A. *Casualty roll for the Crimea, 1854-55.* 286pp. 0-903754-10-X. 1976. £40.00.

CREAGH, O'MOORE, SIR, & HUMPHRIS, E.M. *The Distinguished Service Order, 1886-1923.* 806pp. 0-903754-12-6. 1978. Originally published 1924. £95.00 + p&p £3.00.

CREAGH, O'MOORE, SIR, & HUMPHRIS, E.M. *The Victoria Cross, 1856-1920.* 336pp. 0-903754-22-3. 1985. Originally published 1924. £44.00 + p&p £3.00.

HOBSON, CHRIS. *Airmen died in the Great War 1914-1918: the roll of honour of the British and Commonwealth air services of the First World War.* 468pp. 0-871505-81-X. 1995. £45.00.

MCDERMOTT, PHILIP. *For distinguished conduct in the field: the register of the Distinguished Conduct Medal 1920-1992.* 2 vols. 1068pp. 0-903754-65-7. 1995. £70.00 + p&p £4.50.

MESSAGE, COLIN. *Naval General Service Medal roll, 1793-1840: alphabetical list of recipients.* 600pp. 1996. £160.00.

O'BYRNE, W.R. *Naval biographical dictionary: comprising the life and services of every living officer in H.M.'s navy from the rank of admiral to that of lieutenant.* 2 vols. 1400pp. 0-903754-26-6. 1990. Originally published 1849. £120.00.

PHILLIPART, JOHN. *Royal military calendar: army service and commission book containing the services and progress of promotion of the generals, lieutenant generals, major generals, colonels and majors of the army.* 5 vols. 2200pp. 0-903754-30-4. 1985. Originally published 1820. £125.00.

PURVES, ALEC A. *Medals, decorations and orders of the Great War, 1914-1918.* 2nd ed. 192pp. 0-903754-38-X. 1988. £18.00.

The Royal Air Force list 1918. 432pp. 0-903754-46-0. 1990. £28.00.

The South African war casualty roll: the South African Field Force 1899-1902. 782pp. 0-903754-96-7. 1982. £34.00.

The South Africa war casualty roll: Natal Field Force 1899-1900. 237pp. 0-903754-95-9. 1980. £18.00.

Soldiers died in the Great War 1914-1919. 80 pts in 74 vols. 1988. Originally published 1921. Also available on CD-Rom from Naval & Military Press, see above, p. 34.

Pt.1. *Household cavalry and cavalry of the Line (including Yeomanry and Imperial Camel Corps).* 96pp. 1-871505-01-1. £16.00.

Pts.2 & 3. *Royal Horse and Royal Field Artillery, Regulars and Territorial Force (including Honourable Artillery Company Batteries, Royal Garrison Artillery).* 430pp. 1-871505-02-X. £44.00.

Pt.4. *Corps of Royal Engineers.* 214pp. 1-871505-04-6. £27.00.

Pt.5. *Foot Guards (including Guards Machine Gun Regiment).* 148pp. 1-871505-05-4. £22.00.

Pt.6. *The Royal Scots (Lothian Regiment).* 116pp. 1-871505-06-2. £16.00.

Pt.7. *The Queen's (Royal West Surrey Regiment).* 96pp. 1-871505-07-0. £16.00.

Pt.8. *The Buffs (East Kent Regiment).* 72pp. 1-871505-08-9. £16.00.

Pt.9. *The King's Own (Royal Lancaster Regiment).* 62pp. 1-871505-09-7. £16.00.

Pt.10. *The Northumberland Fusiliers.* 158pp. 1-871505-10-0. £22.00.

Pt.11. *The Royal Warwickshire Regiment.* 124pp. 1-871505-11-9. £20.00.

Pt.12. *The Royal Fusiliers (City of London Regiment).* 174pp. 1-871505-12-7. £22.00.

Pt.13. *The King's (Liverpool Regiment).* 142pp. 1-871505-13-5. £22.00.
Pt.14. *The Norfolk Regiment.* 58pp. 1-871505-14-3. £16.00.
Pt.15. *The Lincolnshire Regiment.* 88pp. 1-871505-15-1. £16.00.
Pt.16. *The Devonshire Regiment.* 60pp. 1-871505-16-X. £16.00.
Pt.17. *The Suffolk Regiment.* 70pp. 1-871505-17-8. £16.00.
Pt.18. *Prince Albert's (Somerset Light Infantry).* 54pp. 1-871505-18-6. £16.00.
Pt.19. *The Prince of Wales's Own (West Yorkshire Regiment).* 116pp. 1-871505-19-4. £18.00.
Pt.20. *The East Yorkshire Regiment.* 76pp. 1-871505-20-8. £16.00.
Pt.21. *The Bedfordshire Regiment.* 70pp. 1-871505-21-6. £16.00.
Pt.22. *The Leicestershire Regiment.* 70pp. 1-871505-22-4. £16.00.
Pts.23 & 32. *The Royal Irish Regiment and Royal Inniskillen Fusiliers.* 96pp. 1-871505-23-2. £16.00.
Pt.24. *Alexandra, Princess of Wales's Own (Yorkshire Regiment).* 76pp. 1-871505-24-0. £16.00.
Pt.25. *The Lancashire Fusiliers.* 128pp. 1-871505-25-9. £20.00.
Pt.26. *The Royal Scots Fusiliers.* 56pp. 1-871505-26-7. £16.00.
Pt.27. *The Cheshire Regiment.* 84pp. 1-871505-27-5. £16.00.
Pt.28. *The Royal Welsh Fusiliers.* 104pp. 1-871505-28-3. £18.00.
Pt.29. *The South Wales Borderers.* 56pp. 1-871505-29-1. £16.00.
Pt.30. *The King's Own Scottish Borderers.* 82pp. 1-871505-30-5. £16.00.
Pt.31. *The Cameronians (Scottish Rifles).* 66pp. 1-871505-31-3. £16.00.
Pt.32. *The Royal Inniskilling Fusiliers —* see pt. 23.
Pt.33. *The Gloucestershire Regiment.* 82pp. 1-871505-33-X. £16.00.
Pt.34. *The Worcestershire Regiment.* 96pp. 1-871505-34-8. £16.00.
Pt.35. *The East Lancashire Regiment.* 70pp. 1-871505-35-6. £16.00.
Pt.36. *The East Surrey Regiment.* 68pp. 1-871505-36-4. £16.00.
Pt.37. *The Duke of Cornwall's Light Infantry.* 50pp. 1-871505-37-2. £16.00.
Pt.38. *The Duke of Wellington's (West Riding Regiment).* 76pp. 1-871505-38-0. £16.00.
Pt.39. *The Border Regiment.* 76pp. 1-871505-39-9. £16.00.
Pt.40. *The Royal Sussex Regiment.* 66pp. 1-871505-40-2. £16.00.
Pt.41. *The Hampshire Regiment.* 86pp. 1-871505-41-0. £16.00.
Pt.42. *The South Staffordshire Regiment.* 62pp. 1-871505-42-9. £16.00.
Pt.43. *The Dorsetshire Regiment.* 48pp. 1-871505-43-7. £16.00.
Pt.44. *The Prince of Wales's Volunteers (South Lancashire Regiment).* 56pp. 1-871505-44-5. £16.00.
Pt.45. *The Welch Regiment.* 80pp. 1-871505-45-3. £16.00.
Pt.46. *The Black Watch (Royal Highlanders).* 84pp. 1-871505-46-1. £16.00.
Pt.47. *The Oxfordshire and Buckinghamshire Light Infantry.* 64pp. 1-871505-47-X. £16.00.
Pt.48. *The Essex Regiment.* 90pp. 1-871505-48-8. £16.00.
Pt.49. *The Sherwood Foresters (Nottinghamshire and Derbyshire Regiment).* 106pp. 1-871505-49-6. £18.00.
Pt.50. *The Loyal North Lancashire Regiment.* 78pp. 1-871505-50-X. £16.00.
Pt.51. *The Northamptonshire Regiment.* 60pp. 1-871505-51-8. £16.00.
Pt.52. *Princess Charlotte of Wales's (Royal Berkshire Regiment).* 74pp. 1-871505-52-6. £16.00.
Pt.53. *The Queen's Own (Yorkshire Light Infantry).* 88pp. 1-871505-53-4. £16.00.
Pt.54. *The King's Own (Yorkshire Light Infantry).* 94pp. 1-871505-54-2. £16.00.
Pt.55. *The King's (Shropshire Light Infantry).* 54pp. 1-871505-55-0. £16.00.
Pt.56. *The Duke of Cambridge's Own (Middlesex Regiment).* 124pp. 1-871505-56-9. £20.00.
Pt.57. *The King's Royal Rifle Corps.* 140pp. 1-871505-57-7. £22.00.
Pt.58. *The Duke of Edinburgh's (Wiltshire Regiment).* 60pp. 1-871505-58-5. £16.00.
Pt.59. *The Manchester Regiment.* 134pp. 1-871505-59-3. £20.00.

Pt.60. *The Prince of Wales's (North Staffordshire Regiment).* 56pp. 1-871505-60-7. £16.00.

Pt.61. *The York and Lancaster Regiment.* 90pp. 1-871505-61-5. £16.00.

Pt.62. *The Durham Light Infantry.* 118pp. 1-871505-62-3. £16.00.

Pt.63. *The Highland Light Infantry.* 102pp. 1-871505-63-1. £18.00.

Pt.64. *Seaforth Highlanders (Ross-shire, Buffs, The Duke of Albany's).* 88pp. 1-871505-64-X. £16.00.

Pt.65. *The Gordon Highlanders.* 84pp. 1-871505-65-8. £16.00.

Pt.66. *The Queen's Own (Cameron Highlanders).* 74pp. 1-871505-66-6. £16.00.

Pts. 67, 68, 69. *Princess Victoria's (Royal Irish Fusiliers), The Connaught Rangers.* 138pp. 1-871505-67-4. £22.00.

Pt.70. *Princess Louise's (Argyll and Sutherland Highlanders).* 80pp. 1-871505-70-4. £16.00.

Pts. 71, 72, 73. *The Prince of Wales's Leinster Regiment (Royal Canadians), Royal Munster Fusiliers, Royal Dublin Fusiliers.* 108pp. 1-871505-71-2. £18.00.

Pt.74. *The Rifle Brigade (The Prince Consort's Own).* 138pp. 1-871505-74-7. £22.00.

Pt.75. *Machine Gun Corps, Tank Corps.* 194pp. 1-871505-75-5. £25.00.

Pt.76. *The London Regiment, Honourable Artillery Company (Infantry), Inns of Court Officers Training Corps.* 313pp. 1-871505-76-3. £36.00.

Pt.77. *Monmouthshire Regiment, Cambridge Regiment, Hertfordshire Regiment, Herefordshire Regiment, Army Cyclist Corps, Northern Cyclist Battalion, Highland Cyclist Battalion, Kent Cyclist Battalion, Huntingdonshire Cyclist Battalion.* 60pp. 1-871505-77-1. £16.00.

Pt.78. *Royal Army Service Corps.* 80pp. 1-871505-78-X. £16.00.

Pt.79. *Royal Army Medical Corps.* 56pp. 1-871505-79-8. £16.00.

Pt.80. *Labour Corps, Royal Army Ordnance Corps, Royal Army Veterinary Corps, Royal Army Pay Corps, Corps of Army Schoolmasters, Channel Islands Militia, Corps of Military Mounted Police, Corps of Military Foot Police, Corps of Small Arms School, Military Provost Staff Corps, Non-Combatant Corps, Queen Mary's Army Auxiliary Corps.* 94pp. 1-871505-80-1. £16.00.

The Air Force list, October 1940: the official Air Force list for the Battle of Britain period August 1940. 720pp. 0-903754-45-2. 1990. Originally published 1940. £28.00.

PURVES, ALEC A. *Medals, decorations and orders of W.W.II., 1939-1945.* 200pp. 0-903754-36-3. 1986. £18.00.

Prisoners of war: British army 1939-45. 560pp. 0-903754-61-4. 1990. Originally published 1945.

Prisoner of war: naval and air forces of Great Britain and the Empire 1939-45. 146pp. 0-903754-62-2. 1990. £28.00 + p&p £3.00.

Cross of sacrifice series
    v.1. *Officers who died in the service of British, Indian, and East African regiments and corps, 1914-1919.* £34.99.
    v.2. *Officers who died in the service of the Royal Navy, Royal Naval Volunteer Reserve, Royal Marines, Royal Naval Air Service and Royal Air Force, 1914-1919.* £24.99.
    v.3. *Officers who died in the service of the British Commonwealth and colonial navies, regiments, corps and air forces, 1914-1919.* £24.99.
    v.4. *Non-commissioned officers, men and women of the United Kingdom, Commonwealth and Empire who died in the service of the Royal Navy, Royal Marines, Royal Naval Air Service, Royal Flying Corps, and the Royal Air Force, 1914-1919.* £34.99.

Scarecrow Press
4720, Boston Way, Suite A, Lanham, Maryland 20706-4310, USA.

FITZSIMMONS, LINDA, & MCDONALD, ARTHUR W. *The Yorkshire stage 1766-1803: a calendar of plays together with cast lists for Tate Wilkinson's circuit of theatres (Doncaster, Hull, Leeds, Pontefract, Wakefield and York) and the Yorkshire Company's engagements in Beverley, Halifax, Newcastle, Sheffield and Edinburgh.* 1103pp. 0-8108-2187-7. $US92.00.

WEARING, J.P. *The London stage: a calendar of plays and players.*
- *1890-1899.* 1242pp. 0-8108-0910-9. $US83.50.
- *1900-1909.* 1202pp. 0-8108-1403-X. $US72.50.
- *1910-1919.* 1370pp. 0-8108-1596-6. $US89.50.
- *1920-1929.* 1808pp. 0-8108-1715-2. $US97.50.
- *1930-1939.* 1999pp. 0-8108-2349-7. $US144.50.
- *1940-1949.* 1284pp. 0-8108-2500-7. $US121.00.
- *1950-1959.* 1807pp. 0-8108-2690-9. $US136.00.

HORWITZ, BARBARA J. *British women writers 1700-1850: an annotated bibliography of their works and works about them.* 256pp. 0-8108-3315-8. $US37.00.

Scarthin Books
The Promenade, Cromford, Derbyshire, DE4 3QF.

KITCHING, COLIN. *Squire of Calke Abbey: the journals of Sir George Crewe, 1815-1834.* 0-907758-84-3. £9.45.

Scholarly Resources
104, Greenhill Avenue, Wilmington, DE., 19805-1897, U.S.A.
Email: sales@scholarly.com

KEMP, THOMAS J. *Virtual roots: a guide to genealogy and local history on the World Wide Web.* 304pp. 1996. 0-8420-2420-3 (limp). $US24.95. 0-8420-2718-1 (hardback). $US65.00.

PRATT, DAVID H. *Researching British probates 1354-1858: Vol. 1. Province of York.* 219pp. 0-8420-2420-4. 1992. $US75.00. Guide to the probate resources of the Family History Library of the Church of Jesus Christ of Latter Day Saints.

Scottish Academic Press
56, Hanover Street, Edinburgh, EH2 2DX.
Phone: (031) 2257483

YOUNG, MARGARET D. *The Parliaments of Scotland: burgh and shire commissioners.* 2 vols. 466 + 424pp. 0-7073-0705-8. £35.00 per volume. Biographical dictionary.

KIRK, JAMES, TANNER, ROLAND J., & DUNLOP, ANNIE I., eds. *Calendar of Scottish supplications to Rome. Vol. V. 1447-1471.* 528pp. 0-7073-0757-0. £30.00. Includes matrimonial dispensations, with many other names.

Sessions of York
The Ebor Press, Huntingdon Road, York, YO3 9HS.

BESSE, JOSEPH. *Sufferings of early Yorkshire Quakers.* 88pp. 1998 facsimile reprint; originally published 1753. £12.00 + p&p.

SESSIONS, E. MARGARET. *Rowntree's of Riseborough: family genealogy.* 1-85072-115-7. £15.00 + p&p £1.70.

SESSIONS, E.M., & SESSIONS, WILLIAM K. *The Tukes of York.* 1-85072-020-7. 1989. £3.00 + p&p £1.00.

Shire Publications Ltd.
Cromwell House, Church Street, Princes Risborough, Buckinghamshire, HP17 9AA.
Phone: (01844) 344301
Email: shire@shirebooks.co.uk
http://www.shirebooks.co.uk

BARRETT, JOHN, & IREDALE, DAVID. *Discovering old handwriting.* 184pp. 0-7478-0268-8. £5.99 + p&p £1.00.

CHAPMAN, LEIGH. *Church memorial brasses and brass rubbing.* 32pp. 0-85263-905-8. £2.95 + p&p £1.00.

FEARN, JACQUELINE. *Discovering heraldry.* 96pp. 0-85263-476-5. £3.95 + p&p £1.00.

FREEMAN, J.W. *Discovering surnames.* 72pp. 0-85263-007-7. £3.95 + p&p £1.00.
IREDALE, DAVID, & BARRETT, JOHN. *Discovering your family tree.* 0-85263-767-5. 80pp. £3.95 + p&p £1.00.
IREDALE, DAVID, & BARRETT, JOHN. *Discovering your old house.* 0-7478-0143-6. 112pp. £4.50 + p&p £1.00.
KEMP, BRIAN. *Church monuments.* 32pp. 0-85263-768-3. £2.50 + p&p £1.00.
WRIGHT, GEOFFREY N. *Discovering epitaphs.* 96pp. 0-7478-0324-2. £3.95 + p&p £1.00.

Shropshire Record Series
University of Keele Centre for Local History, Shropshire Records and Research Centre, Castle Gates, Shrewsbury, SY1 2AQ
Phone: (01743) 255357

2. WANKLYN, M.D.G., ed. *The diary of George Gitton of Bridgnorth for 1866.* 0-951371-38-X. 1998. £13.50 (inc. p&p).

Sigma Press
1, South Oak Lane, Wilmslow, Cheshire, SK9 6AR.

BRADLEY, ALAN. *Family history on your P.C: a book for beginners.* 1-85058-502-4. £9.95.

Janice Simons
36, Old Hospital Mews, Hospital Walk, London Road, Kings Lynn, Norfolk, PE30 5RU.

SIMONS, JANICE. *Marriage and obituary notices . . . (Lynn Advertiser, Norfolk).*
1851 1-873237-06-5. 1994 £5.00.
1881. 1-873237-03-0. [199-] £4.50
1882 1-873237-05-7. 1992 £5.00.
1900. 1-873237-02-2. [199-] £4.50.
Volumes for *1880* and *1890* forthcoming.

Spanish & Portuguese Jews Congregation
2, Ashworth Road, London W9 1JY
Phone: (0171) 2892573
Bevis Marks records, being contributions to the history of the Spanish and Portuguese Congregation of London.

2. BARNETT, LIONEL D., ed. *Abstracts of the Ketubot or marriage-contracts of the Congregation from earliest times until 1837.* 1949. £17.50 + p&p £2.50. Published by Oxford University Press.
3. WHITEHILL, G.H., ed. *Abstracts of the Ketubot or marriage-contracts and of the civil marriage registers of the Spanish and Portuguese Jews Congregation for the period 1837-1901.* 1973. £17.50 + p&p £2.50.
4. BARNETT, R.D., ed. *The circumcision registers of Isaac and Abraham de Paiba (1715-1775)* ... 1991. £17.50. Includes RODRIGUES-PEREIRA, MIRIAM, ed. *A record of circumcisions 1679-99, marriages 1679-89, and some female births 1679-99.* 1991. £17.50 + p&p £2.50.
5. RODRIGUES-PEREIRA, MIRIAM, ed. *The birth register (1767-1881) of the Spanish & Portuguese Jews congregation, London, together with the circumcision registers of Elias Lindo (1767-1785), David Abarbanel Lindo (1803-1820), Solomon Almosnino (1815-1827), David Buero de Mesquita (1855-1869) ... and including the Jewish births (1707-1763) in the 18th-century register books of the College of Arms.* 1993. £25.00 + p&p £2.50.
6. RODRIGUES-PEREIRA, MIRIAM, & LOEWE, CHLOE, eds. *The burial register (1733-1918) of the Novo (New) Cemetery of the Spanish & Portuguese Jews Congregation, London (with some later entries).* £35.00 + p&p £6.00.

Dr Jack T. Spencer
1303, Azalea Lane, Dekalb, Illinois, 60115-2329, U.S.A.

SPENCER, JACK TAIF, & SPENCER, EDITH WOOLLEY. *The Spencers of the great migration. Vol.1. 1300 A.D. - 1783 A.D. The history and genealogy of the five Spencer siblings of Bedfordshire who came to New England 1630-1631, and the lineage of some of their descendants in America.* 1997. $US45.00. Published by Gateway Press.

R.G. Spiers
7, Nightingale Court, Nightingale Road, Rickmansworth, Herts., WD3 2BX.

SPIERS, R.G. *Searching for Spiers: a history.* 242pp. 0-9527491-0-6. 1996. £15.00 + p&p.

Spink & Son Ltd.
Book and Publishing Department, 5-7 King Street, St James's, London, SW1Y 6QS
Phone: (0171) 9307888

HENDERSON, A.C. *Hop tokens of Kent & Sussex and their issuers.* 0-907605-30-3.

Roy Stockdill
6, First Avenue, Harston, Watford, Herts., WD2 6PZ

STOCKDILL, ROY. *Family history newsletters from the desktop: creating and publishing family & one-name journals.* 12pp. 1998. £1.00. Published by Stockdill Family History Society.

STOCKDILL, ROY. *Rhyming relations: genealogy in verse.* 0-9533023-0. 1998. £3.95.

Sutton Publishing Ltd.
Phoenix Mill, Thrupp, Stroud, Gloucestershire, GL5 2BU.
Phone (01453) 731114
E mail: sales@sutton-publishing.co.uk
http://www.bookshop.co.uk/sutton
Distributor: Littlehampton Book Services, Units 10-14, Eldon Way, Lineside Estate, Littlehampton, W. Sussex, BN17 7HE.

AYRES, JACK, ed. *The diary of William Holland, a Somerset parson 1799-1818.* 0-86299-052-1. £6.99

BERESFORD, MAURICE. *History on the ground.* 256p. 0-7509-1884-5. 1998. £14.99.

COLLINS, RAE P. *Forward to the past: another journey in ancestry.* 160pp. 0-7509-0893-9. [199-?] £8.99.

COLWELL, STELLA. *Family history: a guide and troubleshooter.* 224pp. 0-7509-1187-5. 1998. £14.99.

CURRIE, C.R.J., & LEWIS, C.P., eds. *A guide to English county histories.* 496pp. 0-7509-1505-6. [199-?] £14.99.

FRANKLIN, PETER, ed. *The taxpayers of medieval Gloucestershire.* 192pp. 0-81299-980-4. [199-?] £40.00. Subsidy, 1327.

FRIAR, STEPHEN. *Heraldry.* 288pp. 0-7509-1085-2. [199-]. £14.99.

HAMMOND, PETER. *The complete peerage. Vol. XIV: addenda and corrigenda.* 0-7509-0154-3. 1998. £95.00.

HAWKINGS, DAVID. *Criminal ancestors: a guide to historical criminal records in England and Wales.* 416pp. 0-7509-1084-4. [199-?] £14.99.

HAWKINGS, DAVID. *Railway ancestors: a guide to the staff records of the railway companies of England and Wales, 1822-1947.* 528pp. 0-7509-0883-1. 1992. £25.00.

HEBER, MARK D. *Ancestral trails: the complete guide to British genealogy and family history.* 0-7509-1418-1. 1997. £25.00.

LAFFIN, JOHN. *British V.C.'s of World War 2.* 288pp. 0-7509-1026-7. [199-?] £18.99.

MADGE, NICK. *English roots: a family history.* 192pp. 0-7509-1139-5. 1996. £14.99. Ashton family of Derbyshire.

SNELLING, STEVE. *V.C.s of the First World War: Passchendaele 1917.* 288pp. 0-7509-1108-5. 1998. £19.99. Various other campaigns are also covered in this series.

TILLER, KATE. *English local history: an introduction.* 0-86299-958-8. 256pp. [1996?] £12.99.

TUCKER, GEORGE HOLBERT. *A history of Jane Austen's family.* 240pp. 0-7509-1663-X. 1998. £9.99.

Thames and Hudson
30, Bloomsbury Street, London, WC1B 3QP

PASTOUREAU, MICHEL. *Heraldry: its origin and meaning.* 0-500-30074-7. 1997. £6.95.

This England
P.O.Box 52, Cheltenham, Gloucestershire, GL50 1YQ

The register of the Victoria Cross. 3rd ed. 0-906324-27-0. 1997. £25.00.

Ruth Tinley
16, Lincoln Road, North Hykeham, Lincoln, LN6 8HE

TINLEY, RUTH. *The Tinley-Glasier connection: a history of tenant farming families.* 94pp. 0-9521336-2-8. 1998. £6.00 + p&p £1.50. Of Lincolnshire and Nottinghamshire, 16-20th c.

TINLEY, RUTH. *Treadgold tracery.* 63pp. 1993. £5.50 (inc. p&p). Of Great Gonerby, Lincolnshire, 18-20th c.

TINLEY, RUTH. *Dusty Almonds.* 31pp. 1996. £2.50 (inc. p&p). Almond family of Lincolnshire, 17-20th c.

Tuckwell Press Ltd.
The Mill House, Phantassie, East Linton, East Lothian, EH40 3DG.
Phone: (01620) 860164

HOLTON, GRAHAM, & WINCH, JACK. *My ain folk: a beginners guide to Scottish family history.* 160pp. 1-86232-024-1. 1997. £5.99.

Twining's Secretarial
313 Pimpala Road, Mt. Hurtle, Woodcraft, S.A., 5162, Australia
Sterling prices include airmail p&p; $A prices include p&p within Australia.

TWINING, ANDREW, & TWINING, SANDRA. *Dictionary of old trades & occupations.* 2nd ed. 0-646-25712-9. 1995. $A17.00; £9.00.

TWINING, ANDREW, & TWINING, SARAH. *The Battle of Waterloo, 1815: an alphabetical list of officers killed and wounded from the official returns.* 0-646-13853-7. 1993. $A7.00; £4.00.

United Synagogue Publications
Woburn House, Tavistock Square, London, WC1H 0EZ

SUSSER, BERNARD. *Alderney Road Jewish Cemetery, London, E1, 1697-1853.* 1-873474-50-4. 1997. £10.00.

University of Exeter Press
Reed Hall, Streatham Drive, Exeter, EX4 4QR

GUY, SUSANNAH. *English local studies handbook: an essential guide to sources of information for professional and amateur local historians.* 2nd ed. 0-85989-590-4. Forthcoming 1999. Guide to record offices, libraries and societies.

University of Hertfordshire Press
College Lane, Hertfordshire, AL10 9AD

GOOSE, NIGEL. *Population, economy and family structure in Hertfordshire in 1851.* 12 vols. 1996-.
- v.1. *Berkhamstead Region.* 0-900458-73-9. 1996. £14.95.
- v.2. *St. Albans Region.* 0-900458-83-6. 1998. £17.95.

University of Nottingham Dept. of Adult Education
Publications Unit, University Park, Nottingham, NG7 2RD

MARCOMBE, DAVID. *Sounding boards: oral testimony and the local historian.* 1995. £5.95.

University of Reading
Administration House (Room 307), Whiteknights, Reading, Berkshire, RG6 7AH
Phone: (0118) 9875123 Ext. 8117

TATE, W.E. *A domesday of English enclosure acts and awards.* 0-7049-0486-1. 1978. £30.00.

University of Wales Press
6, Gwennyth Street, Cardiff, CF2 4YD

MORGAN, T.J., & MORGAN, PRYS. *Welsh surnames.* v, 211pp. 0-7083-0936-4. 1994. £10.95.

Mrs G Warner
62, Poulett Gardens, Twickenham, Middlesex, TW1 4QR

WARNER, JILL. *The Bennetts of Lyme Regis, 1762-1911.* 1997. £12.95 + £1.05 p&p.

Judy Webster
P.O. Box 2044, Salisbury East, Queensland 4107, Australia

WEBSTER, JUDY. *Specialist indexes in Australia: a genealogist's guide.* 120pp. 1-875333-12-6. 1998. $A28.50 (surface mail). Includes indexes to British sources.

Brooke Westcott
14, Daisy Hill Drive, Adlington, Chorley, Lancs, PR6 9NE

WESTCOTT, B.F. *More about wills and other testamentary records.* 1997. £3.00 (inc. p&p).

Ray Westlake Military Books
53, Claremont, Malpas, Newport, Gwent NP9 6PL

SLEIGH, ARTHUR. *Royal Militia & Yeomanry Cavalry list, 1850.* xxxviii, 190pp. 1-871167-18-3. 1991. Reprint; originally published 1850. £35.00.

Westland Publications
P.O. Box 117, McNeal, AZ 85617-0117, U.S.A.
Email: worldrt@primenet.com

SMITH, CLIFFORD N. *British deportees to America.* British American Genealogical Research Series. 8 pts. 1977-87. British-American genealogical research monographs **1-8**.
- Pt.1. *1760-1763.* 97pp. 0-915162-25-3. 1977. $US20.00.
- Pt.2. *1764-1765.* 100pp. 0-915162-26-1. 1979. $US20.00.
- Pt.3. *1766-1767.* 73pp. 0-915162-27-X. 1981. $US20.00.
- Pt.4. *1768-1769.* 34pp. 0-915162-29-6. 1986. $US20.00.
- Pt.5. *1770-1771.* 31pp. 0-915162-30-X. 1986. $US20.00.

Pt.6. *1772-1773*. 36pp. 0-915162-31-8. 1987. $US20.00.
Pt.7. *1774-1775*. 37pp. 0-915162-31-8. 1987. $US20.00.
Pt.8. *Cumulative surname index 1760-1775*. 22pp. 0-915162-33-4. 1987. $US20.00.

SMITH, CLIFFORD N. *British and German deserters, dischargees, and prisoners of war who may have remained in Canada and the United States, 1774-1783*. British-American Genealogical Research Monograph 9. 2 pts. 1988-9.
Pt.1. 24pp. 0-915162-34-2. 1988. $US20.00.
Pt.2. 18pp. 0-915162-35-0. 1989. $US20.00.

SMITH, CLIFFORD N. *Deserters and disbanded soldiers from British, German and Loyalist military units in the South, 1782*. British-American Genealogical Research Monograph 10. 0-915162-36-9. 1991. $US20.00.

K. Willans
9, The Ridge Way, Kenton, Newcastle Upon Tyne, NE3 4LP
http://www.btinternet.com/~jwill/index/htm

1891 census surname index: Registration sub-district of Consett, Co. Durham.
1. *Benfieldside, Shotley Bridge, and Blackhill (part). Piece number RG12/4089.* 1996. £2.00 (inc. p&p).
2. *Conside and Knitsley (part). Piece number RG12/4090.* 1996. £2.00 (inc. p&p).
3. *Conside and Knitsley (part), Healeyfield, Castleside, Muggleswick, and Medomsley (part). Piece number RG12/4091.* £2.00 (inc. p&p).

Willow Bend Books
Route 1, Box 15A, Lovettsville, VA. 22080-9703, U.S.A.

WILSON, JOHN. *The gazetteer of Scotland.* 475pp. Reprint 1996 (originally published 1882). $US28.00.

Wincanton Press
National School, North Street, Wincanton, Somerset BA9 9AT

MUNCTON, THELMA. *Somerset paupers: unremembered lives.* 208pp. 0-948699-28-0. 1994. £20.00.

G.P. Yelland
3, Kamali Avenue, Nattle Park, S.A., 5066, Australia

YELLAND, GEOFFREY P. *Feudalism to freedom: 400 years of Yelland family history; including Abbott, Russell, Turner and Mann.* 300pp. 0-646-27805-3. 1996. $A50.00 + p&p $A4.00 (surface). Of Devon, Cornwall, and South Australia.

Ye Olde Genealogie Shoppe
9605, Vandergriff Road, P.O. Box 39128, Indianapolis, IN., 46239, USA

CAMPBELL, R.G. *Scotch-Irish family research made simple.* $US10.00.
KONRAD, J. *Scottish family research.* $US10.00.

Yorkshire Wolds Publications
Mill Farm, Church Street, Bainton, East Yorkshire, YO25 9NJ

WITHERS, COLIN BLANSHARD. *Yorkshire parish registers.* 1998. £24.99 + p&p £4.00.

PART 2
Societies

Association of Genealogists and Record Agents
29, Badgers Close, Horsham, W. Sussex, RH12 5RU
List of members. £2.50.

British Academy
Orders to: Oxford University Press, Great Clarendon Street, Oxford OX2 6PD
Phone: (01865) 556767

English Episcopal Acta
2-3. CHENEY, C.R., et al. *Canterbury, 1162-1190; Canterbury 1193-1205.* 0-19-726104-3. 1991. £35.00.
6. HARPER-BILL, CHRISTOPHER, ed. *Norwich 1070-1214.* 0-19-726091-8. 1990. £60.00.
7. BARROW, JULIA, ed. *Hereford, 1079-1214.* 0-19-726091-8. 1990. £60.00.
8. FRANKLIN, M.J., ed. *Winchester, 1070-1204.* 0-19-72-6123-X. 1993. £40.00.
9. VINCENT, NICHOLAS, ed. *Winchester, 1205-1238.* 0-19-7261230-2. 1994. £40.00.
10. RAMSEY, FRANCES M.R., ed. *Bath and Wells, 1061-1205.* 0-19-726131-0. 1996. £45.00.
11. BARLOW, FRANK, ed. *Exeter, 1046-1184.* 0-19-726144-2. 1996. £40.00.
12. BARLOW, FRANK, ed. *Exeter, 1186-1257.* 0-19-726145-0. 1996. £40.00.
13. HOSKIN, PHILIPPA M., ed. *Bishops' Acta Worcester, 1218-1268.* 0-19-726171-X. 1997. £25.00.
14. FRANKLIN, M.J., ed. *Coventry and Lichfield, 1072-1159.* 0-19-726172-8. 1997. £25.00.
15. NEININGER, FALKO, ed. *London, 1075-1187.* 0-19-726179-5. Forthcoming
16. FRANKLIN, M.J., ed. *Coventry and Lichfield, 1160-1182.* 0-19-726181-7. 1998. £20.00.
17. FRANKLIN, M.J., ed. *Coventry and Lichfield, 1183-1208.* 0-19-726189-2. Forthcoming

Records of the social and economic history of England and Wales
Orders for this series to: Periodicals Service Company, 11 Main Street, Germanstown, N.Y., 12526, U.S.A.
The set $US620.00.
1. VINOGRADOFF, PAUL, & MORGAN, FRANK, eds. *Survey of the Honour of Denbigh, 1334.* Reprint. Originally published 1914.
2-3. TURNER, J.G., & SALTER, H.E., eds. *The register of St. Augustine's Abbey, Canterbury, commonly called the black book.* 2 vols. Reprint. Originally published 1915-24.
4. NEILSON, N., ed. *A terrier of Fleet, Lincolnshire, from a manuscript in the British Museum;* BALLARD, ADOLPHUS, ed. *An eleventh-century inquisition of St. Augustine's, Canterbury.* Reprint. Originally published 1920.
5. STENTON, F.M., ed. *Documents illustrative of the social and economic history of the Danelaw, from various collections.* Reprint. Originally published 1920.
[6.] LODGE, ELEANOR C., ed. *The account book of a Kentish estate, 1616-1704.* Reprint. Originally published 1927.
7. NEILSON, N. ed. *The cartulary and terrier of the Priory of Bilsington, Kent.* Reprint. Originally published 1928.
8. DOUGLAS, D.C., ed. *Feudal documents from the abbey of Bury St. Edmunds.* Reprint. Originally published 1932.
9. LEES, BEATRICE A., ed. *Records of the Templars in England in the twelfth century: the inquest of 1185 with illustrative charters and documents.* Reprint. Originally published 1935.

Records of social and economic history. New series.
Orders to: Oxford University Press, Great Clarendon Street, Oxford OX2 6PD
Phone: (01865) 556767
3. MACFARLANE, ALAN, ed *The diary of Ralph Josselin, 1616-1683.* 0-19-726103-5. 1991. £32.50.

13. SPALDING, RUTH, ed *The diary of Bulstrode Whitelocke, 1605-1675.* 0-19-726080-2. 1992. £70.00.
14. SPALDING, RUTH, ed. *Contemporaries of Bulstrode Whitelocke, 1605-1675: biographies, illustrated by letters and other documents.* 0-19-726081-0. 1990. £55.00.
19. JOHN, TREVOR, ed. *The Warwickshire hundred rolls of 1279-80: Stoneleigh and Kineton Hundreds.* 0-19-726122-1. 1992. £40.00.
20. HASSALL, WILLIAM, & BEAUROY, JAQUES, ed. *Lordship and landscape in Norfolk, 1250-1350: the early records of Holkham.* 0-19-726093-4. 1993. £60.00.
21. KIRK, JAMES, ed. *The books of assumption of the thirds of benefices: Scottish ecclesiastical rentals at the Reformation.* 0-19-726125-6. 1995. £55.00.
23. GERVERS, MICHAEL, ed. *The cartulary of the Knights of St. John of Jerusalem in England, part 2: Prima Camera, Essex.* 0-19-726138-8. 1996. £50.00.
24. DYMOND, DAVID, ed. *The register of Thetford Priory, part 1. 1482-1517.* 0-19-726160-4. 1995. £40.00.
25. DYMOND, DAVID, ed. *The register of Thetford Priory, part 2. 1518-1540.* 0-19-726161-2. 1996. £50.00.
26. CROWTHER, JANICE E, & CROWTHER, PETER A., eds. *The diary of Robert Sharp of South Cave: life in a Yorkshire village, 1812-1837.* 0-19-7226173-6. 1997. £35.00.
27. FENWICK, CAROLYN C., ed. *The poll taxes of 1377, 1379 and 1381, part 1: Bedfordshire-Leicestershire.* 0-19-726186-8. 1998. £50.00.

British Association for Local History

24, Lower Street, Harnham, Salisbury, SP2.
Orders to: Phillimore & Co., Shopwyke Manor Barn, Chichester, PO20 6BG
Email: bookshop@phillimore.co.uk

BECKETT, J.V. *Local taxation.* 56pp. 0-7199-1030-7. 1980. £2.95.
DYMOND, DAVID. *Writing local history.* 112pp. 0-85033-695-3. 1996. £6.95.
EVANS, ERIC J. *Tithes: maps, apportionments, and the 1836 Act.* 32pp. 0-85033-857-3. 1997. £8.00.
FOSTER, DAVID. *The Rural Constabulary Act 1839.* 56pp. 0-7199-1072-2. 1982. £2.95.
GRAY, VIC., & LIDDELL, BILL. *Running a local history fair.* 16pp. 0-85033-710-0. 1989. £2.00.
MUNBY, LIONEL. *Time and dating handbook for local historians.* 88pp. 0-86077-074-6. 1997. £8.00.
MUNBY, LIONEL. *Reading Tudor and Stuart handwriting.* 16pp. 0-85033-638-4. 1988. £2.00.
REID, ANDY. *The Union workhouse: a study guide for teachers and local historians.* 112pp. 0-85033-914-6. 1994. £10.95.
MURPHY, MICHAEL. *Newspapers and local history.* 24pp. 0-85033-782-8. 1991. £2.95.

British Records Association

c/o London Metropolitan Archives, 40, Northampton Rd., London, EC1R 0HB
Phone: (0171) 8330428
Members are entitled to discounts.

BRIDGEMAN, IAN. *Records for the history of policing.* Forthcoming.
CREATON, HEATHER. *Sources for the history of London, 1939-45: a guide and bibliography.* xii, 196pp. 1998. £12.50.
HARVEY, P.D.A. *Manorial records.* Reprint forthcoming.
HUNNISETT, R.F. *Editing records for publication.* 1977. £6.75 + p&p 70p.
HUNNISETT, R.F. *Indexing for editor.* 0-900222-02-6. 1972. £12.50 + p&p £1.25.
MULLET, MICHAEL. *Sources for the history of English nonconformity.* 0-900222-09-3. 1972. £6.75 + £1.25.
OWEN, DOROTHY M. *Records of the established church in England.* 0-900222-11-5 1974. £10.00 + p&p 70p.
STEPHENS, W.B., & UNWIN, R.W. *Materials for the local and regional study of schooling.* 0-900222-00-0. 1987. £6.75.

British Record Society

c/o Patric Dickinson, The College of Arms, Queen Victoria Street, London EC4V 4BT

The records of the nation: the Public Record Office, 1838-1988; the British Record Society, 1888-1988. viii, 312pp. 0-85115-538-3. £35.00.

Index Library — reprints

Orders to: Kraus Reprint & Periodicals, Route 100, Millwood, New York, 10546, U.S.A. Vols.1-88 are also available on microfiche from Chadwyck-Healey Ltd. See Raymond's *British Genealogical Microfiche* for details. There is also a *Microfiche series,* for which see ditto.

1. PHILLIMORE, W.P.W., ed. *A calendar of wills relating to the counties of Northampton and Rutland proved in the court of the archdeacon of Northampton, 1510 to 1652.* xvi, 210pp. Reprint; originally published 1888. $US80.00 (with vols. 2 & 3).
2. PHILLIMORE, W.P.W., ed. *A calendar of Chancery proceedings. Bills and answers filed in the reign of King Charles the First. Vol. i.* vi, 265pp. Reprint; originally published 1889. $US80.00 (with vols. 1 & 3).
3. PHILLIMORE, W.P.W., ed. *Index nominum to the royalist composition papers. First and second series. Vol. i: A to F.* viii, 184pp. Reprint; originally published 1889. $US80.00 (with vols. 1 & 2).
4. PHILLIMORE, W.P.W., ed. *An index to bills of privy signet, commonly called signet bills, 1584 to 1596 and 1603 to 1624, with a calendar of writs of privy seal, 1601 to 1603.* xvi, 236pp. Reprint; originally published 1890. $US80.00 (with vols. 5 & 6).
5. PHILLIMORE, W.P.W., ed. *A calendar of Chancery proceedings. Bills and answers ... Vol. ii.* iv, 264pp. Reprint; originally published 1890. $US80.00 (with vols. 4 & 6).
6. PHILLIMORE, W.P.W., ed. *A calendar of Chancery proceedings. Bills and answers ... Vol. iii.* iv, 190pp. Reprint; originally published 1890. $US80.00 (with vols. 4 & 5).
7. PHILLIMORE, W.P.W., ed. *Calendars of wills and administrations in the consistory court of the bishop of Lichfield and Coventry, 1516 to 1652. Also those in the peculiars now deposited in the probate registries at Lichfield, Birmingham and Derby, 1529-1652, 1675-1790, 1753-1790.* xii, 387pp. Reprint; originally published 1892. $US65.00.
8. PHILLIMORE, W.P.W., ed. *Index to wills proved and administrations granted in the court of the archdeacon of Berks, 1508 to 1652.* viii, 199pp. Reprint; originally published 1893. $US90.00 (with vols. 9 & 10).
9. PHILLIMORE, W.P.W., & FRY, GEORGE S., eds. *Abstracts of Gloucestershire inquisitiones post mortem returned into the Court of Chancery in the reign of King Charles the First. Pt. i: 1-11 Charles I, 1625-1636.* x, 233pp. Reprint; originally published 1893. $US90.00 (with vols. 8 & 10).
10. SMITH, J. CHALLENOR C., ed. *Index of wills proved in the Prerogative Court of Canterbury, 1383-1558, and now preserved in the Principal Probate Registry, Somerset House, London. Vol. 1.* xxxvi, 308pp. Reprint; originally published 1893. $US90.00 (with vols. 8 & 9).
11. SMITH, J. CHALLENOR C., ed. *Index of wills proved in the Prerogative Court of Canterbury, 1383-1558 ... Vol. 2.* vii, 392pp. Reprint; originally published 1895. $US36.00.
13. PHILLIMORE, W.P.W., & FRY, GEORGE S., eds. *Abstracts of Gloucestershire inquisitiones post mortem ... Pt. ii: 12-18 Charles I, 1637-1642.* xii, 190pp. Reprint; originally published 1895. $US23.00.
14. FRY, EDWARD ALEXANDER, ed. *A calendar of Chancery proceedings. Bills and answers ... Vol. iv.* viii, 240pp. Reprint; originally published 1896. $US23.00.
15. FRY, GEORGE S., ed. *Abstracts of inquisitiones post mortem relating to the city of London returned into the court of chancery. Pt. i: 1 Henry VII to 3 Elizabeth, 1485-1561.* viii, 259pp. Reprint; originally published 1896. $US23.00.
16. GRANT, FRANCIS J., ed. *The commissariot record of Edinburgh: register of testaments. Pt.1: vols 1 to 35, 1514-1600.* iv, 304pp. Reprint; originally published 1897. $US36.00.
17. FRY, EDWARD ALEXANDER, ed. *A calendar of wills proved in the Consistory Court (city and deanery of Bristol division) of the bishop of Bristol, 1572-1792. And also a calendar of wills in the Great Orphan Books preserved in the Council House, Bristol, 1379-1674.* x, 136pp. Reprint; originally published 1897. $US23.00.

19. PHILLIMORE, W.P.W., ed. *Placita coram domino rege apud Westmonasterium de termino Sancte Trinitatis anno regni regis Edwardii filii regis Henrici vicesimo quinto. The pleas of the court of King's Bench, Trinity term, 25 Edward I, 1297.* xxvii, 315pp. Reprint; originally published 1898. $US36.00.

20. GRANT, FRANCIS J., ed. *The commissariot record of Inverness: register of testaments, 1630-1800.* 32pp. Reprint; originally published 1897. Includes *The commissariot record of Hamilton and Campsie: register of testaments, 1564-1800.* 85pp. Reprint; originally published 1898. $US23.00.

21. FRY, EDWARD ALEXANDER, ed. *Abstracts of Gloucestershire inquisitiones post mortem ... Pt. iii: Miscellaneous series, 1-18 Charles I, 1625-1642.* viii, 175pp. Reprint; originally published 1899. $US23.00.

22. FRY, EDWARD ALEXANDER, ed. *A calendar of wills and administrations relating to the county of Dorset proved in the Consistory Court (Dorsetshire division) of the late diocese of Bristol, 1681-1792, and in the Archdeaconry Court of Dorset 1568-1792, and in the several peculiars, 1660-1799, all now preserved at the probate registry, Blandford.* x, 268pp. Reprint; originally published 1900. $US23.00.

23. FRY, GEORGE S., & FRY, EDWARD ALEXANDER, eds. *Abstracts of Wiltshire inquisitiones post mortem returned into the Court of Chancery in the reign of King Charles the First.* viii, 501pp. Reprint; originally published 1901. $US53.00.

24. HALL, WILLIAM HAMILTON, ed. *Calendar of wills and administrations in the Archdeaconry Court of Lewes in the Bishopric of Chichester, together with those in the Archbishop of Canterbury's peculiar jurisdiction of South Malling and the peculiar of the Deanery of Battle, comprising together the whole of the eastern division of the county of Sussex and the parish of Edburton in West Sussex. From the earliest extant instruments in the reign of Henry VIII to the Commonwealth.* xix, 529pp. Reprint; originally published 1901. $US53.00.

26. MADGE, SIDNEY J., ed. *Abstracts of inquisitiones post mortem for the city of London returned into the Court of Chancery during the Tudor period. Pt. ii: 4-19 Elizabeth, 1561-1577.* x, 223pp. Reprint; originally published 1901. $US23.00.

27. HARTOPP, HENRY, ed. *Calendars of wills and administrations relating to the county of Leicester proved in the Archdeaconry Court of Leicester, 1495-1649, and in the peculiars of St. Margaret, Leicester, Rothley, Groby, Evington, and the unproved wills, etc., previous to 1801, all now preserved in the probate registry at Leicester.* xii, 314pp. Reprint; originally published 1902. $US36.00.

28. FOSTER, C.W., ed. *Calendars of Lincoln wills. Vol. i: 1320-1600.* xvi, 349pp. Reprint; originally published 1902.

29. FRY, EDWARD ALEXANDER, ed. *Index of Chancery proceedings (Reynardson's division) preserved in the Public Record Office, A.D. 1649-1714. Vol. i: A to K.* xxiii, 259pp. Reprint; originally published 1903. $US23.00.

30. MADGE, SIDNEY J., ed. *Abstracts of inquisitiones post mortem for Gloucestershire returned into the Court of Chancery during the Plantagenet period. Pt. iv: 20 Henry III to 29 Edward I, 1236-1300.* xvi, 241pp. Reprint; originally published 1903. $US23.00.

31. FRY, EDWARD ALEXANDER, ed. *Calendar of wills and administrations in the Consistory Court of the Bishop of Worcester, 1451-1600. Also marriage licences and sequestrations now deposited in the probate registry at Worcester.* viii, 535pp. Reprint; originally published 1904. $US53.00.

32. FRY, EDWARD ALEXANDER, ed. *Index of Chancery proceedings (Reynardson's division) ... Vol. ii: L to Z.* vi, 238pp. Reprint; originally published 1904. $US23.00.

33. COKAYNE, GEORGE E., & FRY, EDWARD ALEXANDER, eds. *Calendar of marriage licences issued by the Faculty Office, 1632-1714.* iv, 427pp. Reprint; originally published 1905. $US36.00.

34. FRY, EDWARD ALEXANDER, & PHILLIMORE, W.P.W., eds. *A calendar of wills proved in the Consistory Court of the Bishop of Gloucester. Vol. ii: 1660 to 1800.* viii, 448pp. Reprint; originally published 1907. $US36.00.

35. FRY, EDWARD ALEXANDER, ed. *Calendars of wills and administrations relating to the counties of Devon and Cornwall, proved in the court of the Principal Registry of the Bishop of Exeter, 1559-1799, and of Devon only, proved in the court of the Archdeacon of Exeter, 1540-1799, all now preserved in the probate registry at Exeter.* xxiv, 878pp. Reprint; originally published 1908. $US75.00.

36. FRY, EDWARD ALEXANDER, ed. *Abstracts of inquisitiones post mortem for the city of London ... Pt. iii: 19-45 Elizabeth, 1577-1603.* ix, xxxiii, 348pp. Reprint; originally published 1908. $US36.00.

37. FRY, EDWARD ALEXANDER, ed. *Abstracts of Wiltshire inquisitiones post mortem returned into the Court of Chancery in the reigns of Henry III, Edward I, and Edward II, A.D. 1242-1326.* xv, 505pp. Reprint; originally published 1908. $US53.00.

38. HARTOPP, HENRY, ed. *Leicestershire marriage licences; being abstracts of the bonds and allegations for marriage licences preserved in the Leicester Archdeaconry registry, 1570-1729.* vii, 542pp. Reprint; originally published 1910. $US53.00.

39. FRY, EDWARD ALEXANDER, ed. *Calendar of wills and administrations in the Consistory Court of the Bishop of Worcester, 1601-1652. Also marriage licences and sequestrations now deposited in the probate registry at Worcester.* Reprint; originally published 1910. $US23.00.

40. FRY, EDWARD ALEXANDER, ed. *Abstracts of inquisitiones post mortem for Gloucestershire ... Pt. v: 30 Edward I to 32 Edward III, 1302-1358.* ix, 375pp. Reprint; originally published 1910. $US36.00.

41. *Calendars of Lincoln wills. Vol. ii: Consistory court wills, 1601-1652.* viii, 234pp. Reprint; originally published 1910. $US23.00.

42. NOBLE, W.M., ed. *Calendars of Huntingdonshire wills, 1479-1652.* xii, 222pp. Reprint; originally published 1911. $US23.00

45. FRY, EDWARD ALEXANDER, ed. *Calendar of wills and administrations in the court of the Archdeacon of Taunton. Pts. 1 and 2: Wills only, 1537-1799.* vi, 437pp. Reprint; originally published 1912. $US36.00.

46. FRY, EDWARD ALEXANDER, ed. *Calendar of wills and administrations relating to the counties of Devon and Cornwall proved in the consistory court of the Bishop of Exeter, 1532-1800, now preserved in the probate registry at Exeter.* vi, 324pp. Reprint; originally published 1914. $US36.00.

47. STOKES, ETHEL, ed. *Abstracts of inquisitiones post mortem for Gloucestershire ... Pt. vi: 33 Edward III to 14 Henry IV, 1359-1413.* x, 266pp. Reprint; originally published 1914. $US23.00.

48. STOKES, ETHEL, ed. *Abstracts of Wiltshire inquisitiones post mortem returned into the Court of Chancery in the reign of King Edward III, A.D. 1327-1377.* vi, 461pp. Reprint; originally published 1914. $US48.00.

49. FRY, EDWARD ALEXANDER, ed. *Calendar of wills in the Consistory Court of the Bishop of Chichester, 1482-1800.* viii, 415pp. Reprint; originally published 1915. $US36.00.

50. PLOMER, HENRY R., ed. *Index of wills and administrations now preserved in the Probate Registry at Canterbury, 1396-1558 and 1640-1650.* viii, 603pp. Reprint; originally published 1920. $US60.00.

51. HARTOPP, HENRY, ed. *Index to the wills and administrations proved and granted in the Archdeaconry Court of Leicester, 1660-1750, and in the peculiars of St. Margaret, Leicester, and Rothley, and the Rutland peculiars of Caldecott, Ketton and Tixover, and Liddington prior to 1821, now preserved in the probate registry at Leicester.* viii, 391pp. Reprint; originally published 1920. $US40.00.

52. FOSTER, C.W., ed. *Calendars of administrations in the Consistory Court of Lincoln, A.D. 1540-1659.* xxii, 410pp. Reprint; originally published 1921. $US40.00.

53. FRY, GEORGE S., ed. *Calendars of wills and administrations relating to the county of Dorset.* viii, 184, viii, 130pp. Reprint; originally published 1922. $US30.00.

54. BLAGG, THOMAS M., & MOIR, JOSEPHINE SKEATE, eds. *Index of wills proved in the Prerogative Court of Canterbury. Vol. vii: 1653-1656.* xx, 786pp. Reprint; originally published 1925. $US100.00.

55. FRY, E.A., & JENKINS, CLAUDE, eds. *Index to the act books of the archbishops of Canterbury, 1663-1859. Pt. i: A-K.* iv, 587pp. Reprint; originally published 1929. $US70.00.

56. GLENCROSS, R.M., ed. *Calendar of wills, administrations and accounts relating to the counties of Cornwall and Devon in the connotorial archidiaconal court of Cornwall (with which are included the records of the royal peculiar of St. Burian) now preserved in the district probate office at Bodmin. Pt. i: 1569-1699.* vi, 373pp. Reprint; originally published 1929. $US40.00.

57. FOSTER, C.W., ed. *Calendars of wills and administrations at Lincoln. Vol. iv: Archdeaconry of Stow, peculiar courts, and miscellaneous courts.* xvi, 696pp. Reprint; originally published 1930. $US60.00.

58. BLAGG, THOMAS M., & WADSWORTH, F. ARTHUR, eds. *Abstracts of Nottinghamshire marriage licences. Vol. i: Archdeaconry court, 1577-1700; peculiar of Southwell, 1588-1754.* xvi, 696pp. Reprint; originally published 1930. $US60.00.

59. GLENCROSS, R.M., ed. *Calendar of wills ... relating to the counties of Cornwall and Devon ... Pt. ii: 1700-1799.* vi, 243pp. Reprint; originally published 1932. $US30.00.

60. BLAGG, THOMAS M., & WADSWORTH, F. ARTHUR, eds. *Abstracts of Nottinghamshire marriage licences. Vol. ii: Archdeaconry court, 1701-1753; peculiar of Southwell, 1755-1853.* xii, 751pp. Reprint; originally published 1935. $US70.00

61. BLAGG, THOMAS M., ed. *Index of wills proved in the Prerogative Court of Canterbury. Vol. viii: 1657-1660.* xvi, 891pp. Reprint; originally published 1936. $US70.00.

62. GLENCROSS, REGINALD M., ed. *A calendar of the marriage licence allegations in the registry of the bishop of London. Vol. i: 1597 to 1648.* vii, 436pp. Reprint; originally published 1937. $US75.00.

63. JENKINS, CLAUDE, ed. *Index to the act books of the Archbishops of Canterbury, 1663-1859. Pt. ii: L-Z, with index locorum.* 612pp. Reprint; originally published 1938. $US80.00.

64. FRY, EDWARD ALEXANDER, ed. *Calendar of administrations in the Consistory Court of the bishop of Chichester, 1555-1800; calendar of wills and administrations in the peculiar court of the Archbishop of Canterbury, 1520-1670; calendar of wills and administrations in the peculiar court of the dean of Chichester, 1577-1800.* xii, 269pp. Reprint; originally published 1940. $US95.00 (with vols. 65 & 66).

65. RIDGE, C. HAROLD, ed. *Index of wills and administrations now preserved in the Probate Registry at Canterbury. Vol. ii: Wills and administrations, 1558-1577, and administrations, 1539-1545.* viii, 149pp. Reprint; originally published 1940. $US95.00 (with vols.64 & 66).

66. GLENCROSS, REGINALD M., ed. *A calendar of the marriage licence allegations in the registry of the Bishop of London. Vol. ii: 1660-1700.* vi, 214pp. Reprint; originally published 1940. $US95.00 (with vols.64 & 65).

67. AINSWORTH, JOHN, ed. *Index of wills proved in the Prerogative Court of Canterbury. Vol. ix: 1671-1675.* xii, 292pp. Reprint; originally published 1942. $US100.00 (with vol.68).

68. AINSWORTH, JOHN, ed. *Index to administrations in the Prerogative Court of Canterbury, and now preserved in the Principal Probate Registry, Somerset House, London. Vol. i: 1649-1654.* xiv, 423pp. Reprint; originally published 1944. $US100.00 (with vol.67).

69. FARROW, M.A., ed. *Index to wills proved in the Consistory Court of Norwich and now preserved in the district probate registry at Norwich, 1370-1550, and wills among the Norwich enrolled deeds, 1286-1508.* xiv, 423pp. Reprint; originally published 1945. $US100.00 (with vol.70).

70. DRUCKER, LUCY, ed. *Administrations in the Archdeaconry of Northampton, 1677-1710, now preserved in the District Probate Registry at Birmingham.* vii, 255pp. Reprint; originally published 1947. $US100.00 (with vol.69).

71. RIDGE, C. HAROLD, ed. *Index to wills proved in the Prerogative Court of Canterbury. Vol. x: 1676-1685.* x, 481pp. Reprint; originally published 1948. $US100.00 (with vol.72).

72. RIDGE, C. HAROLD, ed. *Index to administrations in the Prerogative' Court of Canterbury ... Vol. ii: 1655-1660, A-F.* viii, 153pp. Reprint; originally published 1949. $US100.00 (with vol.71).

73. MILLICAN, PERCY, ed. *Index to wills proved in the consistory court of Norwich ... 1550-1603.* vi, 188pp. Reprint; originally published 1950. $US95.00 (with vols.74 & 75)

74. RIDGE, C. HAROLD, ed. *Index to administrations in the Prerogative Court of Canterbury ... Vol. ii: 1655-1660, G-Q.* vi, 175pp. Reprint; originally published 1952. $US95.00 (with vols.73 & 75).

75. RIDGE, C. HAROLD, ed. *Index to administrations in the Prerogative Court of Canterbury ... Vol. ii: 1655-1660, R-Z.* 128pp. Reprint; originally published 1953. $US95.00 (with vols.73 & 74).

Index Library

The following volumes are still available direct from the British Record Society:

83. FITCH, MARC, ed. *Index to administrations in the Prerogative Court of Canterbury. Vol. v: 1609-1619.* viii, 192pp. 1968. £12.00.

89. FITCH, MARC, ed. *Index to testamentary records in the Archdeaconry Court of London now preserved in Guildhall Library, London. Vol. i: (1363)-1649.* xx, 476pp. 0-901505-05-6. 1979. £32.00.

90. GRIMWADE, M.E. *Index of the probate records of the court of the Archdeacon of Suffolk, 1444-1700. Vol. 1: A-K,* eds. W.R. Serjeant and R.K. Serjeant. viii, 319pp. 0-901505-06-4. 1979. £12.50.

91. GRIMWADE, M.E. *Index of the probate records of the court of the Archdeacon of Suffolk, 1444-1700. Vol. 2: L-Z,* eds. W.R. Serjeant and R.K. Serjeant. vi, 321-617pp. 0-901505-07-2. £14.50.

92. LONGDEN, HENRY ISHAM. *Administrations and inventories of the Archdeaconry of Northampton (now preserved in the County Record Office at Northampton). Pt. ii: 1711-1800,* ed. Clare Baggott. x, 158pp. 1980. £11.50.

93-4. CHEYNE, ERNEST. *Probate records of the courts of the Bishop and Archdeacon of Oxford, 1516-1732,* rev. D.M. Barratt. 2 vols. 0-901505-09-9 (v.1); 0-901505-15-3 (v.2). 1981-5. £17.00 per vol.

95-6. GRIMWADE, M.E. *Index of the probate records of the Court of the Archdeacon of Sudbury,* ed. W.R. & R.K. Serjeant. viii, 330pp.; vi, 331, 667pp. 2 vols. 0-901505-13-7 (v.1); 0-901505-14-5 (v.2). 1984. £16.00 per vol.

97. FITCH, MARC, ed. *Index to testamentary records in the Commissary Court of London (London Division) now preserved in Guildhall Library, London. Volume III. 1571-1625.* xiv, 527pp. 0-901505-11-0. 1985. £32.00.

98. FITCH, MARC, ed. *Index to testamentary records in the Archdeaconry Court of London now preserved in Guildhall Library, London. Volume II. 1661-1700.* xiv, 284pp. 0-901505-17-X. 1985. £25.00.

99. WEBB, CLIFF, ed. *Union index of Surrey probate records which survive from before the year 1650.* li, 627pp. 0-901505-27-7. 1990. £39.00.

100. FITCH, MARC, ed. *Index to administrations in the Prerogative Court of Canterbury and now preserved in the Public Record Office, Chancery Lane, London. Vol. VI. 1631-1648.* xii, 572pp. 0-901505-18-8. 1986. £36.00.

101. HAINS, GRACE, & FOSTER, C.W., eds. *Index of Lincoln Consistory Court wills and inventories, 1660-1700.* xvi, 297pp. 0-901505-28-5. 1991. £32.50.

102 & 108. FITCH, MARC, ed. *Index to testamentary records in the Commissary Court of London (London Division) now preserved in Guildhall Library, London. Volume IV. 1626-1649 and 1661-1700.* 2 vols. xviii, 297pp.; xviii, 299-657pp. 0-901505-20-X (pt.1). 0-901505-21-8 (pt.2). Pt.1. £39.00. Pt.2. £36.00.

103 & 106-7. THURLEY, CLIFFORD, & THURLEY, DOROTHEA, et al. *Index of the probate records of the Consistory Court of Ely, 1449-1858.* 3 vols. lxii, 376pp. 0-901505-29-3 (v.1). xii, 377-868pp. 0-901505-30-7 (v.2). xii, 869-1303pp. 0-901505-31-5 (v.3). 1994-6. £36.00 per vol.

104-5. CIRKET, ALAN F. *Index of Bedfordshire probate records, 1484-1858,* ed. Joan Stuart & Peggy Wells. 2 vols. xxx, 382pp. 0-901505-33-1 (v.1). vi, 383-783pp. 0-901505-34-X (v.2). 1993-4. £32.50 (v.1). £35.00 (v.2).

109. BARRATT, D.M., HOWARD-DRAKE, JOAN, & PRIDDEY, MARK, eds. *Index to the probate records of the courts of the Bishop and Archdeacon of Oxford, 1733-1857, and of the Oxfordshire peculiars, 1547-1856.* xxvi, 390pp. 0-901505-36-6. 1997. £19.00.

Canterbury & York Society
c/o Institute of Historical Research, University of London, Senate House, London WC1E 7HU
Orders to: Boydell & Brewer Ltd., P.O. Box 9, Woodbridge, Suffolk, IP12 3DF
Members are entitled to a substantial discount. Prices on application.

1. PHILLIMORE, W.P.W., ed. *Rotuli Hugonis de Welles, episcopi Lincolniensis, A.D. MCCIX-MCCXXXV. Vol. i.* 1909.
2. GRIFFITHS, R.G., ed. *Registrum Thome de Cantilupo, episcopi Herefordensis, A.D. MCCLXXV-MCCLXXXII.* 1907.
3. DAVIS, F.N, SALTER, H.E., & PHILLIMORE, W.P.W., eds. *Rotuli Hugonis de Welles, episcopi Lincolniensis, A.D. MCCIX-MCCXXXV. Vol. ii.* 1907.
4. DAVIS, F.N., ed. *Rotuli Hugonis de Welles, episcopi Lincolniensis, A.D. MCCIX-MCCXXXV. Vol. iii.* 1908.
5. BANNISTER, A.T., ed. *Registrum Ade de Orleton, episcopi Herefordensis, A.D. MCCCXVII-MCCCXXVII.* 1908.
6. CAPES, WILLIAM W., ed. *Registrum Ricardi de Swinfield, episcopi Herefordensis, A.D. MCCLXXXIII-MCCCXVII.* 1909.
12. THOMPSON, W.N., ed. *The register of John de Halton, bishop of Carlisle, A.D. 1292-1324. Vol. i.* 1913.
17. THOMPSON, A. HAMILTON, ed. *Visitations of religious houses in the Diocese of Lincoln. Vol. i: Injunctions and other documents from the registers of Richard Flemyng and William Gray, bishops of Lincoln, A.D. 1420-1436.* 1915.
24. THOMPSON, A. HAMILTON, ed. *Visitations of religious houses in the Diocese of Lincoln. Vol. ii: Records of visitations held by William Alnwick, bishop of Lincoln, A.D. 1436-1449. Pt.1.* 1919.
31. DAVIS, F.N., FOSTER, C.W., & THOMPSON, A. HAMILTON, eds. *Rotuli Ricardi Gravesend, diocesis Lincolniensis.* 1925. For 1258-79.
33. THOMPSON, A. HAMILTON, ed. *Visitations of religious houses in the Diocese of Lincoln. Vol. iii: Records of visitations held by William Alnwick, bishop of Lincoln, A.D. 1436-1449. Pt.2.* 1927.
35. THOMPSON, E. MARGARET, ed. *Registrum Matthei Parker, diocesis Cantuariensis, A.D. 1559-1575. Vol. 1,* ed. Margaret Frere. 1928.
39. THOMPSON, E. MARGARET, ed. *Registrum Matthei Parker, diocesis Cantuariensis, A.D. 1559-1575. Vol. 3.* 1933.
44. GOODMAN, A.W., ed. *Registrum Henrici Woodlock, diocesis Wintoniensis, A.D. 1305-1316. Vol. 2.* 1941.
45. JACOB, E.F., ed. *The register of Henry Chichele, archbishop of Canterbury, 1414-1443. Vol. i.* 1943.
46. JACOB, E.F., ed. *The register of Henry Chichele, archbishop of Canterbury, 1414-1443. Vol. iii.* 1945.
49. JOHNSON, CHARLES, ed. *Registrum Hamonis Hethe, diocesis Roffensis, A.D. 1319-1352. Vol. 2.* 1948.
51. GRAHAM, ROSE, ed. *Registrum Roberti Winchelsey, Cantuariensis archiepiscopi, A.D. 1294-1313. Vol. 1.* 1952.
53. WOOD, A.C., ed. *Registrum Simonis de Langham, Cantuariensis archiepiscopi (1366-8).* 1956.
54. DU BOULAY, F.R.H., ed. *Registrum Thome Bourgchier, Cantuariensis archiepiscopi, A.D. 1454-1486.* 1957.
55. EDWARDS, KATHLEEN, ed. *The registers of Roger Martival, bishop of Salisbury, 1315-1330. Vol. i: The register of presentations and institutions to benefices.* 1959.
56. MAYR-HARTING, H., ed. *The acta of the bishops of Chichester, 1075-1207.* 1964.
57. ELRINGTON, C.R., ed. *The registers of Roger Martival, bishop of Salisbury, 1315-1330. Vol. ii: The register of divers letters (first half).* 1973.
58. ELRINGTON, C.R., ed. *The registers of Roger Martival, bishop of Salisbury, 1315-1330. Vol. ii: The register of divers letters (second half).* 1972.
59. REYNOLDS, SUSAN, ed. *The registers of Roger Martival, bishop of Salisbury, 1315-1330. Vol. iii: Royal writs.* 1965.
60. DUNSTAN, G.R., ed. *The register of Edmund Lacy, bishop of Exeter, 1420-1455. Registrum commune. Vol. i.* 1963.

61. DUNSTAN, G.R., ed. *The register of Edmund Lacy, bishop of Exeter, 1420-1455. Registrum commune. Vol. ii.* 1966.
63. DUNSTAN, G.R., ed. *The register of Edmund Lacy, bishop of Exeter, 1420-1455. Registrum commune. Vol. iv.* 1971.
64. DAVIS, F.N., ed. *The register of John Pecham, archbishop of Canterbury, 1279-1292. Vol. i.* 1969.
65. DOUIE, DECIMA, ed. *The register of John Pecham, archbishop of Canterbury, 1279-1292. Vol. ii.* 1968.
66. DUNSTAN, G.R., ed. *The register of Edmund Lacy, bishop of Exeter, 1420-1455. Vol. v.* 1972.
67. RICHTER, MICHAEL, ed. *Canterbury professions.* 1973.
68. OWEN, DOROTHY M., ed. *The registers of Roger Martival, bishop of Salisbury, 1315-1330. Vol. iv: General introduction to the registers, by Kathleen Edwards, and the register of inhibitions and acts.* 1975.
69. BARKER, ERIC E., ed. *The register of Thomas Rotherham, archbishop of York, 1480-1500.* Vol. i. 1976.
70. HILL, ROSALIND M.T., ed. *The register of William Melton, archbishop of York, 1317-1340. Vol. i.* 1977.
71. ROBINSON, DAVID, ed. *The register of William Melton, archbishop of York, 1317-1340. Vol. ii.* 1978.
72. HORN, JOYCE, ed. *The register of Robert Hallum, bishop of Salisbury, 1407-17.* 1982.
73. BENNETT, N.H., ed. *The register of Richard Fleming, bishop of Lincoln, 1420-1431. Vol.1.* 1984.
75. WRIGHT, D.P., ed. *The register of Thomas Langton, bishop of Salisbury, 1485-93.* 1985.
76. HARPER-BILL, C., ed. *The register of John Morton, archbishop of Canterbury, 1486-1500.* 1987.
77. SWANSON, R.N., ed. *The register of John Catterick, bishop of Coventry and Lichfield, 1415-19.* 112pp, 0-90723-935-8. £25.00.
78. HARPER-BILL, CHRISTOPHER, ed. *The register of John Morton, archbishop of Canterbury, 1486-1500. Vol. II.* 268pp. 0-90723-947-1. £25.00.
79. STOREY, R.L., ed. *The register of John Kirkby, bishop of Carlisle, 1332-1352, vol. I; and the register of John Ross, bishop of Carlisle, 1325-32.* 192pp. 0-90723-948-X. £29.50.
80. TIMMINS, T.C.B., ed. *Register of John Waltham, bishop of Salisbury, 1338-1395.* 355pp. 0-90723-949-8. £25.00.
81. STOREY, R.L., ed. *The register of John Kirby, bishop of Carlisle, 1332-1352, vol. II.* 147pp. 0-90723-950-1. £29.50.
82. ROBINSON, O.F., ed. *The register of Walter Bronescombe, bishop of Exeter, 1258-1280. Vol. I.* 208pp. 0-90723-951-X. £25.00.
83. VINCENT, NICHOLAS, ed. *The letters and charters of Cardinal Guala Bicchieri, papal legate in England, 1216-1218.* 290pp. 0-90723-953-6. £25.00.
84. POBST, PHYLLIS E., ed. *The register of William Bateman, bishop of Norwich, 1344-1355. Vol. I.* 176pp. 0-90723-954-4. £29.50.
85. BROCKLESBY, REGINALD, ed. *The register of William Melton, archbishop of York, 1317-1340. Vol. IV.* 256pp. 0-90723-956-0. £29.50.

Catholic Record Society

Agents: St Philip's Books, 85, Lock Crescent, Kidlington, Oxon., OX5 1HG. Phone: (01865) 377578.

1. *Miscellanea, I.* Reprint. Originally published 1905. £15.00 + p&p. Contents include: BURTON, E., ed., 'The registers of the Catholic Mission of Winchester, 1721-1826; HANSOM, S. J., ed., 'Catholic registers: Cowdray, Eastbourne and Midhurst'; MATTHEWS, J.H., ed., 'The Catholic registers of Perthir in the County of Monmouth', *etc., etc.*
2. *Miscellanea, II.* Reprint. Originally published 1905. £15.00 + p&p. Contents include: MATTHEWS, JOHN HOBSON, ed., 'Records relating to Catholicism in the South Wales marches, 17th and 18th centuries,' GILLOW, JOSEPH, ed. 'Catholic registers of Towneley Hall, Lancashire ... 1705-1727 ...', HANSOM, J.S., ed., 'The Catholic registers of Cheam in Surrey' [1755-1843]; HANSOM, J.S., ed. 'The Catholic registers of Wootton Wawen, Warwickshire, [1765-1843]'; *etc., etc.*

3. *Miscellanea III.* Reprint. Originally published 1906. £15.00 + p&p. Contents include: HOOK, PAUL, ed. 'The catholic registers of Holywell, Flintshire, [1698-1829]'; TRAPPES-LOMAX, RICHARD, ed. 'The Catholic registers of Nidd Hall, N.R. of Yorkshire, 1780-1833'; HANSOM, J.S., ed. 'The old registers of the Catholic mission of Llanarth, in the county of Monmouth, 1780-1833'; HANSOM, J.S., ed. 'Registers of St Joseph's Chapel, Trenchard Lane (now Street), Bristol, 1777-1808'; *etc. etc.*
4. *Miscellanea IV.* Reprint. Originally published 1907. £18.00 + p&p. Contents include: HANSOM, JOSEPH S., ed. 'The Catholic registers of Holme-on-Spalding Moor, East Riding of York, [1744-1804]'; HANSOM, J. S. 'The nuns of the Institute of Mary at York from 1677 to 1825'; HANSOM, J. S. 'Papist returns for the City of York and part of the Ainsty, 1735'; MATTHEWS, JOHN HOBSON, ed. 'Catholic registers of Courtfield, in the parish of Welsh Bicknor, Monmouthshire 1773-1832'; *etc., etc.*
5. POLLEN, JOHN HUNGERFORD, ed. *Unpublished documents relating to the English martyrs. Vol. 1. 1584-1603.* Reprint. Originally published 1908. £18.00 + p&p.
6. *Miscellanea V.* Reprint. Originally published 1909. Contents include: HANSOM, JOSEPH S., ed. 'A list of convicted recusants in the reign of Charles II'; LANGTON, FRANCIS A.R., & HANSOM, JOSEPH S., eds. 'The catholic registers of the domestic chapel formerly at Crondon Park, Essex, with some notes relating to Hopcar, Lancashire'; GILLOW, JOSEPH, ed. Registers of the Catholic Chapel, Lulworth Castle, Dorset ... [1755-1840]'; *etc.*
7. *Miscellanea VI. Bedingfield papers, etc.* Reprint. Originally published 1909. £15.00. Contents include: POLLEN, J.H., ed. 'Bedingfield papers'; 'Monmouthshire recusants 1719'; GILLOW, JOSEPH, ed. 'Catholic registers of St Mary's domestic chapel, Everingham Park, Yorkshire'; GILLOW, JOSEPH, ed. 'Catholic registers of St Elizabeth's Church, Richmond, Surrey [1794-1839]'; GILLOW, JOSEPH, ed. 'The catholic registers of the domestic chapel at Callay Castle, Northumberland, 1796-1839'; GILLOW, JOSEPH, ed. 'The Catholic registers of the domestic chapel at Slindon House and St Richard's Church, Slindon, Sussex, [1698-1840]'; *etc.*

9. *Miscellanea VII.* Reprint. Originally published 1911. £15.00 + p&p. Contents include: MATTHEWS, JOHN HOBSON, ed. 'Some records of the Monmouth mission'; HANSOM, JOSEPH S., ed. 'The Catholic registers of Liverpool, now St Mary's, Highfield Street. Book 1. 1741-1773', *etc.*
53. *Miscellanea. Recusant records.* 1961. £10.00 + p&p. Primarily relating to Yorkshire and the North.
54. KENNY, ANTHONY, ed. *The responsa scholarum of the English College, Rome. Pt. 1. 1598-1621.* 1962. £10.00 + p&p
55. KENNY, ANTHONY, ed. *The responsa scholarum of the English College, Rome. Pt. 2. 1622-1685.* 1963. £10.00 + p&p.
57. BOWLER, HUGH, ed. *Recusant roll no. 2, 1593-1594: an abstract in English.* 1965. £10.00 + p&p.
61. BOWLER, HUGH, ed. *Recusant roll no. 3. (1594-1595), and recusant roll no. 4 (1595-1596): an abstract, in English.* 1970. £10.00 + p&p.
63. HARRIS, P.R., ed. *Douai College documents, 1639-1794.* 1972. £10.00 + p&p.
65. WILLIAMS, J. ANTHONY, ed. *Post-Reformation Catholicism in Bath. Vol. I.* 1975. £10.00 + p&p.
66. *Post-Reformation Catholicism in Bath. Vol II. Registers, 1780-1825.* 1976. £10.00 + p&p.
69. HOLT, GEOFFREY. *St. Omer and Bruges colleges, 1593-1773: a biographical dictionary.* 1979. £10.00 + p&p.
70. HOLT, GEOFFREY. *The English Jesuits, 1650-1829.* 1984. £10.00 + p&p.
72. SHARRATT, MICHAEL, ed. *Lisbon College register, 1628-1813.* 1991. £10.00 + p&p.
73. MURPHY, MARTIN. *St. Gregory's College, Seville, 1592-1767.* 1992. £10.00 + p&p.
74-5. MCCOOG, THOMAS M. *English and Welsh Jesuits, 1555-1650.* 2 vols. 1994-5. £10.00 + p&p per volume.
76. LA ROCCA, JOHN. *Jacobean recusant rolls for Middlesex.* 1997. £10.00 + p&p.

Monograph series

1. WILLIAMS, J.A. *Catholic recusancy in Wiltshire, 1660-1791.* 1968. £20.00 + p&p.
2. AVELING, J.C.H. *Catholic recusancy in the City of York, 1558-1791.* £18.00 + p&p.

Occasional publications

2. WORRALL, E. S., ed. *Returns of papists, 1767: dioceses of England and Wales except Chester.* 1989. £15.00 + p&p.

Cory Society
c/o Vernon Cory, 40, The Oval, Harrogate, N. Yorkshire, HG2 9BA
CORY, MICHAEL, & CORY, VERNON. *The English Corys.* 1995. £22.15.

Council for British Archaeology
111, Walmgate, York, YO1 2UA
Phone: (01904) 671417
COX, MARGARET. *Life and death in Spitalfields, 1700-1850.* 1997. £15.00.

Goddard Association of Europe
11, Chandos Road, Newbury, Berkshire, RG14 7EP.
Goddard families: the Goddards of the High Peak of Derbyshire. Pt.1 Chinley and Buxworth. 1996. 26pp. £3.00 (inc. p&p).
Goddard families: the Goddards of North Gloucestershire. 1996. 2 pts.
 Pt.1. *Chipping Campden and Quinton.* 15pp. £3.00.
 Pt.2. *Stanway and the Vale of Evesham.* 1996. 15pp. £3.00.
Goddard families: the Goddards of North Wiltshire. 2 chapters. 1995-7.
 Ch.1. *Early history 1200-1600 Aldbourne, Enfield (Middlesex) & Mere.* 18pp. £3.00 (inc p&p)
 Ch.2. *Berwick Bassett, Clatford & Hidden.* 34pp. £3.00.
The Goddards of the Vale of Pewsey, Wilts. 1999. Forthcoming.
JEFFRIES, RICHARD. *A memoir of the Goddards of North Wiltshire, compiled from ancient records, registers and family papers.* 1987. Originally published 1873. £5.00 (inc. p&p).
GODDARD, JULIE. *The Dunsdon family: an incomplete history.* 2 pts.
 Pt.1. *Origins and dispersion.* 84pp. 1998. £9.50.
 Pt.2. *Steeple Ashton.* 84pp. £5.00 (inc. p&p).

Harleian Society
College of Arms, Queen of Arms, Queen Victoria Street, London EC4V 4BT
Phone: (0171) 2367728

Visitations
117. SQUIBB, G.D., ed. *The visitation of Dorset, 1677, made by Sir Edward Bysshe.* 1977. £35.00.

New series
2-3. CORDER, JOAN, ed. *The visitation of Suffolk, 1561, made by William Hervy.* 2 vols. 0-9500207-4-5 (v.1); 0-9500207-5-3 (v.2). 1981-4. £35.00 per volume.
4. SQUIBB, G.D. ed. *Munimenta heraldica, 1484 to 1984: an anthology of the texts of the royal letters patent granted to the College of Arms, together with other documents of a constitutional character relating to the college, the Earl Marshal, and the officers of arms.* 0-9500207-6-1. 1985. £35.00.
5. SQUIBB, G.D. ed. *The visitation of Nottinghamshire, 1662-1664, made by William Dugdale.* 0-9500207-7-X. 1986. £35.00.
6. SQUIBB, G.D., ed. *Dugdale's Nottinghamshire and Derbyshire visitation papers.* 0-9500207-8-8. 1987. £35.00.
7. JONES, FRANCIS, ed. *A catalogue of Welsh manuscripts in the College of Arms.* 0-9500207-9-6. 1988. £35.00.
8. SQUIBB, G.D., ed. *The visitation of Derbyshire, 1662-1664, made by William Dugdale.* 0-9513335-0-X. 1989. £35.00.
9. GWYNNE-JONES, P.L.I. *An index to the genealogical manuscripts of Ralph Bigland, Garter King of Arms, in the College of Arms.* 0-9513335-1-8. 1990. £35.00.
10. SQUIBB, G.D. ed. *The visitation of Hampshire 1686, made by Sir Henry St. George, Knight.* 0-9513335-2-6. 1991. £35.00.
11. SQUIBB, G.D. ed. *The visitation of Somerset and the City of Bristol (1672), made by Sir Edward Bysshe.* 0-9513335-3-4. 1992. £35.00.
12. SQUIBB, G.D. ed. *The visitations of Oxfordshire 1669 and 1675, by Sir Edward Bysshe.* 1993. £35.00.
14. SIDDONS, M.P., ed. *Visitation by the heralds in Wales.* 0-951333-6-9. 1995/6. £50.00.
HOLDEN, JOAN, ed. *Visitation of London, 1687.* Forthcoming.

Register Section
89. WARD, WINIFREDE, ed. *The registers of St. Margaret's Westminster. Part iii: burials, March 1666-March 1673; June 1681-March 1688; marriages Feb. 1681-Sep. 1699.* 1977. £35.00.

Historical Geography Research Group

c/o Dr. P.M.R. Howell, Department of Geography, University of Cambridge, Downing Place, Cambridge, CB2 3EN

7. FINLAY, ROGER. *Parish registers: an introduction.* £4.95. Aimed at historical geographers.
23. MILLS, DENNIS, & PEARCE, CAROL. *People and places in the Victorian census: a review and bibliography of publications based substantially on the manuscript census enumerators' books, 1841-1911.* 1-870074-05-X. 1989. £7.95.

Huguenot Society of Great Britain and Ireland

Huguenot Library, University College, Gower Street, London WC1E 6BT
Phone: (0171) 3807094
Email: s.massil@ucl.ac.uk
Members are entitled to a substantial discount
Most earlier volumes are available on microfiche; see *British Genealogical Microfiche* for details.

48. OAKLEY, ANNE M., ed. *Actes du consistoire de l'église française de Threadneedle Street, Londres. Vol II. 1571-1577.* 1969. £15.00.
49. HANDS, A. P., & SCOULOUDI, IRENE, eds. *French protestant refugees relieved through the Threadneedle Street church, London, 1681-1687.* 1971. £15.00.
50. SMITH, RAYMOND, ed. *The archives of the French protestant church of London: a handlist.* 1972. £15.00.
51. SMITH, RAYMOND, ed. *Records of the Royal Bounty and connected funds, the Burn donation, and the Savoy church, in the Huguenot library, University College, London: a handlist.* 1974. £15.00.
52 & 53. MARMOY, CHARLES F. A., ed. *The French protestant hospital: extracts from the archives of 'La Providence' relating to inmates and applicants for admission, 1718-1957, and to recipients of and applicants for the Coqueau charity, 1745-1901.* 2 vols. £24.00 per set.
54. GWYNNE, ROBIN D., ed. *A calendar of the letter books of the French church of London from the civil war to the restoration, 1643-1659.* 1979. £15.00.
55. MARMOY, CHARLES F. A., ed. *The case book of 'La maison de charité de Spittlefields', 1739-41.* 1981. £15.00.
56. GRAY, IRVINE. *Huguenot manuscripts: a descriptive catalogue of the remaining manuscripts in the Huguenot library.* 1983. £15.00.
57. SCOULOUDI, IRENE, ed. *Returns of strangers in the metropolis 1593, 1627, 1635, 1639.* 1985. £15.00.
58. GWYNN, ROBIN, ed. *Minutes of the Consistory Court of the French church of London, Threadneedle Street, 1679-92.* 1994.
59. BOERSMA, O., & JELSMA, A. J., eds. *Unity in multiformity: the minutes of the Coetus of London, 1575; and the consistory minutes of the Italian church of London, 1570-1591.* 1997. 0-906100-25-9. 178pp.

New Series
3. SPICER, ANDREW. *The French-speaking Reformed community and their church in Southampton, 1567-c.1620.* 1998. 0-906-100-30-5. 198pp.
JOHN GANDON, ed. *Master index to the Proceedings of the Huguenot Society of Great Britain and Ireland, vols. 1-26, 1886-1997.* 0-906100-35-6. 300pp. Forthcoming.

Jewish Historical Society of England

33, Seymour Place, London, W1H 5AP
GOLDSCHMIDT-LEHMANN, RUTH, MASSIL, S.W., & SALINGER, P.S. *Anglo-Jewish bibliography 1971-1990.* 1992. £35.00.
LEHMANN, RUTH P. *Anglo-Jewish bibliography 1937-1970.* 1973. £20.00.
RIGG, J.M., & JENKINSON, HILARY, SIR. *Exchequer of the Jews, vol. IV.* 1972. £10.00.
Plea rolls of the Exchequer of the Jews, vol. V. 1992. £50.00.
For *Bevis Marks records*, see Spanish and Portuguese Jews Congregation.

Library Association Publishing

7, Ridgmount Street, London, WC1E 7AE
Phone: (0171) 6367543
Email: lapublishing@la-hq.org.uk
CREATON, HEATHER. *Bibliography of printed works on London history to 1939.* xxxiv, 809pp. 1-85604-074-7. 1994. £80.00.

HARVEY, RICHARD. *Genealogy for librarians.* 2nd ed. 0-85157-408-4. 1992. £31.00 + p&p £1.95.

List and Index Society
Public Record Office, Ruskin Avenue, Kew, Richmond, Surrey TW9 4DU
Members are entitled to substantial discounts.

218. *Chancery patent rolls C66: calendar, 16-17 Jas. I.* 1986. £16.00 + p&p £2.50.
221. *Prerogative Court of Canterbury: parchment inventories post 1660 (PROB 4/1-6416).* 1886. 15. 1986. £15.00 + p&p £2.50.
229. *Chancery patent rolls (C66): calendar, 18-19 Jas. I.* 1988. £13.50 + p&p £2.50.
232. *Catalogue of indexes (IND1) and obsolete lists and indexes (OBS1).* 1988. £7.50 + p&p £2.50.
233. *Chancery patent rolls (C66): calendar, 20-23 Jas. I.* 1989. £22.50 + p&p £2.50.
234. *Records of the Royal Mint, 16-20th c. (MINT 1-29).* 1989. £30.00 + p&p £3.00.
241. *Chancery patent rolls: calendar, 27 Eliz. I., 1584-1585, with index to grantees, 23-27 Eliz. I.* 1990. £30.50 + p&p £3.05.
242. *Chancery patent rolls: calendar, 28-29 Eliz. I, 1585-1587. (C66/1271-91). Pt.1.* 1991. £22.50 + p&p £2.50.
243. *Chancery patent rolls: calendar, 28-29 Eliz I., 1585-1887 (C66/1271-91). Pt.2. (with index to grantees).* 1991. £22.50 + p&p £2.50.
247. *Chancery patent rolls: calendar, 30 Eliz. I, 1587-1588.* 1992. £24.00 + p&p £2.50.
248. *Ships musters series I and II (ADM 36-37). Pt. I.* 1992. £30.00 + p&p £3.00.
249. *Ships' musters series I and II (ADM 36-37). Pt. II.* 1992. £30.00 + p&p £3.00.
253-4. *Calendar of Chancery decree rolls, C78/46-85, C78/86-130.* 2 vols. £30.00 + p&p £3.00.
255. *Draft calendar of patent rolls, 31 Elizabeth I, 1588-9.* 1994/5. £27.00 + p&p £2.70.
257. HORWITZ, HENRY, & MORETON, CHARLES. *Samples of Chancery pleadings and suits, 1627, 1685, 1735 and 1785.* 332pp. 1995/6. £20.00 + p&p £2.50.
261. *Supreme Court of Judicature: documents exhibited or deposited in court, pt. 2. J90/1131-1894, with indexes to J90/1-1893.* 300pp. 1999/6. £18.00 + p&p £2.50.
265-6. *RG4, RG8. Non-parochial registers of births, marriages and deaths.* 448pp. 2 vols. 1996-7. £30.00 + p&p £3.00.
267. *RG6. Society of Friends registers deposited with the General Register Office.* 128 pp. £12.50 + p&p £2.50.

Special series

S18. SAINTY, J.C. *Officers of the Exchequer.* 1983. £15.00 + p&p £2.50.
S22. *Huntington Library: Hastings mss. (13th - 19thc.)* 1987. £15.00 + p&p £2.50.
S24. CLWYD RECORD OFFICE. *A handlist of the Glynne-Gladstone mss in St. Deiniol's library, Harwarden.* 1990. £30.00 + p&p £3.00.
S25. *Papers of Sir Nicholas Bacon in the University of Chicago Library.* [199-?] £30.00 + p&p £3.00.
S26. AXTON, MARIE, & AXTON, RICHARD, eds. *Calendar and catalogue of Sark Seigneuric archive 1526-1927.* 1991. £22.50 + p&p £2.50.

Local Population Studies Society
Sir David Cooke, Bt., Secretary, 78, Harlow Terrace, Harrogate, N. Yorkshire HG2 0PN

MILLS, DENNIS, & SCHÜRER, KEVIN. *Local communities in the Victorian census enumerators books.* £12.50.

Monumental Brass Society
c/o Society of Antiquaries, Burlington House, Piccadilly, London WIV 0HS

Monumental brasses of Cornwall. 1997. £12.50.

North West Catholic History Society
10, Ellesmere Road, Pemberton, Wigan, Lancashire, WN5 9LA
Email: J.A.Hilton@btinternet.com

GARDNER, NORMAN, ed. *Lancashire quarter sessions records: register of recusants 1678.* 1998. £30.00 (inc. p&p).
MITCHINSON, A.J., ed. *The return of the Papists of the diocese of Chester, 1705.* £3.50 (inc. p&p).

Pipe Roll Society
Hon. Treasurer, Public Record Office, Ruskin Avenue, Kew, Richmond, Surrey, TW9 4DU

17. *Feet of fines of the reign of Henry II and of the first seven years of the reign of Richard I, A.D. 1182 to A.D. 1196.* 1894. £8.00. (unbound).

20. *Feet of fines of the seventh and eighth years of the reign of Richard I, A.D. 1196 to A.D. 1197.* 1896. £8.00 (unbound)
22. *The great roll of the pipe for the twenty-first year of the reign of King Henry the Second, A.D. 1174-1175.* 1897. £10.00.
23. *Feet of fines of the ninth year of the reign of King Richard I, A.D. 1197 to A.D. 1198.* 1898. £10.00.
24. *Feet of fines of the tenth year of the reign of King Richard I, A.D. 1198 to A.D. 1199, excepting those for the counties of Bedford, Berkshire, Buckingham, Cambridge, Devon and Dorset; also a roll of the King's court in the reign of King Richard I.* 1900. £10.00.
46. STENTON, DORIS M., ed. *The great roll of the pipe for the ninth year of the reign of King Richard the First, Michaelmas 1197 (Pipe roll 43).* 1931. £10.00.
47. STENTON, DORIS M., ed. *The great roll of the pipe for the tenth year of the reign of King Richard the First, Michaelmas 1198 (Pipe roll 44).* 1932. £10.00.
48. STENTON, DORIS M., ed. *The great roll of the pipe for the first year of the reign of King John, Michaelmas 1199 (Pipe roll 45).* 1933. £10.00.
65. DODWELL, BARBARA, ed. *Feet of fines for the county of Norfolk for the tenth year of the reign of King Richard the First 1198-1199, and for the first four years of the reign of King John, 1199-1202.* 1952. £8.00 (unbound).
70. DODWELL, BARBARA, ed. *Feet of fines for the county of Norfolk for the reign of King John, 1201-1215; for the County of Suffolk for the reign of King John, 1199-1214.* 1958. £8.00 (unbound).
74. BARNES, PATRICIA M., & SLADE, C.F., eds. *A medieval miscellany for Doris Mary Stenton.* 1962. £9.00 (unbound).
75. BROWN, R.A., ed. *Pipe roll, 17 John.* 1964. £10.00. Includes HOLT, J.C., ed. *Praestitia roll, 14-18 John, roll of summons 1214, scutage roll, 16 John.* 1964. £10.00.
76. DARLINGTON, R.R., ed. *The cartulary of Worcester Cathedral Priory (Register I).* 1968. £20.00.
77. EBDEN, E. PAULINE, ed. *The great roll of the pipe for the second year of the reign of King Henry III, Michaelmas 1218 (Pipe roll 62).* 1972. £10.00.

Royal Historical Society
University College London, Gower Street, London WC1E 6BT
Orders for volumes over 5 years old to: Oxbow Books, Park End Place, Oxford, OX1 1HN.
Orders for more recent works to: Cambridge University Press, Edinburgh Buildings, Shaftesbury Road, Cambridge, CB2 2RU.

Guides and handbooks
2. PRYDE, E.B., et al. *Handbook of British chronology.* 3rd ed. 0-521-56350-X. 1996. £40.00.
4. CHENEY, C.R. *Handbook of dates for students of British history.* 0-521-55151-X. 1995. £15.95.
5. NORTON, J.E. *Guide to national and provincial directories of England and Wales, excluding London, published before 1856.* 0-861931-14-9. 1950. £12.00.
9. MILNE, ALEXANDER TAYLOR. *A centenary guide to the publications of the Royal Historical Society, 1868-1968, and of the former Camden Society, 1838-1897.* 0-901050-0-8. 1968. £5.00.
10. YOUNGS, FREDERIC A., ed. *Guide to local administrative units. vol. 1. Southern England.* 0-901050-67-9. 1980. £25.00.
11. SMITH, D. *Guide to Bishops' registers of England and Wales: a survey from the middle ages to the abolition of episcopacy in 1646.* 0-901050-72-5. 1981. £15.00.
12. MULLINS, E.L.C. *Texts and calendars II: an analytical guide to serial publications, 1957-1982.* 0-861931-00-9. 1983. £15.00.
14. STEVENSON, D. *Scottish texts and calendars.* 1987. 0-861931-11-4. £15.00.

Camden Third series
66. MIDGLEY, L.MARGARET, ed. *Ministers accounts of the Earldom of Cornwall, 1296-7. Vol.1.* 0-861930-68-1. 1942. £19.50.
71. HASSALL, W.O., ed. *Cartulary of St. Mary, Clerkenwell.* 0-861930-71-1. 1949. £19.50.
73. CHIBNALL, M., ed. *Select documents of the English lands of the Abbey of Bec.* 0-861930-73-8. 1951. £35.00.

Camden Fourth series
2. HARVEY, B.F., ed. *Documents illustrating the rule of Walter de Wenlok, Abbot of Westminster, 1283-1307.* 0-901050-63-6. 1965. £15.00.
10. FARADAY, M.A., ed. *Herefordshire militia assessments of 1663.* 0-901050-08-3. 1972. £15.00.
16. HOCKEY, S.F., ed. *Account book of Beaulieu Abbey.* 0-901050-27-X. 1975. £15.00.
17. COCKBURN, J.S., ed. *Western Circuit assize orders, 1629-1648.* 0-901050-29-6. 1976. £15.00.
20. TANNER, N.P., ed. *Norwich heresy trials, 1428-31.* 0-901050-39-3. 1977. £15.00.
28. SEARLE, A., ed. *Barrington family letters, 1628-1632.* 0-86193-098-3. 1983. £15.00.
31. KEMP, B., ed. *Reading Abbey cartularies I.* 0-86193-108-4. 1986. £15.00.
33. KEMP, B., ed. *Reading Abbey cartularies ... II. Berkshire documents, Scottish charters, and miscellaneous documents.* 0-86193-112-2. 1981. £19.50.

Camden Fifth series
2. O'CONNOR, S.J., ed. *Calendar of the cartularies of John Pyel and Adam Fraunces, mayors and merchants of London.* 1995. £40.00.
6. ADAMS, SIMON, ed. *Household accounts and disbursement books of Robert Dudley, Earl of Leicester, 1558-1561, 1584-86.* 1996. £40.00.
8. KIRBY, JOAN, ed. *The Plumpton letters and papers.* 1997. £40.00

Camden Classic Reprints
1. CARPENTER, CHRISTINE, ed. *Kingsford's Stonor letters and papers, 1290-1683.* 1996. £45.00(hb); £15.95(pb).

Society of Antiquaries
Burlington House, Piccadilly, London W1V 0HS

WAGNER, A.R. *Aspilogia, being materials on heraldry, volume I. A catalogue of English medieval rolls of arms.* 1950. £25.00
TREMLETT, T.R., ed. *Aspilogia, being materials on heraldry, volume II: Rolls of arms of Henry III.* 1967. £15.00.
BRAULT, GERARD, ed. *Aspilogia, being materials on heraldry, volume III: Rolls of arms of Edward I (1272-1307).* 0-85115-66-9. 1997. £150.00.

Dictionary of British arms: medieval ordinary. 2 vols.
v.1. ed. D.H.B.Chesshyre & T. Woodcock. 0-85431-258-7. 1992. £42.00.
v.2. ed. T. Woodcock, Janet Grant, & Ian Graham. 0-85431-268-4. 1996. £60.00.

BEDFORDSHIRE
Bedfordshire Historical Record Society
10 Kimbolton Ave, Bedford, MK40 3AD

16. MARSHALL, LYDIA M., ed. *The Bedfordshire hearth tax return for 1671.* 0-85155-051-7. 1990. £7.50 (inc. p&p).
50. CIRKET, ALAN, ed. *Samuel Whitbread's notebooks, 1810-11, 1813-4.* 1971. £5.00 (inc. p&p). Notes detailing cases heard before a J.P.
51. TIBBUTT, H.G., ed. *Some early nonconformist church books.* 1972. £5.00 (inc. p&p). For Kensworth, Keysoe, Brook End, Stevington, Carlton, Rothwell, Kimbolton, Bedford, Southill, Hail Weston and St. Neots.
52. BAKER, DAVID, ed. *The inhabitants of Cardington in 1782.* 0-85155-034-7. 1973. £5.00 (inc. p&p).
55. TIBBUTT, H.G., ed. *The minutes of the First Independent Church (now Bunyan Meeting) at Bedford, 1656-1766.* 0-85155-037-1. 1976. £6.00 (inc. p&p).
58. MCGREGOR, MARGARET, ed. *Bedfordshire wills proved in the Prerogative Court of Canterbury, 1383-1548.* 0-85155-040-1. 1979. £7.00 (inc. p&p).
63-4. NICHOLLS, YVONNE, ed. *Court of Augmentations accounts for Bedfordshire.* 0-85155-045-2 (v.63); 0-85155-046-0 (v.64). 1984-5. £8.00 per vol., £12.50 for both.
65. LEE, ROSS, ed. *Law and local society in the time of Charles I: Bedfordshire and the Civil War.* 0-85155-047-9. 1986. £8.00 (inc. p&p). Includes inventories of Royalist 'delinquents', lists of Catholic recusants, etc.
66. MORGAN, RICHARD, ed. *The diary of a Bedfordshire squire.* 0-85155-048-7. 1987. £10.00 (inc. p&p). Diary of John Thomas Brooks of Flitwick, 1829-58.
67. BUSHBY, DAVID, ed. *The Bedfordshire schoolchild: elementary education before 1902.* 0-85155-050-9. 1988. £12.00 (inc. p&p).

68. WELCH, EDWIN, ed. *The Bedford Moravian church in the eighteenth century.* 1989. £12.00 (inc. p&p).
69. THOMPSON, JOHN S., ed. *Hundreds, manors, parishes and the church: a selection of early documents for Bedfordshire.* 0-85155-052-5. 1990. £12.00 (inc. p&p). Includes the Hundred rolls, 1274 and 1279, account rolls for Higham Gobion and Streatley, 1379-82, tithe and expenditure accounts for Blunham rectory 1520-39, Turvey churchwardens' accounts 1551-2, Archdiaconal visitations 1578, and Egginton manorial court rolls, 1297-1572.
71. LUTT, NIGEL, ed. *Bedfordshire muster rolls 1539-1831.* 0-85155-054-1. 1992. £15.00 (inc. p&p).
74. COLLETT-WHITE, JAMES, ed. *Inventories of Bedfordshire country houses, 1714-1830.* 0-85155-057-6. 1995. £15.00 (inc. p&p).
75. WELCH, EDWIN, ed. *Bedfordshire chapels and meeting houses: official registration, 1672-1901.* 0-85155-058-4. 1996. £15.00 (inc. p&p).
76. BELL, PATRICIA, ed. *Bedfordshire wills 1484-1533.* 0-85155-059-2. 1997 £15.00 (inc. p&p).

Supplement, 1961-65, to a Bedfordshire bibliography. 1967. £3.50 (inc. p&p).

Second supplement 1966-70, to a Bedfordshire bibliography. 1971. £3.50 (inc. p&p).

Third supplement, 1971-75, to a Bedfordshire bibliography. 0-85155-039-8. 1978. £3.50 (inc. p&p).

BERKSHIRE

Berkshire Record Society
c/o Berkshire Record Office, Shire Hall, Shinfield Park, Reading, RG2 9XD

1. CLARK, GILLIAN, ed. *Correspondence of the Foundling Hospital inspectors in Berkshire, 1757-1768.* 0-9524946-0-4. 1994. £25.00 + p&p £2.50.
2. MORTIMER, IAN, ed. *Berkshire glebe terriers, 1634.* 0-9524946-1-2. 1997. £25.00 + p&p £2.50.
3. DURRANT, PETER, ed. *Berkshire overseers records, 1654-1834.* 0-9524946-2-0. 1997. £25.00 + p&p £2.50.

Berkshire probate accounts, 1583-1712. Forthcoming.

Reading mayors' and cofferers' accounts 1356-1516. Forthcoming.

BUCKINGHAMSHIRE

Buckinghamshire Record Society
Record Office, County Hall, Aylesbury, Bucks., HP20 1UA.
Phone: (01296) 382586 or 382588.
Members are entitled to substantial discounts.

11. GREAVES, R. W., ed. *The first ledger book of High Wycombe.* xix, 330pp. 1961. £5.00.
12. JENKINS, J. G., ed. *The cartulary of Missenden Abbey: Part III.* xxvi, 262pp. 1962. £4.50. Jointly published with the Historical Manuscripts Commission.
13. BONSEY, CAROL G., & JENKINS, J.G., ed. *Ship money papers and Richard Grenville's notebook.* xv, 131pp. 1965. £5.00.
15. ELVEY, G. R., ed. *Luffield Priory charters. Part I.* xviii, 289pp. 1968. £5.00. Jointly published with the Northamptonshire Record Society.
16. PUGH, R. K., ed. *The letter-books of Samuel Wilberforce, 1843-68.* xviii, 438 pp. 1970. £5.00.
17. CHIBNALL, A. C., ed. *The certificate of musters for Buckinghamshire in 1522.* vii, 418pp. 1973. £5.00. Jointly published with the Historical Manuscripts Commission.
18. ELVEY, G. R., ed. *Luffield Priory charters. Part II.* lxxix, 495 pp. 1975. £10.00. Jointly published with the Northampton Record Society.
19. ELVEY, E. M., ed. *The courts of the Archdeaconry of Buckingham.* xxx, 449pp. 1975. £15.00.
20. DONALD, JOYCE, ed. *The letters of Thomas Hayton, vicar of Long Crendon, 1821-1887.* xx, 185pp. 1979. £8.00.
21. WILSON, JOHN, ed. *Buckinghamshire contributions for Ireland, 1642, and Richard Grenville's military accounts, 1642-1645.* xxviii, 171pp. 1983. £15.00
23. KUSSMAUL, ANN, ed. *The autobiography of Joseph Mayett of Quainton (1783-1839).* xxxii, 101 pp. 1986. £10.00 (hb); £5.50 (pb).
24. REED, MICHAEL, ed. *Buckinghamshire probate inventories, 1661-1714.* xx, 330 pp. 1988. £18.00.
25. TRAVERS, ANITA, ed. *A calendar of the feet of fines for Buckinghamshire, 1259-1307, with an appendix, 1179-1259.* xvi, 153pp. 1989. £14.00.

28. BROAD, JOHN, ed. *Buckinghamshire dissent and parish life, 1669-1712.* xlvi, 292pp. 1993. £20.00.
29. BOATWRIGHT, LESLEY, ed. *Buckinghamshire inquests and indictments from late fourteenth century Buckinghamshire.* lvxi, 336pp. 1995. £25.00.
30. REED, MICHAEL, ed. *Buckinghamshire glebe terriers, 1578-1640.* 1998. £25.00.

CAMBRIDGESHIRE
Cambridgeshire Record Society
County Record Office, Shire Hall, Cambridge, CB3 OAP

1. KNIGHT, F., ed. *Letters to William Frend from the Reynolds family of Little Paxton and John Hammond of Fenstanton, 1793-1841.* 0-904323-00-5. 1974. £6.00.
2. WILKERSON, J.C., ed. *John Norden's survey of Barley, Hertfordshire, 1593-1603.* 0-904323-01-3. 1974. £6.00.
3. HALL, CATHERINE P., & RAVENDALE, JACK, eds. *The West Fields of Cambridge.* 0-904353-02-1. 1976. £12.00. Terrier, c.1360.
4. KIMBALL, ELISABETH G., ed. *A Cambridgeshire gaol delivery roll, 1332-1334.* 0-904323-03-X. 1978. £4.00.
5. OWEN, DOROTHY M., & THURLEY, DOROTHEA, eds. *The Kings School, Ely: a collection of documents relating to the history of the school and its scholars.* 0-904323-04-8. £10.00.
6. PARSONS, KENNETH A. C., ed. *The church book of the Independent Church (now Pound Lane Baptist), Isleham, 1693-1805.* 0-904323-06-4. £15.00.
7. GOODISON, J.W., ed. *Catalogue of the portraits in Christ's, Clare, and Sidney Sussex Colleges.* 0-904323-07-2. £10.00. Includes biographies of sitters.
8. BRASSLEY, PAUL, LAMBERT, ANTHONY, & SAUNDERS, PHILIP, eds. *Accounts of the Reverend John Crakanthorp of Fowlmere, 1682-1710.* 0-904323-08-0. £15.00.
10. BURY, M. E., & PICKLES, J. D., eds. *Romilly's Cambridge diary, 1842-1847.* 0-904323-10-2. £19.50.
11. COLEMAN, M. CLARE, ed. *A court roll of the manor of Downham, 1310-1327.* 0-903423-11-0. £15.00.
12. BOURGEOIS, E. J., ed. *A Cambridgeshire lieutenancy letterbook, 1595-1605.* 0-904323-12-9. £19.50.

CHANNEL ISLANDS
La Société Guernesiase
Candie Gardens, St. Peter Port, Guernsey, GY1 1UG

KRECKELER, DAVID W. *Guernsey emigrants to Australia, 1828-1899: family histories.* 0-9518075-2. 1996.

CHESHIRE
See Lancashire

CORNWALL
See Devon

CUMBERLAND
Cumberland & Westmorland Antiquarian & Archaeological Society
c/o Ian Caruana, 10, Peter Street, Carlisle, Cumbria, CA3 8QP

Extra series
23. HUDLESTON, C.R., & BOUMPHREY, R.S., eds. *Cumberland families and heraldry.* 429pp. 1978. £12.00 (inc. p&p).
27. WINCHESTER, A.J.L., ed. *The diary of Isaac Fletcher of Underwood, Cumberland, 1756-1781.* xlii, 518pp. 1-8731244-20-1. 1994. £36.00 (inc. p&p).

Tract series
14. BARNES, F., & HOBBS, J.L. *A hand-list of newspapers published in Cumberland, Westmorland & North Lancashire.* 1951. £1.50 (inc. p&p).
17. FARADAY, M.A., ed. *Westmorland protestation returns, 1641-2.* 86pp. 1971. £3.00 (inc. p&p).
19. DICKINSON, R., &DICKINSON, F. *Monumental inscriptions at Ulverston.* 113pp. 1973. £4.50 (inc. p&p).

Record series
11. TODD, JOHN M., ed. *The Lanercost cartulary.* 0-85444-060-1. 1997. Jointly published with the Surtees Society, which see.
12. BUTLER, L.A.S., ed. *The Cumbria parishes 1714-1725 from Bishop Gastrell's notitia, with additions by Bishop Porteus, 1778-1779.* 1-873124-24-4. £20.00 (inc. p&p).

DERBYSHIRE
Derbyshire Record Society
9, Caernarvon Close, Walton, Chesterfield, Derbyshire, S40 3DY
Members receive a substantial discount.

3. DOE, VANESSA S., ed. *The diary of James Clegg of Chapel-en-le-Frith, 1708-55. Part 2: 1737-47.* 1981. £8.00 (inc. p&p).
5. DOE, VANESSA S., ed. *The diary of James Clegg of Chapel-en-le-Frith, 1708-55. Part 3: 1748-55.* 1981. £8.00 (inc. p&p).
11. GARRATT, H.J.H., & RAWCLIFFE, CAROLE. *Derbyshire feet of fines 1323-1546.* 1985. £20.00 (inc. p&p).
12. WALTON, MARY, & RIDEN, PHILIP, eds. *Chesterfield parish register, 1558-1660.* 1986. £20.00 (inc. p&p).
13. FOWKES, D.V., & POTTER, G.R., eds. *William Senior's survey of the estates of the first and second Earls of Devonshire, c. 1600-28.* 1988. £20.00 (inc. p&p).
15. NOLAN, DOROTHY M., WATKINSON, WILFRID J., & RIDEN, PHILIP, eds. *Chesterfield parish register, 1600-35.* 15. 1990. £20.00 (inc. p&p).
17. CRAVEN, MAXWELL. *A Derbyshire armory.* 1991. £20.00 (inc. p&p).
18. KETTLE, PAMELA, & RIDEN, PHILIP, eds. *Sutton-cum-Duckmanton parish register, 1662-1837.* 1992. £20.00 (inc. p&p).
20. *A seventeenth-century Scarsdale miscellany.* 1993. £20.00 (inc. p&p). Includes Scarsdale surveys of 1651 and 1662.
21. CLIFFORD, JOHN G., & CLIFFORD, FRANCINE, eds. *Eyam parish register, 1630-1700.* 1993. £20.00 (inc. p&p).
22. BECKETT, J.V., & HEATH, JOHN E., eds. *Derbyshire tithe files, 1836-50.* 1995. £20.00 (inc. p&p).

Occasional papers.
1. MILWARD, ROSEMARY. *A glossary of household, farming and trade terms from probate inventories.* 3rd ed. 1986. £4.00 (inc. p&p).
5. CLARK, RICHARD, ed. *The Derbyshire papist returns of 1705-6.* 1983. £4.00 (inc. p&p).
6. CLARK, RICHARD, ed. *Derbyshire pedigrees: an index to the holdings of Derby Local Studies Library.* 1984. £4.00 (inc. p&p).
7. BATTYE, KATHLEEN M., ed. *The diary of Joseph Jenkinson of Dronfield, 1833-43.* 1987. £5.00 (inc. p&p).

DEVON
Devon & Cornwall Record Society
c/o Devon & Exeter Institution, 7, The Close, Exeter, EX1 1EZ
Items marked* now available only when complete sets are ordered, or when secondhand copies are in stock.

1. YOUINGS, JOYCE, ed. *Devon monastic lands: calendar of particulars for grants 1536-1558.* 0-901853-04-6. 1955. £15.00.*
2. HOSKINS, W.G. *Exeter in the seventeenth century: tax and rate assessments 1602-1699.* 0-901853-05-4. 1957. £15.00.
3. COOK, MICHAEL, ed. *The Diocese of Exeter in 1821: Bishop Carey's replies to queries before visitation, vol. 1. Cornwall.* 0-901853-06-2. 1958. £15.00.*
4. COOK, MICHAEL, ed. *The Diocese of Exeter in 1821: Bishop Carey's replies to queries before visitation, vol. 2. Devon.* 0-901853-07-0. 1960. £15.00.*
5. HULL, P.L., ed. *The cartulary of St. Michael's Mount.* 0-901853-08-9. 1965. £15.00.*
6. BROCKETT, ALLAN, ed. *The Exeter assembly: minutes of the assemblies of the United Brethren of Devon and Cornwall 1691-1717 as transcribed by the Reverend Isaac Gilling.* 0-901853-09-7. 1963. £15.00.
7. 10. 13. 16. 18. DUNSTAN, G.R., ed. *The register of Edmund Lacy, Bishop of Exeter 1420-1455.* 5 vols. 0-901853-10-0 (v. 7); 0-901853-12-7 (v. 10); 0-901853-15-1 (v. 13); 0-901853-02-X (v.16); 0-901853-17-8 (v.18). 1963. £15.00 each, obtainable from the Canterbury & York Society, q.v.
8. LONDON, VERA C.M., ed. *The cartulary of Canonsleigh Abbey.* 0-901853-16-X. 1965. £15.00.*
11. CASH, MARGARET., ed. *Devon inventories of the sixteenth and seventeenth centuries.* 0-901853-13-5. 1965. £15.00.*
12. WELCH, EDWIN, ed. *Plymouth building accounts of the sixteenth and seventeenth centuries.* 0-901853-14-3. 1967. £15.00.*
14. ERSKINE, AUDREY M., ed. *The Devonshire lay subsidy of 1332.* 0-901853-00-3. 1969. £15.00

15. HANHAM, ALISON., ed. *Churchwardens' accounts of Ashburton, 1479-1580.* 0-901853-01-1. 1970. £15.00.
17. HULL, P.L., ed. *The caption of seisin in the Duchy of Cornwall, 1377.* 0-901853-03-8. 1971. £15.00.*
19. POTTS, RICHARD., ed. *A calendar of Cornish glebe terriers, 1673-1735.* 0-901853-19-4. 1974. £15.00.
21. GARDINER, DOROTHY A., ed. *A calendar of early Chancery proceedings relating to West Country shipping, 1388-1493.* 0-901853-20-8. 1976. £15.00.
22. ROWE, MARGERY M., ed. *Tudor Exeter: tax assessments, 1489-1595.* 0-901853-21-6. 1977. £15.00.
23. CHAPMAN, STANLEY G., ed. *The Devon cloth industry in the eighteenth century: Sun Fire Office inventories of merchants and manufacturers property, 1726-1770.* 0-901853-22-4. 1978. £15.00.
24. ERSKINE, AUDREY M., ed. *The accounts of the fabric of Exeter Cathedral, 1279-1353, part I.* 0-901853-24-0. 1981. £15.00
25. POUNDS, N.J.G., ed. *The Parliamentary survey of the Duchy of Cornwall, Part I.* 0-091853-25-2. 1982. £15.00.
26. ERSKINE, AUDREY M., ed. *The accounts of the fabric of Exeter Cathedral, 1279-1353. Part II.* 0-901853-26-7. 1983. £15.00.
27. POUNDS, N.J.G., ed. *The Parliamentary survey of the Duchy of Cornwall. Part II.* 0-901853-27-5. 1984. £15.00.
28. SUMMERSON, HENRY, ed. *Crown pleas of the Devon eyre, 1238.* 0-901853-28-3. 1885. £15.00.
29. BOURNE, JOHN, ed. *Georgian Tiverton: the political memoranda of Beavis Wood, 1768-98.* 0-901583-29-1. 1986. £15.00.
30. HULL, P.L., ed. *The cartulary of Launceston Priory (Lambeth Palace MS.719): a calendar.* 0-901853-30-5. 1987. £15.00.
31. PONSFORD, C.N. ed. *Shipbuilding on the Exe: the memoranda book of Daniel Bishop Davy (1799-1874) of Topsham.* 0-901853-31-3. 1988. £15.00.
32. ROWE, MARGERY., & DRAISEY, J.M., eds. *The Receivers' accounts of the City of Exeter, 1304-1353.* 0-901853-32-1. 1989. £15.00.
33. GRAY, TODD, ed. *Early Stuart mariners and shipping: the maritime surveys of Devon and Cornwall, 1619-35.* 0-901853-33-X. 1990. £15.00
36. KOWALESKI, MARYANNE, ed. *The local port customs accounts of Exeter, 1266-1321.* 0-901853-36-4. 1994. £15.00
37. BEARMAN, R., ed. *Charters of the Redvers family and the earldom of Devon, 1090-1217.* 0-901853-37-2. 1994. £15.00.
38. GRAY, TODD, ed. *Devon household accounts, 1627-59, Part I: Sir Richard and Lady Lucy Reynell of Forde House, 1627-43, John Willoughby of Leyhill, 1644-6 and Sir Edward Wise of Sydenham, 1656-9.* 0-901853-38-0. 1995. £15.00.
39. GRAY, TODD, ed. *Devon household accounts, 1627-59, Part II: Henry, Earl of Bath and Rachel, Countess of Bath, of Tawstock and London, 1639-54.* 0-901853-39-9. 1996. £15.00.
40. WYATT, PETER, ed. *The Uffculme wills and inventories, 16th to 18th centuries.* Introduction by Robin Stanes. 0-901853-40-2. 1997. £15.00.
FOX, H.S.A., & PADEL, O., eds. *The Cornish estate of the Arundell family, fourteenth to eighteenth centuries.* Forthcoming.

Extra series

1. ROWE, MARGERY M., & JACKSON, ANDREW M. *Exeter freemen, 1266-1967* 0-901853-18-6. 1973. £15.00.
2. PESKETT, HUGH. *Guide to the parish and non-parochial registers of Devon and Cornwall, 1538-1837.* 0-901853-23-2. 1979. Supplement, 1983. £15.00. New edition forthcoming.
STRIDE, S. *Shelflist of the Society's collections.* 1986. £2.00 + p&p 30p.

Uffculme Archive Group

c/o R.G.F.Stanes, Culver House, Payhembury, Honiton, Devon, EX14 0HR.

WYATT, PETER, & STANES, ROBIN. *Uffculme: a peculiar parish. A Devon town from Tudor times.* xviii, 322p. 0-952-9850-0-4. 1997. £12.00 + p&p. £2.00.

DORSET

Dorset Record Society

Dorset County Museum, High West Street, Dorchester, Dorset DT1 1XA

1. WEINSTOCK, MAUREEN, ed. *Weymouth & Melcombe Regis minute book, 1625-1660.* 108pp. 1964. £8.00 + p&p £1.00.

4. MILLS, A.D., ed. *The Dorset lay subsidy roll of 1332.* xii, 123pp. 1971. £10.00 + p&p £1.00.
5. COOPER, LETTICE ASHLEY, ed. *Two 17th century Dorset inventories.* 24pp. 1974. £2.00. Includes probate inventory of Anthony Cooper, Earl of Shaftesbury, 1699.
6. RUMBLE, ALEXANDER R., ed. *The Dorset lay subsidy roll of 1327.* xxxv, 160pp. 1980. £10.00 + p&p £1.00.
7. BETTEY, J.H., ed. *The case book of Sir Francis Ashley, J.P., recorder of Dorchester, 1614-1635.* xiii, 131pp. 1981. £6.50 + p&p £1.00.
8. MACHIN, R., ed. *The building accounts of Mapperton Rectory, 1699-1703.* xiv, 35pp. 0-900339-07-1. 1983. £4.00 + p&p £1.00.
11. WILLIAMS, C.L.SINCLAIR, ed. *Puddletown: house, street and family: an account of the inhabitants of Piddletown parish, 1724, Dorsetshire.* 93pp. 0-900339-10-1. 1988. £5.75 + p&p £1.00. An 18th c. census.
12. *William Whiteway of Dorchester: his diary, 1618 to 1635.* 193pp. 0-900339-11-X. 1991. £9.75 + p&p £1.00.
13. JAMES, J.F., & BETTEY, J.H., eds. *Farming in Dorset: diary of James Warne, 1758; letters of George Boswell, 1787-1805.* 180pp. 0-900339-12-8. 1993. £10.75 + p&p £1.00.

Poole Historical Trust
c/o Ian Andrews, 103, Orchard Avenue, Parkstone, Poole, Dorset, BH14 8AH

The Sydenhams of Poole. 0-9504914-5-4. 16pp. £1.50.

DURHAM
Surtees Society
5 The College, Durham, DH1 3EQ
Members are entitled to a discounted price.

2. RAINE, J., ed. *Wills and inventories illustrative of the history, manners, language, statistics, etc., of the northern counties of England, from the eleventh century downwards. Pt.1.* 1835. £21.00 (inc. p&p). Mainly from the Registry of Durham.
32. GREENWELL, WILLIAM, ed. *Bishop Hatfield's survey. A record of the possessions of the see of Durham, made by order of Thomas Hatfield, Bishop of Durham.* 1857. £21.00 (inc. p&p). 14th c.
38. GREENWELL, W., ed. *Wills and inventories from the registry at Durham. Vol. 2.* 1860. £21.00 (inc. p&p). 16th c.
112. HODGSON, J.C., ed. *Wills and inventories from the registry at Durham. Vol. 3.* 1906. £21.00 (inc. p&p). 16th c.
116. [CLAY, J.W., ed.] *North country wills, being abstracts of wills relating to the counties of York, Nottingham, Northumberland, Cumberland and Westmorland, at Somerset House and Lambeth Palace. [Vol.I.] 1383-1558.* 1908. £21.00 (inc. p&p).
122. DENDY, F.W., ed. *Visitations of the North, or, some early heraldic visitations of, and collections of pedigrees relating to, the north of England. Vol.1.* 1912. £21.00 (inc. p&p). 16th c.
124. *North country diaries (second series).* 1915. £21.00 (inc. p&p).
128. BROWN, W., ed. *The registers of John le Romeyn, lord archbishop of York (1286-1296), pt. ii; and of Henry of Newark, lord archbishop of York (1296-1299).* 1917. £21.00 (inc. p&p).
133. DENDY, F.W., ed. *Visitations of the North ... Vol. 2.* 1921. £21.00 (inc. p&p).
137. OLIVER, A.M., ed. *Early deeds relating to Newcastle upon Tyne.* 1924. £21.00 (inc. p&p). Medieval.
138. BROWN, W., ed. *The register of Thomas of Corbridge, lord archbishop of York, 1300-1304. Vol. 1.* 1925. £21.00 (inc. p&p).
139. BOUTFLOWER, D.S., ed. *Fasti Dunelmenses: a record of the beneficed clergy of the Diocese of Durham down to the dissolution of the monasteric and collegiate churches.* 1926. £21.00 (inc. p&p).
142. WOOD, H.M., ed. *Wills and inventories from the registry at Durham, vol. 4.* 1929. £21.00 (inc. p&p).
144. BLAIR, C.H. HUNTER, ed. *Visitations of the North. Pt.3. A visitation of the North of England circa 1480-1500.* 1930. £21.00 (inc. p&p).
146. BLAIR, C.H. HUNTER, ed. *Visitations of the North. Pt.4. Visitations of Yorkshire and Northumberland in A.D. 1575, and a book of arms from Ashmole ms.no.834.* 1932. £21.00 (inc. p&p).
147. HOWDEN, M.P., ed. *The register of Richard Fox, lord bishop of Durham (1494-1501).* 1932. £21.00 (inc. p&p).

149. *The register of William Greenfield ... Vol. 2.* 1934. £21.00 (inc. p&p). For the Archdeaconry of York.
150. THOMPSON, A. HAMILTON. *The Surtees Society 1834-1934, including a catalogue of its publications, with notes on their sources and contents, and a list of the members of the society from its beginnings to the present day.* 1939. £21.00 (inc. p&p).
151. *The register of William Greenfield ... Vol. 3.* 1936. £21.00 (inc. p&p). For the Archdeaconries of Cleveland and East Riding.
152. *The register of William Greenfield ... Vol.4.* 1938. £21.00 (inc. p&p). For the Archdeaconries of Nottingham and Richmond.
153. *The register of William Greenfield ... Vol.5.* 1940. £21.00 (inc. p&p). For the Archdeaconry of Nottingham.
158-159. THOMPSON, A. HAMILTON, ed. *Northumbrian pleas from De Banco rolls 1-[37] (1-[8] Edward I).* 1950. £42.00 (inc. p&p).
161. HINDE, G., ed. *The registers of Cuthbert Tunstall, bishop of Durham 1530-1559, and James Pilkington, bishop of Durham, 1561-1576.* £21.00 (inc. p&p).
162. FRASER, C.M., ed. *Records of Antony Bek, bishop and patriarch, 1283-1311.* 1953. £21.00 (inc. p&p).
168. HUDLESTON, C.R., ed. *Naworth estate and household accounts, 1648-1660.* 1958. £21.00 (inc. p&p).
169. *The register of Thomas Langley, ... vol. 3.* 1959. £21.00 (inc. p&p).
170. *The register of Thomas Langley, vol. 4.* 1961. £21.00 (inc. p&p).
173. HUDLESTON, C.R., ed. *Durham recusants estates, 1717-1778, vol. 1.* 1962. £21.00 (inc. p&p).
175. HUDLESTON, C.R. & FORSTER, A.M.C., eds. *Miscellanea. Vol. iii.* Contents: *Durham recusant estates, 1717-1778, pt. 2.* FORSTER, ANN M.C., ed. *Durham entries on the recusants rolls, 1636-7.* 1965. £21.00 (inc. p&p).
176. FRASER, C.M., ed. *Ancient petitions relating to Northumberland.* 1966. £21.00 (inc. p&p).
178. DICKINSON, H.T., ed. *The correspondence of Sir James Clavering.* 1967. £21.00 (inc. p&p).
180. FORSTER, A.M.C., ed. *Selections from the disbursements book, 1691-1709, of Sir Thomas Haggerston, Bart.* £21.00 (inc. p&p).
181. ROWE, D.J., ed. *The records of the Company of Shipwrights of Newcastle upon Tyne, 1622-1967. Vol. 1.* 1970. £21.00 (inc. p&p).
182. *The register of Thomas Langley. Vol. 6.* 1970. £21.00 (inc. p&p).
183. KIRBY, D.A., ed. *Parliamentary surveys of the Bishopric of Durham. Vol. 1.* 1971. £21.00.
184. *The records of the Company of Shipwrights of Newcastle upon Tyne, 1622-1967. Vol. 2.* 1971. £21.00 (inc. p&p).
185. *Parliamentary surveys of the Bishopric of Durham. Vol. 2.* 1972. £21.00 (inc. p&p).
186. PERCY, J.W., ed. *York memorandum book B/Y.* 1973. £21.00 (inc. p&p). 1371-1596.
187. KITCHING, C.J., ed. *The royal visitation of 1559: act book for the Northern Province.* 1975. £21.00 (inc. p&p).
188. PLAYNE, ELIZABETH, & DE BOER, G., eds. *Lonsdale documents.* 1976. £21.00 (inc. p&p).
189. HAINSWORTH, D.R., eds. *Commercial papers of Sir Christopher Lowther, 1611-1644.* 1977. £21.00 (inc. p&p).
191. PHILLIPS, C.B., ed. *Lowther family estate papers, 1617-1675.* 1979. £21.00 (inc. p&p).
192. DOBSON, R.B., ed. *York City chamberlains' account rolls, 1396-1500.* 1980. £21.00 (inc. p&p).
194. FRASER, C.M., ed. *Northern petitions illustrative of life in Berwick, Cumbria and Durham in the fourteenth century.* 1981. £21.00 (inc. p&p).
195. MILBURN, G.E., ed. *The diary of John Young, Sunderland chemist and Methodist lay preacher, covering the years 1841-1843.* 1983. £21.00 (inc. p&p).
197. ELLIS, J.M., ed. *The letters of Henry Liddell to William Cotesworth (1708-17).* 1987. £21.00 (inc. p&p).
198. LOMAS, R.A. & PIPER, A.J., eds. *Durham Cathedral Priory rentals, volume I: bursars' rentals.* 1989. £21.00 (inc. p&p).
199. FRASER, C.M. & EMSLEY, K., eds. *Durham quarter sessions rolls, 1471-1625.* 1991. £21.00 (inc. p&p).
201. ATKINSON, J.A., FLYNN, B., PORTASS, V., SINGLEHURST, K. & SMITH, H.J., eds. *Darlington wills and inventories, 1600-1625.* 1993. £21.00 (inc. p&p).

202. WADE, J.F., ed. *Customs accounts of Newcastle upon Tyne, 1454-1500.* 1995. £21.00 (inc. p&p).
203. TODD, J.M., ed. *The Lanercost cartulary.* 1997. £21.00 (inc. p&p).

GLOUCESTERSHIRE & BRISTOL
Bristol & Gloucester Archaeological Society
D.Smith, 22, Beaumont Road, Gloucester, GL2 0EJ
Members are entitled to a substantial discount.

Gloucestershire Record Series
1. WYATT, IRENE, ed.*Transportees from Gloucestershire to Australia, 1783-1842.* 0-900197-26-9. 1988. £20.00 (inc. p&p).
2-3, 5 & 8. FRITH, BRIAN, ed. *Biglands Gloucestershire collections.* 4 vols. 0-900197-28-5 (v.1). 0-900197-30-7 (v.2). 0-900197-34-X (v.3). 0-900197-40-4 (v.4). 1989-95. £30.00 per volume (inc. p&p).
6. HOYLE, R.W., ed. *The military survey of Gloucestershire, 1522.* 0-900197-36-3. £30.00 (inc. p&p).
7. LITZENBERGER, C.J., ed. *Tewkesbury churchwardens' accounts, 1563-1624.* 0-900197-40-4. 1995. £30.00 (inc. p&p).
9. HODSDON, JAMES. *An historical gazetteer of Cheltenham.* 0-900197-43-9. 1997. £30.00 (inc. p&p).
10. WALKER, DAVID, ed. *The cartulary of St. Augustine's Abbey, Bristol.* 0-900197-46-3. 1998. £30.00 (inc. p&p).
PATTERSON, R.B., ed. *The original acta of St Peter's Abbey, Gloucester, c. 1122-1263.* Forthcoming.
SALE, A.J.H., ed. *Cheltenham wills and inventories, 1660-1740.* Forthcoming.
FENDLEY, JOHN, ed. *Bishop Benson's survey, 1735-50.* Forthcoming. Survey of the Diocese of Gloucester.
EDWARD, SUZANNE, ed. *The Chapter act book of Gloucester Cathedral, 1616-87.* Forthcoming.
RHODES, JOHN, ed. *Registers of Llanthony Priory, 1457-65, 1501-25.* Forthcoming. Estate records.
BARLOW, JILL, ed. *Register of Gloucester apprentices from 1595.* Forthcoming.
ELRINGTON, C.R., ed. *Abstract of feet of fines for Gloucestershire, 1199-1272.* Forthcoming.

Bristol Record Society
c/o Dept of Historical Studies, University of Bristol, 13-15, Woodland Road, Bristol, BS8 1TB
3. RALPH, ELIZABETH, & HARDWICK, NORA M., eds. *Calendar of the Bristol apprentice book, 1532-1565. Part II. 1544-1552.* 1980. xii, 196pp. 1980. £15.00 + p&p.
38. RICHARDSON, DAVID, ed. *Bristol, Africa, and the eighteenth-century slave trade to America. Vol. 1 The years of expansion, 1698-1729.* xxix, 203pp. 0-901583-0-0. 1986. £15.00 + p&p. Many names of shipmasters, merchants, slave factors, etc.
39. RICHARDSON, DAVID, ed. *Bristol, Africa, and the eighteenth-century slave trade to America. Vol.2. The years of ascendancy 1730-1745.* xxv, 145pp. 0-901538-08-6. 1987. £15.00 + p&p.
41. STANFORD, MAUREEN, ed. *The ordinances of Bristol, 1506-1598.* xxv, 117pp. 0-901538-11-6. 1990. £15.00 + p&p.
42. RICHARDSON, DAVID, ed. *Bristol, Africa and the eighteeth-century slave trade to America. Vol. 3. The years of decline, 1746-1769.* xxxiv, 249pp. 1991. £15.00 + p&p.
43. RALPH, ELIZABETH, ed. *Calendar of the Bristol apprentice book. Part III. 1552-1565.* ix, 155pp. 0-901538-13-2. 1992. £15.00 + p&p.
44. LANG, SHEILA, ed. *Tudor wills proved in Bristol 1546-1603.* xiii, 145pp. 1993. £15.00 + p&p.
45. BARRY, JONATHAN, & MORGAN, KENNETH, eds. *Reformation and revival in eighteenth-century Bristol.* xv, 183pp. 0-86292-418-9. 1994. £15.00 + p&p. Many names of nonconformists, etc.
46. BURGESS, CLIVE, ed. *The pre-Reformation records of All Saints, Bristol. Part I.* 1, 150pp. 0-901538-16-7. 1995. £15.00 + p&p.
47. RICHARDSON, DAVID, ed. *Bristol, Africa and the eighteenth-century slave trade to America. Vol. 4. The final years, 1770-1807.* xl, 279pp. 1996. £15.00 + p&p.
48. LEECH, ROGER H., ed. *The topography of medieval and early modern Bristol, Part I. Property holdings in the early walled town and marsh suburb north of the Avon.* xxvii, 220pp. 1996. £15.00 + p&p. Identifies numerous owners and occupiers.

49. STEMBRIDGE, P.K. *The Goldney family: a Bristol merchant dynasty*. x, 173pp. 0-901538-19-1. 1998. £15.00 + p&p.

HERTFORDSHIRE
Hertfordshire Record Society
14 Westbury Close, Hitchin, Hertfordshire, SG5 2NE
Members are entitled to substantial discounts

9. FLOOD, SUSAN, ed. *St. Albans wills 1471-1500*. xiv, 197pp. 0-9510728-8-9. 1994. £17.80 + p&p £1.78.
5. DOREE, STEPHEN, ed. *Parish register and tithing book of Thomas Hassall of Amwell*. xlvii, 281pp. 0-9510728-4-6. 1989. £3.75 + p&p 37p.
8. SHELDRICK, GILLIAN, ed. *The accounts of Thomas Green, 1742-1790*. xxix, 167pp. 0-9510728-7-0. £3.75 + p&p 37p. Accounts of a musician.
10. DOREE, STEPHEN, ed. *The early churchwardens accounts of Bishops Stortford, 1431-1558*. xxv, 365pp. 0-9510728-9-7. £19.95 + p&p £1.99.
12. KING, ANN, ed. *Muster books 1580-1605*. xxxv, 269pp. 0-9523779-1-8. £19.75 + p&p £1.97.
13. ADAMS, BEVERLY, ed. *Lifestyle and culture in Hertford: wills and inventories, 1660-1725*. 0-9523799-2-6. 1997. £19.50 + p&p £1.95.

KENT
The Faversham Society
Fleur de Lis Heritage Centre, Preston Street, Faversham, Kent, ME13 8NS

GOULDEN, RICHARD. *The Faversham book trade, 1730-1900*. 0-900532-89-0. £4.45. Biographical dictionary.

LANCASHIRE
Lancashire Parish Register Society
c/o Mr T. O'Brien, 16, Rothay Drive, Penarth, Warrington, WA5 2PG

103. SHAW, R. CUNLIFFE, ed. *The registers of Woodplumpton, part II. 1659-1784*. 1964. £20.00 + p&p £1.50.
114. DICKINSON, ROBERT,& DICKINSON, FLORENCE, eds. *The register of Prescot parish church, Part II. 1632-1666*. 1975. £20.00 + p&p.
120. BROMLEY, ROBERT, ed. *The register of the chapel of St. Helen, Hollinfare: baptisms, 1654-1837; marriages, 1705-1744; burials, 1709-1837*. 1981. £20.00 + p&p £1.50.
121. FOSTER, IRENE, ed. *The register of the chapel of St Thomas, Heaton Norris: baptisms, 1769-1845; burials 1767-1850*. 1982. £20.00 + p&p £1.50.
122. FOSTER, IRENE, ed. *The register of the parish of Childwall. Part II. 1681-1753*. 1983. £20.00 + p&p £1.50.
124. FOSTER, I., ed. *The register of the chapel of Chorlton cum Hardy: baptisms 1639, 1737-1837, marriages, 1737-1751; burials, 1753-1837*. 1985. £20.00 + p&p £1.50.
125. FOSTER, IRENE, ed. *The registers of the parish church of Warrington: baptisms, marriages and burials, 1680-1706*. 1986. £20.00 + p&p £1.50.
126. ALCOCK, S., & ALCOCK, E., eds. *The register of the parish church of Halton, 1727-1837*. 1987. £20.00 + p&p £1.50.
127. DICKINSON, ROBERT, ed. *The register of the chapel of Ireleth: baptisms 1745-1784; marriages 1745-1753*. 1988 £20.00 + p&p £1.50.
129. ROGERS, C.D., ed. *The registers of St Peter's, Ashton-under-Lyne: baptisms 1824-1837; burials 1835-1837*. ROGERS, C.D., ed. *The registers of St Lawrence, Chorley: baptisms and burials 1653-1708*. ROGERS, C.D., ed. *The registers of St Peters', Blackley: baptisms and burials, 1754-1783*. 1990. £20.00 + p&p £1.50.
131. ROGERS, C.D., ed. *The registers of the parish church of Eccles, in the County of Lancaster. Part II. Baptisms 1632/3-1665-6; marriages, 1632/3-1664; burials 1632-1663*. 1990. £20.00 + p&p £1.50.
132. *The register of the parish of Urswick, part II: 1696-1837*. 1992. £20.00 + p&p £1.50.
133. ROGERS, C.D., ed. *The registers of Colton, 1813-1842*. ROGERS, C.D., ed. *The registers of the Priory church of Lancaster: marriages, 1754-1777*. ROGERS, C.D., ed. *The register of the chapel of Rusland, 1782-1851*. 1992. £20.00 + p&p £1.50.
134. ROGERS, C.D., ed. *The registers of St James's, George Street, Manchester: baptisms and burials, 1708-1837*. 1993. £20.00 + p&p £1.50.

135. STONES, AIDAN C., ed. *The registers of Egton-cum-Newland: baptisms and burials, 1792-1841.* 1993. £20.00 + p&p £1.50.

136. ROGERS, C.D., ed. *The registers of Rivington, [1637]-1702-1837.* 1994. £20.00 + p&p £1.50.

137. PERKINS, JOHN, ed. *The registers of the parish of Prescot, 1531-1595.* 1995. £20.00 + p&p £1.50.

138. TAYLOR, K.T., ed. *The registers of Hindley, 1644-1814.* 1995. £20.00 + p&p £1.50.

139. PERKINS, J., & SIMPSON, JOHN, eds. *The registers of Haslingden: baptisms 1603-1683; marriages, 1603-1698; burials, 1603-1679.* 1995.

140. *The register of the parish church of St Mary, Todmorden. Pt 2.* 1995. £20.00 + p&p £1.50. 1781-1812.

141. BULMER, JOHN R., ed. *The registers of St Thomas, Ashton-in-Makerfield. Baptisms, 1810-27; burials 1806-44.* 1997.

142. PERKINS, JOHN, ed. *The register of St Thomas, Ashton-in-Makerfield: baptisms 1828-1873.* 1997. £20.00 + p&p £1.50.

143. *The registers of St Michaels-on-Wyre, 1707-1837, the registers of Copp Chapel (St Anne): marriages 1737, baptisms 1728-1837.* 1998. £20.00 + p&p £1.50.

Record Society of Lancashire & Cheshire

c/o Greater Manchester Record Office, 56, Marshall Street, New Cross, Manchester M4 5FU

Members receive substantial discounts.

110, 112 & 114. BAGLEY, J.J., ed. *The great diurnal of Nicholas Blundell of Little Crosby, Lancashire.* 3 vols. 1968. v.1. 1702-1711. v.2. 1712-1719. v.3. 1720-28. The set £30.00.

111. WILSON, K.P., ed. *Chester customs accounts, 1301-1566.* 1969. £9.00.

113. DICKINSON, ROBERT, ed. *Index to wills and administrations formerly preserved in the Probate Registry, Chester, 1826-1830.* 1972. £9.00.

115. DICKINSON, ROBERT, ed. *Marriage bonds for the Deaneries of Lonsdale, Kendal, Furness, Copeland & Amounderness, in the Archdeaconry of Richmond now preserved at Preston. Pt. vii. 1746-55.* 1975.

116. IVES, E.W., ed. *Letters and accounts of William Brereton of Malpas.* 1976. £9.00. Early 16th c.

117. FRANCE, R. SHARPE, ed. *The registers of estates of Lancashire papists, 1717-1788. Volume III. 1717, with lists of persons registered 1718-1785.* 1977. £9.00.

118. DICKINSON, ROBERT, & DICKINSON, FLORENCE, eds. *Index to wills and administrations formerly preserved in the Probate Registry, Chester, 1831-1833, prefaced by a history of the Society & guide to publications volumes I-CXVII, 1878-1977',* by Brian E. Harris. 1978. £9.00.

119. LAWTON, G.O., ed. *Northwich Hundred poll tax 1660 and hearth tax 1664.* 0-902593-08-0. 1979. £9.00.

122. BRIGG, MARY, ed. *The journals of a Lancashire weaver, 1856-60, 1860-64, 1872-75.* 0-902593-12-9. 1982. £7.50. Diary of John O'Neil of Carlisle and Clitheroe.

124 & 131. PHILIPS, C.B., & SMITH, J.H., eds. *Stockport probate records, 1578-1619.* 2 vols. 0-902593-4-5 (v.1); 0-902593-22-6 (v.2). 1985-92. The set £15.00.

125. BOOTH, P.H.W., & CARR, A.D., eds. *Account of Master John de Burnham the younger, Chamberlain of Chester, of the revenues of the counties of Chester and Flint, Michaelmas 1361 to Michaelmas 1362.* 0-902593-20-X. 1991. £25.00.

126. BARRACLOUGH, GEOFFREY, ed. *The charters of the Anglo-Norman Earls of Chester, c.1071-1237.* 0-902593-17-X. 1988. £25.00.

127, 132 & 133. ADDY, JOHN, & MCNIVEN, PETER, eds. *The diary of Henry Prescott, Ll.B., Deputy Registrar of Chester Diocese.* 3 vols. 0-902593-16-1 (v.1); 0-902593-23-4 (v.2); 0-902593-28-5 (v.3). 1987-96. £75.00 the set.

128. DORE, R.N., ed. *The letter books of Sir William Brereton. Volume two: June 18th 1645 - February 1st 1645/6.* 0-902593-19-6. 1990. £35.00.

129. DUTTON, DAVID J., ed. *Odyssey of an Edwardian Liberal: the political diary of Richard Durning Holt.* 0-902593-18-8. 1989. £18.00.

130. CROSBY, ALAN G., ed. *The family records of Benjamin Shaw, mechanic, of Dent, Dolphinholme and Preston, 1772-1841.* 0-902593-21-8. 1991. £20.00.

134. CUST, RICHARD, ed. *The papers of Sir Richard Grosvenor, 1st Bart. (1585-1645).* 0-902593-33-1. 1996. £20.00.
135. MARTIN, J.D., ed. *The account book of Clement Taylor of Finsthwaite, 1712-42.* 1998.
136. POWER, M., ed. *The Liverpool town book, 1649-71.* 0-902593-38-2. Forthcoming.
BOOTH, P., ed. *The accounts of the officials of the manor and hundred of Macclesfield, 1831-2.* Forthcoming.

Helmshore Local History Society

c/o John Simpson, The Cottage, Tor View Farm, Helmshore, Rossendale, Lancs., BB4 4AB

SIMPSON, JOHN, ed. *The court roll of the Honor of Clitheroe, 1567-1568.* 0-906881-08-0. 1996. £3.00 + p&p 70p.
ASPIN, CHRISTOPHER, & SIMPSON, JOHN. *Memories of village life: a memorial to Derek Pilkington.* 0-906881-06-4. 1992. £1.95 + p&p 70p. Includes information on the Pilkington family of Helmshore, *etc.*

LEICESTERSHIRE

Leicestershire Archaeological and Historical Society

The Guildhall, Leicester, LE1 5FQ

GREENHILL, F.A. *Incised slabs of Leicestershire and Rutland.* 1958. £15.00 + p&p £2.00.
Various offprints from the society's transactions are also available.

LINCOLNSHIRE

Lincoln Record Society

Lincoln Cathedral Library, The Cathedral, Lincoln, LN2 1PZ
Orders to: Messrs Boydell and Brewer, P.O. Box 9, Woodbridge, Suffolk IP12 3DF.

26. PEYTON, S.A., ed. *Minutes of proceedings in Quarter Sessions held for the parts of Kesteven, in the County of Lincoln, 1674-1695. Vol.2.* 1931. £25.00.
27. FOSTER, C.W., ed. *The Registrum Antiquissimum of the Cathedral Church of Lincoln. Vol. I.* 1931. £25.00. Charters, 13-16th c.
28. FOSTER, C.W., ed. *The Registrum Antiquissimum ... Vol.2.* 1933. £25.00.
29. FOSTER, C.W., ed. *The Registrum Antiquissimum ... Vol.3.* 1935. £25.00.
30. SILLEM, ROSAMOND, ed. *Records of some Sessions of the Peace in Lincolnshire, 1360-1375.* 1936. £25.00.
32. FOSTER, C.W., & MAJOR, KATHLEEN, eds. *The Registrum Antiquissimum ... Vol.4.* 1937. £25.00.
33. THOMPSON, A. HAMILTON, ed. *Visitations in the Diocese of Lincoln, 1517-1531. Vol.I. Visitations of rural deaneries by William Atwater, Bishop of Lincoln, and his commissaries, 1517-1520.* 1940. £25.00.
34. MAJOR, KATHLEEN, ed. *The Registrum Antiquissimum ... Vol.5.* 1940. £25.00.
35. THOMPSON, A. HAMILTON, ed. *Visitations in the Diocese of Lincoln, 1517-1531. Vol.2. Visitations of rural deaneries by John Longland, bishop of Lincoln, and of religious houses by Bishops Atwater and Longland, and by his and their commissaries, 1517-1531.* 1944. £25.00.
36. THOMSON, W.S., ed. *A Lincolnshire assize roll for 1298.* 1944. £25.00.
37. THOMPSON, A. HAMILTON, ed. *Visitations in the Diocese of Lincoln, 1517-1531, Vol.3. Visitations of religous houses (concluded) by bishops Atwater and Longland, and by their commissaries, 1517-1531.* 1947. £25.00.
38. BRACE, H.W., ed. *The first minute book of the Gainsborough monthly meeting of the Society of Friends, 1669-1719. Vol.1. 1669-1689.* 1948. £25.00.
39. HILL, ROSALIND M.T., ed. *The rolls and register of Bishop Oliver Sutton, 1280-1299. Vol.1. Institutions to benefices and confirmations of heads of religious houses in the Archdeaconry of Lincoln.* 1948. £25.00.
40. BRACE, H.W., ed. *The first minute book of Gainsborough monthly meeting of the Society of Friends, 1669-1719. Vol.2. 1689-1709.* 1949. £25.00.
41. MAJOR, KATHLEEN, ed. *The Registrum Antiquissimum ... Vol.6.* 1950. £25.00.
42. *The Registrum antiquissimum ... Facsimiles of charters in vols. v & vi.* 1950. £25.00.
43. HILL, ROSALIND M.T., ed. *The rolls and register of Bishop Oliver Sutton, 1280-1299. Vol.2. Institutions to benefices and confirmations of heads of religious houses in the Archdeaconry of Northampton.* 1950. £25.00.

44. BRACE, H.W., ed. *The first minute book of Gainsborough monthly meeting of the Society of Friends. Vol.3. 1709-1719.* 1951. £25.00.
45. HILL, J.W.F. *Letters and papers of the Banks family of Revesby Abbey, 1704-1760.* 1952. £25.00.
46. MAJOR, KATHLEEN, ed. *The Registrum Antiquissimum ... Vol.7.* 1953. £25.00.
48. HILL, ROSALIND M.T., ed. *The rolls and register of Bishop Oliver Sutton, 1280-1299. Vol.3. Memoranda, May 19, 1290-May 18, 1292.* 1954. £25.00.
49. KIMBALL, ELIZABETH G., ed. *Records of some Sessions of the Peace in Lincolnshire, 1381-1396. Vol.1. The Parts of Kesteven and the Parts of Holland.* 1955. £25.00.
50. HINTON, R.W.K., ed. *The port books of Boston, 1601-1640.* 1956. £25.00.
51. MAJOR, KATHLEEN, ed. *The Registrum Antiquissimum ... Vol.8.* 1958. £25.00.
52. HILL, ROSALIND M.T., ed. *The rolls and register of Bishop Oliver Sutton, 1280-1299. Vol.4. Memoranda, May 19, 1292-May 18, 1294.* 1958. £25.00.
53. HODGETT, G.A.J., ed. *The state of the ex-religious and former chantry priests in the Diocese of Lincoln, 1547-1573, from returns in the Exchequer.* 1959. £25.00.
54. KIRKUS, A.M., ed. *The records of the Commissioners of Sewers in the Parts of Holland, 1547-1603. Vol.1.* 1959. £25.00.
56. KIMBALL, ELIZABETH G., ed. *Records of some Sessions of the Peace in Lincolnshire, 1381-1396. Vol.2. The Parts of Lindsey.* 1962. £25.00.
57. ARCHER, MARGARET, ed. *The register of Bishop Philip Repingdon, 1405-1419. Vol.1. Memoranda, 1405-1411.* 1963. £25.00.
58. ARCHER, MARGARET, ed. *The register of Bishop Philip Repingdon, 1405-1419. Vol.2. Memoranda, 1411-1414.* 1963. £25.00.
60. HILL, ROSALIND M.T., ed. *The rolls and register of Bishop Oliver Sutton, 1280-1299. Vol.5. Memoranda, May 19, 1294-May 18, 1296.* 1965. £25.00.
61. BOWKER, MARGARET, ed. *An episcopal court book for the Diocese of Lincoln, 1514-1520.* 1967. £25.00.
62. MAJOR, KATHLEEN, ed. *The Registrum Antiquissimum ... Vol.9.* 1968. £25.00.
63. OWEN, A.E.B., ed. *The records of the Commissioners of Sewers in the Parts of Holland, 1547-1603. Vol.2.* 1968. £25.00.
64. HILL, ROSALIND M.T., ed. *The rolls and register of Bishop Oliver Sutton, 1280-1299. Vol.6. Memoranda, May 19, 1297-September 12, 1299.* 1969. £25.00.
65. KIMBALL, ELIZABETH G., ed. *Records of some Sessions of the Peace in the City of Lincoln, 1351-1354, and the Borough of Stamford, 1351.* 1971. £25.00.
66. LLOYD, C.M., ed. *Letters from John Wallace of Harpswell to Madam Whichcot, 1721-1727;* FINCH, MARY E., ed. *Correspondence of John Fardell, Deputy Registrar, 1802-1805.* 1973. £25.00.
67. MAJOR, KATHLEEN, ed. *The Registrum Antiquissimum ... Vol.10.* 1973. £25.00.
68. *The Registrum Antiquissimum ... Facsimiles of charters in vols. viii, ix & x).* 1973. £25.00.
69. HILL, ROSALIND M.T., ed. *The rolls and register of Bishop Oliver Sutton, 1280-1299. Vol.7. Ordinations, May 19, 1290-September 19, 1299.* 1975. £25.00.
71. OWEN, A.E.B., ed. *The records of the Commissioners of Sewers in the Parts of Holland, 1547-1603. Vol.3.* 1977. £25.00.
73. OWEN, DOROTHY M., ed. *The minute book of the Spalding Gentlemen's Society, 1732.* 1981. £25.00.
74. ARCHER, MARGARET, ed. *The register of Bishop Philip Repingdon, 1405-1419, Vol.3. Memoranda, 1414-1419.* 1982. £25.00.
75. SPURRELL, MARK, ed. *Stow church restored, 1846-1866.* 0-901503-39-8. 1984. £25.00.
76. HILL, ROSALIND M.T., ed. *The rolls and register of Bishop Oliver Sutton, 1280-1299, Vol.8. Institutions, collations and sequestations, all archdeaconries except Lincoln and Northampton.* 0-901503-40-1. 1986. £25.00.
77. CLARK, PETER, & CLARK, JENNIFER, eds. *The Boston Assembly minutes, 1545-1575.* 0-901503-50-9. 1987. £25.00.
78. MCLANE, BERNARD WILLIAM, ed. *The 1341 royal inquest in Lincolnshire.* 0-901503-51-7. 1988. £25.00.
79. SHORT, D.MARY. *A bibliography of the printed items relating to the City of Lincoln.* 0-901503-52-5. 1990. £25.00.
80. JOHNSTON, J.A., ed. *Probate inventories of Lincoln citizens, 1661-1714.* 0-901503-53-3. 1991. £25.00.
81. MCHARDY, A.K., ed. *Clerical poll taxes of the Diocese of Lincoln, 1377-1381.* 1992. 0-901503-54-1. 1992. £25.00. includes Leicestershire, Rutland and Bedfordshire.

82. NEVILLE, GRAHAM, ed. *The diaries of Edward Lee Hicks, Bishop of Lincoln 1910-1919.* 0-901503-55-X. 1993. £25.00.
83. COUTH, BILL, ed. *Grantham during the Interregnum: the hall book of Grantham, 1641-1649.* 0-901503-56-8. 1995. £25.00.
85. OWEN, A.E.B., ed. *The medieval Lindsey Marsh: select documents.* 0-901503-58-4. 1996. £25.00.

LONDON
London Record Society
c/o Institute of Historical Research, Senate House, London, WC1E 7HU
Email: creaton@sas.ac.uk
Members are entitled to substantial discounts.

1. CHEW, HELENA M., ed. *London possessory assizes: a calendar.* 1963. £20.00 + p&p £3.50.
2. GLASS, D., ed. *London inhabitants within the walls, 1695.* 1966. £20.00 + p&p £3.50. Index to the marriage tax returns.
3. DARLINGTON, I., ed. *London Consistory Court wills, 1492-1547.* 1967. £20.00 + p&p £3.50.
7. HODGETT, G.A.J., ed. *The cartulary of Holy Trinity, Aldgate.* 1971. £20.00 + p&p £3.50.
10. CHEW, HELENA M., & KELLAWAY, W., eds. *London assize of nuisance, 1301-1431: a calendar.* 1973. £20.00 + p&p £3.50.
12. WEINBAUM, M., ed. *The London eyre of 1276.* 1973. £20.00 + p&p £3.50.
13. MCHARDY, A.K., ed. *The church in London 1375-92.* 1977. £20.00 + p&p £3.50. Includes clerical poll tax returns, 1379-81.
16. KITCHING, C.J., ed. *London and Middlesex chantry certificates, 1548.* 1980. £20.00 + p&p £3.50.
18. BASING, PATRICIA, ed. *Parish fraternity register, fraternity of the Holy Trinity and Ss. Fabian and Sebastian in the parish of St. Botolph without Aldersgate.* 1982. £20.00 + p&p £3.50.
19. HARRIS, G.G., ed. *Trinity House of Deptford transactions, 1609-35.* 1983. £20.00 + £3.50.
20. MASTERS, BETTY R., ed. *Chamber accounts of the 16th century.* 1984. £20.00 + p&p £3.50.
22. KEENE, DEREK, & HARDING, VANESSA. *A survey of primary sources for property holding in London before the Great Fire.* 1985. £20.00 + p&p £3.50.
24. HITCHCOCK, T.V., ed. *Richard Hutton's complaint book.* 1987. £20.00 + £3.50 p&p. Notebook of the steward of the Quaker workhouse at Clerkenwell.
25. MASON, E. EMMA, ed. *Westminster Abbey charters, c.1066-1214.* 1988. £20.00 + p&p £3.50.
26. LOENGARD, J.S., ed. *London viewers and their certificates, 1508-1588.* 1989. £20.00 + p&p £3.50. The viewers were responsible for resolving disputes over property.
28. PALEY, R., ed. *Justice in 18th century Hackney: the justicing notebook of Henry Norris and the Hackney petty sessions book.* 1991. £20.00 + p&p £3.50.
29. LANG, R.G., ed. *Two Tudor subsidy assessment rolls for the City of London, 1541 and 1582.* 1993. £20.00 + p&p £3.50.
31. HARDING, VA & WRIGHT, L., eds. *London Bridge: selected accounts and rentals 1381-1538.* 1995. £20.00 + p&p £3.50.
32. GIESE, L., ed. *London Consistory Court depositions, 1586-1611: lists and indices.* Forthcoming.
33. HITCHCOCK, T.V. & BLACK, J., eds. *The settlement and bastardy examinations of St. Luke, Chelsea, 1730-66.* Forthcoming.

London Topographical Society
c/o Bishopsgate Institute, 230, Bishopsgate, London, EC2M 4QH

SCHOFIELD, JOHN, ed. *The London surveys of Ralph Treswell.* 0-902087-25-8. £16.00.

NORFOLK
Norfolk Record Society
c/o Mrs B. Miller, O.B.E., Secretary, 17, Christchurch Road, Norwich NR2 2AE

15. SACHSE, WILLIAM L., ed. *Minutes of the Norwich court of mayoralty, 1630-1631.* 1942. £5.00 + p&p £2.50.
19. WATKIN, AELRED, ed. *Archdeaconry of Norwich: inventory of church goods, temp. Edward III.* 1947. £5.00 + p&p £2.50.
35. BEDINGFELD, A.L., ed. *A cartulary of Creake Abbey.* 1966. £5.00 + p&p £2.50.
39. RUTLEDGE, P., ed. *Great Yarmouth assembly minutes, 1538-1545.* RICHWOOD, D.L., ed. *The Norwich accounts for the customs on strangers' goods and merchandise, 1582-1610.* 1970. £5.00 + p&p £2.50.

41. FERNIE, E.C., & WHITTINGHAM, A.B., eds. *The early communar and pitancer rolls of Norwich Cathedral Priory, with an account of the building of the cloister.* 1972. £5.00 + p&p £2.50.
43. HOULBROOKE, R.A., ed. *The letter book of John Parkhurst, Bishop of Norwich, compiled during the years 1571-5.* 1974-5. £5.00 + p&p £2.50.
45. DUNN, RICHARD MINTA, ed. *Norfolk Lieutenancy journal, 1660-1676.* 1977. £5.00 + p&p £5.50.
46. SMITH, A. HASSELL, ed. *The papers of Nathaniel Bacon of Stiffkey. Vol.1. 1556-1577.* 1978-9. £5.00 + p&p £2.50.
47. FROSTICK, CLAIRE. *Index of wills proved in the Consistory Court of Norwich, 1819-1857, and now preserved in the Norfolk Record Office.* 1980. £5.00 + p&p £2.50.
48. OWEN, A.E.B., ed. *The records of a Commission of Sewers for Wiggenhall, 1319-1324.* 1981. £5.00 + p&p £2.50.
49. SMITH, A. HASSELL, & BAKER, GILLIAN M., ed. *The papers of Nathaniel Bacon of Stiffkey. Vol.2. 1578-1585.* 1982-3. £5.00 + p&p £2.50.
50. YAXLEY, DAVID, ed. *Survey of the Houghton Hall estate by Joseph Hill 1800.* 1984. £5.00 + p&p £2.50. Estates of Cholmondeley family.
51. METTERS, G.A., ed. *The Parliamentary survey of Dean and Chapter properties in and around Norwich in 1649.* 1985. £5.00 + p&p £2.50.
52. HAINES, TIMOTHY. *An index to Norwich city officers, 1453-1835.* 1986. £5.00 + p&p £2.50.
53. SMITH, A. HASSELL, ed. *The papers of Nathaniel Bacon of Stiffkey. Vol.3. 1586-1595.* 1987-88. £5.00 + p&p £2.50.
54. ROSENHEIM, JAMES M., ed. *The notebook of Robert Doughty, 1662-1665.* 1989. £15.00 + p&p £3.50. J.P.'s notebook.
55. STOKER, DAVID A., ed. *The correspondence of the Reverend Francis Blomefield (1705-52).* 1990. £15.00 + p&p £3.50.
57. PRIESTLEY, URSULA, ed. *The letters of Philip Stannard, Norwich textile manufacturer (1751-1763).* 1994. £15.00 + p&p £3.50.
58. MARTINS, SUSANNA WADE, & WILLIAMSON, TOM, eds. *The farming journal of Randall Burroughes (1794-1799).* 1995. £15.00 + p&p £3.50.
59. DYMOND, DAVID, ed. *The register of Thetford Priory. Part 1. 1482-1517.* 1995. £15.00 + p&p £3.50. Jointly published by Oxford University Press for the British Academy. Accounts rather than a chartulary.
60. DYMOND, DAVID, ed. *The register of Thetford Priory. Part 2. 1518-1540.* 1996. £15.00 + p&p £3.50. Jointly published by Oxford University Press for the British Academy.
61. *Farming and gardening in late medieval Norfolk.* 1997. £15.00 + p&p £3.50. Includes NOBLE, CLAIRE, ed. *Norwich Cathedral Priory gardeners' accounts, 1329-1530,* and MORETON, CHARLES, ed *Skayman's book, 1516-1518.* 1997. £15.00 + p&p £3.50. The latter is the account book of Robert Skayman, steward of the Townshead family of East Raynham.

NORTHUMBERLAND
See also Durham

Society of Antiquaries of Newcastle upon Tyne
The Black Gate, Castle Garth, Newcastle upon Tyne, NE1 1RQ

WILLS, MARGARET. *Gibside and the Bowes family.* 114pp. 1995. £14.95.

Felton and Swarland Local History Society
c/o Peter Cook, 23 Berlow Grove, Felton, Morpeth, Northumberland, NE65 9NG

Index of births, deaths and marriages from the Morpeth Herald.
  v.1. *April 1860 - March 1861.* 1996. £4.00 (inc. p&p).
  v.2. *April 1861 - March 1862.* 1997. £4.00 (inc. p&p).
  v.3. *April 1862 - March 1863.* 1998. £4.00 (inc. p&p).
  v.4. *April 1893 - March 1864.* Forthcoming.
Index of the census returns for the Felton district of Northumberland. 3 vols. 1992-3.
  v.1. *1841-1851.* 1992. £4.00 (inc. p&p).
  v.2. *1861-1871.* 1993. £4.00 (inc. p&p).
  v.3. *1881-1891.* 1993. £4.00 (inc. p&p).
Index of the monumental inscriptions of the Felton district of Northumberland. 1991. £5.00 (inc. p&p).

Index of baptismal records of Felton Presbyterian church, 1880-1893. 1994. £3.00 (inc. p&p).

NOTTINGHAMSHIRE
Thoroton Society of Nottinghamshire

c/o Nottinghamshire Archives, Castle Meadow Road, Nottingham, NG2 1AG
Item marked* to be ordered from:
Jermy & Westerman, 203 Mansfield Road, Nottingham, NG1 3FS

25. HUNNISETT, R.F., ed. *Calendar of Nottinghamshire coroners inquests, 1485-1558.* xxxi, 242pp. 1969.*
29-30, 32 & 34. HOLDSWORTH, C.J., ed. *Rufford charters.* 4 vols. 1972-81. £30.00 + p&p.
31, 35 & 36. SEDDON, P.R., ed. *Letters of John Holles, 1587-1637.* 3 vols. 1975-86. £20.00 + p&p.
37. WEBSTER, W.F., ed. *Nottinghamshire hearth tax, 1664, 1674.* lxii, 183pp. 1988. £13.50.
39. BENNETT, M., ed. *A Nottinghamshire village in war and peace: the accounts of the Constables of Upton, 1640-1666.* 1995. £14.95.

Centenary index to the Transactions (vols 1-100) and Record Series (vols 1-40). 1997. £5.00.

OXFORDSHIRE
Oxford Historical Society

38, Randolph Street, Oxford, OX4 1XZ
Members are entitled to substantial discounts.

1. BOASE, C.W., ed. *Register of the University of Oxford. Vol. 1. 1449-63, 1505-71.* 0-901775-46-0. Reprint. Originally published 1885. £18.00.
2, 7, 13 & 34. HEARNE, THOMAS. *Remarks and collections of Thomas Hearne.* ed. C. Doble, et al. 11 vols. 0-901775-14-2 (v.1); 0-901775-15-0(v.2); 0-901775-16-9(v.3); 0-901775-18-5(v.4); 0-901775-18-5(v.5); 0-901775-19-3(v.6); 0-901775-20-7(v.7); 0-901775-21-5(v.8); 0-901775-22-3(v.9); 0-901775-23-1(v.10); 0-901775-24-X(v.11). Reprint. Originally published 1885-1921. £18.00 per vol.
9. EVANS, MARGARET, ed. *Letters of Richard Radcliffe and John James of Queens College, Oxford, 1755-83, with additions, notes, and appendices.* 0-901775-45-2. Reprint. Originally published 1887. £18.00.
10. CLARK, ANDREW, ed. *Register of the University of Oxford. Vol. II, 1571-1622. Pt I. Introductions.* 0-901775-47-9. Reprint. Originally published 1887. £18.00.
11. CLARK, ANDREW, ed. *Register of the University of Oxford. Vol. II. 1571-1622. Pt. 2. Matriculations and subscriptions.* 0-901775-48-7. Reprint. Originally published 1887. £18.00.
12. CLARK, ANDREW, ed. *Register of the University of Oxford. Vol. II. 1571-1622. Pt. 3. Degrees.* 0-901775-98-3. Reprint. Originally published 1888. £18.00.
14. CLARK, ANDREW, ed. *Register of the University of Oxford. Vol. 2. 1571-1622. Pt. 4. Indexes.* 0-901775-02-9. Reprint. Originally published 1889. £18.00.
18. ROGERS, J.E. THOROLD, ed. *Oxford city documents, 1268-1665.* 0-901775-50-9. Reprint. Originally published 1891. £18.00.
19, 21, 26, 30 & 40. CLARK, ANDREW, ed. *The life and times of Anthony Wood, antiquary, of Oxford, 1632-1695, described by himself. Collected from his diaries and other papers.* 5 vols. 0-901775-84-3(v.1); 0-901775-85-1(v.2); 0-901775-86-X(v.3); 0-901775-83-5(v.4); 0-901775-87-8(v.5). Reprints. Originally published 1891-1900. v 1-3, £18.00 per volume; v.4-5 currently reprinting.
24. STAPLETON, BRYAN, MRS. *Three Oxfordshire parishes: Kidlington, Yarnton, and Begbroke.* 0-901775-79-7. Reprint. Originally published 1893. £18.00. Many pedigrees.
27. BOASE, C.W., ed. *Registrum collegii Exoniensis. Register of the rectors, fellows, and other members on the foundation of Exeter College, Oxford, with a history of the College and illustrative documents.* New ed. 0-901775-07-X. Reprint. Originally published 1894. £18.00.
28 & 31. WIGRAM, SPENCER ROBERT, ed. *The cartulary of the monastery of St. Frideswide at Oxford.* 2 vols. 0-901775-81-9(v.1); 0-901775-82-7(v.2). Reprints. Originally published 1895-6. £18.00 per volume.

35-6. ANSTEY, HENRY, ed. *Epistolae academicae Oxon (Registrum F).* A collection of letters and other miscellaneous documents illustrative of academical life and studies at Oxford in the fifteenth century. 2. vols. 0-901775-05-3(v.1); 0-901775-06-1(v.2). Reprint. Originally published 1898. £18.00 per volume.

44, 62 & 79. MAGRATH, JOHN RICHARD, ed. *The Flemings in Oxford,* being documents selected from the Rydal papers in illustration of the lives and ways of Oxford men, 1650-1700. 3 vols. 1904-23. £18.00 per vol. Fleming family letters.

49 & 51. SALTER, HERBERT, ed. *Eynsham cartulary.* 2 vols. 0-901775-56-8(v.1); 0-901775-57-6(v.2). Reprint. Originally published 1907-8. £18.00 per volume.

64. SALTER, H.E., ed. *The Oxford deeds of Balliol College.* 1913. £18.00.

66, 68 & 69. SALTER, H.E., ed. *A cartulary of the Hospital of St John the Baptist.* 3 vols. 0-901775-58-4(v.1); 0-901775-59-2(v.2); 0-901775-60-6(v.3). Reprints. Originally published 1914-17. £18.00 per volume.

70 & 73. SALTER, H.E., ed. *Mediaeval archives of the University of Oxford.* 2 vols. 0-901775-61-4(v.1); 0-901775-62-2(v.2). Reprint. Originally published 1920-21. £18.00 per volume.

76. SALTER, H.E., ed. *Registrum annalium collegii Mertonensis. 1483-1521.* 1923. £18.00.

84. RICHARDS, G.C., ed. *The Dean's register of Oriel, 1446-1661.* 1926. £18.00.

87. SALTER, H.E., ed. *Oxford Council acts, 1583-1626.* 1927. £18.00.

88. SALTER, H.E., ed. *The Boarstall cartulary.* 1927. £18.00. Private cartulary of Rede family, 15th c.

89-91, 97-8, & 101. SALTER, H. E., ed. *Cartulary of Oseney Abbey.* 6 vols. 0-901775-64-9(v.1); 0-901775-65-7(v.2); 0-901775-66-5(v.3); 0-901775-67-3(v.4); 0-901775-68-1(v.5); 0-901775-77-0(v.6). Reprints. Originally published 1929-36.

93-4. SALTER, H.E., ed. *Registrum cancellarii Oxoniensis, 1434-1469.* 2 vols. 0-901775-72-4(v.1); 0-901775-73-8. Reprint; originally published 1932. £18.00 per volume.

95. HOBSON, M.G., & SALTER, H.E., eds. *Oxford council acts, 1626-1665.* 0-901775-26-6. Reprint. Originally published 1932.

New Series

2. HOBSON, M.G., ed. *Oxford Council acts, 1665-1701.* 0-901775-27-4. Reprint. Originally published 1939. £18.00.

6-8 & 30. PANTIN, W.A. *Canterbury College, Oxford.* 4 vols. 0-901775-39-8(v.1); 0-901775-41-X(v.2); 0-904107-09-4(v.3); 0-904107-09-4(v.4). 1941-85. v.1-3. £18.00 per volume; v.4. £28.00.

10. HOBSON, M.G., ed. *Oxford Council acts, 1701-1752.* 0-901775-95-9. 1948. £18.00.

11. CORDEAUX, E.H., & MERRY, D.H. *A bibliography of printed books relating to Oxfordshire (excluding the University and the City of Oxford).* 0-9014107-07-8. Reprinted 1981. Originally and published 1955.

14 & 20. SALTER, H.E. *Survey of Oxford.* ed W.A.Pantin & W.T. Mitchell. 2 vols. 0-901775-75-4(v.1). 0-901775-00-2(v.2.) 1960-9. £18.00 per volume. Traces landowners & tenants.

15. HOBSON, M.G., ed. *Oxford Council acts, 1752-1801.* 0-901775-28-2. 1962. £18.00.

17. SPOKES, P.S. *Summary catalogue of manuscripts in the Bodleian Library relating to the City, County and University of Oxford. Accessions from 1916 to 1962.* 1964. Available from Publications Officer, Bodleian Library, Oxford OX1 3BG, price on application.

19. AVELING, HUGH, DOM, &, PANTIN, W.A., eds. *The letter book of Robert Joseph, monk-scholar of Evesham and Gloucester College, Oxford, 1530-3.* 1967. £18.00

21. HARGREAVES-MAWDESLEY, W.N., ed. *Woodforde at Oxford, 1759-1776.* 1969. £18.00. Diary, etc.

22. PANTIN, W.A., & MITCHELL, W.T., eds. *The register of Congregation, 1448-1463.* 1972. £18.00.

23-4 FLETCHER, JOHN M., ed. *Registrum annalium collegii Mertonensis, 1521-[1603].* 2 vols. 0-904107-01-9(v.1); 0-904107-04-3(v.2). 1974-6. £18.00 per volume.

25. CORDEAUX, E.H., & MERRY, D.H., eds. *A bibliography of printed works relating to the City of Oxford.* 1976. £18.00.

26. MITCHELL, W.T., ed. *Epistolae academicae, 1508-1596.* 1980. £18.00.

27. MITCHELL, W.T., ed. *Registrum cancellarii, 1498-1506.* 0-904107-06-X. 1980. £28.00.
28. CORDEAUX, E.H., & MERRY, D.H. *Bibliography of printed works relating to Oxfordshire (excluding the University and City of Oxford). Supplementary volume.* 0-904107-08-6. 1981. £18.00.
30. PANTIN, W.A. *Canterbury College, Oxford. Volume IV.* 1985. £28.00.
31. GRAHAM, MALCOLM, ed. *Oxford city apprentices, 1697-1800.* 1987. £28.00.
32-3. SLADE, C.F.,& LAMBRICK, GABRIELLE, eds. *Two cartularies of Abingdon Abbey.* 2 vols. 1990-92. £28.00 per volume.
34. FLETCHER, JOHN M., & UPTON, CHRISTOPHER A., eds. *The domestic accounts of Merton College, Oxford, 1 August 1482-1 August 1494.* 1996. £28.00.
35. ADAMS, REGINALD H., ed. *Memorial inscriptions in St. John's College, Oxford.* 1986. £10.00.
36. HUTCHINSON, F.E., & CRASTER, EDMUND, SIR. *Monumental inscriptions in All Soul's College, Oxford.* 1998. £12.50.
37-8. MITCHELL, W.T., ed. *Register of Congregations, 1507-16.* 2 vols. 1994-7. £28.00 per volume.

Oxfordshire Record Society
c/o S. Tomlinson, Bodleian Library, Oxford, OX1 3BG

39. WEAVER, J.R.H., & BEARDWOOD, A., eds. *Some Oxfordshire wills proved in the Prerogative Court of Canterbury, 1393-1510.* £9.00.
41. BRIERS, P.M., ed. *Henley borough records: assembly books i-iv, 1393-1543.* 1966. £9.00.
42. TOYNBEE, MARGARET, ed. *The papers of Captain Henry Stevens, waggon-master general to King Charles I.* 1962. £9.00. Includes biographical notes on obscure royalists.
45. HASSALL, W.O., ed. *Index of persons in Oxfordshire deeds acquired by the Bodleian Library, 1578-1963.* 1966. £9.00.
46. STONE, E., HYDE, PATRICIA, eds. *Oxfordshire hundred rolls of 1279. 1. The Hundred of Bampton. 2. The Borough of Witney.* 1969. £9.00.

47. PUGH, R.K., ed. *The letter-books of Samuel Wilberforce, 1843-68.* 1970. £9.00. Jointly published with Buckinghamshire Record Society.
49. ROY, IAN, ed. *The Royalist ordnance papers, 1642-1646. Pt.2.* 1975. £9.00.
51. HORN, PAMELA, ed. *Village education in nineteenth-century Oxfordshire: the Whitchurch school log book, 1868-93.* 1979. £12.00.
52. CLAPINSON, MARY, ed. *Bishop Fell and nonconformity: visitation documents from the Oxford Diocese, 1682-83.* 1980. £12.00.
53. KIMBALL, ELIZABETH, G., ed. *Oxfordshire sessions of the Peace in the reign of Richard II.* 1983. £12.00.
54. BOLTON, JAMES L., & MASLEN, MARJORIE, eds. *Calendar of the court books of the Borough of Witney, 1538-1610.* 1985. £12.00.
56. COOPER, JANET, ed. *The Oxfordshire eyre, 1241.* 1989. £12.00
57. JENKINS, A.P., ed. *The correspondence of Thomas Secker, Bishop of Oxford, 1737-58.* 1991. £15.00.
58. MASLEN, MARJORIE, ed. *Woodstock chamberlains' accounts, 1609-50.* 1983. £15.00.
59. GIBSON, JEREMY, ed. *Oxfordshire and North Berkshire protestation returns and tax assessments, 1641-42.* 1994. £15.00.
60. BEAUCHAMP, PETER C., ed. *The Oxfordshire muster rolls, 1539, 1542, 1569.* 1996. £15.00.
61. BARRATT, D.M., HOWARD-DRAKE, JOAN, & PRIDDY, MARK, eds. *Probate records of the courts of the Bishop and Archdeacon of Oxford, 1733-1857, and of Oxfordshire Peculiars, 1547-1856.* 1997. £15.00. Jointly published with the British Record Society.

Banbury Historical Society
c/o Banbury Museum, 8 Horsfair, Banbury, OX16 0AA.

4. BEESON, F.C. *Clockmaking in Oxfordshire, 1400-1850.* 3rd ed. 1989. Published by, and available from, the Museum of the History of Science, Oxford.
11. PRICE, F.D., ed. *The Wigginton constables' book, 1691-1836.* 1971. £15.00 + p&p £1.50.

13-14. BRINKWORTH, E.R.C., & GIBSON, J.S.W., eds. *Banbury wills and inventories.* 2 vols. 1976-85. Pt.1. *1591-1620.* 1985. £10.00 + p&p £2.00. Pt.2. *1621-1650.* 1976. £15.00 + p&p £1.50.

15. GIBSON, J.S.W., & BRINKWORTH, E.R.C., eds. *Banbury Corporation records, Tudor and Stuart.* 1977. £15.00 + p&p £2.00.

17. *Administrations and inventories of the Archdeaconry of Northampton. Pt.2. 1711-1800.* 1980. Jointly published with the British Record Society, q.v.

18. GIBSON, J.S.W., ed. *Banbury burial registers 1723-1812.* [198-]. £10.00 + p&p £1.50.

21. RENOLD, PENELOPE, ed. *Banbury gaol records.* 1987. £15.00 + p&p £1.50.

22. GIBSON, J.S.W., ed. *Baptism and burial registers of Banbury, Oxfordshire. Part 4. 1813-1838.* 1988. £15.00 + p&p £1.50.

24. GIBSON, JEREMY, ed. *Oxfordshire and North Berkshire protestation returns and tax assessments, 1641-42.* 1994. £15.00 + p&p £2.00.

26. GILKES, R.K., ed. *The 'Bawdy Court' of Banbury: the act book of the Peculiar Court of Banbury, 1625-1638.* 1998. £15.00 + p&p £2.00.

RUTLAND

Rutland Local History Record Society

Rutland County Museum, Catmos Street, Oakham, Leicestershire, LE15 6HW
Phone: (01572) 723654
Members are entitled to substantial discounts.

CORNWALL, JULIAN, ed. *Tudor Rutland: the county community under Henry VIII.* Rutland record series **1**. 0-907464-01-7. 1980. £3.00. Military survey, 1522; lay subsidy, 1524.

BOURN, JILL, & GOODE, AMANDA. *The Rutland hearth tax, 1665.* Rutland record series **3**. 0-907464-08-4. 1991. £3.50.

CHINNERY, ALLEN, ed. *The Oakham survey, 1305.* Occasional publications **2**. 0-907464-01-7. 1991. £3.50.

The Oakham Lordshold survey of 1787. Forthcoming.

SOMERSET
Somerset Record Society

c/o Somerset Studies Library, Paul Street, Taunton, TA1 3PF

BAILEY, DERRICK SHERWIN, ed. *Wells Cathedral chapter act book, 1666-1683.* 0-11-440041-5. 1973. £15.00 + p&p. Jointly published with the Historical Manuscripts Commission.

COCKBURN, J.S., ed. *Somerset assize orders 1640-1659.* 0-901732-02-8. 1971. £15.00 + p&p.

COSTEN, M.D., ed. *Wesleyans and Bible Christians in South Somerset: accounts and minutes, 1808-1907.* 0-901732-26-5. 1984. £18.00 + p&p.

GERARD, THOMAS. *The particular description of the County of Somerset.* 0-901732-16-8. 1900 (1973 reprint; originally written 1633). £15.00 + p&p.

HARLEY, J.B., & HORROCKS, D.M.M., eds. *Medieval deeds of Bath and district.* 0-901732-20-6. 1974. £15.00 + p&p.

MORLAND, STEPHEN C., ed. *The Somersetshire quarterly meeting of the Society of Friends, 1668-1699.* 0-901732-21-4. 1978. £15.00 + p&p.

WATKIN, AELRED, ed. *The great chartulary of Glastonbury.* 3 vols. 0-901732-17-6; 0-901732-18-4; 0-901732-19-2. 1947-56. £15.00 per volume + p&p.

WIGFIELD, W.M., ed. *The Monmouth rebels, 1685.* 0-901732-27-3. 1985. £15.00 + p&p.

WOODWARD, G.H., ed. *Calendar of Somerset chantry grants, 1548-1603.* 0-901732-25-7. 1982. £15.00 + p&p.

Nailsea & District Local History Society

c/o Peter Wright, 5, The Perrings, Nailsea, Bristol, BS19 2YD

Backwell: the 1891 census. Some observations. 1997. £4.50 + 50p p&p.

WRIGHT, PETER. *Holy Trinity churchyard, Nailsea: tombstone inscriptions, 1978.* 0-9516258-6-1. New ed. 1994.

Staffordshire Parish Register Society

c/o Sue Parkes, Hon. Secretary, 60, Pool Hayes Lane, Willenhall, WV12 4PY

Alton parish register: bapts., mar., & bur., 1681-1746; banns, 1754-1769; BTs 1676-1682, 1746-1758. £3.00 (inc. p&p).

Biddulph parish register: bapts., mar., & bur., 1558-1642 & 1653-1684. £3.00 (inc. p&p).
Bradeley parish register: bapts. 1540-1779; mar. & bur. 1538-1779. £3.00 (inc. p&p).
Brierley Hill parish register: bapts. & bur., 1766-1800. £3.00 (inc. p&p).
Dudley parish register: bapts. 1540-1779; mar. & bur., 1541-1649. £3.00 (inc. p&p).
Milwich parish register, part 2 (with index to part 1): bapts., mar., & bur., 1713-1812. £3.00 (inc. p&p).
Penn parish register: bapts., 1748-1812; mar., 1754-1837; bur., 1754-1812. £3.00 (inc. p&p).

Staffordshire Record Society
c/o William Salt Library, Eastgate Street, Stafford, Staffs ST16 2LZ

Staffordshire Advertiser index to births, marriages and deaths, 1821-1840. 1986. £4.00 (including p&p).
GATLEY, D.A., ed. *The Stoke-upon-Trent parish listing, 1701.* 1994. £4.25 (inc. p&p).

Burntwood Family History Group
c/o Len Wenman, 10 Squirrels Hollow, Boney Hay, Burntwood, Staffs
Email: lawman@lineone.net

St. Mary's Hospital burials, 1867-1920. £4.00 (inc. p&p).
St. Mary's Hospital burials, 1921-1956. £4.00 (inc. p&p).
A surname index to the parish registers of Christchurch church, Burntwood, 1820-1920. £3.00 (inc. p&p).
A surname index to the census returns for Burntwood, Edial and Woodhouses, 1841 to 1871. £3.00 (inc. p&p).
A surname index to the census returns for Burntwood, Edial and Woodhouses, 1881 and 1891. £3.00 (inc. p&p).
Surname index to the Methodist chapels in the Burntwood area. Forthcoming.
Surname index to the parish registers of St. Joseph's and St. Theresa's, Chasetown. Forthcoming.
Christchurch, Burntwood monumental inscriptions. Forthcoming.
Burntwood School admission books. Forthcoming.
Parish registers of St. Anne's, Chasetown. Forthcoming.
Parish registers of St. John's, Chase Terrace. Forthcoming.
Burntwood poor law records, enclosure awards, and tythe records. Forthcoming.

SUFFOLK
Suffolk Record Society
c/o Libraries & Heritage, St. Andrew House, County Hall, Ipswich, IP4 1LJ
Orders to: Boydell & Brewer, P.O. Box 9, Woodbridge, Suffolk, IP12 3DF
Phone: (01394) 411320

2. DENNY, A.H., ed. *The Sibton Abbey estates: select documents, 1325-1509.* 166pp. 0-900716-12-6. 1960. £25.00.
4. BECKETT, R.B., ed. *John Constable's correspondence. [v.1.] The family of East Bergholt.* 336pp. 0-85115-064-0. 1962. £25.00.
5. GRANSDEN, ANTONIA, ed. *The letter-book of William of Hoo, sacrist of Bury St. Edmunds, 1280-1294.* 0-900716-11-8. 1963. £25.00.
6. *John Constable's correspondence, ii: early friends and Maria Bicknell (Mrs. Constable).* 1224pp. 0-900716-05-3. 1964. £25.00.
9. WEBB, JOHN. *Poor relief in Elizabethan Ipswich.* 167pp. 0-900716-03-7. 1966. £25.00.
11. *John Constable's correspondence v: various friends, with Charles Boner and the author's children.* 1224pp. 0-900716-08-8. 1967. £25.00.
13. HOLMES, CLIVE, ed. *The Suffolk Committee for Scandalous Ministers, 1644-46.* 128pp. 0-900716-00-2. 1970. £25.00.
16. MARTIN, G.H., ed. *The Ipswich recognizance rolls, 1294-1327: a calendar.* 151pp. 0-900716-14-2. 1973. £25.00.
17. DODD, KENNETH MELTON, ed. *The field book of Walsham-le-Willows, 1577.* 168pp. 0-900716-16-9. 1974. £25.00.
20. STEWARD, A.V. *A Suffolk bibliography.* 477pp. 0-85115-115-9. £30.00.
21. THOMSON, RODNEY M., ed. *The archives of the abbey of Bury St. Edmunds.* 190pp. 0-85115-087-X. 1980. £25.00.
22. REED, MICHAEL, ed. *The Ipswich probate inventories, 1583-1631.* 126pp. 0-85115-148-5. 1981. £25.00.

23. NORTHEAST, PETER, ed. *Boxford churchwardens accounts, 1530-1561.* 124pp. 0-85115-160-4. 1982. £25.00.
27. RIDGARD, JOHN, ed. *Medieval Framlingham: selected documents, 1270-1524.* 176pp. 0-85115-432-8. 1985. £25.00.
28. POUND, JOHN, ed. *The military survey of 1522 for Babergh Hundred.* 166pp. 0-85115-438-7. 1986. £25.00.
29. EVANS, NESTA, ed. *The wills of the Archdeaconry of Sudbury, 1630-1635.* 574pp. 0-85115-492-1. 1987. £25.00.
34. BAILEY, MARK ed. *The bailiffs minute book of Dunwich, 1404-1440.* 159pp. 0-85115-306-2. 1992. £25.00.
35. ALLEN, MARION E., ed. *Wills of the Archdeaconry of Sudbury, 1620-1624.* 360pp. 0-85115-345-3. 1989. £25.00.
37. ALLEN, MARION E., ed. *Wills of the Archdeaconry of Suffolk, 1625-6.* 298pp. 0-85115-644-4. 1995. £25.00.
38. WEBB, JOHN. *The town finances of Elizabethan Ipswich.* 198pp. 0-85115-643-6. 1996. £25.00.
40. LOCK, RAY, ed. *The court rolls of Walsham le Willows.* 382pp. 0-85115-616-9. 1998. £30.00.
Extra vol. CORDER, JOAN. *A dictionary of Suffolk crests.* 255pp. 0-85115-554-5. 1998. £30.00.

Suffolk charters series
1. MORTIMER, RICHARD, ed. *Leiston Abbey cartulary and Butley Priory charters.* 0-85115-106-X. 1979. £25.00.
2. HARPER-BILL, CHRISTOPHER, ed. *Blythburgh Priory cartulary. Part One.* 0-85115-128-0. 1980. £25.00.
3. HARPER-BILL, CHRISTOPHER, ed. *Blythburgh Priory cartulary. Part Two.* 0-85115-152-3. 1981. £25.00.
4. HARPER-BILL, CHRISTOPHER, ed. *Stoke by Clare cartulary: B.L. Cotton appx. xxi. Part one.* 0-85115-165-5. 1982. £25.00.
5. HARPER-BILL, CHRISTOPHER, & MORTIMER, RICHARD, ed. *Stoke by Clare cartulary: B.L. Cotton appx. xxi. Part two.* 0-85115-179-5. 1983. £25.00.
6. HARPER-BILL, CHRISTOPHER, & MORTIMER, RICHARD, ed. *Stoke by Clare cartulary: B.L. Cotton appx. xxi. Part three.* 0-85115-198-1. 1984. £25.00.
7. BROWN, PHILIPPA, ed. *Sibton Abbey cartularies and charters. Part one.* 0-85115-413-1. 1985. £25.00.
8. BROWN, PHILIPPA, ed. *Sibton Abbey cartularies and charters. Part two.* 0-85115-443-3. 1986. £25.00.
9. BROWN, PHILIPPA, ed. *Sibton Abbey cartularies and charters. Part three.* 0-85115-474-3. 1987. £25.00.
10. BROWN, PHILIPPA, ed. *Sibton Abbey cartularies and charters. Part four.* 0-85115-499-9. 1988. £25.00.
11. HARPER-BILL, CHRISTOPHER, ed. *Cartulary of the Augustinian Friars of Clare.* 0-85115-295-3. 1991. £25.00.
12. BROWN, VIVIEN, ed. *Eye Priory cartulary & charters, I.* 0-85115-322-4. 1992. £30.00.
13. BROWN, PHILIPPA, ed. *Eye Priory cartulary & charters, II.* 0-85115-347-X. 1994. £25.00.
14. HARPER-BILL, CHRISTOPHER, ed. *Charters of the medieval hospitals of Bury St.Edmunds.* 0-85115-558-8. 1994. £25.00.
15. MORTIMER, RICHARD, ed. *Charters of St. Bartholomew's Priory, Sudbury.* 0-85115-574-X. 1996. £25.00.
16. HARPER-BILL, CHRISTOPHER, ed. *Charters of Dodnash Priory.* 0-85115-372-0. 1998. £25.00.

SURREY
Surrey Record Society
c/o Surrey Record Office, County Hall, Penrhyn Road, Kingston upon Thames, KT1 2DN

7. MILLS, M.H., ed. *The pipe roll for 1295: Surrey membrane.* 1968. £5.00 + p&p £2.00.
19. MEEKINGS, C.A.F., ed. *Surrey fines, 1509-1558.* 1968. £5.00 + p&p £2.00.
25. DANCE, ENID M., ed. *Wimbledon vestry minutes, 1747-1788.* 1964. £5.00 + p&p £2.00.
27. BERRYMAN, BLANCH, ed. *Mitcham settlement examinations, 1784-1814.* 1973. £5.00 + p&p £2.00.
28. DALY, ANNE, ed. *Kingston upon Thames register of apprentices, 1563-1703.* 1974. £5.00 + p&p £2.00.
30. SILVERTHORNE, E., ed. *The deposition book of Richard Wyatt, J.P., 1767-76.* 1978. £5.00 + p&p £2.00.
31. *The 1235 Surrey eyre. Pt.1. Introduction and biographies.* 1979. £12.75 + p&p £2.00.
32. *The 1235 Surrey eyre. Text and translation.* 1983. £15.00 + p&p £2.00.

34. WARD, W.R., ed. *Parson and parish in eighteenth-century Surrey: replies to bishops' visitations*. 1994. £15.00 + p&p £2.00.
1524 lay subsidy for Surrey. Forthcoming.
Elizabethan Surrey probate inventories. Forthcoming.
Survey of crown lands, Surrey, temp Edward VI. Forthcoming.

SUSSEX
Sussex Record Society
Barbican House, High Street, Lewes, East Sussex, BN7 1YE
Members are entitled to substantial discounts

1. DUNKIN, H.W., ed. *Calendar of Sussex marriage licences recorded in the Consistory Court of the Bishop of Chichester for the Archdeaconry of Lewes, August 1586 to March 1642/3*. 1902. Reprint forthcoming.
2. SALZMANN, L.F., ed. *An abstract of feet of fines relating to the County of Sussex from 2 Richard I to 33 Henry III*. 1903. Reprint forthcoming.
3. SALZMANN, L.F., ed. *A calendar of post mortem inquisitions relating to the County of Sussex, 1 to 25 Elizabeth*. 1904. Reprint forthcoming.
4. *Miscellaneous records*. 1905. Contents include 'A poll for the election of members of Parliament for the County of Sussex in 1705', SALZMANN, L.F., ed. 'A calendar of the entries relating to Sussex in the Harleian manuscripts', DEEDES, CECIL, ed. 'Extracts from the episcopal register of Richard Praty, S.T.P., lord bishop of Chichester, 1438-1445', *etc*. Reprint forthcoming.
5. RICE, R. GARRAWAY, ed. *West Sussex protestation returns, 1641-2*. 1906. Reprint forthcoming.
6. DUNKIN, EDWIN H.W. *Calendar of Sussex marriage licences ... for the Archdeaconry of Lewes, August 1670 to March 1728/9, and in the peculiar court of the Archbishop of Canterbury for the Deanery of South Malling, May 1620 to December 1732*. 1907. Reprint forthcoming.
7. SALZMANN, L.F., ed. *An abstract of feet of fines ... from 34 Henry III to 35 Edward I*. 1908. Reprint forthcoming.
8. DEEDES, CECIL, ed. *The episcopal register of Robert Rede, ordinis predicatorum, lord bishop of Chichester, 1397-1415. Pt.1*. 1908. Reprint forthcoming.
48. SALZMANN, L.F., ed. *The town book of Lewes, 1542-1701*. 1945-6. £2.50.
61. STEER, FRANCIS W., ed. *A catalogue of Sussex estate and tithe award maps*. 1962. £10.00.
64. DELL, RICHARD F. *Rye shipping records, 1566-1590*. 1965-66. £5.00 (unbound copies only available).
65. SEARLE, ELEANOR, & ROSS, BARBARA, eds. *The cellarers' rolls of Battle Abbey, 1275-1513*. 1967. £10.00.
70. SMITH, VERENA, ed. *The town book of Lewes, 1837-1901*. 1975. £10.00.
71. TITTLER, ROBERT, ed. *Accounts of the Roberts family of Boarzell, Sussex, c.1568-1582*. 1977-9. £2.50.
72. KINGSLEY, DAVID. *Printed maps of Sussex, 1575-1900*. 1982. £5.00. Includes biographies of cartographers.
73. MCCANN, TIMOTHY J., ed. *The correspondence of the Dukes of Richmond and Newcastle, 1724-1750*. 0-85445-032-7. 1984. £5.00.
74. HUNNISETT, R.F., ed. *Sussex coroners inquests, 1485-1558*. 0-85445-033-5. 1985. £12.00.
76. CROSSLEY, DAVID, & SAVILLE, RICHARD, eds. *The Fuller letters, 1728-1755: guns, slaves and finance*. 0-85445-037-8. 1991. £24.00.
77. DAVEY, ROGER, ed. *East Sussex land tax, 1785*. 0-85445-038-6. 1991. £24.00.
78. FORD, WYN K. *Chichester Diocesan surveys, 1686 and 1724*. 0-85445-039-4. 1994. £29.00. Visitation returns, 1686, and replies to bishops' queries, 1724.
80. SHORT, BRIAN, ed. *The Ashdown Forest dispute, 1876-1882: environmental politics and custom*. 0-85445-041-0. 1997. £18.50. Dispute concerned rights in the Forest. Includes much biographical information.
81. *Sussex schools in the eighteenth century*. 1998. £25.00.

Rye Local History Group
c/o Mrs P. Kingswood, 12 Rock Channel Quay, Rye, E. Sussex, TN31 7DL
Monumental inscriptions in Rye Cemetery. 1996. £3.00 + 50p p&p.

WILTSHIRE
Wiltshire Record Society
c/o Mr. M.J. Lansdown, 53, Clarendon Road, Trowbridge, Wilts., BA14 7BS
Members are entitled to substantial discounts.

1. PUGH, R.B., ed. *Abstract of feet of fines relating to Wiltshire for the reigns of Edward I and Edward II.* xx, 190pp. 1939 (1966 reprint). £20.00 + p&p.
2. PAFFORD, J.H.P., ed. *Accounts of the Parliamentary garrisons of Great Chalfield and Malmesbury, 1645-1646.* 112pp. 1940 (1966 reprint). £20.00 + p&p.
3. PUGH, R.B., ed. *Calendar of Antrobus deeds before 1625.* lvi, 165pp. 1947 (1972 reprint). £20.00 + p&p. Relates to Amesbury and district.
4. JOHNSON, H.C., ed. *Wiltshire county records: minutes of proceedings in sessions, 1563 and 1574 to 1592.* xxviii, 246pp. 1949. £20.00 + p&p.
5. RATHBONE, M.G., ed. *List of Wiltshire borough records earlier in date than 1836.* xiv, 108pp. 1951 (1974 reprint). £20.00 + p&p.
6. BECKINSALE, R.P., ed. *The Trowbridge woollen industry as illustrated by the stock books of John and Thomas Clark, 1803-1824.* xxvi, 249pp. 1951 (1973 reprint). £20.00.
7. MABBS, A.W., ed. *Guild stewards' book of the Borough of Calne, 1561-1688.* xxxiv, 150pp. 1953. £20.00 + p&p.
9. KERRIDGE, E., ed. *Surveys of the manors of Philip, Earl of Pembroke and Montgomery, 1631-2.* xiv, 178pp. 1953 (1969 reprint). £20.00 + p&p.
10. RAMSAY, G.D., ed. *Two sixteenth century taxation lists, 1545 and 1576.* xxiv, 242pp. 1954 (1969 reprint). £20.00 + p&p. Includes the clergy benevolence of 1545, and the subsidy of 1576.

FOWLE, J.P.M., ed. *Wiltshire quarter sessions and assizes, 1736.* lxvi, 214pp. 1955 (1972 reprint). £20.00 + p&p.

13. RICKARD, R.L., ed. *Progress notes of Warden Woodward for the Wiltshire estates of New College, Oxford, 1659-1675.* xx, 116pp. 1957 (1969 reprint). £20.00 + p&p. The estates were in Alton Barnes, Colerne and Stert.
14. FARR, M.W., ed. *Accounts and surveys of the Wiltshire lands of Adam de Stratton, 1268-86.* xxxviii, 266pp. 1959. £20.00 + p&p. Highworth area.
15. WILLIAMS, N.J., ed. *Tradesmen in early Stuart Wiltshire: a miscellany.* xxii, 146pp. 1960 (1979 reprint). £20.00 + p&p.
16. MEEKINGS, C.A.F., ed. *Crown pleas of the Wiltshire eyre, 1249.* viii, 334pp. 1961 (1969 reprint). £20.00 + p&p.
17. DALE, CHRISTABEL, ed. *Wiltshire apprentices and their masters, 1710-1760.* xvi, 224pp. 1961. £20.00 + p&p.
18. CHEW, HELENA M., ed. *Hemingby's register.* xii, 288pp. 1963. £20.00 + p&p. Act book of the Dean and Chapter of Salisbury, early 14th c.
21-2. FARR, BRENDA, ed. *The rolls of Highworth Hundred, 1275-1287.* 2 vols. viii, 190; vii, 196pp. 1966-8. £20.00 per vol + p&p.
23. MURPHY, W.P.D., ed. *The Earl of Hertford's lieutenancy papers 1603-1612.* viii, 235pp. 1969. £20.00 + p&p.
24. PUGH, R.B., ed. *Court rolls of the Wiltshire manors of Adam de Stratton.* viii, 224pp. 0-901333-01-8. 1970. £20.00 + p&p.
25. SANDELL, R.E., ed. *Abstracts of Wiltshire inclosure awards and agreements.* xii, 210pp. 0-901333-02-6. 1971. £20.00 + p&p.
26. CLANCHY, M.T., ed. *Civil pleas of the Wiltshire eyre, 1249.* viii, 215pp. 0-901333-03-4. 1971. £20.00 + p&p.
27. RANSOME, MARY, ed. *Wiltshire returns to the bishop's visitation queries 1783.* viii, 271pp. 0-901333-04-2. 1972.
28. CONYERS, ANGELA, ed. *Wiltshire extents for debts, Edward I - Elizabeth I.* viii, 196pp. 0-901333-05-0. 1973. £20.00 + p&p.
29. ELRINGTON, C.R., ed. *Abstracts of feet of fines relating to Wiltshire for the reign of Edward III.* viii, 224pp. 0-901333-06-9. 1974.
30. SANDELL, R.E., ed. *Abstracts of Wiltshire tithe apportionments.* viii, 164pp. 0-901333-07-7. 1975. £20.00 + p&p.
31. SLACK, PAUL, ed. *Poverty in early Stuart Salisbury.* viii, 183pp. 0-901333-08-5. 1975. £20.00 + p&p. Includes register of passports for vagrants, and various surveys - effectively censuses — of the poor.

32. WILLIAMS, B., ed. *The subscription book of Bishops Tounson and Davenant, 1620-40.* viii, 122pp. 0-901333-09-3. 1977. £20.00 + p&p. Subscriptions to the 39 articles by clergy.
33. PUGH, R.B., ed. *Wiltshire gaol delivery and trailbaston trials, 1275-1306.* ix, 273pp. 0-901333-10-7. 1978.
34. ROGERS, K.H., ed. *Lacock Abbey charters.* vi, 147pp. 0-901333-11-5. 1979. £20.00 + p&p.
35. LONDON, VERA C.M., ed. *The cartulary of Bradenstoke Priory.* x, 252pp. 0-901333-12-3. 1979. £20.00 + p&p.
36. HUNNISETT, R.F., ed. *Wiltshire coroners' bills, 1752-1796.* liv, 240pp. 0-901333-13-1. 1981. £20.00 + p&p.
37. CRITTALL, ELIZABETH, ed. *The justicing notebook of William Hunt, 1744-1749.* xii, 131pp. 0-901333-14-X. 1982. £20.00 + p&p.
38. WALL, ALISON D., ed. *Two Elizabethan women: correspondence of Joan and Maria Thynne, 1575-1611.* xxxiv, 79pp. 0-901333-15-8. 1983. Of Longleat.
39. TIMMINS, T.C.B., ed. *The register of John Chandler dean of Salisbury, 1404-17.* xxxix, 246pp. 0-901333-16-6. 1984. £20.00 + p&p.
40. CHANDLER, J.H., ed. *Wiltshire dissenters' meeting house certificates and registrations, 1689-1852.* xxxvii, 226pp. 0-901333-17-4. 1985. £20.00 + p&p.
41. KIRBY, J.L., ed. *Abstracts of feet of fines relating to Wiltshire, 1377-1509.* v, 248pp. 0-901333-18-2. 1986. £20.00 + p&p.
42. STEVENSON, JANET H., ed. *The Edington cartulary.* xxxiv, 236pp. 0-901333-19-X. 1987. £20.00 + p&p.
43. FREEMAN, JANE, ed. *The commonplace book of Sir Edward Baynton of Bromham.* xxii, 80pp. 0-901333-20-4. 1988. £20.00 + p&p.
44. REEVES, MARJORIE & MORRISON, JEAN, eds. *The diaries of Jeffery Whitaker, schoolmaster of Bratton, 1739-1741.* lxiv, 117pp. 0-901333-21-2. 1989.
45. CROWLEY, D.A., ed. *The Wiltshire tax list of 1332.* xxi, 188pp. 0-901333-22-0. 1989.
46. HEMBRY, PHYLLIS, ed. *Calendar of Bradford-on-Avon settlement examinations and removal orders, 1725-98.* xxii, 164pp. 0-901333-23-9. 1990. £20.00 + p&p.
47. ROGERS, K.H., ed. *Early trade directories of Wiltshire.* xiii, 215pp. 0-901333-24-7. 1992. £20.00 + p&p.
48. WARNEFORD, F.E., ed. *Star Chamber suits of John and Thomas Warneford.* xix, 108pp. 0-901333-25-5. 1993. £20.00 + p&p. Of Sevenhampton.

KIRBY, J.L., ed. *The Hungerford cartulary: a calendar of the Earl of Radnor's cartulary of the Hungerford family.* xix, 300pp. 0-901333-26-3. 1994. £20.00 + p&p. 15th c.

COWAN, MICHAEL, ed. *The letters of John Peniston, Salisbury architect, catholic and yeomanry officer, 1823-30.* xx, 268pp. 0-901333-27-1. 1996. £20.00 + p&p.

HENLY, H.R., ed. *The apprentice registers of the Wiltshire Society, 1817-1922.* 1997. £20.00 + p&p.

WILLIAMS, S.A., ed. *Wiltshire papist returns and estate enrolments, 1705-87.* Forthcoming.

FARR, BRENDA, ed. *Crown pleas of the Wiltshire eyre, 1268.* Forthcoming.

CARR, D.R., ed. *Salisbury city ledger A.* Forthcoming.

HOBBS, S.D., & AVERY, SUSAN, eds. *Wiltshire glebe terriers.* Forthcoming.

KIRBY, J.L., ed. *The Hungerford cartulary vol. 2: the Hobhouse cartulary.* Forthcoming.

WORCESTERSHIRE

Worcestershire Historical Society

c/o J.H.Brown, 7, Prestwich Avenue, Worcester, WR5 1QA
Members are entitled to a substantial discount.

New series

3. BABER, A.F.C., ed. *The court rolls of the manor of Bromsgrove and King's Norton, 1494-1504: a calendar.* viii, 176pp. 1963. £5.50.
6. RANSOME, MARY, ed. *The state of the bishopric of Worcester, 1782-1808.* 252pp: 1968. £9.00. Mainly replies to bishop's queries.
7. MARETT, WARWICK PAUL, ed. *A calendar of the register of Henry Wakefield, Bishop of Worcester, 1375-95.* xlviii, 280pp. 1972. £10.00.

8. BOND, SHELAGH, ed. *The Chamber order book of Worcester, 1601-1650.* viii, 495pp. £13.50.
9 & 13. SCHAFER, R.G., ed. *A selection from the records of Philip Foley's Stour Valley iron works, 1668-74.* 2 vols. xxiii, 128; xxiv, 42pp. 1978-90. £12.00 + £20.00.
11. MEEKINGS, C.A.F., PORTER, S., & ROY, I, eds. *The hearth tax collectors book for Worcester, 1678-1680.* 139pp. 1983. £15.00.
12. MORGAN, PAUL, ed. *Inspections of churches and parsonage houses in the Diocese of Worcester, in 1674, 1676, 1684 and 1687.* 118pp. 1986. £16.50.
14. ROBERTS, STEPHEN K., ed. *Evesham borough records of the seventeenth century, 1605-1687.* xxx, 122pp. 1994. £15.00.
15. HAINES, ROY MARTIN, eds. *Calendar of the register of Simon de Montacute, Bishop of Worcester, 1334-1337.* xxviii, 432pp. 1996. £35.00.

Occasional publications
8. COOPER, MARGARET. *The Worcester book trade in the eighteenth century.* 48pp. 1997. £3.50. Includes list of book trade apprentices.

YORKSHIRE
Yorkshire Archaeological Society
Claremont, 23, Clarendon Road, Leeds LS2 9NZ
Members are entitled to substantial discounts. Many older registers are available on microfiche; these are listed in *British Genealogical Microfiche.*

Parish Register Section
Map of ancient parishes and chapelries of Yorkshire. Sheet map. £5.00 + p&p £1.50.

Acomb
129. RICHARDSON, HAROLD, ed. *The parish register of Acomb, an ancient village of the West Riding of Yorkshire, now incorporated with the City of York.* Vols. 1-10, 1663-1837 (bishops transcripts 1634-1760). 1966. £20.00 + p&p £2.25.

Almondbury
139. TAYLOR, HARRY, ed. *The parish register of Almondbury volume 1 (part 1). 1557-1598.* 1974. £20.00 + p&p £2.25.
140. TAYLOR, HARRY, ed. *The parish register of Almondbury. Volume 1 (part 2). 1598-1652.* 1975. £20.00 + p&p £2.25.
148. TAYLOR, HARRY, & TAYLOR, JESSICA, eds. *The parish register of Almondbury, volume 2. 1653-1682.* 1984. £20.00 + p&p £2.25.
153. TAYLOR, HARRY, & TAYLOR, JESSICA, eds. *The parish register of Almondbury, volume 3. 1683-1703.* 1988. £20.00 + p&p £2.25.

Askham Bryan
131. RICHARDSON, HAROLD, ed. *The parish registers of Askham Bryan vols 1-6, 1695-1837 (bishops transcripts 1604-1694), and Askham Richard, 1813-1837.* 1967. £20.00 + p&p £2.25.

Austerfield
39. LUMB, GEORGE DENISON, ed. *The registers of the chapel of Austerfield, in the parish of Blyth and in the County of York, 1559-1812.* 1910. £20.00 + p&p £2.25.

Birstall
146. NUSSEY, JOHN, ed. *The parish register of Birstall. Volume 1. 1558-1635.* 1983. £20.00 + p&p £2.25.
152. NUSSEY, JOHN, ed. *The parish register of Birstall. Volume 2. 1636-1687.* 1987. £20.00 + p&p £2.25.

Bishopthorpe
150. BRUNSKILL, ELIZABETH, ed. *The parish register of Bishopthorpe, 1631-1837.* 1986. £20.00 + p&p £2.25.

Bowes
127. ALDERSON, BASIL ROXBY, ed. *The parish register of Bowes, 1670-1837 (bishops transcripts 1615-1700).* 1964. £20.00 + p&p £2.25.

Braithwell
132. TILLOTT, P.M., ed. *The parish register of Braithwell, volume 1. 1559-1774.* £20.00 + p&p £2.25.

Brandsburton
142. HICKS, J.D., ed. *The parish register of Brandsburton, 1558-1837.* 1979. £20.00 + p&p £2.25.

Bubwith
99. CHARLESWORTH, JOHN, ed. *The parish register of Bubwith: baptism and burials 1600-1767; marriages 1600-1753. Part 1.* 1935. £20.00 + p&p £2.25.

Bulmer
160. WILSON, ELLEN, ed. *The parish register of Bulmer, 1571-1837.* 1995. £20.00 + p&p £2.25.

Collingham
141. EXWOOD, ELISABETH, ed. *The parish register of Collingham, 1579-1837.* 1978. £20.00 + p&p £2.25.

Easingwold
145. GURNEY, NORAH K.M., ed. *The parish registers of Easingwold, Raskelf and Myton upon Swale, 1813-1837.* 1983. £20.00 + p&p £2.25.

Giggleswick
147. HOYLE, R.W., ed. *The parish register of Giggleswick. Volume 1. 1558-1669.* 1984. £20.00 + p&p £2.25.
151. HOYLE, R.W., ed. *The parish register of Giggleswick. Volume 2. 1669-1769.* 1986. £20.00 + p&p £2.25.

Heslington
SMITH, MARGARET E., ed. *The parish register of Heslington 1639-1837.* 1982. £20.00 + p&p £2.25.

Howden
21. WEDDALL, G.E., ed. *The registers of Howden, Co. York. Vol. I. (1543-1659).* 1904. £20.00 + p&p £2.25.
24. WEDDALL, G.E., ed. *The registers of the parish of Howden, Co. York. Vol II (1543-1702).* 1905. £20.00 + p&p £2.25.
48. WEDDALL, G.E., ed. *The parish registers of Howden, 1725-1770.* 1913. £20.00 + p&p £2.25.

Kirk Deighton
159. MORTON, MAISIE, & PRESTON, CYRIL, eds. *The parish register of Kirk Deighton, 1600-1837.* 1994. £20.00 + p&p £2.25.

Kirklington
35. MCCALL, H.B., ed. *The parish registers of Kirklington in the County of York, 1568-1812.* 1909. £20.00 + p&p £2.25.

Lythe
137. HANSELL, M.W., ed. *The parish register of Lythe, volumes I, II & III, 1634-1768 (bishops transcripts, 1619-1640).* 1973. £20.00 + p&p £2.25.
138. HANSELL, M.W., ed. *The parish register of Lythe, volumes IV-XI, 1754-1837.* 1973. £20.00 + p&p £2.25.

Masham
161. SMITH, DAVID M., ed. *The parish register of Masham, 1599-1716.* 1996. £20.00 + p&p £2.25.

Oswaldkirk
135. ROWLEY, PATRICK, ed. *The parish register of Oswaldkirk, vols. I-X, 1538-1837.* 1976. £20.00 + p&p £2.25.

Owston
157. BRENT, ANDREW, ed. *The parish register of Owston, 1600-1837.* 1993. £20.00 + p&p £2.25.

Riccall
124. HAMSHAW, ROBERT GORDON, ed. *The parish register of Riccall, Yorks., 1669-1813 [marriages end 1753].* 1960. £20.00 + p&p £2.25.

Rokeby
128. ALDERSON, BASIL ROXBY, ed. *The parish register of Rokeby, Yorks., vols I-VII, 1598-1837.* 1965. £20.00 + p&p £2.25.

Scruton
156. PRESTON, C.S., ed. *The parish register of Scruton, 1572-1837.* 1991. £20.00 + p&p £2.25.

Settrington
38. COLLINS, FRANCIS, ed. *The register of Settrington, 1559-1812.* 1910. £20.00 + p&p £2.25.

Sheffield
60. DRURY, CHARLES, & HALL, T. WALTER, eds. *The parish register of Sheffield in the County of York. Part II. Burials 1560 to 1634; baptisms, marriages 1635 to 1653.* 1918. £20.00 + p&p £2.25.
68. DRURY, CHARLES, & HALL, T. WALTER, eds. *The parish register of Sheffield in the County of York. Part III. Burials, 1635 to 1653; baptisms, marriages, 1653 to 1686.* 1921. £20.00 + p&p £2.25.

74. DRURY, CHARLES, & HALL, T. WALTER, eds. *The parish register of Sheffield in the County of York. Part IV. Burials 1653 to 1686; baptisms 1687 to 1703; marriages 1687 to 1703.* 1924. £20.00 + p&p £2.25.
143. OWEN, W.S., & WALTON, MARY, eds. *The parish register of Sheffield, volume VI. 1720-1736.* 1981. £20.00 + p&p £2.25.
154. WALTON, MARY, & OWEN, W.S., eds. *The parish register of Sheffield. Volume 7. Burials 1703-1719; baptisms 1736-1752.* 1989. £20.00 + p&p £2.25.

Thorpe Bassett
155. RUDDOCK, N.P., ed. *The parish register of Thorpe Bassett, 1604-1837.* 1990. £20.00 + p&p £2.25.

Wadworth
162. PRESTON, CYRIL, ed. *The parish register of Wadworth, 1575-1837.* 1997. £20.00 + p&p £2.25.

Walton in Ainsty
51. FLETCHER, D.E., & FLETCHER, C.E., eds. *The parish register of Walton in Ainsty, vols I-IV. 1619-1837.* 1962. £20.00 + p&p £2.25.

Wensley
130. THWAITE, HARTLEY, ed. *The parish register of Wensley. Vol. II. 1701-1837.* 1967. £20.00 + p&p £2.25.

York. St.Crux
149. SMITH, MARGARET E., ed. *The parish register of St. Crux, York. Volume II. Baptisms 1716-1837; marriages and burials 1678-1837.* 1985. £20.00 + p&p £2.25.

York. St.Mary Bishophill Junior
52. COLLINS, FRANCIS, ed. *The parish register of St. Mary, Bishophill Junior 1602 to 1812.* 1915. £20.00 + p&p £2.25.

York. St.Mary Castlegate
134. MULGREW, M. LOYOLA, ed. *The parish register of St. Mary, Castlegate, York. Volume I. 1604-1705.* 1970. £20.00 + p&p £2.25.
136. MULGREW, MARGARET F.M., ed. *The parish register of St. Mary, Castlegate, York. Volumes II, III & IV, 1705-1837 (bishops transcripts 1813-1837).* 1972. £20.00 + p&p £2.25.

York. Saint Olave
158. WHITEHEAD, BARBARA, ed. *The parish register of St. Olave, York, 1650-1785.* 1993. £20.00 + p&p £2.25.

Record Series
31. BROWN, WILLIAM, ed. *Yorkshire inquisitions 1245, 1282 and 1294-1303, vol iii.* 1902. £24.00 + p&p £2.50.
37. BROWN, WILLIAM, ed. *Yorkshire inquisitions 1300-07, vol iv.* 1906. £24.00 + p&p £2.50.
40. CLAY, JOHN WILLIAM, ed. *Paver's marriage licences 1630-44, vol i.* 1909. £24.00 + p&p £2.50.
41. BROWN, WILLIAM, ed. *Yorkshire Star Chamber proceedings 1485-1549, vol i.* 1909. £24.00 + p&p £2.50.
126. KING, H, & HARRIS, A., eds. *A survey of the manor of Settrington (1600).* 1962. £24.00 + p&p £2.50.
128. WENHAM, PETER, ed. *Letters of James Tate.* 1966. £24.00 + p&p £2.50.
129. LAWRANCE, N.A.H., ed. *Fasti parochiales, vol iii, Deanery of Dickering.* 1967. £24.00 + p&p £2.50.
131. RICHARDSON, HAROLD, ed. *Court rolls of the manor of Acomb, vol i (1544-1761).* 1969. £24.00 + p&p £2.50.
132. KERSHAW, IAN, ed. *Bolton Priory rentals and ministers' accounts, 1473-1539.* 1970. £24.00 + £2.50.
133. GURNEY, NORAH KM, & CLAY, C..HARLES TRAVIS, eds. *Fasti parochiales, vol iv; being notes on the advowson and pre-Reformation incumbents of the parishes in the Deanery of Craven.* 1971. £24.00 + p&p £2.50.
134. BREARS, PETER C.D., ed. *Yorkshire probate inventories, 1542-1689.* 1972. £24.00 + p&p £2.50.
136. ROEBUCK, PETER, ed. *Constable of Everingham estate correspondence, 1726-43.* 1976. £24.00 + p&p £2.50.
137. RICHARDSON, HAROLD, ed. *Court rolls of the manor of Acomb, vol ii (1762-1846).* 1976. £24.00 + £2.50 p&p.
138. SUTTON, DEBORAH, ed. *York civic records, vol ix (1588-90).* 1978. £24.00 + p&p £2.50.
139. MORTIMER, JEAN E, & MORTIMER, RUSSELL S., eds. *Leeds Friends' minute book, 1692-1712.* 1980. £24.00 + p&p £2.50.
140. MICHELMORE, DAVID J.H., ed. *The Fountains Abbey lease book.* 1981. £24.00 + p&p £2.50.

141. HORROX, ROSEMARY, ed. *Selected rentals and accounts of medieval Hull (1203-1528)*. 1983. £24.00 + p&p £2.50.
142. ROMNEY, P., ed. *The diary of Charles Fothergill, 1805. An itinerary to York, Flamborough and the north-western dales of Yorkshire*. 1984. £24.00 + p&p £2.50.
143. LAWRANCE, N.A.H., ed. *Fasti parochiales, vol v, Deanery of Buckrose*. 1985. £24.00 + p&p £2.50.
144. CHILDS, WENDY R., ed. *The customs accounts of Hull, 1453-1490*. 1986. £24.00 + p&p £2.50.
145. HOYLE, RICHARD W., ed. *Early Tudor Craven: subsidies and assessments, 1510-1547*. £24.00 + p&p £2.50.
146. BUTLER, LAWRENCE A.S., ed. *The archdeaconry of Richmond in the eighteenth century: Bishop Gastrell's 'Notitia', the Yorkshire parishes, 1714-1725*. 1990. £24.00 + £2.50.
148. TRINGHAM, NIGEL J., ed. *Charters of the vicars choral of York Minster: city of York and its suburbs to 1546*. 1993. £35.00 + p&p £3.50.
149. MCDERMID, RICHARD T.W., ed. *Beverley Minster fasti: being biographical notes on the provosts, prebendaries, officers and vicars in the church of Beverley prior to the Dissolution*. 1993. £24.00 + p&p £2.50.
150. CROSS, CLAIRE, & VICKERS, NOREEN, eds. *Monks, friars and nuns in sixteenth century Yorkshire*. 1995. £39.00 + p&p £3.50.
151. ENGLISH, BARBARA, ed. *Yorkshire hundred and quo warranto rolls*. 1996. £30.00 + p&p £3.50.

Record Series Extra series
9. CLAY, CHARLES TRAVIS, ed. *Early Yorkshire charters, vol. XI: The Percy fee*. 1963. Price on application.
10. CLAY, CHARLES TRAVIS, ed. *Early Yorkshire charters, vol. XII: The Tison fee*. 1965. Price on application.

Wakefield Court Rolls series
1. FRASER, C.M., & EMSLEY, KENNETH, ed. *The court rolls of the manor of Wakefield, from October 1639 to September 1640*. 1977. £12.00 + p&p £1.75.
2. JEWELL, HELEN M., ed. *The court rolls of the manor of Wakefield from September 1348 to September 1350*. 1981. £12.00 + p&p £1.75.
3. WEIKEL, ANN, ed. *The court rolls of the manor of Wakefield from October 1331 to September 1333*. 1983. £12.00 + p&p £1.75.
4. WEIKEL, ANN, ed. *The court rolls of the manor of Wakefield from October 1583 to September 1585*. 1984. £12.00 + p&p £1.75.
5. FRASER, CONSTANCE, & EMSLEY, KENNETH, ed. *The court rolls of the manor of Wakefield from October 1664 to September 1665*. 1986. £12.00 + p&p £1.75.
6. HABBERJAM, MOIRA, O'REGAN, MARY, & HALE, BRIAN, eds. *The court rolls of the manor of Wakefield from October 1350 to September 1352*. 1987. £12.00 + p&p £1.75.
7. WEIKEL, ANN, ed. *The court rolls of the manor of Wakefield from October 1550 to September 1552*. 1989. £12.00 + p&p £1.75.
8. ROBINSON, LILIAN, ed. *The court rolls of the manor of Wakefield from 1651 to 1652*. 1990. £12.00 + p&p £1.75.
9. WEIKEL, ANN, ed. *The court rolls of the manor of Wakefield from 1537 to 1539*. 1993. £12.00 + p&p £1.75.
10. BRENT, ANDREW, ed. *The court rolls of the manor of Wakefield from 1790 to 1792*. 1994. £12.00 + p&p £1.75.
11. FRASER, C.M., eds. *The court rolls of the manor of Wakefield from 1608/9*. 1996. £12.00 + p&p £1.75.

Boothferry Family & Local History Group
c/o Mrs M Howard, 17, Airmyn Avenue, Goole, Yorkshire, DN14 6PF

Goole Cemetery monumental inscriptions, vol. 1. 1997. £3.50 + p&p 60p. Vol. 2 is forthcoming.

Thoresby Society
Claremont, 23, Clarendon Road, Leeds, LSZ 9NZ
Members are entitled to substantial discounts.

8. LANCASTER, W.T., & BAILDON, W. PALEY, ed. *The coucher book of the Cistercian abbey of Kirkstall in the West Riding of the County of York*. 1904. In 3 pts. £1.50 + p&p per pt.

10. LUMB, GEORGE DENISON, ed. *The registers of the parish church of Leeds from 1667 to 1695: seventh and eighth books.* 1901. Pt.3. (incl. index) £4.50 + p&p.
14. WILSON, EDMUND, ed. *Leeds Grammar School admission books from 1820 to 1900.* 1906. £4.50 + p&p.
19. LUMB, GEORGE DENISON, ed. *Testamenta Leodiensia: wills of Leeds, Pontefract, Wakefield, Otley and district, 1539 to 1553.* 1913. Pt. 2. £1.50 + p&p.
27. LUMB, GEORGE DENISON, ed. *Wills of Leeds, Pontefract, Wakefield, Otley and district, 1553 to 1561.* 1930. Pts 1 & 2. £1.50 + p&p per pt.
34. CLARK, J.G., ed. *The court book of the Leeds Corporation. First book. January 1662 to August 1705.* 1936. £4.50 + p&p.
40. LUMB, G.D., PLACE, J.B, & BECKWITH, F., eds. *Extracts from the Leeds Intelligencer and the Leeds Mercury, 1777-1782, with an introductory account of the Leeds Intelligencer, 1754-1866.* 1955. Pts. 1 & 3. £4.50 + p&p per pt.
45. LE PATOUREL, JOHN, ed. *Documents relating to the manor and borough of Leeds, 1066-1400.* 1956. £4.50 + p&p.
57. KIRBY, JOAN, ed. *The manor and borough of Leeds, 1425-1662: an edition of documents.* 1981. £6.50 + p&p.

Second series
6. SHARPLES, MARION. *The Fawkes family and their estates in Wharfedale, 1819-1936.* 1997. £15.00 + p&p.

SCOTLAND

Saltire Society
9, Fountain Close, 22, High Street, Edinburgh, EH1 1TF.
Orders to: Scottish Book Source, 137, Dundee Street, Edinburgh, EH11 1BG.
Phone: (0131) 2296800.
JAMES, ALWYN. *Scottish roots.* 0-85411-066-6. £4.99.

Scottish Association of Family History Societies
c/o Miss S. M. Spiers, 27, Woodland Drive, Aberdeen, AB15 6YJ
DOBSON, DAVID. *Scottish seafarers, 17th cent.* 1-874722-00-5.
DOBSON, DAVID. *Scottish seafarers, 18th cent.* 1-874722-11-0.
DOBSON, DAVID. *Jacobites of the '15.* 1-874722-04-8.

Scottish Genealogy Society
15, Victoria Terrace, Edinburgh EH1 2JL
Phone: (0131) 2203677
Email: scotgensoc@sol.co.uk
http://www.scotland.net.scotgensoc/
Bathgate mortality records 1860-1925. 218pp. £7.00.
CARSTAIRS, N.R. & CARSTAIRS, S. *Edinburgh 1851 census.* 2 vols.
  v.1. *Canongate.* 279pp. £25.00.
  v.2. *Old Town.* 446pp. £32.00.
  v.3. *New Town.* 671pp. £55.00.
Scottish names bibliography. 2nd ed. 26pp. 1993. £1.75.
TORRANCE, D.R., ed. *Lady Glenorchy communion rolls.* 77pp. £5.25. For 1785-1835. This is an Edinburgh church.
Lady Glenorchy Free Church baptisms. 15pp. £1.25. For 1843-56.
RUTHVEN-MURRAY, P., ed. *Edinburgh police register, 1815-1859.* 71pp. £3.00. List of constables.
The McClellans in Galloway. 2 vols. £12.00 per volume. Set £22.00.
TORRANCE, D.R. *Kirkcudbright burgesses 1576-1975.* 66pp. £4.00.
Scottish clock and watchmakers, 1445-1900. £6.00.
Troon parish poll tax, 1694. 89pp. £4.50.
Index to Scottish genealogist. £4.00.
Holdings list no. 1: Microfilms held in the library. 80p.
Members' interests 1997. £1.50.

Monumental inscriptions.
Angus 1. The environs of Forfar, Kirriemuir & Brechin. 331pp. £13.00.
Angus 2. The environs of Arbroath and Montrose. 300pp. £13.00.
Angus 3. The environs of Dundee. 126pp. £8.00.
Angus 4. Dundee & Broughty Ferry. 300pp. £12.00.
Bute, Arran & Cumbrae: the old county of Bute. 123pp. £5.00.
Caithness 1. Bower, Canisbay, Dunnet, Olrig. 142pp. £5.50.
Caithness 2. Watten and Wick. 171pp. £5.50.
Caithness 3. Halkirk, Reay, Thurso. 141pp. £5.50.
Caithness 4. Latheron. 108pp. £5.50.

Carrick, the southern part of Ayrshire. 208pp. £9.00.
Dean Cemetery. £6.75. An Edinburgh cemetery.
Duddingston, part of Edinburgh. £2.00. Includes poll tax 1694.
Dunbartonshire. £8.50.
Dunfermline Abbey. 51pp. £3.00.
Inverness West. 80pp. Includes Abertarff, Urquhart, Glenormiston, Kiltarlty, Conwinth, Kilmorack and Kirkhill.
Inverness West. £6.50. Includes Boleskine, Dores, Inverness, Bone, Moy, Dalarossie, Devlot, Dunlichity, Croy, Dalcross, Petty and Andersier.
Isla Munda. 12pp. £1.50. Burial isle in Loch Leven, Argyll.
Kilmarnock & Loudoun. 189pp. £9.00.
Kilmun, Argyllshire. 112pp. £5.00.
Kinlochlaigh & Keil. £1.00.
Kincardine. £12.00. Includes 19 parishes.
Kirkcudbright 1. Auchencairn, Balmaclellan, Balmaghie, Borgue, Kirkandrews, Senwick, Buittle and Carsphairn. 130pp. £6.00.
Kirkcudbright 2. Colvend, Southwick, Corsock, Crossmichael, Dalbeattie, Dalry. 81pp. £5.00.
Kirkcudbright 3. Dundrennan Abbey, Dunrod, Galtway, Girthon (Sandgreen & Gatehouse), Kelton, Gelston, Kirkcormack, Kells. 114pp. £6.00.
Kirkcudbright 4. Kirkcudbright, Kirkgunzeon, Kirkpatrick Durham. £6.00.
Kirkcudbright 5. Lochrutton, Parton, Perrick, Tongland, Twynholm, Kirkchrist (Stell), Orr. £8.00.
Kirkcudbright 6. Kirkmabrech, Kirkdale, Creetown, Minnigaff. 51pp. £3.50.
Kirkcudbright 7. Kirkirkbean, Kirkpatrick Irongray, Newabbey, Terregles with Lincluden College, Troqueer. 193pp. £8.00.
Lanarkshire Upper Ward. £13.00.
Peebleshire. 137pp. £16.00.
Perthshire, East. 263pp. £12.00. Covers Strathmore and the Carse of Gowrie.
Perthshire, North, vol. 1. Perth. 306pp. £12.00.
Perthshire, North, vol. 2. Dunkeld and environs. 282pp. £12.00.
Renfrewshire 1. Arthurlie, Bridge of Weir, Cathcart, Eaglesham, Eastwood, Erskine, Gourock, Greenock, Houston, Inchannan, Inverkipp, Johnstone, Kilbarchan, Kilellan. £8.00.
Renfrewshire 2. Kilmacolm, Lochwinnoch, Mearns, Neilston, Paisley, Pollokshaws, Port Glasgow, Renfrew. £8.00.
Speyside. 2nd ed. 155pp. £6.50. Laggan, Kingussie, Insh, Alvie, Rothiemurchus, Garten & Kincardine, Abernethy, Duthil, Inverallan, Cromdale, Advie, Inveraven, Knockando, Aberlour, Rothes Speymouth, Bellie.
Stirling West, covering the parishes of Baldernock, Balfron, Buchanan, Buchlyvie, Campsie, Denny, Dennyloanhead, Drymen, Dunipace, Fintry, Gargunnock, Inchcaillench, Killearn, Kilsyth, Kippen, Kirk O'Muir, Lennoxtown, Strathblane. £12.00.
Stirling East, covering the parishes of Airth, Bothkennar, Cambuskenneth, Falkirk, Larbert, Logie, Muiravonside, Plean, Polmont, St. Ninians, Slamannan, Stirling. £10.00.
Sutherland. Former county of Sutherland & Kincardine (Ardgay). 321pp. £12.00.
Upper Deeside: parishes of Crathie & Braemar to Kincardine O'Neil & Birse. 122pp. £6.00.
Upper Donside: parishes of Strathdon to Keig, now in Gordon District. 120pp. £4.50.
West Lothian. 178pp. £7.50.
Wester Ross. 63pp. £4.00.
MITCHELL, A. *Burial grounds: an index of unpublished M.I.'s.* 14pp. 80p.

Scottish History Society

Orders to: Bridge of Allan Books, 2, Henderson Street, Bridge of Allan, Stirlingshire, FK9 4HT.
Phone: (01786) 834483

Third series
16. *Register of the consultations of the ministers of Edinburgh and some other brethren of the ministry. Vol.II: 1657-60.* 1930. £9.00.
17. MALCOLM, CHARLES A., ed. *The minutes of the justices of the peace for Lanarkshire, 1707-1723.* 1931. £9.00
23. LINDSAY, E.R., & CAMERON, ANNIE I., eds. *Calendar of Scottish supplications to Rome, 1418-1422.* 1934. £9.00.
32. EASSON, D.E., & MACDONALD, ANGUS, eds. *Charters of the abbey of Inchcolm.* 1938. £9.00.

Fourth series

12. BURNS, CHARLES, ed. *Calendar of Papal letters to Scotland of Clement VII of Avignon, 1378-1394.* 1976. £9.00.
13. MCGURK, FRANCIS, ed. *Calendar of Papal letters to Scotland of Benedict XIII of Avignon, 1394-1419.* 1976. £9.00.
15. ADAMS, IAN H., ed. *Papers on Peter May, land surveyor, 1749-1793.* 1979. £9.00. Mainly letters; includes 'biographical index' of persons mentioned.
16. FYFE, JANET, ed. *Autobiography of John McAdam (1806-1883), with selected letters.* 1980. £9.00. Includes 'biographical appendix', with brief lives of persons mentioned.
17. KIRK, JAMES, ed. *Stirling Presbytery records, 1581-1587.* 1981. £9.00.

Fifth series

4. ADAM, R.J., ed. *The calendar of Fearn: text and additions, 1471-1667.* 1991. £9.00. Mainly obituary notices.

Scottish Library Association

Motherwell Business Centre, Coursington Road, Motherwell, ML1 1PW

COX, MICHAEL, ed. *Exploring Scottish History: a directory of resource centres for Scottish local and national history in Scotland.* 0-900649-79-8. 1992. £6.95.

Scottish Record Society

Dept of Scottish History, University of Glasgow, Glasgow, G12 8QG
Prices on application.

ADAMS, IAN H., ed. *Directory of former Scottish commonties.* xiii, 281pp. 1971.
GILCHRIST, G., ed. *Annan parish censuses, 1801-21.* ix, 139pp.
BARCLAY, R.S., ed. *Orkney testaments and inventories, 1573-1615.* ix, 198pp. 1977.
APTED, M.R., & HANNABUSS, S., eds. *Painters in Scotland, 1301-1700: biographical dictionary.* viii, 166pp. 1978.
TRANTER, N.L., ed. *The Urquhart censuses of Portpatrick, 1832-1853.* 160pp. 1980.
ADAMSON, DUNCAN, ed. *West Lothian hearth tax lists, 1691 (with county abstracts for Scotland.)* 152pp. 1981.
KIRK, JAMES, ed. *Visitations of the Diocese of Dunblane and other churches, 1586-1589.* lviii, 115pp. 1984.

TORRIE, E.P.D., ed. *The gild book of Dunfermline, 1433-1597.* xxxiv, 198pp. 1986.
DAVIDSON, F., ed. *Examination roll of Arbroath, 1752; town's duty roll, 1753.* xiv, 165pp. 1987.
BEATON, E.A., & MACINTYRE, S.W., eds. *The burgesses of Inveraray, 1655-1963.* x, 230pp. 1990.
DUNLOP, A. IAN, ed. *The Kirks of Edinburgh, 1560-1984.* 517pp. 1988.
STEWART, A.I.B., ed. *List of inhabitants upon the Duke of Argyle's property in Kintyre, in 1792.* 1991.
MUNRO, JEAN, ed. *The inventory of Chisholm writs, 1556-1810.* 1992.
COWPER, A.S., ed. *Scottish Society for the Propagation of Christian Knowledge schoolmasters, 1709-1872.* 1997.

Stair Society

Saltire Court, 20, Castle Terrace, Edinburgh, EH1 2ET
Phone: (0131) 2289900
Email: Mail.Desk@Shepwedd.co.uk

25. IMRIE, JOHN, ed. *The justiciary records of Argyll and the Isles, 1664-1742, vol. II.* 1969. £12.00.
29. PINKERTON, JOHN M., ed. *The minute book of the Faculty of Advocates, 1661-1712. Vol. 1.* 1976. £15.00.
30. KIRK, JAMES, ed. *The synod records of Lothian and Tweeddale, 1589-1596.* 1977. £15.00.
34. PINKERTON, JOHN M., ed. *The court of the official in pre-Reformation Scotland.* 1982. £15.00.
38. HUNTER, DOREEN M., ed. *The court of the Barony and Regality of Falkirk and Callendar. Vol. I. 1638-1656.* £25.00.
Guide to the national archives of Scotland. 1996. £25.00. Jointly published with the Scottish Record Office.

Aberdeen & N.E. Scotland Family History Society

164, King Street, Aberdeen, AB24 5BD
Phone: (01224) 646323
Email: anesfhs@rsc.co
www.rsc.co.uk/anesfhs

BEVERLY, W., & BEVERLY, S. *30 years at Portlethen: day book, 1840-1869 of the Rev. William Low.* Ref AA430. £4.80 + p&p.

CRAIG, H. *The family record: a unique way of recording your family tree.* Ref AA535. £3.00 + p&p.
DIACK, LESLEY. *North-East roots: a guide to sources.* 4th ed. Ref AA570. £2.25 + p&p. (Forthcoming).
FERGUSON, K. *Black Kalendar of Aberdeen, 1746-1878: victims and perpetrators of crime.* Ref AA518. £.25 + p&p.
JOHNSON, G. *Census records for Scottish families.* 3rd ed. Ref AA520. £6.00 + p&p.
LAWSON, J. *The emigrant Scots: ships manifests in Canadian archives pre 1900.* Ref AA530. £4.20 + p&p.
LEITH, R. *Membership roll, Frederick Street Congregational Chapel, Aberdeen, 1807-1859.* Ref AA410. £2.25 + p&p.
MORTIMER, E. *Roll of inhabitants of Aberdeen in 1795.* Ref AA580. £3.75.
SMITH, S., & WILSON, M. *Aberdeen Royal Infirmary deaths recorded.* 3 vols.
  v.1. *1743-1822.* Ref AA511. £4.50 + p&p.
  v.2. *1838-1855.* Ref AA512. £4.50 + p&p.
  v.3. *1855-1870.* Ref AA513. £4.50 + p&p.
WALLACE, M., WALLACE, N., & MERSON, D. *Grange Kirk session records, 1703-1859.* Ref AA425. £5.10 + p&p.
WALLACE, M., WALLACE, N., & MERSON, D. *Grange Kirk session records, 1694-1702.* Ref AA420. £5.10 + p&p.
WATSON, F. *In sickness and in health: N.E. Health records as a source for family history.* Ref AA550. £2.25.
Craig near Montrose, 1788 [census] with description of 1791. Ref AA230. £5.00 + p&p.
Hands across the water: emigration from Northern Scotland. Proceedings of the 6th annual conference of the the Scottish Association of Family History Societies. Ref AA547. £2.40 + p&p.
Index to names in Banffshire 1851 census. 5 vols.:
  v.1. *Marnoch, Forglen, Inverkeithny and Rothiemay.* Ref AA211. £5.00.
  v.2. *Gamrie and Alvah.* Ref AA212. £5.00.
  v.3. *Banff, Boyndie and Ordiquhill.* Ref AA213. £5.00.
  v.4. *Fordyce, Cullen and Deskford.* Ref AA214. £5.00.
  v.5. *Rathven.* Ref. AA215. £5.00.
Melvin family story, 1750-1900s: Ellon, Bourtie & Keithhall. Ref AA565. £5.40.
Peterhead Parish, 1801. Ref AA240. £4.20. Census.

Monumental Inscriptions:
Aberdour MIs. Ref. AA102. £2.25 + p&p.
Aboyne St Mary's / Kirkton of Aboyne MIs. Ref. AA103. £2.25 + p&p.
Alford MIs. Ref. AA105. £2.25 + p&p.
Alvah MIs. Ref. AA108. £2.25 + p&p.
Auchindoir MIs. Ref AA110. £2.25 + p&p.
Belhelvie MIs. Ref. AA112. £2.25 + p&p.
Bourtie / Old Meldrum Episcopal MIs. Ref AA114. £2.25 + p&p.
Braemar MIs. Ref AA115. £2.25 + p&p.
Chapel of Garioch / Logie Durno MIs. Ref AA116. £2.25 + p&p.
Cluny MIs. Ref AA118. £2.25 + p&p.
Crimond / Rattray MIs. Ref. AA120. £2.25 + p&p.
Culsalmond MIs. Ref. AA122. £2.25 + p&p.
Daviot MIs. Ref AA123. £2.25 + p&p.
Drumblade MIs. Ref AA125. £2.25 + p&p.
Dunnottar MIs. Ref AA127. £2.25 + p&p.
Durris MIs. Ref AA128. £2.25 + p&p.
Dyce MIs. Ref AA129. £2.25 + p&p.
Echt MIs. Ref AA130. £2.25 + p&p.
Fetterangus MIs. Ref AA132. £2.25 + p&p.
Fettercairn MIs. Ref AA133. £2.25 + p&p.
Forglen MIs. Ref AA134. £2.25 + p&p.
Fyvie MIs. Ref AA136. £2.25 + p&p.
Glenbervie MIs. Ref AA137. £2.25 + p&p.
Glenmuick / Glen Tanar MIs. Ref AA138. £2.25 + p&p.
Hatton of Fintray MIs. Ref AA139. £2.25 + p&p.
Inverkeithny MIs. Ref AA142. £2.25 + p&p.
John Knox (Aberdeen) MIs. Ref AA145. £2.25 + p&p.
Keithhall & Kinkell MIs. Ref AA147. £2.25 + p&p.
Kincardine O'Neil MIs. Ref AA148. £2.25 + p&p.
King Edward MIs. Ref AA150. £2.25 + p&p.
Leslie MIs. Ref AA154. £2.25 + p&p.
Lonmay MIs. Ref AA157. £2.25 + p&p.
Marnoch MIs. Ref AA160. £2.25 + p&p.
Marykirk MIs. Ref AA161. £2.25 + p&p.
Millbrex & Woodhead of Fyvie MIs. Ref AA162. £2.25 + p&p.
Monymusk MIs. Ref AA164. £2.25 + p&p.
New Deer MIs. Ref AA165. £2.25 + p&p.
Newhills MIs. Ref AA166. £2.25 + p&p.
Oldmeldrum MIs. Ref AA169. £2.25 + p&p.
Peathill MIs. Ref AA172. £2.25 + p&p.
Peterculter MIs. Ref AA174. £2.25 + p&p.

Rathen MIs. Ref AA177. £2.25 + p&p.
Rhynie MIs. Ref AA180. £2.25 + p&p.
St Clements (Aberdeen) MIs. Ref AA183. £2.25 + p&p.
Strachan MIs. Ref AA185. £2.25 + p&p.
Tough MIs. Ref AA188. £2.25 + p&p.
Tyrie MIs. Ref AA190. £2.25 + p&p.
Udny MIs. Ref AA192. £2.25 + p&p.

Pollbooks
Aberdeen & Freedom Lands Poll Book, 1696. Ref AA308. £2.25 + p&p.
Aberdour & Tyrie Poll Book, 1696. Ref AA316. £2.25 + p&p.
Auchredie (New Deer) Poll Book, 1696. Ref AA324. £2.25 + p&p.
Drumoak Poll Book, 1696. Ref AA332. £2.25 + p&p.
Dyce, Fintray and Newhills 1696. Ref AA336. £2.25 + p&p.
Fraserburgh & Pitsligo Poll Book, 1696. Ref AA340. £2.25 + p&p.
Lonmay & Crimond Poll Book, 1696. Ref AA349. £2.25 + p&p.
Old Deer & Longside Poll Book, 1696. Ref AA356. £2.25 + p&p.
Old Machar & Old Toun Aberdeen Poll Book, 1696. Ref AA358. £2.25 + p&p.
Peterhead Poll Book, 1696. Ref AA364. £2.25 + p&p.
Rathen & Strichen Poll Book, 1696. Ref AA372. £2.25 + p&p.
Skene & Kinellar 1696. Ref AA378. Ref AA738. £2.25 + p&p.
Strathbogie Poll Book, 1696 Vol 1: Dumbennan, Gartly, Rhynie, Essie. Ref AA381. £2.25 + p&p.
Strathbogie Poll Book, 1696 Vol 2: Glass, Kinnoir, Ruthven / Botarie. Ref AA382. £2.25 + p&p.

Borders Family History Society
c/o Miss Jean Sanderson, 12, Woodside Park, Kelso, Roxburghshire, TD5 7RE.

Borders, kin, blood and stone: proceedings of the Scottish Association of Family History Societies, 1996. £4.00.
Register of members interests. £3.00.

Monumental Inscriptions
Berwickshire
Eccles, Birgham & Leitholm. £8.00.
Fogo. £5.00.
Greenlaw. 104pp. £8.00.
Mertoun. 54pp. £5.00.
Polwarth. 54pp. £5.00.

Roxburghshire
Bedrule. 43pp. £5.00.
Crailing & Nisbet. 52pp. £5.00.
Eckford. 52pp. £5.00.
Edgerston. 40pp. £5.00.
Ednam. 44pp. £5.00.
Hounam & Linton. 54pp. £5.00.
Kelso. £5.00.
Makerstoun. 45pp. £5.00.
Maxton. 47pp. £5.00.
Morebattle. 51pp. £5.00.
Oxnam. 60pp. £5.00.
Roxburgh. 58pp. £5.00.
Smailholm. 52pp. £5.00.
Sprouston & Lempitlaw. 54pp. £5.00.
Stichill & Hume. 60pp. £5.00.
Yetholm. 54pp. £5.00.

Central Scotland Family History Society
c/o Mrs Carol Sergeant, 4, Fir Lane, Larbert, Stirlingshire, FK5 3LW

Stirling burgess list 1600-1699. £3.00 + p&p 35p.
Stirling burgess list 1700-1799. £3.00 + p&p 35p.
Stirling burgess list 1800-1899. £3.00 + p&p 35p.

Dumfries and Galloway Family History Society
Dumfries and Galloway Family History Research Centre, 9, Glasgow Street, Dumfries, Scotland, DG2 9AF

Members interest booklet 1992. 1-873977-01-8. 1992. £1.00.
Members interest booklet 1995. 1-872350-71-2. 1995. £3.00.
Dumfries and Galloway: some sources for local and family history. 1-873977-08-5. 1995. £3.00.
Portpatrick old kirkyard. 1-873977-0-93. 1995. £3.75. Monumental inscriptions, hearth tax list 1692, and parish list 1684.
Irregular marriages: Annan, Dumfriesshire, 1794-1854. 1-873977-13-1. 1997. £5.00.
Irregular marriages: Portpatrick, Wigtownshire, 1759-1826. 1-873977-12-3. 1997. £5.00.

GRAY, ADAM. *A Scots agricultural glossary.* 1-873977-14-X. 1997.

1841 census (Stewartry of Kirkcudbright) indexed by surname. 1998.
  Balmaghie. 1-873977-32-8. £1.80.
  Buittle. 1-873977-20-4. £1.60.
  Carsphairn. 1-873977-19-0. £1.40.
  Creetown. 1-873977-31-10. £1.80.
  Crossmichael. 1-873977-22-0. £1.80.
  Dalry. 1-873977-29-8. £2.00.
  Girthon. 1-873977-26-3. £2.10.
  Kirkbean. 1-873977-18-2. £1.40.
  Kirkcudbright. 1-873977-28-10. £1.40.
  Kirkgunzeon. 1-873977-24-7. £1.20.
  Kirkmabreck. 1-873977-30-1. £1.40.
  Lochrutton. 1-873977-17-4. £1.20.
  Minnigaff. 1-873977-25-5. £2.10.
  Parton. 1-873977-21-2. £1.40.
  Terregles. 1-873977-27-1. £1.40.
  Tongland. 1-873977-23-9. £1.40.
All other Stewartry parishes are due for publication.

1851 census indexed by surname. 1992.
  Applegarth. 1-873977-03-4. £3.00.
  Canonbie. 1-873977-04-2. £5.00.
  Cummertrees. 1-873977-05-0. £3.00.
  Durisdeer. 1-873977-06-9. £3.00.
  Johnstone. 1-873977-00-X. £3.00.

Fife Family History Society
30, Duddingston Drive, Kirkealdy, Fife, KY2 6JP

CAMPBELL, A.J. *Fife emigrants and their ships. Pt. 1. Australia and New Zealand.* 78pp. 1998. £3.00 (incl. p&p).

CAMPBELL, A.J. *Recorded indentures of apprenticeship.* 1998. £3.00 (incl. p&p).

CAMPBELL, A.J. *Fife convict transportees, 1752-1867.* 1998. £2.50 + p&p.

CAMPBELL, A.J. *Baptismal registers.* £3.00 (incl. p&p). For St. Peters, Kirkcaldy (1812-54), Holy Trinity, Dunfermline (1840-1854), Inverkeithing (1753-55), and Cairneyhill (1746-1768).

Wills, 1824-1892, registered with the sheriff court of Fife at Cupar. 4 vols. £3.00 per vol. or £10.00 the set (incl. p&p).

ROSS, JANET, & MAYLOR, ARKLEY. *Fife Family History pedigree charts index, and old parish records of Fife and Kinross.* 1995. £2.50 (incl. p&p).

CAMPBELL, ANDREW. *The archives of Fife.* £3.00 (incl. p&p).

Kirkcaldy burials, 1767-1854, from the lair registers. 2 vols. £3.00 per vol or £5.75 the set (incl. p&p).

DUNSIRE, ANDREW. *The Dunsire families of Fife.* 150pp. £5.70 (incl. p&p).

Glasgow & West of Scotland Family History Society
Unit 5, 22, Mansfield Street, Glasgow, G11 5QP.

MILLER, S. *Strathclyde sources.* 1995. Guide to sources in Argyll and Bute, Ayrshire, Dunbartonshire, Glasgow, Lanarkshire, Renfrewshire and parts of Stirlingshire.

WILLING, J.A., & FARIE, J.S. *Burial grounds of Glasgow.* Rev. ed. 1997. £2.40 + p&p 36p.

Highland Family History Society
c/o Reference Room, Public Library, Farraline Park, Inverness, IV1 1NH.

Register of members interests, August 1997. £3.00.

1851 census indexes:
  Killearnon (Roc). £1.50
  Kiltearn (Roc). £1.50
  Kincardine (with Croick) (Roc). £1.50
  Knockbain (Roc). £1.80
  Tain (Roc). £2.10
  Wick (Cai). £2.70

Monumental inscriptions:
  Old Alness (Roc). £3.00
  Avoch (Roc). £2.70
  Easter Suddie (Roc). £1.80
  Fortrose (Roc). £1.80
  Geddes (Nai). £1.80
  Old Hugh, Inverness (Inv). £3.00
  Killearnan (Roc). £1.80
  Kilmuir (Black Isle) (Roc). £2.10
  St. Clements, Dingwall (Roc). £4.50.

Largs and North Ayrshire Family History Society
c/o Mrs C. Craig, Hon Secretary, 2, Raillies Road, Largs, KA30 8QZ.

Largs and North Ayrshire OPR references to officers and seamen in the Cumbrae Revenue cutters. £1.50 (inc. p&p).

Index to 1841 census for Largs. £4.50 (inc. p&p).

Members interests. 1995. £3.50 (inc. p&p).

Midlothian Family History Society
c/o Lasswade High School Centre, Eskdale Drive, Bonnyrigg, EH19 2LA

Index of Midlothian Censuses, 1841:
Borthwick. 1-902434-00-5. £2.00 + p&p 38p.
Carrington. 1-902434-01-3. £1.50 + p&p 31p.
Colinton. 1-902434-03-X. £2.50 + p&p 45p.
Cockpen. 1-902434-02-1. £2.50 + p&p 45p.
Cranston. 1-902434-36-6. £2.00 + p&p 38p.
Fala/Soutra. 1-902434-11-0. £1.00 + p&p 20p.
Glencross. 1-902434-12-9. £1.50 + p&p 31p.
Heriot. 1-902434-13-7. £1.00 + p&p 20p.

Index of Midlothian Censuses, 1851:
Borthwick. 1-902434-30-7. £2.50 + p&p 45p.
Carrington. 1-902434-31-5. £2.00 + p&p 38p.

Shetland Family History Society
6, Hillhead, Lerwick, Shetland, ZE1 0ED

BEATTIE, ALAN M. *Shetland pre-1855 parish sources for family historians.* 1995. £3.50.

Tay Family History Society
Family History Research Centre, 179, Princes Street, Dundee, DD4 6DQ.

Abernyte monumental inscriptions. 38pp. Ref. M101. £3.50 + p&p 31p.
Inchture churchyard, Perthshire. 32pp. Ref. M104. £2.50 + p&p 31p.
Kinnoul graveyard, Perthshire. 31pp. £2.50 + p&p 31p.
Longforgan churchyard, Perthshire. 44pp. Ref. M106. £2.80 + p&p 31p.
Old Pert graveyard, Angus. 18pp. Ref M110. £2.00 + p&p 31p.
PELLOW, A. *Cases from Perth court, 1840.* 38pp. £3.00 + p&p.
Tay Valley source book. 38pp. £2.50 + p&p 31p.

Troon & District Family History Society
c/o M.E.R.C., Troon Library, South Beach, Troon, Ayrshire, KA10 6EF.

Directory of members interests 1995. £1.50 + p&p.

Dundonald burial register 1763-1854. 21pp. £3.15 + p&p.
Newton Green burial ground. £3.15 + p&p.
Sources for family history in Ayrshire. 48pp. £3.60 + p&p.

Monumental inscriptions:
Ayr Auld Kirk. 98pp. £6.60 + p&p.
Coylton. 34pp. £3.15 + p&p.
Craigie. 32pp. £3.15 + p&p.
Crosbie Kirkyard, Ayr. £3.15 + p&p.
Dundonald. 33pp. £3.15 + p&p.
Kyle graveyards: Barnwell, Culzean, Fairfield, Newton-on-Ayr, Coodham, St Margarets R.C. 43 pp. £3.15.
Monkton. 36pp. £3.15.
Old Alloway Kirk. 48pp. £3.15.
St Nicholas, Prestwick. 29pp. £3.15.
St.Quivox churchyard. 47pp. £3.15.
Symington. 42pp. £3.15.
Troon. £3.15.
Wallacetown cemetery, Ayr. 49pp. £3.15.

WALES

Carmarthenshire Antiquarian Society
c/o John Davies, Carmarthen County Archivist, County Hall, Carmarthen, SA31 1JP

DAVIES, JOHN, ed. *The Carmarthenshire book of ordinances, 1569-1606.* 1996. £3.95 + p&p £1.05.

South Wales Record Society
12, The Green, Radyr, Cardiff, CF4 8BR

Diaries of John Bird, 1790-1803. 0-9508676-3-2. 1987. £12.00 + p&p £1.50. Jointly published with Glamorgan Archive Service.
CROUCH, DAVID, ed. *Llandaff episcopal acta, 1140-1287.* 0-9508676-4-0. 1989. £20.00 + p&p £1.50.
GUY, JOHN R., ed. *Diocese of Llandaff in 1763.* 0-9508676-6-7. 1991. £18.95 + p&p £1.55. Ecclesiastical visitation answers to queries.
PARKINSON, ELIZABETH, ed. *The Glamorgan hearth tax assessment of 1670.* 0-9508676-9-1. 1994. £16.50 (inc. p&p).
DENNING, R.W.T., ed. *The diary of William Thomas, 1762-1795.* 0-9525961-0-5. 1995. £19.95 (inc. p&p).

JONES, JUDITH, ed. *Monmouthshire wills proved in the Prerogative Court of Canterbury, 1560-1601.* 0-9525961-2-1. 1997. £24.00 (inc. p&p).
BARROW, JULIA, ed. *St. Davids episcopal acta, 1085-1280.* Forthcoming.
EDMUNDS, MICHAEL J., ed. *The manor court book of Pennard, 1673-1701.* Forthcoming.
CULLIFORD, MARTIN, ed. *The letterbooks of Henry Brown, Tredegar estate agent, 1797-1806.* Forthcoming.

OVERSEAS

National Genealogical Society
4527, 17th Street N., Arlington, VA., 22207-2399, U.S.A.

EMMISON, F.G., ed. *Wills of the County of Essex, England, 1558-1565.* 369pp. 0-915156-51-2. 1982. $US35.00.
COLDHAM, PETER WILSON. *Lord mayor's court of London: depositions relating to Americans, 1641-1736.* 119pp. 0-915156-23-7 (cloth); 0-686-27217-X (pb). $US12.00 (cloth); $US10.00 (pb).
EMMISON, F.G., ed. *Wills of the County of Essex (England) 1558-1565.* 369pp. 0-915156-51-2. 1982. $US35.00.

New England Historic Genealogical Society
160, N.Washington Street, Boston, MA., 02114-2120, U.S.A.
Email: nehgs@nehgs.org
http://www.nehgs.org

ALLEN, MARION, E., & EVANS, NESTA, eds. *Wills from the Archdeaconry of Suffolk.*
v.1. *1629-1636.* 585pp. 1986. $US25.00 + p&p.
v.2. *1637-1640.* 566pp. 1986. $US25.00 + p&p.
See under **Essex Record Office** in part 3 for further volumes in this series.
ANDERSON, ROBERT CHARLES. *The great migration begins: immigrants to New England 1620-1633.* 3vols. 2386pp. $US125.00 + p&p.
BARBER, HENDRY. *British family names: their origin and meaning.* 286pp. Photocopied reprint. Originally published 1902.
BLAYDES, FREDERICK AUGUSTUS. *Genealogia Bedfordiensis: a collection of evidences relating chiefly to the landed gentry of Bedfordshire, 1538-1700.* ix, 507pp. Photocopied reprint; originally published 1890. $US82.00 + p&p.

CLEVELAND, DUCHESS OF. *Battle Abbey roll.* 3 vols. 388pp; 398pp; 528pp. Photocopied reprint. Originally published 1889. $US214.00 + p&p.
COLBY, FREDERICK THOMAS. *The visitation of the County of Devon in the year 1564.* vi, 249pp. Photocopied reprint. Originally published 1881. $US46.00 + p&p.
EMMERTON, JAMES A., & WATERS, HENRY F. *Gleanings from English records about New England families.* 147pp. Photocopied reprint. Originally published 1880. Mainly concerned with Bigge, Champernon, Fletcher, Gilbert, Hathorne, Manning, and Smith.
FILBY, P.WILLIAM. *American and British genealogy and heraldry: a selected list of books.* 3rd ed. 940pp. 1983. $US15.00 + p&p.
FILBY, P.WILLIAM. *American and British genealogy and heraldry: 1982-1985 supplement.* 230pp. 1987. $US5.00 + p&p.
REDMONDS, GEORGE. *Surnames and genealogy: a new approach.* 235pp. 1997. $US20.00 + p&p.
WATERS, HENRY F. *Genealogical gleanings in England.* 132pp. Photocopied reprint. Originally published 1892. $US28.00 + p&p.
Catalogs to the N.E.H.G.S. circulating library. 2 vols. 1998.
v.1. Genealogies. 325pp. $US10.00 + p&p.
v.2. Histories & references. 264pp. $US20.00 + p&p.
The New England historical and genealogical register, 1874-1994 on CD-Rom. 1996. $US265.50 + p&p. Includes much information on English ancestors of American colonists.

Ontario Genealogical Society
40, Orchard View Boulevard, Suite 251, Toronto, M4R 1B9, Canada.

WHYTE, DONALD. *A dictionary of Scottish emigrants to Canada before Confederation.* 433pp. 0-920036-09-0. 1986. $C25.00 + p&p.
WHYTE, DONALD. *A dictionary of Scottish emigrants to Canada before Confederation.* Vol. 2. 1996. $C33.00 + p&p.
WHYTE, DONALD. *Scottish ancestry: a brief guide.* 47pp. 0-912951-23-0. 1984. $C3.00 + p&p.

PART 3
Libraries and Record Offices

Public Record Office
Sales and Marketing, Kew, Surrey, TW9 4DU
Phone: (0181) 3925271
Email: bookshop@pro.gov.uk
http://www.pro.gov.uk

BARNES, T.G. *The court of Star Chamber and its records.* Forthcoming.

BEVAN, AMANDA, ed. *Tracing your ancestors in the Public Record Office.* PRO reader's guide 16. 1-873162-61-8. 1998. £12.00.

CALE, MICHELLE. *Law and society: an introduction to sources for criminal and legal history from 1800.* PRO readers guide 14. 1-873162-30-8. 1996. £12.99.

COX, JANE. *New to Kew?* PRO reader's guide 16. 1-873162-40-5. 1997. £5.99.

COX, JANE, & COLWELL, STELLA. *Never been here before? A genealogist's guide to the Family Records Centre.* PRO reader's guide 17. 2nd ed. 1-873162-41-3. 1997. £5.99.

ELLIS, MARY. *Using manorial records.* PRO reader's guide 6. Rev. ed. 1-873162-38-3. Rev. ed. 1997. £7.99.

FOOT, WILLIAM. *Maps for family history.* PRO reader's guide 9. 1-873162-17-0. 1994. £8.95. Covers records of tithe redemption, the Valuation Office, and the National Farm Survey of England and Wales, 1836-1943.

FOWLER, SIMON, et al. *R.A.F. records in the P.R.O.* PRO reader's guide 8. 1-873162-14-6. 1994. £4.99.

FOWLER, SIMON. *Sources for labour history.* PRO reader's guide 7. 1-873162-21-9. 1995. £10.95.

FOWLER, SIMON, & SPENCER, WILLIAM. *Army records for family historians.* Rev. ed. PRO reader's guide 3. 1-873162-59-6. November 1998. £6.99.

FOWLER, SIMON, SPENCER, WILLIAM, & TAMBLIN, STUART. *Army service records of the First World War.* PRO reader's guide 19. Rev. ed. 1-873162-55-3. 1998. £6.99.

GRANNUM, GUY. *Tracing your West Indian ancestors.* PRO reader's guide 11. 1-873162-20-0. 1995. £8.95.

HORWITZ, H. *Chancery and Equity records and proceedings, 1600-1800.* Rev. ed. 1-873162-63-4. 1998. £15.00.

HOYLE, RICHARD. *Tudor taxation records.* PRO reader's guide 5. 1-873162-11-1. 1994. £5.95.

HUNNISETT, R.F., ed. *Sussex coroners' inquests, 1588-1603.* 1-873162-28-6. 1996. £20.00.

HUNNISETT, R.F., ed. *Sussex coroners' inquests, 1603-1688.* 1-873162-53-7. August 1998. £25.00.

JURKOWSKI, M., SMITH, C., & CROOK, D. *Lay taxes in England and Wales, 1188-1688.* 1-873162-64-2. 1998. £25.00.

LUMAS, SUSAN. *Making use of the census.* PRO reader's guide 1. Rev. ed.. 1-873162-43-X. 1997. £5.99.

RODGER, N.A.M. *Naval records for genealogists.* PRO handbook 22. 1-873162-58-8. 1998. £15.00.

SCOTT, MIRIAM. *Prerogative Court of Canterbury wills and other probate records.* PRO reader's guide 15. 1-873162-23-5. 1997. £5.99.

SHORNEY, DAVID. *Protestant nonconformity and Roman Catholicism.* PRO reader's guide 13. 1-873162-27-8. 1996. £9.99.

SMITH, KELVIN, WATTS, CHRISTOPHER T., & WATTS, MICHAEL J. *Records of merchant shipping and seamen.* PRO reader's guide 20. 1-873162-49-9. 1998. £6.99.

SPENCER, WILLIAM. *Records of the Militia and volunteer forces.* PRO reader's guide 3. 1-873162-44-8. 1997. £7.99.

THOMAS, GARTH. *Records of the Royal Marines.* PRO reader's guide 10. 1-873162-19-7. 1994. £8.95.

MORTIMER, IAN. ed. *Record repositories in Great Britain.* 10th ed. 1-873162-54-5. 1997. £3.99. Co-published with the Royal Commission on Historical Manuscripts.

Royal Commission on Historical Manuscripts

Quality House, Quality Court, Chancery Lane, London WC2A 1HP

Accessions to repositories ... in 1989. 74pp. 0-11-440241-8. 1990. £8.50.
Accessions to repositories ... in 1990. 72pp. 0-11-440228-0. 1991. £9.50.
Later issues are available on line.
MORTIMER, IAN, ed. *Record repositories in Great Britain.* 10th ed. 1-873162-54-5. 1997. £3.99. Co-published with the Public Record Office.
Surveys of historical manuscripts in the United Kingdom: a select bibliography. 3rd ed. iv, 35pp. 0-9539239-0-7. 1997. £3.00.

Guides to sources for British history.

3. *Guide to the location of collections described in the Reports and calendars series 1870-1980.* 71pp. 0-11-440144-6. 1982. £2.50.
8. *Records of British business and industry 1760-1914: textiles and leather.* 130pp. 0-11-440226-4. 1990. £5.50.
9. *Records of British business and industry 1760-1914: metal processing and engineering.* 202pp. 0-11-440232-9. £17.95.
10. *Principal family and estate collections: family names A-K.* xviii, 118pp. 0-11-440265-5. 1996. £30.00.
11. *Principal family and estate collections: family names L-W.* Forthcoming.

Joint publications series.

24. ALTMAN, AVROM, ed. *The Kniveton leiger.* xxxiv, 316pp. 0-11-440065-2. 1977. Jointly published with the Derbyshire Archaeological Society.
25. ROBINSON, DAVID, ed. *Visitations of the Archdeaconry of Stafford, 1829-1841.* xxxvii, 150pp. 0-11-440066-0. 1980. Jointly published with the Staffordshire Record Society. £10.00.
26. NUTTAL, GEOFFREY F., ed. *Calendar of the correspondence of Philip Doddridge, D.D., (1702-1751).* li, 420pp. 0-11-440067-9. 1979. Jointly published with the Northamptonshire Record Society. £15.00.

27. HAINES, R.M., ed. *Calendar of the register of Adam de Orleton, Bishop of Worcester, 1327-1333.* xxvi, 305pp. 0-11-440093-8. 1979. £10.00.

Reports and calendars

9. *Manuscripts of the Marquess of Salisbury (Cecil).*
   vol. *XXIII. Addenda 1562-1605,* ed. G.Dyfnallt Owen. xiii, 281pp. 0-11-440042-3. 1973. £3.50.
   vol. *XXIV. Addenda 1605-1668,* ed. G.Dyfnallt Owen. xvi, 401pp. 0-11-440062-8. 1976. £10.00.
58. *Manuscripts of the Marquess of Bath.*
   Vol. *V. Talbot, Dudley and Devereux papers 1533-1659.* 376pp. 0-11440092-X. 1980. £10.00.
71. *Manuscripts of Allan George Finch.*
   Vol. *IV: 1692 and addenda 1690-1691,* ed. Francis Bickley. xliii, 583pp. 0-11-440140-3.
   Vol. *V. 1693 and secret service papers 1691-1693,* ed. Francis Bickley and Sonia P. Anderson. Forthcoming.
75. *Manuscripts of the Marquess of Downshire.*
   Vol. *IV. Papers of William Trumbull the elder, 1613-1614,* ed. A.B. Hinds. xxiv, 580pp. 0-11-440134-9. 1940. £3.15.
   Vol. *V. Papers of William Trumbull the elder, September 1614 - August 1616,* ed. G. Dyfnallt Owen. xix, 663pp. 0-11-440217-5. 1988. £38.00.
   Vol. *VI. Papers of William Trumbull the elder, September 1616 - December 1618,* ed. G. Dyfnallt Owen & Sonia P. Anderson. ix, 710pp. 0-11-440230. £60.00.

BEDFORDSHIRE

Bedfordshire County Record Office

County Hall, Cauldwell Street, Bedford, MK42 9AP

The old poor law. Archive teaching unit 1. £3.00 + p&p £1.00.
A guide to educational sources. £4.00 + p&p £1.00.
CIRKET, ALAN. *Bedfordshire probate records, 1484-1858.* 2 vols. Vol. 1. £32.50 + p&p £2.00. Vol. 2. £35.00 + p&p £2.50.
Discovering your old house. £3.95 + p&p 55p.

How to discover the history of your house in Bedfordshire. £1.00 + p&p 50p.
Guide to the Russell estate collection for Bedfordshire & Devon to 1910. 50p + p&p 25p.
Luton manor court roll, 1470-1559. £3.00 + p&p 50p.
WARD, KEVIN T. *Pre-registration title deeds: the legal issues of ownership, custody and abandonment*. £9.50 + p&p £1.00.
Short guide to sources (extracts from newsletters). £6.00 + p&p £1.00.
Bedford Methodist Circuit membership book 1781-1806. £3.00 + p&p £1.00.
Blunham Old Meeting Baptist Church book 1724-1891. £3.00 + p&p £1.00.
Southill Independent Church book, 1693-1851. £3.50 + p&p £1.00.
Woburn Congregational Church book 1791-1837. £3.00 + p&p £1.00.

Bedfordshire parish registers series
These are also available on fiche; see the listing in *British Genealogical Microfiche*.
Ampthill. **17**. £14.50.
Arlesey. **66**. £10.50.
Aspley Guise. **72**. £9.75.
Astwick. **26**. £4.50.
Barton le Clay. **4**. £9.50.
Battlesden. **37**. £5.00.
Bedford. St. Cuthbert. **1**. £9.50.
Bedford. St. John. **1**. £9.00.
Bedford. St. Mary. **35**. £11.50.
Bedford. St. Paul. **58**. £28.40.
Bedford. St. Peter. **40**. £8.00.
Biddenham. **16**. £7.00.
Biggleswade. **30**. £11.50.
Billington. **33**. £4.50.
Bletsoe. **24**. £7.00.
Blunham. **19**. £12.50.
Eaton Socon (2 sections). **74**. £24.75.
Edworth. **2**. £5.50.
Eggington (with Leighton Buzzard). **31-3**. £21.50.
Elstow. **1**. £13.00.
Eversholt. **75**. £10.00.
Everton. **80**. £8.75.
Eyeworth. **2**. £6.50.
Farndish. **59**. £6.00.
Felmersham. **9**. £7.50.
Flitton. **18**. £12.50.
Flitwick. **21**. £7.50.
Goldington. **40**. £7.00.
Great Barford. **5**. £9.00.
Harlington. **20**. £7.50.

Harrold. **34**. £8.50.
Hatley Cockayne. **2**. £6.00.
Henlow. **26**. £8.50.
Highham Gobion. **13**. £4.50.
Hockcliffe. **33**. £5.00.
Houghton Conquest. **41**. £10.00.
Houghton Regis. **65**. £12.25.
Hulcote. **29**. £4.50.
Husborne Crawley. **68**. £10.75.
Kempston. **39**. £13.00.
Kensworth. **76**. £9.25.
Keysoe. **60**. £8.75.
Knotting. **7**. £5.00.
Langford. **70**. £9.25.
Leighton Buzzard (including the chapelries of Heath, Reach and Eggington). **31-3**. £21.50.
Lidlington. **29**. £8.00.
Little Barford. **6**. £5.50.
Little Staughton. **45**. £7.25.
Lower Gravenhurst. **13**. £4.50.
Luton 1602-1754 (3 parts). **53**. £26.00.
Luton 1755-1812. **54**. £11.50.
Marston Moretaine. **44**. £10.50.
Maulden. **22**. £10.50.
Melchbourne. **7**. £5.50.
Meppershall. **38**. £8.00.
Millbrook. **20**. £8.00.
Milton Bryan. **37**. £7.50.
Milton Ernest. **11**. £8.00.
Northill. **13**. £12.50.
Oakley. **16**. £8.00.
Odell. **11**. £8.00.
Old Warden. **10**. £8.50. Fiche. £5.00.
Pavenham. **9**. £7.50.
Pertenhall. **50**. £7.75.
Podington. **69**. £8.50.
Potsgrove. **37**. £5.00.
Potton (2 sections). **61**. £20.50.
Pulloxhill. **22**. £6.50.
Ravensden. **47**. £7.50.
Renhold. **5**. £6.50.
Ridgmont. **57**. £8.75.
Riseley. **28**. £7.50.
Roxton. **5**. £7.50.
Salford. **29**. £5.50.
Sandy. **6**. £15.50.
Sharnbrook. **24**. £7.00.
Shefford (with Campton). **52**. £11.50.
Shelton. **7**. £5.50.
Shillington. **36**. £13.50.
Souldrop. **7**. £5.50.
Southill. **12**. £15.50.
Stagsden. **63**. £9.25.
Stanbridge. **33**. £5.50.

Steppingley. 51. £7.25.
Stevington. 9. £7.50.
Stotfold. 38. £8.00.
Streatley. 4. £6.00.
Studham. 77. £10.00.
Sundon. 4. £6.50.
Sutton. 2. £10.00.
Swineshead. 7. £7.00.
Tempsford. 19. £8.00.
Thurleigh. 28. £7.00.
Tilbrook. 79. £9.00.
Tilsworth. 33. £5.50.
Tingrith. 17. £6.50.
Toddington. 23. £12.00.
Tottenhoe. 71. £8.25.
Turvey. 78. £11.25. Fiche. £7.50.
Upper Gravenhurst. 13. £6.00.
Upper Stondon. 26. £4.50.
Westoning. 20. £9.00.
Whipsnade. 25. £4.50.
Wilden. 46. £8.25.
Willington. 10. £6.00.
Wilshampstead. 49. £10.50.
Woburn. 3. £18.50.
Wootton. 43. £11.50.
Wrestlingworth. 2. £9.50.
Wymington. 67. £7.50.
Yelden. 7. £5.50.

CAMBRIDGESHIRE

Cambridge University Library
West Road Cambridge CB3 9DR

Libraries directory. 17th ed. 1996/7. £1.50.
OWEN, A.E.B. *Summary guide to accessions of western manuscripts (other than medieval) since 1867.* 48pp. 1966. £1.00.
OWEN, D.M. *Catalogue of the records of the Bishop and Archdeaconry of Ely.* xii, 89pp. 1971. £5.00 (unbound). Published by the Marc Fitch Fund.

Cambridgeshire Libraries Publications
Resource Unit, 19 Gordon Avenue, Cambridgeshire, PE15 8AL
Phone (01354) 660940

Annual reports of the county archivist. 1965-1994. £1.00 per year (some early years out of print).
BLACK, ANGELA. *Guide to education records in the County Record Office, Cambridge.* 85pp. 1972. £1.00.

FARRAR, MICHAEL. *Genealogical sources in Cambridgeshire.* 100pp. 2nd ed. 1-870724-73-9. 1994. £2.50 + 50p p&p (includes cumulative supplement).
HESELTINE, PETER. *The brasses of Huntingdonshire.* 96pp. 09042436392. 1987. £1.50.
PHILLIPSON, LAUREL. *The Wisbech Quaker's roll of 1723.* Forthcoming.
SLATER, JOHN, & LIQUORICE, MARY. *A Crowland journey with the Slater family.* 48pp. 1-870724-09-7. 1994. £4.50.

CHESHIRE

Cheshire Record Office
Duke Street, Chester, CH1 1RL
Phone: (01244) 602574

DAVENPORT, I.T. *Cheshire place names: an index to the census, 1841 to 1891.* £3.95 + p&p 31p.
DUNN, F.I. *The ancient parishes, townscapes and chapelries of Cheshire.* 40pp + sheet map. 1987. £4.50 + p&p 45p.
IRVING, JOAN. *Guide to family history: research resources for the Macclesfield area.* £1.75 + p&p 20p.
LANGSTON, B. *Cheshire parish registers: a summary guide.* 1996. £3.95 + p&p 31p.
THACKER, A.T. *The Chester Diocesan records and the local historian.* 1981. £1.30 + p&p 20p. Offprint from *Transactions of the Historical Society of Lancashire and Cheshire.*
A map of the Diocese of Chester divided into deaneries, c. 1740. £3.00 + p&p £1.55.
Archives on Merseyside: a guide to local repositories. 50p + p&p 20p.
Cheshire Record Office guide. £8.50 + p&p. £1.25.
Family history: Chester archives. 90p + p&p 31p.
Saltney ancestors: the 1881 census. £3.20 + p&p 45p.

Tameside Local Studies Library
Astley Cheetham Public Library, Trinity Street, Stalybridge, Cheshire SK15 2BN
Email: tamelocal@dial.pipex.com

Guide to the Tameside Archive Service. £12.95.

Stockport Central Library
Local Heritage Librarian,
Wellington Road South, Stockport,
SK1 3RS
Phone (0161) 4744530
Genealogy in Stockport: a guide to sources in the Heritage Library. 6th ed. Forthcoming.

CORNWALL
Cornwall Record Office
County Hall, Truro, TR1 3AY
Phone: (01872) 323127
Guide to sources at Cornwall Record Office. 79p. 1995. £5.00 + £1.00 p&p.
Sources for Cornish family history. 1997. £2.50 + £1.00 p&p.
Review and accession list.
  1994-5. £2.00 + 75p p&p.
  1995-6. £2.00 + 75p p&p.
  1996-7. £2.00 + 75p p&p.
Index to accessions 1979-1993. 57p. 1993. £2.50 + £1.00 p&p.
Guide to Cornish probate records. Rev. ed. 1996. £4.50 + £1.50 p&p.
Index to Cornish probate records 1600-1649. 5 pts. 1984-88.
  Pt.1. *A-D.* £2.00 + £1.00 p&p.
  Pt.2. *E-K.* £2.00 + £1.00 p&p.
  Pt.3. *L-R.* £2.00 + £1.00 p&p.
  Pt.4. *S-Z.* £2.00 + £1.00 p&p.
  Pt.5. *Parishes/Occupations.* 110p. £2.50 + £1.00 p&p.
Index to Cornish Estate Duty and Deanery of St. Buryan wills. 49p. 1987.
Pedigrees and heraldic documents. Handlist **3**. Rev. ed. 1985. £2.00 + 75p p&p.
Parish poor law papers. Handlist **4**. 20pp. Rev. ed. 1993. £2.00 + 75p p&p.
Tuneful tongues. Handlist **6**. 48p. 1997. £2.50 & £1.00 p&p. Documentary sources for church bells and bellringing, including full list of Cornish churchwardens' accounts.
A list of Cornish manors. Rev. ed. Forthcoming.
Introduction to the Arundell archive. 36p. 1996. £2.00 + 50p p&p.

CUMBERLAND
Cumbria County Council Archive Service
Cumbria Record Office, The Castle, Carlisle, CA3 8UR.
Phone: (01228) 607285
Cumbrian ancestors: notes for genealogical searchers. 3rd ed. 0-9500371-5-X. Forthcoming, approx. £6.95 + p&p.
ASHCROFT, LORAINE. *Vital statistics: the Westmorland 'census' of 1787.* Curwen archive texts **1**. 414pp. 1-89759000-8. 1992. £9.50 + p&p £1.50.
Fleming Senhouse papers. Cumbria County Council record series **2**. 174pp. 1961. Concerns the papers of Sir George Fleming, Bishop of Carlisle (died 1747), and his son William, Archdeacon of Carlisle.

DERBYSHIRE
Derbyshire Record Office
County Offices, Matlock, DE4 3AG
Local studies in Derbyshire: a guide to library resources. 0-903-46344-X. 1996. £2.50.

DEVON
Devon County Council
County Local Studies Librarian, Exeter Central Library, Castle Street, Exeter. EX4 3PQ.
Many publications are also available on fiche; see *British Genealogical Microfiche* for details.
Abbots Bickington to Zeal Monachorum: a handlist of parish histories compiled on the occasion of the centenary of parish councils. 1-85522-331-7. 1994. £2.95.
Devon bibliography. 1985-96. Annual. £2.95 per issue. Earlier issues published by Devon History Society.
Handlist of local directories in Devon libraries. 60p.
Local studies in Devon: a guide to its resources. £2.00. Directory of societies, libraries, museums, *etc.*
The Burnet Morris index 1940-1900. 1990. 70p.

GUY, ANDREW. *An index of brass rubbings in the West Country Studies Library.* 1-855222-098-9. £4.50.
A variety of free leaflets are also available.

Devon Record Office
Castle Street, Exeter, EX4 3PU
Phone: (01392) 384253
http://www.devon-cc.gov.uk
Annual report 1986-87. £1.00 + p&p.
List of accessions. Annual, 1987/8-1994/5. £2.00 per issue.
Guide to sources. £2.00 + p&p.
Map of Devon parishes. 20p. + p&p
Parish, non-parochial and civil registers in the Devon Record Office. 1996. £2.50 + p&p.
VAGE, J.E. *Records of the Bishop of Exeter's Consistory Court to 1660.* Handlist 1. 0-86114-975-0. 1980. £1.00 + p&p.
THORNE, R.F.S. *Methodism in Devon: a handlist of chapels and their records.* 2nd ed. Handlist 2. 0-86114-975-0. 1989. £1.50 + p&p.
Ship's crew lists: a handlist of records in the Devon Record Office. Handlist 3. 0-86114-655-7. 1987. £4.75 + p&p.

DORSET
Dorset County Record Office
Bridport Road, Dorchester, Dorset DT1 1RP
Phone: (01305) 267933
Guide to the location of the parish registers of Dorset. £1.50 + p&p 78pp.
Guide to the location of nonconformist & Roman Catholic registers. £1.00 + p&p 70pp.
Guide to the transcripts held in the County Record Office. 75pp. + p&p 72p.
List of documents in the Record Office relating to precautions in the county against the threat of French invasion, 1797-1814. 10pp. + p&p 41p.
The archives of Dorset: catalogue of an exhibition to mark the 30th anniversary of the Dorset Record Office held at the County County Museum 1986. £2.00 + p&p 62p.
A map of the parishes of Dorset c.1900 + p&p. 40pp. + p&p 26p.

Dorset Record Office annual reports. 1983-5. 50p + p&p 56p per year; 1986-, £1.00 + p&p 57p per year.
Dorset motor taxation records: a short guide. 75p + p&p 56p.

Poole Museums Services
4 High Street, Poole, Dorset BH15 1BW
PRECIOUS, JANET, ed. *Book of the Staple, 1589-1727.* 0-86251-026-0. 1997. £2.95.

CO. DURHAM
Durham Record Office
County Hall, Durham, DH1 5UL
Phone: (0191) 3864411
Email: alm@durham/gov.uk
The Londonderry papers, catalogue of documents. xiv + 166pp. 1969. £4.00 + £1.00 p&p.
Map of parish and chapelry boundaries, circa 1800. 1983. £1.00 + 50p postage.
Streatlam and Gibside: the Bowes and Strathmore families in County Durham. [vi] + 45p. 1984. £3.50 + £1.25 p&p.
Durham places in the mid-nineteenth century. iii + 135pp. 1996. £6.50 + p&p £1.00.
Durham family history gazetteer. ii + 41pp. 1996. £3.00 + 75p postage.
Many leaflets are also available.

ESSEX
Essex Record Office
PO Box 11, County Hall, Chelmsford, SM1 1LY
ALLEN, D.H. *Essex Quarter Sessions order book, 1652-1661.* 300pp. 0-900360-44-5. (Cat. no. 65). 1974. £5.95.
APPLEBY, DAVID, & APPLEBY, JOHN. *The magic boxes: professional photographers and their studies in North Essex, 1845-1937.* 72pp. 0-900360-83-. (Cat no. 115). 1992. £6.95. Includes directory of photographers.
EMMISON, F.G. *Elizabethan life: morals and the church courts.* 356pp. 0-900360-41-0. (Cat no. 63) 1973. £6.99.
EMMISON, F.G. *Elizabethan life: home, work and land.* 364pp. 0-900360-78-X. (Cat no. 69) 1976. £9.95.
EMMISON, F.G., ed. *Elizabethan life: Essex gentry's wills in the Prerogative Court of Canterbury.* 361pp. 0-900360-50-X. (Cat no. 71). 1978. £6.99.

EMMISON, F.G., ed. *Essex wills* 10 vols.
  v.1. *1558-1565 (Archdeaconries of Essex, Colchester and Middlesex (Essex Division).* 369pp. 091515652. 1982. £14.95. (published by the National Genealogical Society)
  v.2. *1565-1571 (Ditto.)* 292pp. 0-880820-05-5. 1983. £14.95. (published by the New England Genealogical Society)
  v.3. *1571-1577 (Ditto.)* 538pp. 0-880820-16-0. 1986. £14.95. (published by the New England Genealogical Society)
  v.4. *1577-1584 (Ditto.)* 272pp. 0-900360-69-0. (Cat no. 96) 1989. £14.95.
  v.5. *1584-1591 (Ditto.)* 401pp. 0-900360-73-9. (Cat no. 101) 1989. £14.95.
  v.6. *1591-1597 (Ditto.)* 279pp. 0-900360-80-1. (Cat no. 104) 1991. £14.95.
  v.7. *1597-1603 (Ditto.)* 230pp. 0-900360-79-8. (Cat no. 107) 1990. £14.95.
  v.8. *1558-1569 Bishop of London's Commisary Court.* 274pp. 0-900360-96-8. (Cat no. 124) 1993. £14.95.
  v.9. *1569-1578 (Ditto.)* 274pp. 0-900360-99-2 (Cat no. 127) 1994. £14.95.
  v.10. *1578-1588 (Ditto.)* 303pp. 1-898529-01-9 (Cat no. 129) 1995. £14.95.
Two further volumes are in preparation.
GRIEVE, HILDA E.P. *Examples of English handwriting, 1150-1750.* 33pp. 0-900360-31-3 (Cat no. 21) 1954.
MASON, A. STUART. *Essex on the map: the 18th century land surveyors of Essex.* 138pp. 0-900360-75-5. (Cat no. 105). 1990. £14.95.
QUINTRELL., B.W., ed. *The Maynard Lieutenancy book 1608-1839.* 2 vols. 550pp. 0-900360-95-X. (Cat no. 123) 1993.
SHARPE, J.A., ed. *William Holcroft his booke: local office-holding in late Stuart Essex.* 124pp. 0-900360-66-6. (Cat no. 90) 1986. £6.50.
WARD, J.C., ed. *The medieval Essex community: the lay subsidy of 1327.* 139pp. 0-9003360-64-X (Cat no.88) 1983. £5.50.
Essex family history: a genealogists guide to the Essex Record Office. 4th ed. 0-900360-94-1. (Cat no. 122) 1995. £6.50.
Essex parishes and hundreds. Map. (Cat no. 77). £1.25.
Essex in London: a guide to the records of the London boroughs formerly in Essex, deposited in the Essex Record Office. 2nd ed. 160pp. 1-898529-06-X (Cat no. 117). 1996. £5.50.

GLOUCESTERSHIRE AND BRISTOL

Gloucestershire Record Office

Clarence Row, Alvin Street, Gloucester, GL1 3DW

Handlist of the contents of the Gloucestershire Record Office. 0-904950-93-X. 1995. £12.50 + p&p £3.00.
Handlist of genealogical records. 0-904950-77-8. 1992. £6.00 + p&p £1.90.
Records of the Bishops and Archdeacons. 1968. £5.00 + p&p £1.90.
Records of the Dean and Chapter. 1967. £5.00 + p&p £1.90.
Gloucestershire quarter sessions archives (1660-1889) and other official records. 1958. £3.00 + p&p 75p.
Gloucestershire family history. 3rd ed. 0-904950-91-3. 1993.
Your house has history. 0-904950-88-3. 1993. 80p + p&p 27p.
Gloucestershire parishes. Map. 60p + p&p £1.27.

Bristol Historical Databases Project

University of the West of England, St. Matthias Campus, Oldbury Court Road, Fishponds, Bristol, BS16 2JP
Phone: (0117) 9655384 ext. 4487
Please specify whether you require computer disks in ASCII format, or in *Idealist for Windows.* The latter requires Microsoft Windows 3.1 or above, a 386 processor, at least 1.5 Mb free space, and at least 4 MB RAM.

Bibliography of Bristol and Bath. Disc. £3.00.
Matthews' commercial directory, 1792. Disc. £3.00.
Reed's commercial directory, 1794. Disc. £3.00.
Matthews' commercial directory, 1801. Disc. £3.00.
Matthews' commercial directory, 1851. Disc. £3.00.
Bristol obituaries, 1871-1921. Disc. £3.00.
Bristol poll book, 1722. Disc. £3.00.
Bristol poll book, 1774. Disc. £3.00.
Guide to the Port of Bristol archives. Disc. £3.00.
Bristol business archives. Disc. £3.00.

Bristol Record Office
'B' Bond Warehouse, Smeaton Road, Bristol, BS1 6XN
Phone: (0117) 9225692

Registers and bishops transcripts of births, baptisms, marriages and burials in Bristol Record Office; includes Anglican and nonconformist registers. £1.00.

School admission records and log books in Bristol Record Office: a comprehensive alphabetical listing of schools and educational establishments records. Rev. ed. £3.00.

Fact sheet on Bristol probate records. £1.20.

Index to Bristol wills 1793-1858. £1.20.

Bristol: the home front. Records in Bristol Record Office relating to World War II. 50p.

The poor law in Bristol: a handlist of records relating to the administration of the poor law in Bristol Record Office. £2.00.

Family history at Bristol Record Office. £1.50.

HAMPSHIRE
Bournemouth Libraries
Town Hall, Bourne Avenue, Bournemouth BH2 6DY

MARSH, JAN. *Genealogical sources in the Dorset county reference libraries.* 3rd ed. 1994. £1.25.

A guide covering Bournemouth only is in preparation; the town was in Hampshire pre-1974.

Hampshire Record Office
Sussex Street, Winchester, Hampshire, SO23 8TH
Phone: (01962) 846154

Hampshire record series.
Subscribers receive substantial discounts.
1. *Sir Henry Whithed's letter book volume 1: 1601-1614.* xiv, 127pp. 1976. £5.00. Letter book of a J.P. and sheriff; many names.
2. GREATREX, JOHN, ed. *The register of the common seal of the Priory of St. Swithun, Winchester 1345-1497.* xl, 312pp. 1979. £8.00.
3. STAGG, D.J., ed. *A calendar of New Forest documents 1244-1334.* xii, 330pp. 0-906680-00-x. 1979. £8.00.
4. DAVEY, C.R., ed. *The Hampshire lay subsidy rolls, 1586.* xi, 180pp. 0-906680-01-8. 1981. £8.00.
5. STAGG, D.J., ed. *A calendar of New Forest documents 15th-17th centuries.* 0-906680-02-6. 1983. £8.00.
6. CROOK, J., ed. *The wainscot book.* xxxvii, 184pp. 0-906680-03-4. 1984. £8.00. Concerns houses in Winchester Cathedral Close.
7. HOCKEY, S.F., ed. *The register of William Edington, Bishop of Winchester 1346-1366, part 1.* xxvi, 317pp. 0-906680-04-2. 1986. £15.00.
8. HOCKEY, S.F., ed. *The register of William Edington, Bishop of Winchester 1346-1366, part 2.* v, 289pp. 0-906680-05-0. 1987. £15.00.
9. HANNA, K.A., ed. *The cartularies of Southwick Priory, part 1.* lxviii, 305pp. 0-906680-06-9. 1988. £15.00.
10. HANNA, K.A., ed. *The cartularies of Southwick Priory, part 2.* vi, 551pp. 0-906680-07-7. 1989. £15.00.
11. HUGHES, ELIZABETH, & WHITE, PHILIPPA, eds. *The Hampshire hearth tax assessment 1665.* xxi, 468pp. 1-873595-08-5. 1991. £15.00.
13. WARD, W.R., ed. *Parson and parish in eighteenth-century Hampshire: replies to bishops visitations.* xxxvi, 384pp. 1-85975-30-1. 1995. £15.00.
14. PAGE, MARK, ed. *The pipe roll of the Bishopric of Winchester, 1301-2.* 1-85975-108-3. 1996. £15.00.
15. CHAPMAN, JOHN, & SEELIGER, SYLVIA, eds. *A guide to enclosure in Hampshire 1700-1900.* xxiv, 403pp. 1-85975-109-1. 1997. £15.00.

Portsmouth record series.
1. WILLIS, ARTHUR J,. & HOAD, MARGARET J., eds. *Borough sessions papers 1653-1688.* 1971. £15.00.
2. ALBERT, W., & HARVEY, P.D.A., eds. *Portsmouth and Sheet turnpike commissioners' minute book, 1711-1754.* 1973. £15.00.
3. SURRY, N.W., & MHOMAS, J.H., eds. *Book of original entries 1731-1751.* 1976. £15.00.
7. LOWE, J.A., ed. *Records of the Portsmouth Division of Marines 1764-1800.* 1991. £15.00.
8. HAMPSON, G., ed. *Portsmouth customs letter books 1748-1750.* 1995. £15.00.

Hampshire Record Office leaflets
Sources for the history of Winchester buildings. 50p.
A guide to Winchester city archives in Hampshire Record Office. £1.50.
Parish registers of Hampshire and the Isle of Wight. £1.00.
Estate records of the Bishops of Winchester in Hampshire Record Office. £1.00.
Quarter sessions records in Hampshire Record Office. £1.00.
Records of the Diocese of Winchester in Hampshire Record Office. £1.00.
Sources for family history at Hampshire Record Office. £1.00.

Southampton Archive Services
Civic Centre, Southampton, SO14 4LY
Phone: (01703) 832251

A guide to the records of Southampton Corporation and absorbed authorities. Southampton records 1. 72pp. 1964. 60p. + p&p.
Southampton crew lists, 1863-1913. 2nd ed. 1989. £5.75 + p&p.
Sources for family history in Southampton Archives Office. 1997. £3.00 + p&p.

Southampton City Libraries
Civic Centre, Southampton, SO14 7LW

Men and women of Southampton. 1983. £2.50.
Guide to genealogical sources. 1-87065-160-X. 1989. £2.00. In Southampton Reference Library.

Isle of Wight County Record Office
26 Hillside Street, Newport, Isle of Wight PO30 2EB
Phone: (01983) 523821

HOCKEY, S.F., ed. *Cartulary of Carisbrooke Priory.* 0-906328-13-6. 1981. £8.00 + p&p £2.00.
HOCKEY, S.F., ed. *The charters of Quarr Abbey.* 0-90632-847-0. 1991. £16.00 + p&p £2.30.

Herefordshire Record Office
The Old Barracks, Harold Street, Hereford, HR1 2QX
Phone: (01432) 265441

Parish registers available at Herefordshire Record Office. £1.00 + p&p 50p.
Parish officers: records available at Herefordshire Record Office. £1.00 + p&p 50p.
School records available at Herefordshire Record Office. £1.00 + p&p 50p.
Census records available at Herefordshire Record Office. £1.00 + p&p 50p.

KENT

Bexley Libraries and Museums Department
Local Studies Section, Hall Place, Bourne Road, Bexley, DA5 1PQ
Phone: (01322) 526574

REILLY, LEONARD. *Family history in Bexley: a guide to tracing your Bexley ancestors.* 24pp. 0-902541-31-5. 1993.

LANCASHIRE

Bolton Archive Service
Central Library, Civic Centre, Le Mans Crescent, Bolton, BL1 1SE

LAMARA, J.D. *Handlist of registers.* 4th ed. 1997. £2.00 + p&p 50p.

Lancashire Record Office
Bow Lane, Preston, PR1 2RE
Phone: (01772) 263034

Finding folk: a handlist of basic sources for family history in the Lancashire Record Office. 2nd ed. 0-904663-05-1. 1997. £8.50 + p&p £2.55.
FRANCE, R. SHARPE. *Guide to the Lancashire Record Office.* 3rd ed. 0-90222852-8. 1985. £12.75 + p&p £2.90.
MARTIN, JANET D. *Guide to the Lancashire Record Office: a supplement, 1977-1989.* 1992. £14.95 + p&p £1.61 (published by Lancashire County Books).

Liverpool Record Office
City Libraries, William Brown Street, Liverpool, L3 8EW
Phone: (0151) 2255443

A handlist of Church of England parish records. 1996. £2.50 + p&p 38p.
Map of Church of England parishes in Liverpool and district. 1996. £3.99 + p&p 41p.
A handlist of Roman Catholic parish records. 0-902990-19-5. 1997. £3.00 + p&p 38p.

Salford Archives Centre
658/662 Liverpool Road, Irlam, Manchester, M30 5AD
Phone: (0161) 7755643
CROSS, ANDREW. *A handlist of Salford City Archives.* 8pp. [199-?] Free.
Various other free leaflets are also available.

Wigan Heritage Services
Town Hall, Leigh, WN7 2DY
Phone: (01942) 404559
A guide to genealogical sources. 1994. £1.95.
A guide to the archives. 1996. £2.95.

LEICESTERSHIRE
Leicestershire Record Office
Long Street, Wigston Magna, Leicester, LE18 2AH
Phone: (0116) 2571080
FARRELL, JEROME. *Family forbears.* 0-85022-219-2. 1987. £3.45.
LEE, JOYCE. *Who's buried where in Leicestershire.* 0-85022-291-5. 1991. £5.99.
Handlist of Leicestershire bishops transcripts. 0-9500435-5-9. 1987. £1.00.
Handlist of parish and non-conformist church registers in Leicestershire Record Office. £3.00.

Leicester University Library
P.O. Box 248, University Road, Leicester, LE1 9QD
BURCH, BRIAN, & CLARK, JENNY. *Leicester University Library: a handlist of the manuscript collection.* 1-898489-08-4. £3.00.

LINCOLNSHIRE
Lincolnshire Books
Sam Hayes, Education and Cultural Services Directorate, County Offices, Newland, Lincoln, LN1 17L
Phone: (01522) 510800
Lincolnshire convicts. 0-86111-135-4. 1988. £1.00 + p&p 50p. Includes list of transportees to Australia, 1789-1840.

LONDON
Guildhall Library
Aldermanbury, London, EC2P 2EJ
Phone: (0171) 3321858
London local archives: a directory of local authority record offices and libraries. 3rd ed. 0-900422-38-6. 1994. £3.75. Joint publication with the Greater London Archive Network.

Guildhall Library research guides
1. HARVEY, RICHARD. *A guide to genealogical resources in Guildhall Library.* 4th ed. 0-900422-41-6. 1997. £3.95.
2. *The British overseas: a guide to births, marriages and deaths of British persons overseas before 1945.* 3rd ed. 0-900422-39-4. 1995. £5.75.
3. *City livery companies and related organisations: a guide to their archives in Guildhall Library.* 3rd ed. 0-900422-29-7. 1989. £5.00.
4. *City of London parish registers: a handlist of parish registers, register transcripts and related records at Guildhall Library.* 6th ed. 0-900422-30-0. 1990. £3.50.
5. *Greater London parish registers: registers of Church of England parishes outside the City of London, non-parochial registers, registers of foreign denominations, burial grounds and marriage documents.* 7th ed. 0-900422-40-8. 1995. £3.50.
6. *A handlist of non-conformist, Roman Catholic, Jewish, and burial ground registers at Guildhall Library.* 2nd ed. 0-900422-35-1. 1993. £3.25.
7. BARRISKILL, D. *A guide to the Lloyd's marine collection and related marine sources at Guildhall Library.* 2nd ed. 0-900422-37-8. 1994. £4.25.

Supplementary series
2. BULLOCK-ANDERSON, JOAN. *A handlist of business archives at Guildhall Library.* 2nd ed. 0-900422-34-3. 1991. £4.00.

Corporation of London Records Office
PO Box 270, Guildhall, London, EC2P 2EJ
Phone: (0171) 3321251
DEADMAN, H., & SLUDDER, E. *An introductory guide to the Corporation of London Record Office.* 0-85203-038-X. 1994. £5.00
City freedom archives. Research guide 1. Free.
Sworn brokers archives. Research guide 2. Free.
Transportation and emigration. Research guide 3. Free.
Various free *information sheets* are also available.

MIDDLESEX
London Borough of Hillingdon
Local Heritage Coordinator, Central Library, High Street, Uxbridge, Middlesex, UB8 1HD
Phone: (01895) 811164

Family history in Hillingdon: a guide to sources. 0-907869-28-9. 1998. £1.50.
BRITTON, T. *From Bedfordshire to Yorkshire: a guide to family history resources in Hillingdon Libraries.* 1997. £9.00. Privately published, but distributed by the library.

London Borough of Tower Hamlets Libraries
Bancroft Library, 227 Bancroft Road, Mile End, London, E1 4DQ
FINCH, HAROLD. *The Tower Hamlets connection: a biographical guide.* 1995. £7.99 + p&p £1.20.
Various free leaflets are also available.

NORFOLK
Norfolk Record Office
Gildengate House, Anglia Square, Upper Green Lane, Norwich, NR3 1AX
Phone: (01603) 761349
E-mail: norfrec.nro@norfolk.gov.uk

Parish registers and transcripts in the Norfolk Record Office. £4.00 + p&p 60p.
Free church registers & related records in the Norfolk Record Office. £1.50 + p&p 43p.
A guide to genealogical sources. 3rd ed. 0-903103-04-4. 1993. £2.50.
Norfolk parish map. 50p + p&p 31p.
A guide to sources for tracing the history of a house or property in Norfolk. 75p + p&p 43p.
MEERES, FRANK. *A guide to the records of Norwich Cathedral.* 0-903103-09-5. 1998. £6.95 + p&p 60p.
Various free leaflets are also available.

NORTHUMBERLAND
Newcastle Libraries & Information Service
Promotion and Arts Unit, Princess Square, Newcastle upon Tyne, NE99 1DX
Phone: (0191) 2610691, ext 232.
BENNISON, BRIAN. *Brewers and bottlers of Newcastle upon Tyne from 1850 to the present day.* 86pp. 1-85795-012-7. £4.99.

Tyne and Wear Archives Service
Blandford House, Blandford Square, Newcastle upon Tyne, NE1 4JA
Phone: (0191) 2326789

A guide to sources for family historians at Tyne and Wear Archive Service. 1997. £2.00 + p&p 50p.

OXFORDSHIRE
Oxfordshire Archives
County Hall, New Road, Oxford, OX1 1ND

Family history: a guide to Oxfordshire resources. £1.00.
HOWARD DRAKE, JACK, ed. *Oxford church courts: depositions 1542-1550.* £3.95 + p&p.
HOWARD DRAKE, JACK, ed. *Oxford church courts: depositions 1570-1574.* £3.95 + p&p.
HOWARD DRAKE, JACK, ed. *Oxford church courts: depositions 1581-1586.* £3.95 + p&p.
HOWARD DRAKE, JACK, ed. *Oxford church courts: depositions 1589-1593.* £3.95 + p&p.
HOWARD DRAKE, JACK, ed. *Oxford church courts: depositions 1592-1596.* £3.95 + p&p.

SHROPSHIRE
Shropshire Records and Research Centre
Castle Gates, Shrewsbury, SY1 2AQ
Phone: (01743) 255350

Shropshire family history: a guide to sources in the Shropshire Records & Research Centre. 32pp. 0-903802-68-6. £3.50 + p&p 70p.

SOMERSET
Somerset Record Office
Obridge Road, Taunton, TA2 7PU
Phone: (01823) 278805
Email: Somerset_Archives@compuserve.com
Http://www.somerset.gov.uk

Summary list of Anglican parish and nonconformist registers of births, baptisms, marriages, deaths and burials, of which originals or copies are held in the Somerset Record Office ... £2.50.

SHORROCKS, DEREK. *Your Somerset house: a guide to tracing the history of your house in the Somerset Record Office.* Rev. ed. 0-86183-133-0. 1998. Approx. £3.00.

BUSH, ROBIN. *Your Somerset family: a guide to tracing your family history in the Somerset Record Office.* Rev. ed. 0-86163-329-5. 1997. £2.00.

STAFFORDSHIRE
Staffordshire Record Office
Eastgate Street, Stafford, ST16 2LZ
Phone: (01785) 278380

Family history pack. Rev. ed. 1998. £6.00 + p&p 98p. Includes a wide range of leaflets, each of which is also separately available.

Registration districts. 70p + p&p 25p. List for Staffordshire.

Staffordshire census returns available in libraries and local studies centres. 60p + p&p 25p.

List of registers of Staffordshire nonconformist churches. £2.40 + p&p 43p.

Outline map of ancient Staffordshire parishes. 40p + p&p 25p.

Black country parish map 1908. Includes dates of earliest entries in parish registers.

Potteries parish map 1908. Includes dates of earliest entries in parish registers.

Family collections. £2.50 + p&p 69p. Summary list of the major family collections in the William Salt Library.

Enclosure acts, awards and maps. £2.20 + p&p 60p. List of those at Staffordshire Record Office and the William Salt Library.

Tithe maps and awards. £2.20 + p&p 60p. List of those at Staffordshire Record Office, Lichfield Record Office and the William Salt Library.

Estate maps before 1840. £1.20 + p&p 69p. List of those at Lichfield Record Office, William Salt Library, Hanley Reference Library, and Keele University Library.

Supplement to the handlist of Staffordshire estate maps before 1840. £3.00 + p&p 60p.

Staffordshire gazetteer. £1.80.

Business records. £1.00. Includes lists of records deposited at Lichfield Record Office and William Salt Library.

A variety of other leaflets are available.

Walsall Local History Centre
Essex Street, Walsall, WS2 7AS
Phone: (01922) 721305

Black Country graveyards, cemeteries, epitaphs. 40p. £4.50.

PEARCE, T. *History and directory of Walsall.* 234pp. Facsimile reprint of an 1813 directory. £5.00.

Trace your family tree in Walsall Metropolitan Borough. 92pp. £2.00.

Wolverhampton Archives and Local Studies
Central Library, 42-50, Snow Hill, Wolverhampton, WV2 4AG
Phone: (01902) 5552480

Family history factsheets. 1997. £1.00 + p&p £1.00.

A variety of free leaflets are also available.

SURREY
Southwark Local Studies Library
211 Borough High Street, London, SE1 1JA
Phone: (0171) 4033507

REILLY, LEONARD. *Family history in Southwark: a guide to tracing your Southwark ancestors.* 0-905849-20-5. 1996. £1.95 + p&p £1.00.

HUMPHREY, STEPHEN. *Guide to the archives in Southwark Local Studies Library.* 1992. £2.50 + p&p £1.00.

BEASLEY, JOHN. *Who was who in Peckham.* £3.00 + p&pp £1.00.

Nunhead cemetery guide. £2.75 + p&p £1.00.

Sutton Heritage Service
Central Library, St Nicholas Way, Sutton, SM1 1EA
Phone: (0181) 7704745
Email: sutton.heritage@dial.pipex.com

Guide to the archive & local studies collections in Sutton. 1992. £2.50 (inc. p&p).

Guide to the copies of Surrey parish registers held by the Sutton Archive & Local Studies searchroom. 1993. £2.50 (inc. p&p).

SUSSEX
East Sussex County Record Office
The Maltings, Castle Precincts, Lewes, BN7 1YT.
Phone: (01273) 482349

BERRY, J.A. *How to trace the history of your family.* 1971. 50p + 45p p&p.
BRENT, J.A. *The Hickstead Place archives.* 1975. £5.00 + 80p p&p.
BRENT, J.A. *The history of a parish or locality.* 1970. 50p + 45p p&p.
BRENT, J.A. *The Battle Abbey archives.* 1973. £1.00 + 63p p&p.
DELL, R. *Winchelsea Corporation records.* 1963. £1.25 + £1.00 p&p.
WARNE, H.M. *The Frewen archives.* 1972. £1.00 + 60p p&p.
WILLIAMS, D.C. *How to trace the history of your house.* 1971. 50p + 45p p&p.
WOOLDRIDGE, J.A. *The Danny archives.* 1966. £3.25 + £1.30 p&p.
A descriptive report on the quarter sessions, other official and ecclesiastical records in the custody of the county councils of East and West Sussex. 1954. 75p + 85p p&p.
Handlist of registers of births, baptisms, marriages, deaths and burials. 1998. £1.75 + 25p p&p.

West Sussex Record Office
County Hall, Chichester, West Sussex PO19 1RN
Phone: (01243) 533911

BOOKER, JOHN M.L. *The Wiston archives.* xiv, 541pp. 0-900801-35-2. 1975. £15.00.
BOOKER, JOHN M.L. *The Clough and Butler archives.* x, 56pp. 0-900801-24-7. 1965. £5.00.
BUTLER, DAVID J., ed. *The land drainage records of West Sussex.* lx, 177pp. 0-900801-28-X. 1973. £10.00.
BUTLER, DAVID J. *Quarter sessions and the Justices of the Peace in West Sussex.* 13pp. 0-900801-30-1. 1972. £1.00.
DIBBEN, A.A. *The Greatham archives.* xviii + 22pp. 0-900801-22-0. 1962. £5.00.
FREETH, STEPHEN. *The Wiston archives, vol. II.* vii, 67pp. 0-900801-43-3. 1982. £10.00.
FREETH, STEPHEN G.H., MASON, IAN A., & WILKINSON, PETER M. *A catalogue of the Horsham Museum mss.* viii, 262pp. 0-86260-331-5.
MCCANN, TIMOTHY J. *West Sussex probate inventories, 1521-1834.* 24pp + 4 fiche. 0-86260-005-7. 1981. £15.00.
MCCANN, ALISON. *The Petworth House archives, vol. II.* xi, 112pp. 0-900801-42-5. 1979. £10.00.
MCCANN, TIMOTHY J. *The Goodwood estate archives, vol. III.* ix, 160pp. 0-86260-019-7. £18.50.
OSBORNE, NOEL H., ed. *The Lytton manuscripts.* ix, 79pp. 0-90081-10-7. £5.00.
READMAN, A.E. *The Royal Sussex Regiment: a catalogue of records.* xi, 290pp. 0-86260-073-1. 1985. £25.00.
STEER, FRANCIS W., & KIRBY, ISABEL M. *A catalogue of the records of the bishop, archdeacons and former exempt jurisdictions. Records of the Diocese of Chichester.* 1. xxiii, 268pp. 0-900801-14-X. 1966. £15.00.
STEER, FRANCIS W. *A catalogue of Sussex estate and tithe award maps, vol. 1.* 240pp. 1962. £10.00. Published as vol. **61.** of the Sussex Record Society's series.
STEER, FRANCIS W., & VENABLES, J.E. AMANDA. *The Goodwood estate archives, vol. I.* xxi, 309pp. 0-900801-03-4. 1970. £15.00.
STEER, FRANCIS W., & VENABLES, J.E. AMANDA. *The Goodwood estate archives vol. II.* xx, 168pp. 0-900801-25-5. 1972. £10.00.
STEER, FRANCIS W. *Arundel Castle archives, vol. II.* vii, 242pp. 0-900801-27-1. 1972. £10.00.
STEER, FRANCIS W., ed. *Arundel Castle archives, vol. III.* ix, 108pp. 0-900801-39-5. 1976. £10.00.
STEER, FRANCIS W., ed. *Arundel Castle archives, vol. IV.* xiv, 179pp. 0-900801-44-1. 1980. £10.00.
STEER, FRANCIS W., & OSBORNE, NOEL H. *Petworth House archives vol. 1.* xvi, 207pp. 0-90081-06-9. 1968. £10.00.
WILKINSON, PETER. *Genealogists guide to the West Sussex Record Office.* 3rd ed. 90pp. 0-86260-300-5. £6.75 + p&p.
Ancient charters of the Dean and Chapter of Chichester, 689-1674. 2nd ed. 41pp. 0-900801-26-3. 1976. £2.00.
Family history in West Sussex. Local history mini-guide to sources. **6.** 1996. £1.25 + p&p.
Index to the consecrations and faculties in the Diocese of Chichester before 1850. 42pp. 0-900801-19-0. £2.00.

WARWICKSHIRE
Birmingham Local Studies & History Services
Central Library, Chamberlain Square, Birmingham B3 3HQ
MCKENNA, JOSEPH. *In the midst of life: a history of the burial grounds of Birmingham.* 0-709301-88-X. 1992. £3.50.

WESTMORLAND
See Cumberland

WILTSHIRE
Wiltshire Buildings Record
Libraries & Heritage Headquarters, Bythesea Road, Trowbridge, Wilts., BA14 8BS
Phone: (01225) 713740
SLOCOMBE, PAM, ed. *Architects and building craftsmen with work in Wiltshire.* 0-9527933-0-X. 1996. £6.00 + p&p 80p.

WORCESTERSHIRE
Dudley Libraries
Archives and Local History Service, Mount Pleasant Street, Coseley, Dudley, WV14 9JR
Phone: (01384) 812770

Handlist of parish registers. 30p + p&p 25p.
Handlist of nonconformist records. 30p + p&p 25p.
Brief checklist of sources for genealogical enquiries. 30p + p&p 25p.
Local newspapers: list of holdings. 30p + p&p 25p.
Census enumerators returns, electoral rolls and rate books: list of holdings. 30p + p&p 25p.
Directories: list of holdings. 50p + p&p 25p.
Reading list for family historians. £1.25 + p&p 50p.

Worcestershire Record Office
County Hall, Spetchley Road, Worcester WR5 2NP
www.worcestershire.gov.uk
Email: RecordOffice@worcestershire.gov.uk
(formerly Hereford & Worcester Record Office)
Genealogical resources in Worcestershire, 1. Parish registers and transcripts. 7th ed. 1996. £3.00.

TOHILL, MARGARET. *A handlist of trade directories, almanacks, etc., held by the Worcester branches of Hereford and Worcester Record Office, and some Worcestershire public libraries.* Handlist 2. 1989. £3.95.
Census returns 1841-1891: holdings available at Worcester Record Office and other local record offices and libraries. Handlist 3. 1996. £1.00.
Various free leaflets are also available.

YORKSHIRE
Borthwick Institute
St. Anthony's Hall, Peasholme Green, York, YO1 2PW
Phone: (01904) 642315

Borthwick papers
22. PURVIS, J.S. *The records of the Admiralty Court of York.* 1962. £3.00 + 35p p&p.
37. ROBINSON, D. *Beneficed clergy in Cleveland and the East Riding, 1305-40.* 1970. £3.00 + 35p p&p.
61. HASTINGS, R.P. *Poverty and the poor law in the North Riding of Yorkshire, 1780-1837.* 1982. £3.00 + 35p p&p.
66. BROWN, SANDRA. *The medieval courts of the York Minster Peculiar.* 1984. £3.00 + 35p p&p.

Many other Borthwick papers are also available; these are the ones most likely to be of genealogical interest.

Borthwick texts and calendars.
2. SMITH, D.M., ed. *A calendar of the register of Robert Waldby, Archbishop of York, 1397.* 1974. £3.00 + 70p p&p
4. SHEILS, W.J., ed. *Archbishop Grindal's visitation to the Diocese of York, 1575.* 1977. £5.00 + 70p p&p.
5. BURTON, J.E., ed. *The cartulary of the treasurer of York Minster and related documents.* 1978. £5.00 + p&p 70p.
6. LONGLEY, K.M., ed. *Ecclesiastical cause papers at York, I: Dean and Chapters court 1350-1843.* 1980. £4.50 + p&p 85p.
8. SWANSON, R., ed. *A calendar of the register of Richard Scrope, Archbishop of York, 1398-1405. Part I.* 1981. £5.50 + p&p 90p.
9. SHEILS, W.J., ed. *Ecclesiastical cause papers at York, II: files transmitted on appeal 1500-1833.* 1983. £5.00 + p&p 80p.

10. CROSS, C., ed. *York clergy wills, 1520-1600, I: minster clergy.* 1984. £5.50 + p&p 90p.
11. SWANSON, R., ed. *A calendar of the register of Richard Scrope, Archbishop of York 1398-1405. Pt.2.* 1985. £5.75 + p&p 90p.
13. SHEILS, W.J., ed. *Restoration exhibit books and the northern clergy, 1662-1664.* 1987. £5.00 + p&p 55p.
14. SMITH, D.M., ed. *Ecclesiastical cause papers at York: the Court of York 1301-1399.* 1988. £6.50 + p&p 65p.
15. CROSS, C., ed. *York clergy wills, 1520-1600, II: city clergy.* 1989. £7.00 + p&p 65p.
16. SMITH, D.M. *A guide to the archives of the Merchant Adventurers of York.* 1990. £10.00 + p&p 90p.
19. EVANS, PETER. *Church fabric in the York Diocese 1613-1899: the records of the Archbishops' faculty jurisdiction. A handlist.* 1995. £11.50 + p&p 90p.
20. WEBB, C.C., ed. *The churchwardens accounts of St. Michael, Spurriergate, York, 1518-1548.* 2 vols. 1997. £17.50 + p&p £2.30.
21. ANNESLEY, C., & HOSKIN, P., ed. *Archbishop Drummond's visitation returns 1714, vol. I: Yorkshire parishes A-G.* 1997. £11.50 + p&p £1.05.
22. BURG, JUDITH. *A guide to the Rowntree and Mackintosh company archives 1862-1969.* 1998. £11.50 + p&p £1.25.

Borthwick Wallets.

1. RYCRAFT, A. *Sixteenth and seventeenth century handwriting, series I.* 1969. £2.50 + p&p 45p.
2. RYCRAFT, A. *Sixteenth and seventeenth century handwriting, series II.* 1969. £2.50 + p&p 45p.
3. RYCRAFT, A. *English medieval handwriting.* 1971. £2.50 + p&p 45p.
4. RYCRAFT, A. *Sixteenth and seventeenth century wills, inventories and other probate documents.* 1973. £2.50 + p&p 45p.
6. SMITH, D.M. *Medieval Latin documents, series I: diocesan records.* 1979. £2.50 + p&p 45p.
7. SMITH, D.M. *Medieval Latin documents, series II: probate records.* 1984. £2.50 + p&p 45p.

Occasional papers

2. WEBB, C.C. *A guide to genealogical sources in the Borthwick Institute of Historical Research.* 3rd ed. 1996. £3.00 + p&p 40p.

Lists and indexes

1. NEWSOME, E.B., & NEWSOME, W.R. *An index of marriage bonds and allegations in the peculiar jurisdiction of the Dean and Chapter of York, 1613-1839.* 1985. £7.00 + p&p £2.00.
2. *A list of deposited parish registers in the Borthwick Institute.* £1.00 (post free).
3. NEWSOME, E.B., & NEWSOME, W.R. *An index to the Archbishop of York's marriage bonds and allegations 1830-1839.* 1986. £10.00 + p&p £3.20.
4. NEWSOME, E.B., & NEWSOME, W.R. *An index to the Archbishop of York's marriage bonds and allegations 1820-1829.* 1983. £10.00 + p&p £3.20.
5. NEWSOME, E.B., & NEWSOME, W.R. *An index to the Archbishop of York's marriage bonds and allegations 1800-1809.* 1989. £10.00 + p&p £3.20.
7. NEWSOME, E.B. *An index to the Archbishop of York's marriage bonds and allegations 1790-1799.* 1990. £10.00 + p&p £3.20.
8. SMITH, D.M. *Historical records available on microfilm in York.* 1990. Free.
9. NEWSOME, E.B. *An index to the Archbishop of York's marriage bonds and allegations 1780-1789.* 1991. £10.00 + p&p £3.20.
10. NEWSOME, E.B. *An index to the Archbishop of York's marriage bonds and allegations 1765-1779.* 1993. £10.00. £3.20.
11. FONGE, C.R. *Tithe awards and maps at the Borthwick Institute: a handlist.* 1994. £3.00 + p&p 55p.
12. SMITH, D.M. *A guide to the archives of the Company of Merchant Taylors in the City of York.* 1994. £2.00 + p&p 40p.
13. NEWSOME, E.B. *An index to the Archbishop of York's marriage bonds and allegations 1750-1764.* 1994. £10.00 + p&p £3.20.
14. *A short guide to historical sources in York.* 1994. Free.
15. NEWSOME, E.B. *An index to the Archbishop of York's marriage bonds and allegations 1735-1749.* 1996. £12.00 + p&p £3.30.

16. SMITH, DAVID M. *Company of Merchant Taylors in the City of York: register of admissions 1560-1835*. 1996. £5.00 + p&p 70p.
17. BISSET, ANNA B. *The Eastland Company, York Residence: register of admissions to the freedom 1646-1689, and register of apprentices, 1642-1696*. 1996. £2.00 + p&p 40p.
18. SMITH, DAVID M. *The Company of Merchant Adventurers in the City of York: register of admissions 1581-1835*. 1996. £4.00 + 55p p&p.
19. BUCHANAN, ALEXANDRINA. *A guide to archival accessions at the Borthwick Institute 1981-1996*. 1997. £10.00 + p&p £1.25.

Barnsley Archive Service

Central Library, Shambles Street, Barnsley, S70 2JF
Phone: (01226) 773930
Email: Library-Librarian@Barnsley.ac.uk
BARNSLEY ARCHIVES AND LOCAL STUDIES DEPARTMENT. *The family history handbook*. £1.25 + p&p.

East Riding Archives and Record Service

East Riding of Yorkshire Council, County Hall, Beverley, HU17 9BA
Phone: (01482) 885007
Handlist of parish registers on deposit. 50p + p&p 31p.
Handlist of non-Anglican church records. 50p + p&p 31p.
Handlist of Society of Friends and non-parochial registers on microfilm. 50p + p&p 20p.
The East Riding register of deeds: a guide for users. 2nd ed. 50p + p&p 31p.
East Riding police: an index, 1843-1927. £2.50 + p&p 61p.
Various free leaflets are also available.

Hull City Record Office

79 Lowgate, Hull, HU1 2AA
Phone: (01482) 885007
STANEWELL, L.M. *Calendar of the ancient records, letters, miscellaneous old documents, in the archives of the Corporation of Kingston upon Hull: deeds, letters and administrative records, 1300-1800*. 494pp. £4.60.
OXLEY, G.W. *Guide to the Kingston upon Hull Record Office. Part I. Records of local authorities whose areas or functions were taken over by the former Borough of Kingston upon Hull*. 14pp. 40p.
The people in Hull in 1695 and 1697: an index to the poll tax assessment. 92pp. 0-904767-23-X. £1.55.

Hull College Local History Unit

Park Street Centre, Hull College, Park Street, Hull HU2 8RR
Phone: (01482) 329943
ABLITT, PETER. *The early history of the Hull Dockers Rugby League Club*. 1997. £1.50 Many names of players.
KETCHELL, C. *Famous local people: a resource guide*. 1997. £1.00.
Hull directory 1784. Reprint. £2.50.
Battle's Hull directory 1791. Reprint. £6.00.
Clayton's Hull directory 1803. 3 pts. £7.00 or £2.50 per pt.
Battle's Hull directory 1806-7. 3 pts. £7.00 or £2.50 per pt.
Battle's Hull directory 1814-15. 3 pts. £7.00 or £2.50 per pt.
Battle's Hull directory 1817. 3 pts. £7.00 or £2.50 per pt.
BARNARD, ROBERT. *Hull poll books as directories*. 1997. £5.00.
READHEAD, MICHAEL J. *Horseplay in Westbourne Avenue: a history of polo in Hull*. 1-898398-26-7. 1998. £2.50.

North Yorkshire County Record Office

County Hall, Northallerton, DL7 8AF
EMSLEY, CLIVE. *North Riding naval recruits: documents relating to the Quota Acts and the quota men, 1795-1797*. £5.00.
ROBERTS, F., & ROBERTS, J. *Bainbridge in the middle of the nineteenth century*. £5.00.
WENHAM, L.P., ed. *Richmond burgages*. £5.00.
Bilsdale surveys, 1637-1851, including the 1851 census returns. £5.00.
Craven muster roll 1803. £7.00.
Fylingdales census returns 1851 and 1861. £5.00.
Malton in the early nineteenth-century: surveys and population analyses. £5.00.
Scarborough records 1600-1640. £12.50.
Scarborough records 1641-1660. £10.00.

Settle in the middle of the nineteenth century: tithe apportionment 1843, and census return 1851. £5.00.

The Swaledale estates of the Wharton family in the 17th century: documents illustrating the development of the lead mines, the relations between landlords and tenants, and the extent and management of the estates. £7.00.

To escape the monster's clutches: notes and documents illustrating the preparations in North Yorkshire to repel the invasion threatened by the French from 1793. £5.00.

Guide no. 1: calendars, transcripts and microfilms in the Record Office. 1995. £7.00.

Guide no. 2: parish registers, census returns, land tax assessment, tithe apportionments, enclosure awards in the Record Office. £1.25.

Guide no. 3: maps and plans. List of North Yorkshire and North Riding maps and plans in the Record Office. £5.00.

Guide no. 4: enclosure awards in the Record Office. £5.00.

Guide no. 5: North Yorkshire parish registers. £1.25.

Guide no. 6: North Yorkshire gazetteer of townships and parishes. £1.25.

Guide no. 7: list of non-conformist and chapel registers, and of monumental inscriptions in the record office. 75p.

Sheffield Archives
52, Shoreham Street, Sheffield, S1 4SP.

Guide to the Fairbank collection. 1936. £1.00.

Catalogue of the Arundel Castle manuscripts in the Sheffield City Libraries. 1965. £15.00.

Manuscript collections in the Sheffield City Libraries. 1956. £2.50.

MEREDITH, ROSAMUND. *Guide to the manuscript collections. Supplement 1956-1976.* 1977. £7.00.

Family history guides
£5.00 + p&p £1.00 the set.
1. *Census returns.* £1.00 + p&p 75p.
2. *Monumental inscriptions.* £1.00 + p&p 75p.
3. *Bishops transcripts.* £1.00 + p&p 75p.
4. *Parish registers.* £1.50 + p&p 75p.
5. *Copies of parish registers held by other register offices.* £1.00 + p&p 75p.

6. *Nonconformist registers.* £1.00 + p&p 75p.
7. *Registers of burials in churchyards, chapelyards and cemeteries.* £1.00 + p&p 75p.

SCOTLAND
General Register Office for Scotland
New Register House, Edinburgh, EH1 3YT
Phone: (0131) 3144422
Email: helen.borthwick@gro.scotland.gov.uk
http://www.origins.net

Civil parish map index. Guide for researchers 1. 1989. £2.50.

Personal names in Scotland. 5th ed. 0951317555. 1991. £2.50. Includes various lists of popular names.

The registration districts of Scotland from 1855. Guide for researchers 2. 1994. £4.50.

Computer system for searching the indexes. £2.50.

Ancestral research. Video. 1993. £8.99. Guide to searching at New Register House.

Microfilm copies of parish registers, census records, etc., are also available.

National Library of Scotland
George IV Bridge, Edinburgh, EH1 1EW
FERGUSON, JOAN P.S. *Scottish family histories.* 2nd ed. 254pp. 0-902220-68-3. 1986. £14.95 + p&p £3.00.

Scottish Record Office
General Register House, Princes Street, Edinburgh EH1 3YY.
Phone: (0131) 5351314
N.B. Some titles listed below are actually published by the Stationary Office, as noted.

Annual report of the Keeper of the Records of Scotland, 1996-7. £5.50. Previous reports also available.

ROSIE, ALISON. *Scottish handwriting 1500-1700: a self-help pack.* 1-870874-04.8. [199-?] £8.00. Joint publication with Scottish Records Association.

SCOTTISH RECORD OFFICE. *A short guide to the records.* 24pp. [199-?] £2.50.

SCOTTISH RECORD OFFICE. *List of gifts and deposits in the Scottish Record Office.* v.1. 122pp. 11-490690-4. 1971. £5.00. v.2. 116pp. 0-11-491431-1. 1976. £5.00.

SCOTTISH RECORD OFFICE. *A military source list part two: a guide to sources on military history in government and other records held by the Scottish Record Office.* 170pp. 1-870874-29-3. £11.00.

SCOTTISH RECORD OFFICE. *A Jacobite source list.* 77pp. 1-870874-20-X [199-?] £7.25.

SCOTTISH RECORD OFFICE. *The guide to the national archives of Scotland.* 253pp. 0-11-495791-6. Stationary Office, 1998. £50.00. Jointly published with the Stair Society.

SINCLAIR, CECIL J. *Tracing Scottish local history in the Scottish Record Offices.* 176 pp. 0-11-495231-0. Stationary Office, 1994. £7.95.

SINCLAIR, CECIL J. *Tracing your Scottish ancestors: a guide to ancestry research in the Scottish Record Office.* 155pp. Rev. ed. 0-11-495865-3. Stationary Office, 1997. £9.99.

WILLS, VIRGINIA, ed. *Statistics of the annexed estates 1755-1769.* 74pp. 0-11-490991-1. H.M.S.O., 1973. £3.00.

Dumfries & Galloway Regional Library Service

Ewart Library, Catherine Street, Dumfries, DG1 1JB
Phone (01387) 253820
Email: alastair__johnston@dumgal.gov.net

The book of the Irvings: the Irvins, Irvines or Erineveines, or any other spelling of the name: an old Scots border clan. 0-946280-20-7. £75.00.

Pigot and Slater's Dumfries and Galloway 19th century trade directories. 0-946280-12-6. £12.50.

Wigtown Free Press index: personal names.
v.1. *1843-1880.* 0-946280-00-2. £20.00.
v.2 *1881-1914.* 0-946280-05-3. £20.00.
v.3. *1915-1925.* 0-946280-10-X. £20.00.

Wigtown Free Press index: subject index 1843-1925. 0-946280-11-8. £14.00.

Census '51 parish indexes:
Applegarth. £2.00.
Canonbie. £4.00.
Cummertrees. £2.00.
Durisdeer. £2.00.
Johnstone. £2.00.
Balmadellan. £2.00.

Information booklets
Ancestor hunting in Dumfries Archives Centre. 60p.
Court records. 25p.
Valuation, taxation and rating records. 40p.
Monumental inscriptions. 25p.
A variety of source lists are also available, priced at 10p - 40p.

Glasgow Libraries and Archives

The Mitchell Library, North Street, Glasgow, G3 7DN

ESCOTT, ANNE. *Census returns and old parochial registers on microfilm: a directory of public library holdings in the West of Scotland.* Rev. ed. 0-906169-14-3. 1986. 50p.

Tracing your ancestors: Mitchell Library and Archive sources. 1998. Free.

Archives and Business Records Centre

University of Glasgow, 77-81, Dumbarton Road, Glasgow, G11 6PE
Phone: (0141) 3305515

Glasgow University Archives and Business Records Centre: list of collections. 1998. £5.00 + p&p £1.00.

WALES

National Library of Wales

Aberystwyth, Dyfed, SY23 3BU
Phone: (01970) 632800

Guide to the Department of Manuscripts and Records, the National Library of Wales. 0-907158-80-3. 1994. £15.00 + p&p £2.00.

HENSON, NIA. *Index of the probate records of the Bangor Consistory Court. Volume I. Pre-1700.* 1-901833-95-9. 1980. £6.00 + p&p £3.00.

IFANS, DAFYDD, ed. *Nonconformist registers of Wales / Cofresti Anghydffurfiol Cymru.* 0-907158-75-7. 1994. £14.50 + p&p £2.35.

JONES, NANSI C. *Archdeaconry of Brecon probate records. Volume I. Pre-1600.* 0-907158-39-0. 1989. £10.00 + p&p £3.00.

OWENS, B.G. *The Ilston book: earliest register of Welsh Baptists.* 0-907158-87-0. 1996. £19.50 + p&p £2.50.

SIDDONS, MICHAEL POWELL. *The development of Welsh heraldry.* 3 vols. 0-907158-51-X. 1991-3. £150 + p&p £15.00.
SIDDONS, MICHAEL POWELL. *Welsh pedigree rolls.* 1-907158-90-0. 1996. £7.00 + p&p £1.00.
WILLIAMS, C.J., & WATTS-WILLIAMS, J. *Parish registers of Wales / Cofresti Plwyf Cymru.* Reprint forthcoming.

Denbighshire Record Office
46, Clwyd Street, Ruthin, LL15 1HP
Phone (01824) 703077
For publications formerly issued by Clwyd Record Office, see Flintshire Record Office.

Flintshire Record Office
The Old Rectory, Rectory Lane, Hawarden, Flintshire, CH5 3NR
Phone: (01244) 532364
Formerly published by Clwyd Record Office.
Guide to the parish registers of Clwyd. xii, 124pp. £7.95 + p&p £1.80.
Handlist of the Denbighshire quarter sessions records. 2 vols. ix, 201pp; v, 196pp. £12.95 + p&p £4.80.
Llangollen directory. 12pp. £1.00 + p&p 55p. Facsimile of a section of the *Postal directory of Flintshire and Denbighshire,* 1886.

Glamorgan Record Office
The Glamorgan Building, Cathays Park, Cardiff, CF3 3NE
Phone (01222) 780282
A vanished house. 24pp. £1.00. Margam.
A glossary of medieval and post-medieval terms for South Wales. 164pp. 1988 (with supplement 1989) £10.00 + p&p £2.00.
Fonmon Castle. 36pp. 3rd ed. 1985. £2.00 + p&p £1.50.
On the parish: the poor law before 1834. Source book. 1988. £6.95 + p&p £1.50.
A catalogue of Glamorgan estate maps. 144 pp. 1992. £25.00 + p&p £3.00.
Poor relief in Merthyr Tydfil Union in Victorian times. 199pp. 1992. £15.00 + p&p £2.50.
Annual reports. Most years available from 1974. £3.0 per issue.
A variety of *guides to sources and methods* and *information sheets* etc., are available free.

OVERSEAS

State Library of New South Wales Press
Macquarie St, Sydney, N.S.W. 2000, Australia
RUDD, EDWINA. *Pathfinder no. 2: sources of information in the State Library of New South Wales on births, deaths and marriages in England.* 0-7305-7005-3. 1990. $A9.50.
HEWITT, LYNNE. *Pathfinder no. 5: sources of information in the State Library of New South Wales on births, deaths and marriages in Scotland.* 0-7305-8929-3. 1995. $A12.95.

Library of Virginia
The Library Shop, 800E Broad Street, Richmond, VA., 23219-1905, U.S.A.
WALNE, PETER. *English wills: probate records in England and Wales.* 1964 (1981 reprint). $US7.95.

Subject Index

Brackets indicate counties, using Chapman's system of county codes.

Aberdeen Royal Infirmary 95
Accounts
  Battle Abbey (Ssx) 85
  Beaulieu Abbey (Ham) 65
  Chancellors Farm (Som) 20
  Cheshire 74
  Clark Family 86
  Cornwall 64
  Exeter Cathedral (Dev) 69
  Fowlmere (Cam) 67
  Godinton (Ken) 51
  Great Chalfield (Wil) 86
  Green, T. 73
  Kent 12
  Kniveton (Dby) 101
  London Bridge 77
  Malmesbury (Wil) 86
  Mapperton (Dor) 70
  Neath (Gla) 33
  Norwich Cathedral (Nfk) 78
  Oxford. Merton College 81
  Plymouth (Dev) 68
  Roberts Family 85
  Taylor, C 75
  Thetford Priory (Nfk) 78
  Wiltshire 86
Act Books
  Canterbury Province 56
  Gloucester 72
  Salisbury Cathedral (Wil) 86
  Wells Cathedral (Som) 82
Actors 46
Acts of Parliament 15
Administration Bonds 56, 57
  America 13, 22
  Berkshire Archdeaconry 53
  Canterbury Diocese 55, 56
  Chester Diocese 74
  Chichester Diocese 56
  Cornwall 55, 56
  Devon 55, 56
  Dorset 54, 55
  Leicester Archdeaconry 54, 55
  Lewes Archdeaconry 54
  Lichfield & Coventry Diocese 53
  Lincoln Diocese 55
  Northampton Archdeaconry 56, 57, 82
  Somerset 20
  Stow Archdeaconry (Lin) 56
  Taunton Archdeaconry (Som) 55

Worcester Diocese 54, 55
Admiralty Court, York 113
Adoption Records 9, 34
Airmen 25, 43, 45, 100
Aliens 62
Ancestral File 30
Annuities 40
Antiquaries Collections
  Gloucestershire 72
  Oxford 79
Apprentices 33
  Aberdeen 31
  Bristol 72
  Fife 97
  Gloucester 72
  Kingston on Thames (Sry) 84
  London 22
  Oxford 81
  Walkhampton (Dev) 17
  Wiltshire 86, 87
  Worcester 88
Architects 32
  Wiltshire 113
Archives 38, 52, 101, 103
  Bibliography 101
  Bodleian Library 36
  Bristol, Port of 106
  Cheshire 103
  Cornwall 104
  Derbyshire 104
  Devon 105
  Dorset 105
  Essex 106
  Fife 97
  Glamorganshire 118
  Glasgow 117
  Gloucestershire 106
  Hampshire 108
  Horsham Museum (Ssx) 112
  Lancashire 108
  Leicester University 109
  London 109
  Newcastle (Nbl) 110
  Norfolk 110
  Oxford University 80
  Oxford. Balliol College 38
  Oxford. New College 30
  Oxfordshire 80, 110
  Salford (Lan) 109
  Sark 63

Archives (*continued*)
  Scotland 94, 116, 117
  Sheffield (Yks) 116
  Shropshire 110
  Southampton (Ham) 108
  Southwark (Sry) 111
  Sussex, West 112
  Sutton (Sry) 111
  Tameside (Chs) 103
  Wales 117
  Wigan (Lan) 109
  Winchester (Ham) 108
  Worcestershire 113
  York 114, 115
  Yorkshire. North Riding 116
Armories 13, 26
  Derbyshire 68
Arms 65
Army Records 12, 100, 117
  World War I 100
Artists 29
Assize Records
  Lincolnshire 75
  Somerset 82
  Western Circuit 65
  Wiltshire 86
Association Oath 23
Authors 19, 46
Bankrupts 33
Baptist Records
  Blunham (Bdf) 102
  Ilston (Gla) 117
Bastards
  Chelsea (Mdx) 77
Battle of Hastings 99
Battle of Waterloo 49
Bengal Army 43
Bibliography 23, 64, 92, 99, 101, 110, 113
  Bath (Som) 106
  Bedfordshire 66
  Bristol 106
  Devon 104
  Dorset 107
  Lancashire 108
  Lincoln 76
  London 32, 52, 62, 109
  Norfolk 12
  Oxford 80
  Oxfordshire 80, 81
  Scotland 116
  Southampton (Ham) 108
  Stockport (Chs) 104
  Suffolk 83
Bigland Manuscripts 61
Biographical Dictionaries 8, 19, 52
  Authors 19
  Buckland in the Moor (Dev) 16, 17
  East Anglia 26

Essex 37
Hull (Yks) 115
Normans 8
Peckham (Sry) 111
Scots in America 23
Southampton (Ham) 108
Tower Hamlets (Mdx) 110
Victorian 8
Wales 14
Women 32
Birth Briefs
  Aberdeen 31
Births, Marriages & Deaths 31, 118
  Aberdeen 95
  Lancaster 33
  Northumberland 78
  Overseas 109
  Scotland 118
  Seamen 28
  Staffordshire 83
Bishops' Acta
  Bath & Wells Diocese 51
  Canterbury Diocese 51
  Chichester Diocese 58
  Coventry & Lichfield Diocese 51
  Exeter Diocese 51
  Hereford Diocese 51
  Llandaff Diocese 33, 98
  London Diocese 51
  Norwich Diocese 51
  Saint Davids Diocese 99
  Winchester Diocese 51
  Worcester Diocese 51
Bishops' Registers 64
  Canterbury Diocese 58
  Canterbury Province 58, 59
  Carlisle Diocese 58, 59
  Chichester Diocese 85
  Coventry & Lichfield Diocese 59
  Durham Diocese 70, 71
  Exeter Diocese 58, 59, 68
  Hereford Diocese 58
  Lincoln Diocese 58, 59, 75, 76
  Norwich Diocese 59
  Nottingham Diocese 71
  Rochester Diocese 58
  Salisbury Diocese 58, 59
  Winchester Diocese 58, 107
  Worcester Diocese 87, 88, 101
  York Diocese 59, 70, 71, 113, 114
Bishops' Transcripts 23
Black People
  Kent 42
Bodleian Library 80, 81
Boer War 43
Boldon Book 38
Book Trades 33
  Devon 33

Faversham (Ken) 73
London 32, 33
Worcester 88
Borough Records 39
   Arbroath (Ans) 94
   Banbury (Oxf) 82
   Boston (Lin) 76
   Bristol 72
   Calne (Wil) 86
   Dunfermline (Fif) 94
   Dunwich (Sfk) 84
   Evesham (Wor) 88
   Exeter (Dev) 69
   Grantham (Lin) 77
   Great Yarmouth (Nfk) 77
   Henley (Oxf) 81
   High Wycombe (Bkm) 66
   Hull (Yks) 115
   Ipswich (Sfk) 83
   Leeds (Yks) 92
   Lewes (Ssx) 85
   Liverpool (Lan) 75
   London 77, 99, 109
   Norwich (Nfk) 77, 78
   Oxford 79, 80
   Paisley (Rfw) 33
   Poole (Dor) 105
   Portsmouth (Ham) 107
   Reading (Brk) 66
   Scarborough (Yks) 115
   Southampton (Ham) 108
   Swansea (Cmn) 33
   Weymouth (Dor) 69
   Wiltshire 86, 87
   Winchelsea (Ssx) 112
   Witney (Oxf) 81
   Woodstock (Oxf) 81
   Worcester 88
   York 71, 90
Borthwick Institute 114, 115
Boundaries 11, 12, 64
Brewers
   Newcastle (Nbl) 110
British Record Society 52
Burgess Rolls 23
   Aberdeen 31
   Banff 31
   Elgin (Mor) 31
   Fife 17
   Inveraray (Arl) 94
   Kirkcudbright 92
   Richmond (Yks) 115
   Saint Andrews (Fif) 17
   Stirling 96
Burnet Morris Index 104
Business Records 101, 109
   Bristol 106
   Foley Family 88

Mackintosh 114
Rowntree 114
Staffordshire 111
Stour Valley (Wor) 88
Cambridge University Library 103
Carpenters 41
Cartularies
   Abingdon (Brk) 81
   Aldgate (Lnd) 77
   Bec (France) 64
   Bilsington (Ken) 51
   Blythburgh Priory (Sfk) 84
   Boarstall (Bkm) 80
   Bradenstoke Priory (Wil) 87
   Bristol. Saint Augustine's Abbey 72
   Canonsleigh Abbey (Dev) 68
   Canterbury (Ken) 51
   Carisbrooke Priory (Ham) 108
   Clare Friary (Sfk) 84
   Clerkenwell (Mdx) 64
   Creake Abbey (Nfk) 77
   Edington (Wil) 87
   Essex 52
   Eye Priory (Sfk) 84
   Eynsham (Oxf) 80
   Fraunces family 65
   Glastonbury (Som) 82
   Hobhouse Family 87
   Hungerford Family 87
   Kirkstall (Yks) 91
   Lanercost (Cul) 67, 72
   Launceston Priory (Con) 69
   Leiston Abbey (Sfk) 84
   Lincoln Cathedral 75, 76
   Missenden Abbey (Bkm) 66
   Oseney (Oxf) 80
   Oxford. St. John the Baptist 80
   Pyel Family 65
   Reading (Brk) 65
   Rede Family 80
   Saint Frideswide, Oxford 79
   Saint Michaels Mount (Con) 68
   Sibton Abbey (Sfk) 84
   Southwick Priory (Ham) 107
   Stoke by Clare (Sfk) 84
   Thetford Priory (Nfk) 52
   Worcester 64
   York Minster 113
Census 7, 23, 27, 31, 62, 63, 100
   Annan (Dfs) 94
   Buckland in the Moor (Dev) 17
   Burntwood (Sts) 83
   Cheshire 103
   Dartmoor (Dev) 17
   Dudley (Wor) 113
   Felton (Nbd) 78
   Herefordshire 108
   Kent 8, 42

Census (*continued*)
  Leeming Bar (Yks) 28
  London 31
  Portpatrick (Wig) 94
  Scotland 95, 116
  Scotland, West 117
  Sheffield (Yks) 116
  Staffordshire 111
  Sussex 35
  Worcestershire 113
  Yorkshire. North Riding 116
  Yorkshire. West Riding 29
Census, Pre-1841 22, 30
  Aberdeen 95
  Bradford (Yks) 28
  Cardington (Bdf) 65
  Craig (Ans) 95
  Puddletown (Dor) 70
  Stoke on Trent 83
  Wakefield (Yks) 28
  Westmorland 104
Census 1801
  Leeds (Yks) 28
  Peterhead (Abd) 95
  Ticehurst (Ssx) 35
  Wednesbury (Sts) 29
  York 29
Census 1811
  Kilburn (Yks) 28
  Lewes (Ssx) 35
  Middleton (Yks) 28
  South Otterington (Yks) 28
  Thirsk (Yks) 29
  York 29
Census 1821
  Chiddingly (Ssx) 35
  Hailsham (Ssx) 35
  Hartfield (Ssx) 35
  Hastings (Ssx) 35
  Oswaldkirk (Yks) 29
  Princes Risborough (Bkm) 9
  Stansfield (Yks) 29
  Thirsk (Yks) 29
  York 29
Census 1831
  East Dean (Ssx) 35
  Friston (Ssx) 35
  Hastings (Ssx) 35
  Lewes (Ssx) 35
  Princes Risborough (Bkm) 9
  Tenterden (Ken) 42
  Ticehurst (Ssx) 35
  Uckfield (Ssx) 35
Census 1838
  Withyham (Ssx) 35
Census 1841
  Buckinghamshire Workhouses 10
  Kirkcudbrightshire 97
  Largs (Ayr) 97
  Midlothian 98
  Yorkshire. West Riding 28
Census 1851
  Aylesbury (Bkm) 10
  Banffshire 95
  Beaconsfield (Bkm) 10
  Bilsdale (Yks) 115
  Devon 19
  Edinburgh (Mln) 92
  Fylingdales (Yks) 115
  Great Hampden (Bkm) 10
  Killearnon (Roc) 97
  Kiltearn (Roc) 97
  Kincardine (Roc) 97
  Kirkcudbrightshire 97
  Knockbain (Roc) 97
  Marlow (Bkm) 9
  Norfolk 19
  Princes Risborough (Bkm) 10
  Settle (Yks) 116
  Tain (Roc) 97
  Warwickshire 19
  West Derby (Lan) 36
  Wick (Cai) 97
  Wigtownshire 117
Census 1861
  Fylingdales (Yks) 115
  Kent 12
Census 1863
  Ewhurst (Ssx) 35
Census 1880
  Castle Bolton (Yks) 29
Census 1881
  Saltney (Chs) 103
Census 1891 32
  Backwell (Som) 82
  Consett (Dur) 50
  Somerset, North 20
Chairmakers 9
Chancery Proceedings 36, 40, 53, 54, 63, 69, 100
Chantry Certificates
  London 77
  Middlesex 77
Charities
  Bledlow (Bkm) 9
Chronology 52, 64
Church Court Records 30, 39
  Banbury (Oxf) 82
  Buckingham Archdeaconry 66
  Canterbury Diocese 39
  Essex 105
  Lincoln Diocese 76
  London Diocese 77
  Norwich Diocese 65
  Oxford Diocese 110
  York Minster 113

Churchwardens' Accounts 15
  Ashburton 69
  Bishops Stortford (Hrt) 73
  Boxford (Sfk) 84
  Chipping Campden (Gls) 11
  Clevedon (Som) 20
  Cornwall 104
  Luxborough (Som) 21
  Tewkesbury (Gls) 72
  Turvey (Bdf) 66
  Walkhampton (Dev) 17
  York. St Michael, Spurriergate 114
Circumcision Registers
  London 47
Civil Registration 100
Civil War
  Bedfordshire 65
Clans 13, 25, 32
Clergy 59
  Beverley (Yks) 91
  Buckrose Deanery 91
  Craven Deanery (Yks) 90
  Dickering Deanery (Yks) 90
  Durham Diocese 70
  Lincoln Diocese 76
  London 77
  Northampton Archdeaconry 75
  Salisbury Diocese 87
  Scotland 8
  Suffolk 83
  Wiltshire 86
  Winchester Diocese 39
  York 114
  York Diocese 114
  Yorkshire 91
  Yorkshire. East Riding 113
Clergy, Nonconformist 42
  Kent 42
Clockmakers
  Gloucestershire 37
  Norfolk 37
  Oxfordshire 81
  Scotland 92
  Shropshire 38
Close Rolls 36
Coats of Arms
  Wales 27
College of Arms 61
Commissioners of Sewers 37
Commonties 94
Computers 15, 25, 47, 116
  Programs 15, 25, 42
Confirmation Register
  Bishop Leyburn's 7
Congregationalist Records
  Aberdeen 95
  Bedford 65
  Isleham (Cam) 67

Southill (Bdf) 102
Woburn (Bdf) 102
Constables 52
Constables Accounts
  Upton (Ntt) 79
Coroners Records
  Buckinghamshire 67
  London 28
  Nottinghamshire 79
  Sussex 85, 100
  Wiltshire 87
Court of Augmentations
  Bedfordshire 65
Court of the Official
  Scotland 94
Crests 23, 27
  Suffolk 84
Crimean War 43
Criminal Records 13, 48, 100
  Aberdeen 95
  Banbury (Oxf) 82
  Bodmin (Con) 41
  Cambridgeshire 67
  Dorset 20
  Hastings (Ssx) 35
  Lincolnshire 109
  Somerset 20
  Wilton (Som) 20, 21
  Wiltshire 87
Curia Regis Rolls 37
Customs Records
  Boston (Lin) 76
  Chester 74
  Exeter (Dev) 69
  Hull (Yks) 91
  Newcastle (Nbl) 72
  Norwich (Nfk) 77
  Portsmouth (Ham) 107
Debtors
  London 12
  Wiltshire 86
Deeds & Charters 15, 36, 37, 51, 59, 102
  Amesbury (Wil) 86
  Antrobus Family 86
  Bath (Som) 82
  Bury St.Edmunds (Sfk) 51, 84
  Butley Priory (Sfk) 84
  Chester, Earldom of 74
  Chichester Cathedral (Ssx) 112
  Chisholm (Inv) 94
  Devon 68, 69
  Dodnash Priory (Sfk) 84
  Hull (Yks) 115
  Inchcolm (Fif) 93
  Lacock Abbey (Wil) 87
  Luffield Priory (Bkm) 66
  New Forest (Ham) 107

Deeds and Charters (*continued*)
  Newcastle (Nbl) 70
  Oxford 80
  Oxfordshire 81
  Percy Fee 91
  Quarr Abbey (Ham) 108
  Redvers Family 69
  Rufford (Ntt) 79
  Scotland 65
  Sheffield (Yks) 116
  Somerset 82
  Sudbury Priory (Sfk) 84
  Tison Fee 91
  Waltham Abbey (Ess) 9
  Westminster Abbey (Mdx) 65, 77
  York Minster 91
  Yorkshire 91
  Yorkshire. East Riding 115
Devon & Cornwall Record Society 69
Diaries 70
  Baynton, E 87
  Bird, J 33, 98
  Blundell, N 74
  Brookes, J 65
  Burroughes, R 78
  Clegg, J 68
  Crewe, G 46
  Fletcher, I 67
  Fothergill, C 91
  Gitton, G 47
  Hicks, E 77
  Holland, W 48
  Holt, R 74
  Jenkinson, J 68
  Josselin, R 51
  Low, W 94
  O'Neil, J 74
  Prescott, H 74
  Romilly 67
  Sharp, R 52
  Thomas, W 98
  Warne, J 70
  Whitaker, J 87
  Whitelocke, B. 52
  Whiteway, W 70
  Wood, A. 79
  Woodforde 80
  Young, J 71
  Directories 33
  Bristol 106
  Buckinghamshire 10
  Devon 104
  Dumfrieshire 117
  Hastings (Ssx) 36
  Hull (Yks) 115
  Llangollen (Den) 118
  Shropshire 26
  Walsall (Sts) 111

Wiltshire 87
Worcestershire 113
Directories, Bibliography 32, 64
  Cardiff (Gla) 33
  London 32
Distinguished Conduct Medal 43
Distinguished Flying Cross 43
Distinguished Service Order 43
Domesday Book 8, 38
Duchy of Cornwall 69
Duchy of Lancaster 38
Earldom of Cornwall 64
Eastland Company, York 115
Ecclesiastical Records 52
  Carlisle Diocese 104
  Chester Diocese 103
  Chichester Diocese 112
  Edinburgh (Mln) 93, 94
  Ely Diocese 103
  Exeter Diocese 105
  Gloucester Cathedral 106
  Gloucester Diocese 106
  Lothian 94
  Norwich Cathedral (Nfk) 110
  Salisbury Cathedral (Wil) 87
  Scotland 52, 93, 94
  Tweeddale 94
  Winchester Diocese 107, 108
  Worcester Diocese 88
  York Diocese 114
  York Minster 113
Editing 48, 52
Educational Records 30, 52
  Bedfordshire 65, 101
  Bratton (Wil) 87
  Bristol 107
  Cambridgeshire 103
  Ely (Cam) 67
  Leeds (Yks) 92
  Sussex 85
  Whitchurch (Oxf) 81
  Yorkshire. West Riding 29
Electoral Registers 23
  Hastings (Ssx) 36
  Somerset 41
  Sussex 36
  Worcestershire 113
Emigration 34, 109
  Bristol to America 14, 22
  Bristol to Australia 36
  England to America 13, 19, 22-24, 37, 49, 50, 99
  England to Australia 31
  Fife to Australasia 97
  Gloucestershire to Australia 72
  Great Britain to America 27
  Guernsey to Australia 67
  Kent 42

Liverpool to America 14, 23
London to America 22
Scotland 18
Scotland to America 13, 14, 18, 23
Scotland to Australasia 18
Scotland to Canada 95, 99
Scotland to New Zealand 34
Scotland to West Indies 18
Scotland, North 95
Enclosure Records 49
  Burntwood (Sts) 83
  Hampshire 107
  Staffordshire 111
  Wiltshire 86
  Yorkshire. North Riding 116
Encyclopedias, Genealogical 8, 35, 41
Estate Duty Office 20
Estate Records 101
  Arundel Castle (Ssx) 112, 116
  Arundell Family 69, 104
  Bacon family 12, 63, 78
  Bath, Marquess of 101
  Battle Abbey (Ssx) 112
  Bolton Priory (Yks) 90
  Brereton Family 74
  Bury St Edmunds Abbey (Sfk) 83
  Butler Family 112
  Clough Family 112
  Constable Family 90
  Cornwall 69, 104
  Danny Family 112
  Downshire, Marquess of 101
  Durham 71
  Durham Cathedral 71
  Everingham (Yks) 90
  Fawkes Family 92
  Finch Family 101
  Fountains Abbey (Yks) 90
  Frewen Family 112
  Goodwood (Ssx) 112
  Greatham (Ssx) 112
  Grosvenor Family 75
  Haggerston (Dur) 71
  Hastings Family 63
  Hickstead Place (Ssx) 112
  Hull (Yks) 91
  Lindsey Marsh (Lin) 77
  Llanthony Priory (Gls) 72
  London Bridge 77
  Londonderry Family 105
  Lowther family 71
  Lytton Family 112
  Naworth (Cul) 71
  Oxford. New College 86
  Petworth House (Ssx) 112
  Revesby Abbey (Lin) 76
  Russell Family 102
  Salisbury, Marquess of 101

Scotland 52, 117
Shaw Family 74
Sibton Abbey (Sfk) 83
Staffordshire 111
Stiffkey (Nfk) 12, 78
Stratton, Adam de 86
Sunk Island (Yks) 71
Swaledale (Yks) 116
Wharfedale (Yks) 92
Wharton Family 116
Wiltshire 86
Winchester Diocese 108
Winchester. St. Swithuns Priory 107
Winchester. The Close (Ham) 107
Wiston (Ssx) 112
Exchequer Commissions of Inquiry
  Dorset 20
  Somerset 20
Exchequer Depositions
  Somerset 19
Exchequer, Jewish 62
Eyres
  Devon 69
  London 77
  Oxfordshire 81
  Surrey 84
  Wiltshire 86, 87
Faculty of Advocates 94
Fairs, Running 52
Family Histories 27
Family Histories, Scottish
  Bibliography 27
Family Records Centre 100
Feet of Fines 63, 64
  Buckinghamshire 66
  Essex 30
  Gloucestershire 72
  Norfolk 64
  Surrey 84
  Sussex 85
  Wiltshire 86, 87
Feudal Aids 37
Fine Rolls 36
Footballers 28
  Hamilton (Lks) 7
  Hull (Yks) 28
Forenames
  Scotland 116
Foundling Hospital 66
Fragmenta Genealogica 26
Freemen
  Exeter (Dev) 69
Gamekeepers
  Kent 42
Gazetteers 24, 32
  Buckinghamshire 10
  Cheltenham (Gls) 72
  Cheshire 103

Gazetteers (*continued*)
  Durham 105
  Scotland 19, 27, 50
  Somerset 20
  Staffordshire 111
  Yorkshire. North Riding 116
GEDCOM 25
Genealogists, Professional 51
Genealogy, History of 39
General Register Office 31
Gentleman's Magazine 42
Glebe Terriers
  Berkshire 66
  Buckinghamshire 67
  Cornwall 69
  Wiltshire 87
Glossaries 68, 97, 118
Goldsmiths
  Oxford 35
  Scotland 17
Guildhall Library 109
Gun Licences
  Kent 42
Gypsies 42
Hatchments 38, 39
Health Records 95
Hearth Tax 23
  Bedfordshire 65
  Faversham (Ken) 7
  Glamorganshire 98
  Hampshire 107
  Nottinghamshire 79
  Rutland 82
  Somerset 20
  West Lothian 94
  Worcester 88
Heirs
  America 23
  Scotland 23
Heraldic design 13
Heraldry 8, 14, 35, 42, 46, 48, 61
  Cumberland 67
  Wales 61, 118
Heresy
  Norwich Diocese 65
High Court of Admiralty 13
House History 15, 47
  Bedfordshire 101, 102
  Gloucestershire 106
  Norfolk 110
  Somerset 111
  Sussex 112
  Winchester (Ham) 108
Household Accounts
  Devon 69
  Dudley, Earls of Leicester 65
  Naworth Castle (Cul) 71
Huguenot Records 37, 62

London 62
Southampton (Ham) 62
Huguenots 62
  Pedigrees 14
  Poor 62
Hundred Rolls
  Bampton Hundred (Oxf) 81
  Bedfordshire 66
  Highworth Hundred (Wil) 86
  Warwickshire 52
  Witney (Oxf) 81
  Yorkshire 91
Illegitimacy 31
Indexes, lists of 23, 28, 49, 63
  Kent 8
  Suffolk 8
Indexing 52
Inquisitions 36
  Canterbury (Ken) 51
  Yorkshire 90
Inquisitions Post Mortem 37
  Gloucestershire 53-55
  London 53-55
  Sussex 85
  Wiltshire 54, 55
Insurance Records 33
  Devon 69
Interest Directories 24
  Ayrshire 97, 98
  Dumfriesshire 96
  Scotland 92
  Scottish Borders 96
International Genealogical Index 7, 8, 25, 31
Internet 15, 23, 25, 27, 32, 46
Introductory Guides & Handbooks 7-11, 15,
    18, 19, 22, 23, 26-28, 30, 31, 32, 35, 38, 39,
    41, 42, 47, 48, 63, 100
  Ayrshire 98
  Barnsley (Yks) 115
  Bedfordshire 30
  Bexley (Ken) 108
  Buckinghamshire 9
  Cambridgeshire 103
  Cumbria 104
  Dumfrieshire 117
  East Midlands 19
  Essex 106
  Gloucestershire 106
  Hillingdon (Mdx) 110
  Ireland 50
  Macclesfield (Chs) 103
  North East England 95
  Northamptonshire 30
  Rutland 30
  Scotland 7, 23, 24, 27, 31, 38, 50, 92, 99, 117
  Somerset 107, 111
  Southwark (Sry) 111

126

Staffordshire 111
Strathclyde 97
Sussex 112
Sussex, East 112
Wales 24
Walsall (Sts) 111
West Indies 100
Italians in London 62
Jacobites 13, 14, 31, 92, 117
  Angus 17
Jesuits 38, 60
Jewish Registers
  London 47
Jews 29
  Bibliography 62
Jurors
  Somerset 20
Justices Papers
  Bedfordshire 65
  Dorchester (Dor) 70
  Essex 106
  Hackney (Mdx) 77
  Hampshire 107
  Norfolk 78
  Surrey 84
  Wiltshire 87
Justiciary Records
  Argyllshire 94
Kings Bench 54
Kirby's Quest
  Somerset 20
Knightage 14
La Providence Hospital 62
Labour History 100
Land Drainage
  Sussex, West 112
Land Tax
  Sandford St Martin (Oxf) 15
  Sussex, East 85
  Yorkshire. North Riding 116
Landowners
  Wootton Courtenay (Som) 20
Landowners & Tenants
  Ashdown Forest (Ssx) 85
  Bristol 72
  Buckland in the Moor (Dev) 17
  London 77
  Nazeing (Ess) 34
  Oxford 80
Latin 114
Latin, Medieval 14, 31, 38, 114
Leeds Intelligencer 92
Leeds Mercury 92
Letters
  Banks Family 76
  Barrington Family 65
  Bicchieri, G 59
  Blomefield, F 78

Boswell, G 70
Brereton, W 74
Brown, H 99
Clavering, J 71
Constable, J. 83
Crawshay, R 33
Doddridge, P 101
Fardell, J 76
Fleming Family 80
Fuller Family 85
Hayton, T 66
Holles, J 79
James, J. 79
Joseph, R. 80
Liddell, H 71
Newcastle, Duke of 85
Oxford University 80
Parkhurst, J 78
Peniston, J 87
Plumpton Family 65
Radcliffe 79
Reynolds Family 67
Richmond, Duke of 85
Secker, T. 81
Sitwell, G 33
Stannard, P 78
Stonor Family 65
Tate, J 90
Thynne Family 87
Wallace, J 76
Wilberforce, S. 66, 81
William of Hoo 83
Wood, B 69
Libraries 41, 49
  Devon 104
  Scotland 94
Licences
  Canterbury Diocese 39
  Hampshire 39
Lieutenancy Records
  Cambridgeshire 67
  Essex 106
  Norfolk 78
  Wiltshire 86
Livery Companies 109
Lloyds Collection 109
Local History 8, 10, 28, 32, 35, 38, 48, 52
  Bibliography 48
  Devon 17
  Dumfries & Galloway 96
  Scotland 24, 117
  Sussex 112
Lynn Advertiser 47
Magazines 17, 19
Manorial Lords
  Burton Agnes (Yks) 28
Manorial Records 15, 31, 38, 52, 100
  Acomb (Yks) 90

Manorial Records (*contued*)
  Bedfordshire 66
  Bromsgrove (Wor) 87
  Buckland in the Moor (Dev) 17
  Callendar (Sti) 94
  Clitheroe (Lan) 75
  Cornwall 104
  Downham (Cam) 67
  Eckington (Dby) 22
  Egginton (Bdf) 66
  Falkirk (Sti) 94
  Framlingham (Sfk) 84
  Holkham (Nfk) 52
  King's Norton (Wor) 87
  Leeds (Yks) 92
  Luton (Bdf) 102
  Macclesfield (Chs) 75
  Ockbrook (Dby) 25
  Pennard (Gla) 99
  Settrington (Yks) 90
  Wakefield (Yks) 91
  Walsham le Willows (Sfk) 83, 84
  Widworthy (Dev) 32
  Wiltshire 86
Maps 38, 100
  Buckinghamshire 10
  Devon 105
  Dorset 105
  Durham 105
  Essex 106
  Glamorganshire 33, 118
  Gloucestershire 106
  Liverpool (Lan) 108
  Norfolk 110
  Scotland 25, 116
  Staffordshire 111
  Stoke on Trent (Sts) 111
  Sussex 85, 112
  Whaddon (Bkm) 10
  Yorkshire 88
  Yorkshire. North Riding 116
Marriage Customs 30
Marriage Licences 54
  Bath & Wells Diocese 21
  Canterbury Diocese 39
  Cumberland 74
  Hampshire 39
  Lancashire, North 74
  Leicester Archdeaconry 55
  Lewes Archdeaconry (Ssx) 85
  Lincoln Diocese 27
  London Diocese 56
  Nottinghamshire 56
  South Malling (Ssx) 85
  Westmorland 74
  York Diocese 114
  Yorkshire 90

Marriage Tax
  London 77
Marriages
  Clandestine 25
  Indexes 23
  Norfolk 47
Marriages, Irregular
  Annan (Dfs) 96
  Portpatrick (Wig) 96
Martyrs 60
Mayflower 22
Medals 43, 45
Members of Parliament 10
  Leicester 26
  Scotland 46
Merchant Adventurers, York 114, 115
Merchant Taylors, York 114, 115
Methodist Records
  Bedford 102
  Devon 105
  Somerset, South 82
Microfilm 114
Militia Records 7, 23, 100
  Aylesbury (Bkm) 10
  Bedfordshire 66
  Buckinghamshire 66
  Chalfonts (Bkm) 10
  Craven (Yks) 115
  Dorset 105
  Exeter (Dev) 38
  Herefordshire 65
  Hertfordshire 73
  Horwoods (Bkm) 10
  Missendens (Bkm) 10
  Oxfordshire 81
  Rochester (Ken) 7
  Rutland 9
  Shenley (Bkm) 10
  Somerset 20, 21
  Sussex 35
  Whaddon 10
  Whaddon (Bkm) 10
  Yorkshire. North Riding 116
Minstrels 8
Missing Persons 32
Mitchell Library 117
Monks
  Yorkshire 91
Monmouth Rebels 82
Monumental Inscriptions 46, 47
  Aberdeenshire 93, 95, 96
  Abernyte (Per) 98
  Aberyscir (Bre) 29
  Angus 92
  Ardgay (Roc) 93
  Avoch (Roc) 97
  Ayr 98

128

Barnwell (Ayr) 98
Berwickshire 96
Birmingham (War) 113
Burntwood (Sts) 83
Bute 92
Caithness 92
Carrick (Ayr) 93
Coodham (Ayr) 98
Cornwall 63
Coylton (Ayr) 98
Craigie (Ayr) 98
Crosbie (Ayr) 98
Culzean (Ayr) 98
Dartmoor (Dev) 16
Dean Cemetry (Mln) 93
Devon 16, 105
Devon, West 16
Dingwall (Roc) 97
Duddingston (Mln) 93
Dumfrieshire 117
Dunbartonshire 93
Dundonald (Ayr) 98
Dunfermline Abbey (Fif) 93
Dunnottar (Kcd) 95
Easter Suddie (Roc) 97
Fairfield (Ayr) 98
Felton (Nbl) 78
Fettercairn (Kcd) 95
Forglen (Ban) 95
Fortrose (Roc) 97
Geddes (Nai) 97
Glasgow (Lks) 97
Glenbervie (Kcd) 95
Huntingdonshire 103
Inchture (Per) 98
Inverkeithny (Ban) 95
Inverness 97
Invernessshire 93
Isla Munda (Arl) 93
Isle of Wight (Ham) 41
Keil (Arg) 93
Killearnan (Roc) 97
Kilmarnock (Arl) 93
Kilmuir (Roc) 97
Kilmun (Arl) 93
Kincardineshire 93
Kinlochlaigh (Arg) 93
Kinnoul (Per) 98
Kirkcudbrightshire 93
Kyle (Ayr) 98
Laggan (Mor) 93
Lanarkshire 93
Leicester 26
Leicestershire 75, 109
Llandefailog (Bre) 29
Llandeilo'rfan (Bre) 29
Llanfihangel (Bre) 29
Llanfihangelnantbran (Bre) 29

Llanpyddid (Bre) 29
Llywel (Bre) 29
Longforgan (Per) 98
Marnoch (Ban) 95
Marykirk (Kcd) 95
Monkton (Ayr) 98
Newton on Ayr 98
Nunhead (Sry) 111
Old Alloway (Ayr) 98
Old Alness (Roc) 97
Old Pert (Ans) 98
Oxford. All Souls College 81
Oxford. Saint Johns College 81
Peebleshire 93
Perthshire 93
Portpatrick (Wig) 96
Prestwick (Ayr) 98
Renfrewshire 93
Roxburghshire 96
Rutland 75
Rye (Ssx) 85
Saint Quivox (Ayr) 98
Scotland 27, 93
Sheffield (Yks) 116
Somerset 82
Spitalfields (Lnd) 61
Sterlingshire 93
Stirlingshire 93
Stoke Damerel (Dev) 16
Strachan (Kcd) 96
Sutherland 93
Symington (Ayr) 98
Troon (Ayr) 98
Ulverston (Lan) 67
Walsall (Sts) 111
West Lothian 93
Wester Ross (Roc) 93
Yorkshire. North Riding 116
Monumental Inscriptions, Jewish 49
Moravians
  Bedford 66
Morpeth Herald 78
Motor Records
  Dorset 105
Musicians 73
Names, Personal
  Norman 8
National Farm Survey 100
National Library of Wales 117
Naval Chronicle 28
Naval General Service Medal 43
Newsletters, Editing 48
Newspaper Readers 33
Newspapers 31, 52
  Cumberland 67
  Lancashire, North 67
  Westmorland 67
  Wigtown 117

Newspapers (*continued*)
  Worcestershire 113
Nomina Villarum
  Somerset 20
Nonconformist Registers 63
  Bradford (Yks) 28, 29
  Burntwood (Sts) 83
  Canterbury (Ken) 42
  Edinburgh (Mln) 92
  Felton (Nbl) 79
  Great Horton (Yks) 28
  Kent 42
  Marlow (Bkm) 10
  Princes Risborough, (Bkm) 9
  Staplehurst (Ken) 42
Nonconformity 31, 52, 100
  Bedfordshire 65, 66
  Bristol 72
  Buckinghamshire 67
  Cornwall 68
  Devon 68
  Edinburgh (Mln) 92
  Hampshire 39
  Oxford Diocese 81
  Wiltshire 87
Norman Conquest 22, 23, 99
Nuns
  York 60
Nurserymen 38
Oaths of Allegiance
  York 29
Obituaries 42
  Aberdeen 31
  Bristol 106
  Fearn (Roc) 94
  Norfolk 47
Occupations
  Dictionaries 49
Oral Evidence 31, 49
Orphans 66
Painters
  Scotland 94
Paleography 14, 31, 37, 38, 46, 52, 106, 114, 116
Parish Clerks
  London 37
Parish Records 15, 39
  Amwell (Hrt) 73
  Arbroath (Ans) 94
  Baldock (Hrt) 18
  Bedfordshire 66
  Bristol. All Saints 72
  Carhampton (Som) 21
  Fowlmere (Cam) 67
  Grange (Ban) 95
  Liverpool (Lan) 108
  Nazeing (Ess) 34
  Norwich Archdeaconry (Nfk) 77

Ockbrook (Dby) 25
Saint Botulph (Lnd) 77
Selworthy (Som) 21
Shetland 98
Stirling 94
Stow (Lin) 76
Uffculme (Dev) 69
Wigginton (Oxf) 81
Wimbledon (Sry) 84
Parish registers 13, 24, 26, 27, 31, 38, 62
  Acomb (Yks) 88
  Aisholt (Som) 21
  Allexton (Lei) 26
  Almondbury (Yks) 88
  Alton (Sts) 82
  Ampthill (Bdf) 102
  Amwell (Hrt) 73
  Arlesey (Bdf) 102
  Arlingham (Gls) 15
  Ashburton (Dev) 17
  Ashreigney (Dev) 14
  Ashton in Makerfield (Lan) 74
  Ashton under Lyne (Lan) 73
  Askham Bryan (Yks) 88
  Askham Richard (Yks) 88
  Aspley Guise (Bdf) 102
  Astwick (Bdf) 102
  Austerfield (Yks) 88
  Australia 7
  Banbury (Oxf) 82
  Barton le Clay (Bdf) 102
  Battlesden (Bdf) 102
  Bedford. St. Cuthbert 102
  Bedford. St. John 102
  Bedford. St. Mary 102
  Bedford. St. Paul 102
  Bedford. St. Peter 102
  Biddenham (Bdf) 102
  Biddulph (Sts) 83
  Biggleswade (Bdf) 102
  Billington (Bdf) 102
  Birstall (Yks) 88
  Bishopthorpe (Yks) 88
  Blackley (Lan) 73
  Bletsoe (Bdf) 102
  Blunham (Bdf) 102
  Blyth (Yks) 88
  Bowes (Yks) 88
  Bradeley (Sts) 83
  Bradford (Yks) 28
  Braithwell (Yks) 88
  Brandsburton (Yks) 88
  Brierley Hill (Sts) 83
  Bristol 107
  Bubwith (Yks) 89
  Buckland in the Moor (Dev) 16, 17
  Bulmer (Yks) 89
  Burntwood (Sts) 83

Cairneyhill (Fif) 97
Campton (Bdf) 102
Canterbury (Ken) 42
Carhampton (Som) 21
Charlinch (Som) 21
Chasetown (Sts) 83
Chesham (Bkm) 27
Cheshire 103
Chesterfield (Dby) 68
Childwall (Lan) 73
Chorley (Lan) 73
Chorlton cum Hardy (Lan) 73
Collingham (Yks) 89
Colton (Lan) 73
Cornwall 69
Creech St.Michael (Som) 21
Culbone (Som) 21
Cutcombe (Som) 21
Dartmoor (Dev) 16, 17
Denbighshire 118
Devon 69
Dorset 105
Dudley (Sts) 83
Dudley (Wor) 113
Dundonald (Ayr) 98
Dunfermline (Fif) 97
Easingwold (Yks) 89
Eastbourne (Ssx) 35
Eaton Socon (Bdf) 102
Eccles (Lan) 73
Edworth (Bdf) 102
Eggington (Bdf) 102
Egton cum Newland (Lan) 74
Elstow (Bdf) 102
Enmore (Som) 21
Eversholt (Bdf) 102
Everton (Bdf) 102
Evington (Lei) 26
Exford (Som) 21
Eyam (Dby) 68
Eyeworth (Bdf) 102
Farndish (Bdf) 102
Felmersham (Bdf) 102
Flintshire 118
Flitton (Bdf) 102
Flitwick (Bdf) 102
Giggleswick (Yks) 89
Goldington (Bdf) 102
Great Barford (Bdf) 102
Gulval (Con) 27
Halifax (Yks) 26
Halton (Lan) 73
Hampshire 108
Hardy (Lan) 73
Harlington (Bdf) 102
Harrold (Bdf) 102
Hatley Cockayne (Bdf) 102
Heath (Bdf) 102

Heaton Norris (Lan) 73
Henlow (Bdf) 102
Herefordshire 108
Heslington (Yks) 89
Highham Gobion (Bdf) 102
Hindley (Lan) 74
Hockcliffe (Bdf) 102
Hollinfare (Lan) 73
Houghton Conquest (Bdf) 102
Houghton Regis (Bdf) 102
Howden (Yks) 89
Hulcote (Bdf) 102
Husborne Crawley (Bdf) 102
Ilsington (Dev) 17
Inverkeithing (Fif) 97
Ireleth (Lan) 73
Kempston (Bdf) 102
Kennington (Ken) 12
Kensworth (Bdf) 102
Keysoe (Bdf) 102
Kingsnorth (Ken) 12
Kirk Deighton (Yks) 89
Kirkcaldy (Fif) 97
Kirklington (Yks) 89
Knotting (Bdf) 102
Lancashire 108
Lancaster (Lan) 73
Langford (Bdf) 102
Leeds (Yks) 92
Leicestershire 109
Leighton Buzzard (Bdf) 102
Lidlington (Bdf) 102
Little Barford (Bdf) 102
Little Staughton (Bdf) 102
London 109
Lower Gravenhurst (Bdf) 102
Luccombe (Som) 21
Luton (Bdf) 102
Luxborough (Som) 21
Lythe (Yks) 89
Manchester (Lan) 73
Marlow (Bkm) 9
Marston Moretaine (Bdf) 102
Masham (Yks) 89
Maulden (Bdf) 102
Melchbourne (Bdf) 102
Meppershall (Bdf) 102
Millbrook (Bdf) 102
Milton Bryan (Bdf) 102
Milton Ernest (Bdf) 102
Milwich (Sts) 83
Myton upon Swale (Yks) 89
Newland (Lan) 74
Norfolk 110
Northill (Bdf) 102
Oake (Som) 21
Oakley (Bdf) 102
Oare (Som) 21

Parish registers (*continued*)
  Odell (Bdf) 102
  Old Warden (Bdf) 102
  Oswaldkirk (Yks) 89
  Owston (Yks) 89
  Pavenham (Bdf) 102
  Penn (Sts) 83
  Pertenhall (Bdf) 102
  Podington (Bdf) 102
  Porlock (Som) 21
  Potsgrove (Bdf) 102
  Potto (Bdf) 102
  Prescot (Lan) 73, 74
  Pulloxhill (Bdf) 102
  Raskelf (Yks) 89
  Ravensden (Bdf) 102
  Reach (Bdf) 102
  Renhold (Bdf) 102
  Riccall (Yks) 89
  Ridgmont (Bdf) 102
  Riseley (Bdf) 102
  Rivington (Lan) 74
  Rokeby (Yks) 89
  Roxton (Bdf) 102
  Rusland (Lan) 73
  Saint Michaels on Wyre (Lan) 74
  Salford (Bdf) 102
  Sandy (Bdf) 102
  Scotland 116
  Scotland, West 117
  Scruton (Yks) 89
  Selworthy (Som) 21
  Settrington (Yks) 89
  Sharnbrook (Bdf) 102
  Sheffield (Yks) 89, 90, 116
  Shefford (Bdf) 102
  Shelton (Bdf) 102
  Shillington (Bdf) 102
  Somerset 110
  Souldrop (Bdf) 102
  Southill (Bdf) 102
  Staffordshire 111
  Stagsden (Bdf) 102
  Stanbridge (Bdf) 102
  Steppingley (Bdf) 103
  Stevington (Bdf) 103
  Stoke on Trent (Sts) 111
  Stoke Pero (Som) 21
  Stotfold (Bdf) 103
  Streatley (Bdf) 103
  Studham (Bdf) 103
  Sundon (Bdf) 103
  Surrey 111
  Sussex 112
  Sutton (Bdf) 103
  Sutton cum Duckmanton (Dby) 68
  Swanbourne (Bkm) 9
  Swineshead (Bdf) 103
  Tempsford (Bdf) 103
  Thornborough (Bkm) 10
  Thorpe Bassett (Yks) 90
  Thurleigh (Bdf) 103
  Tilbrook (Bdf) 103
  Tilsworth (Bdf) 103
  Timberscombe (Som) 21
  Tingrith (Bdf) 103
  Toddington (Bdf) 103
  Todmorden (Lan) 74
  Tong (Yks) 29
  Tottenhoe (Bdf) 103
  Treborough (Som) 21
  Turvey (Bdf) 103
  Upper Gravenhurst (Bdf) 103
  Upper Stondon (Bdf) 103
  Urswick (Lan) 73
  Wadworth (Yks) 90
  Wales 118
  Walkhampton (Dev) 17
  Walton in Ainsty (Yks) 90
  Warrington (Lan) 73
  Wensley (Yks) 90
  Westminster. St.Margaret (Mdx) 61
  Westoning (Bdf) 103
  Whipsnade (Bdf) 103
  Widecombe in the Moor (Dev) 17
  Wigginton (Oxf) 38
  Wilden (Bdf) 103
  Willington (Bdf) 103
  Wilshampstead (Bdf) 103
  Withycombe (Som) 21
  Woburn (Bdf) 103
  Woodplumpton (Lan) 73
  Wootton (Bdf) 103
  Wootton Courtenay (Som) 21
  Worcestershire 113
  Wrestlingworth (Bdf) 103
  Wymington (Bdf) 103
  Yelden (Bdf) 103
  York. St.Crux 90
  York. St.Mary Bishophill Junior 90
  York. St.Mary Castlegate 90
  York. St.Olave 90
  Yorkshire 50, 114
  Yorkshire. East Riding 115
  Yorkshire. North Riding 116
Parliamentary Surveys
  Cornwall, Duchy of 69
  Durham 71
  Durham Diocese 71
  Norwich Cathedral (Nfk) 78
Parochial Surveys
  Cumberland 67
  Richmond Archdeaconry (Yks) 91
  Somerset 82
  Westmorland 67
Passenger Lists 19, 22, 24

Patent Rolls 37, 63
Pedigrees 13, 24, 27
  Bedfordshire 99
  Bibliography 13, 14
  Cornwall 104
  Cumberland 67
  Derbyshire 68
  Design of 31, 38, 95
  Fife 97
  Huguenot 14
  Oxfordshire 79
  Wales 118
Peerage 14, 22, 23, 26, 48
  Scotland 24, 27
Petitions
  Northumberland 71
Pewterers 38
Philosophy of Genealogy 39
Photographers
  Essex 105
  Leicester 26
  London 40
Photographs 8
  Dating 15
Pipe Rolls 64
  Surrey 84
Plea Rolls 54
  Northumberland 71
Plea Rolls, Jewish 62
Poetry, Genealogical 48
Police 52
Police Records
  Edinburgh (Mln) 92
  Hull (Yks) 28
  Yorkshire. East Riding 115
Poll Books 23
  Aberdeen 96
  Aberdeenshire 96
  Bristol 106
  Hull 41
  Hull (Yks) 115
  London 41
  Norfolk 41
  Suffolk 41
  Sussex 85
  Westminster (Mdx) 41
  Yorkshire 41
  Yorkshire. West Riding 41
Poll Tax 52
  Hull (Yks) 115
  Lincoln Diocese 76
  London 77
  Northwich Hundred (Chs) 74
  Paisley (Rfw) 31
  Troon (Ayr) 92
Polo Players
  Hull (Yks) 115
Poor Law 31, 33, 52

Abbey (Rfw) 34
Bedfordshire 101
Berkshire 66
Bristol 107
Burntwood (Sts) 83
Clerkenwell (Mdx) 77
Cornwall 104
Glamorganshire 118
Ipswich (Sfk) 83
Keighley (Yks) 28
Kent 42
Luccombe (Som) 21
Merthyr Tydfil (Gla) 118
Paisley (Rfw) 34
Salisbury (Wil) 86
Yorkshire. North Riding 113
Portraits 67
Posse Comitatus
  Amersham (Bkm) 10
Prerogative Court of Canterbury 13, 22, 42, 53, 55-57, 63, 65, 81, 99, 100, 105
Prisoners of War 45
Probate Accounts
  Berkshire 66
  Cornwall 56
  Devon 56
Probate Inventories 63, 68, 114
  Banbury (Oxf) 82
  Bowdon (Chs) 34
  Buckinghamshire 66
  Cheltenham (Gls) 72
  Cheshire, North East 35
  Darlington (Dur) 71
  Dawley (Sal) 39
  Devon 68
  Dorset 70
  Durham Diocese 70
  Evington (Lei) 26
  Hertford (Hrt) 73
  Ipswich (Sfk) 83
  Kent 42
  Lilleshall (Sal) 39
  Lincoln (Lin) 76
  Lincoln Diocese 57
  Northampton Archdeaconry 57, 82
  Ratby (Lei) 26
  Somerset 21
  Surrey 85
  Sussex, West 112
  Telford (Sal) 39
  Uffculme (Dev) 69
  Wellington (Sal) 39
  Wrockwardine (Sal) 39
  Wymondham (Nfk) 12
  Yorkshire 90
Probate Records 27, 30, 100, 114, 118
  Bangor Diocese 117
  Bedfordshire 57, 101

Probate Records (*continued*)
  Brecon Archdeaconry 117
  Bristol 107
  Cornwall 104
  Ely Diocese 57
  London Archdeaconry 57
  London Diocese 57
  Orkney 94
  Oxford Diocese 57, 58, 81
  Stockport (Chs) 74
  Sudbury Archdeaconry (Sfk) 57
  Suffolk Archdeaconry 57
  Surrey 57
  York Province 46
Protestation Returns
  Berkshire, North 81, 82
  Oxfordshire 81, 82
  Sussex, West 85
  Westmorland 67
Public Record Office 24, 52, 63, 100
Quaker Registers 63
  Yorkshire. East Riding 115
Quakers
  Gainsborough (Lin) 75, 76
  Kent 42
  Leeds (Yks) 90
  Scottish 13
  Somerset 82
  Wisbech (Cam) 103
  Yorkshire 46
Quarter Sessions 23, 31
  Carmarthenshire 98
  Denbighshire 118
  Durham 71
  Essex 105
  Gloucestershire 106
  Hampshire 108
  Holland (Lin) 76
  Kesteven (Lin) 75, 76
  Lanarkshire 93
  Lancashire 63
  Lincoln 76
  Lincolnshire 75
  Lindsey (Lin) 76
  Oxfordshire 81
  Stamford (Lin) 76
  Sussex 112
  Sussex, West 112
  Wiltshire 86
Quo Warranto Rolls
  Yorkshire 91
Railwaymen 48
Rates
  Somerset 20
Record Offices & Repositories 19, 25, 32, 49, 101
  Devon 104
  London 109
  Merseyside 103
  North-East 29
  Scotland 94
Record Publications
  Bibliography 64, 71
Record Publications, Scottish
  Bibliography 64
Regiments 13
  1st (Royal) Regiment of Foot 13
  1st Foot Guards 12
  2nd (Queens) Regiment of Foot 13
  3rd (Buffs) Regiment of Foot 13
  4th (Kings) Regiment of Foot 13
  Army Cyclist Corps 45
  Bedfordshire 44
  Black Watch (Royal Highlanders) 44
  Border 44
  Buffs 13, 45
  Buffs (East Kent) 43
  Cambridge 45
  Cameronians 44
  Channel Islands Militia 45
  Cheshire 44
  Connaught Rangers 45
  Corps of Army Schoolmasters 45
  Corps of Military Foot Police 45
  Corps of Military Mounted Police 45
  Corps of Royal Engineers 43
  Corps of Small Arms School 45
  Devonshire 44
  Dorsetshire 44
  Dragoon Guards 13
  Duke of Albany's 45
  Duke of Cambridge's Own (Middlesex) 44
  Duke of Cornwall's 44
  Duke of Edinburgh's (Wiltshire) 44
  Duke of Wellington's 44
  Durham Light Infantry 45
  East Lancashire 44
  East Somerset Regiment of Volunteer Infantry 20
  East Surrey 44
  East Yorkshire 44
  Essex 44
  Foot Guards 43
  Gloucestershire 44
  Gordon Highlanders 45
  Hampshire 44
  Herefordshire 45
  Hertfordshire 45
  Highland Cyclist Battalion 45
  Highland Light Infantry 45
  Honourable Artillery Company 43, 45
  Horse Guards 13
  Household Cavalry 43
  Huntingdonshire Cyclist Battalion 45
  Imperial Camel Corps 43
  Inns of Court Officers Training Corps 45

Kent Cyclist Battalion 45
King's Own (Royal Lancaster) 43
King's Own Scottish Borderers 44
Kings (Liverpool) 44
Labour Corps 45
Lancashire Fusiliers 44
Leicestershire 44
Life Guards 13
Lincolnshire 44
London 45
Loyal North Lancashire 44
Machine Gun Corps 45
Manchester 44
Military Provost Staff Corps 45
Monmouthshire 45
Natal Field Force 43
Non-Combatant Corps 45
Norfolk 44
Northamptonshire 44
Northern Cyclist Battalion 45
Oxfordshire & Buckinghamshire Light Infantry 44
Prince of Wales Volunteers (South Lancashire) 44
Prince of Wales's (North Staffordshire) 45
Prince of Wales's Leinster 45
Prince of Wales's Own (West Yorkshire) 44
Princess Charlotte of Wales's (Royal Berkshire) 44
Princess Louise's (Argyll & Sutherland Highlanders) 45
Princess Victoria's 45
Queen Mary's Army Auxiliary Corps 45
Queen's (Royal West Surrey) 43
Queen's Own (Cameron Highlanders) 45
Queen's Own (Yorkshire Light Infantry) 44
Rifle Brigade 45
Ross-shire 45
Royal Army Medical Corps 45
Royal Army Ordnance Corps 45
Royal Army Pay Corps 45
Royal Army Service Corps 45
Royal Army Veterinary Corps 45
Royal Canadians 45
Royal Dublin Fusiliers 45
Royal Fusiliers 43
Royal Fusiliers (City of London) 43
Royal Horse Artillery 43
Royal Inniskillen Fusiliers 44
Royal Irish 44
Royal Irish Fusiliers 45
Royal Militia & Yeomanry Cavalry 49
Royal Munster Fusiliers 45
Royal Rifle Corps 44
Royal Scots 43
Royal Scots Fusiliers 44
Royal Sussex 44, 112

Royal Warwickshire 43
Royal Welsh Fusiliers 44
Scottish Borderers 44
Seaforth Highlanders 45
Sherwood Foresters 44
Shropshire Light Infantry 44
Somerset Light Infantry 44
South African Field Force 43
South Staffordshire 44
South Wales 44
Suffolk 44
Tank Corps 45
Welch 44
West Yorkshire 44
Worcestershire 44
York & Lancaster 45
Yorkshire 44
Yorkshire Light Infantry 44
Yorkshire West Riding 44
Registration Districts
  Essex 34
  Hampshire 34
  Kent 34
  Norfolk 34
  Scotland 116
  Staffordshire 111
  Suffolk 34
  Surrey 34
  Sussex 34
Registry Offices 9, 27
Rolls of Arms 8, 13, 65
Roman Catholic Registers 22, 59
  Bath (Som) 60
  Bristol. Trenchard Lane 60
  Callaly Castle (Nbl) 60
  Cheam (Sry) 59
  Cowdray (Ssx) 59
  Crondon Park (Ess) 60
  Eastbourne (Ssx) 59
  Everingham (Yks) 60
  Holme on Spalding Moor (Yks) 60
  Holywell (Fln) 60
  Liverpool. Highfield Street (Lan) 60
  Llanarth (Mon) 60
  Lulworth Castle (Dor) 60
  Midhurst (Ssx) 59
  Nidd Hall (Yks) 60
  Perthir (Mon) 59
  Richmond (Sry) 60
  Slindon (Ssx) 60
  Towneley Hall (Lan) 59
  Welsh Bicknor. Courtfield (Mon) 60
  Winchester (Ham) 59
  Wootton Wawen (War) 59
Roman Catholic Students
  Douai 60
  Lisbon 60
  Rome 60

Roman Catholic Students (*continued*)
  Seville 60
Roman Catholics 22, 60, 100
  Bath (Som) 60
  Bedfordshire 65
  Bibliography 21, 22
  Chester Diocese 7, 63
  Derbyshire 68
  Durham 71
  Lancashire 7, 74
  Liverpool (Lan) 108
  Middlesex 60
  Monmouth 60
  Monmouthshire 60
  Preston (Lan) 41
  Scotland 22
  Wales 22
  Wales, South 59
  Wiltshire 60, 87
  York 60
  Yorkshire 60
Royal Air Force 100
Royal Ancestors 19, 23, 24, 27, 42
Royal Marines 100
  Portsmouth (Ham) 107
Royal Military Calendar 28, 43
Royal Mint 63
Royal Navy 100
Royalist Composition Papers 53
Royalists 81
Rugby Players
  Hull (Yks) 115
Saint Deiniol's Library 63
Sasines
  Aberdeen 31
  Banffshire 31
  Forres 31
  Kincardineshire 31
  Morayshire 31
School Records
  Herefordshire 108
Scottish Record Office 116
Seamen 28, 43, 45, 63, 69, 100, 105, 108
  Cornwall 69
  Devon 69
  Kent 42
  Newhaven (Ssx) 35
  Rye (Ssx) 85
  Scotland 13, 18, 92
  Sussex 35
  Yorkshire. North Riding 115
Seamen, Merchant 100
Settlement Papers
  Bradford on Avon (Wil) 87
  Buckingham (Bkm) 10
  Chalfont St. Peter (Bkm) 10
  Chelsea (Mdx) 77
  Iver (Bkm) 10
  Kent 42
  Mitcham (Sry) 84
  Newport Pagnell (Bkm) 10
  Quainton (Bkm) 10
  Somerset 20, 50
  Stoke Poges (Bkm) 10
  Stony Stratford (Bkm) 10
Sewers, Commissioners of
  Holland (Lin) 76
  Wiggenhall (Nfk) 78
Ship Money
  Buckinghamshire 66
Shipwrights
  Newcastle (Nbl) 71
  Topsham (Dev) 69
Signet Bills 53
Slave Trade
  Bristol 72
Societies 49
Soldiers 23, 28, 34, 43-45, 49, 50
  Scotland 17
  Scottish in America 13
Spalding Gentlemen's Society 76
Staffordshire Advertiser 83
Star Chamber Proceedings 100
  Sevenhampton (Wil) 87
  Yorkshire 90
Subsidies
  Craven (Yks) 91
  Devon 68
  Dorset 70
  Essex 106
  Gloucestershire 48
  Hampshire 107
  London 77
  Rutland 82
  Somerset 19, 20
  Surrey 85
  Wiltshire 86
Supplications
  Scotland 46
Supreme Court of Judicature 63
Surnames 7, 13, 14, 27, 31, 32, 35, 42, 47, 99
  Devon 30
  Lancashire 30
  Leicestershire 26
  Oxfordshire 30
  Scotland 25, 26
  Sussex 30
  Wales 49
  Welsh 24
Surnames, Scotland
  Bibliography 92
Surtees Society 71
Surveyors 94
  Essex 106
Surveys
  Barley (Hrt) 67

Bilsdale (Yks) 115
Cornwall, Duchy of 69
Denbighshire 51
Devonshire, Earls of 68
Durham Diocese 70
Gloucester Diocese 72
Houghton Hall (Nfk) 78
Kintyre (Arl) 94
London 77
Malton (Yks) 115
Oakham (Rut) 82
Pembroke, Earl of 86
Scarsdale (Dby) 68
Settrington (Yks) 90
Surrey 85
Wiltshire 86
Swing Riots 13
  Buckinghamshire 13
  Hampshire 13
  Wiltshire 13
Tax Records 23, 52, 100
  Babergh Hundred (Sfk) 84
  Buckinghamshire 66
  Buckland in the Moor (Dev) 17
  Dumfrieshire 117
  Exeter (Dev) 68, 69
  Gloucestershire 72
  North Petherton Hundred (Som) 20
  Wiltshire 86, 87
Teachers
  Scotland 17, 94
Templars 51
Terriers
  Cambridge 67
  Fleet (Ken) 51
  Hampshire 39
Testa de Nevill 37
Thoroton Society 79
Tithe Records 52, 100
  Blunham (Bdf) 66
  Bradford (Yks) 28
  Dartmoor (Dev) 16
  Derbyshire 68
  Nazeing (Ess) 34
  Settle (Yks) 116
  Staffordshire 111
  Sussex 85, 112
  Wiltshire 86
  Yorkshire 114
Tontines 40
Trade Tokens
  Kent 47
  Sussex 47
Tradesmen
  Cowbridge (Gla) 33
  Wiltshire 86
Transportees 13, 109
  Buckinghamshire 10

England to America 23, 49, 50
Fife 97
Gloucestershire to Australia 72
Lincolnshire to Australia 109
Trinity House 77
Turnpike Records
  Hampshire 107
University Records
  Oxford 80
  Oxford. Canterbury College 80, 81
  Oxford. Merton College 81
  Oxford. Oriel College 80
University Registers
  Aberdeen 31
  Oxford 79-81
  Oxford. Exeter College 79
  Oxford. Keble College 37
  Oxford. Magdalen College 36
  Oxford. Merton College 80
Valuation Office 100
Victoria Cross 43, 48
Virginia Company 27
Visitations, Ecclesiastical 68
  Chichester Diocese 85
  Dunblane Diocese 94
  Exeter Diocese 68
  Hampshire 39, 107
  Lincoln Diocese 58, 75
  Lincolnshire 75
  Llandaff Diocese 33, 98
  Oxford Diocese 81
  Stafford Archdeaconry 101
  Surrey 85
  Wiltshire 86
  Worcester Diocese 87
  York Diocese 113
  York Province 71
  Yorkshire 114
Visitations, Heraldic 14, 41
  Bristol 61
  Derbyshire 61
  Devon 99
  Dorset 61
  Hampshire 61
  London 61
  Northern England 70
  Nottinghamshire 61
  Oxfordshire 61
  Somerset 61
  Suffolk 61
  Wales 61
War Memorials
  Amersham (Bkm) 10
  Aylesbury (Bkm) 10
  Aylesbury Hundred 10
  Buckinghamshire 10
  Dartmoor (Dev) 16
  Eastbourne (Ssx) 35

War Memorials (*continued*)
  Milton Keynes 10
  Missenden (Bkm) 10
Web Publishing 25
Widows
  London 25
Wigtown Free Press 117
Wills 7, 31, 37, 49, 53, 55, 56, 100, 114, 118
  Aberdeen 31
  America 13, 14, 22, 23
  Banbury (Oxf) 82
  Battle Deanery 54
  Bedfordshire 65, 66
  Berkshire Archdeaconry 53
  Bowdon (Chs) 34
  Bristol 53, 72, 107
  Caldecott (Rut) 55
  Canterbury Diocese 55, 56
  Cheltenham (Gls) 72
  Cheshire, North East 35
  Chester Diocese 74
  Chichester Diocese (Ssx) 55, 56
  Cornwall 55, 56, 104
  Darlington (Dur) 71
  Dartmoor (Dev) 16
  Devon 55, 56
  Dorset 54, 55
  Durham Diocese 70
  Essex 99, 105, 106
  Evington (Lei) 54
  Exeter Archdeaconry (Dev) 55
  Fife 97
  Gloucester Diocese 54
  Groby (Lei) 54
  Hertford (Hrt) 73
  Huntingdonshire 55
  Inverness 54
  Ketton (Rut) 55
  Lancashire 7

  Leeds (Yks) 92
  Leicester (Lei) 54, 55
  Leicester Archdeaconry 54, 55
  Lewes Archdeaconry (Ssx) 54
  Lichfield & Coventry Diocese 53
  Liddington (Rut) 55
  Lincoln (Lin) 54
  Lincoln Diocese 55, 57
  London 57, 77
  Monmouthshire 99
  Northamptonshire 53
  Northern England 70
  Norwich Diocese 56, 57, 78
  Otley (Yks) 92
  Oxfordshire 81
  Pontefract (Yks) 92
  Rothley (Lei) 54, 55
  Rutland 53
  Saint Albans (Hrt) 73
  Saint Buryan (Con) 56, 104
  Scotland 23, 53
  Somerset 20
  South Malling (Ssx) 54
  Stow Archdeaconry (Lin) 56
  Sudbury Archdeaconry (Sfk) 84
  Suffolk Archdeaconry (Sfk) 84, 99
  Taunton Archdeaconry (Som) 55
  Tixover (Rut) 55
  Uffculme (Dev) 69
  Virginia 37
  Wakefield (Yks) 92
  Worcester Diocese 54, 55
  York (Yks) 114
World War I 43-45, 100
World War II 29, 45
  Bristol 107
  London 52
Writing a Family History 15

Family Name Index

Abbott 50
Almond 48
Almosnino 47
Alnwick 58
Anderson 39
Andrews 17
Antrobus 86
Arundell 69, 104
Ashton 48
Atwater 75
Austen 48

Bacon 12, 63, 78
Baker 17
Banks 76
Barrington 65
Bastard 17
Bateman 59
Baynton 87
Bedingfield 60
Bek 71
Bellamy 18
Bennet 17
Bennett 49
Benson 72
Bicchieri 59
Bicknell 83
Bigge 99
Bird 33, 98
Blomefield 78
Blundell 74
Bodrugan 30
Boner 83
Bosanquet 39
Boswell 70
Bourchier 17
Bourgchier 58
Bowers 28
Bowes 39, 78, 105
Brereton 74
Brockell 15
Bronescombe 59
Brooks 65
Brown 99
Brumby 17
Burn 62
Burnell 16
Burroughes 78
Butler 112

Cantilupe 58
Carter 39
Catterick 59
Cecil 101
Champernon 99
Chandler 87
Chichele 58
Child 39
Cholmondeley 78
Chrispin 17
Clapp 15
Clark 86
Clavering 71
Clegg 68
Clifford 39
Clough 112
Cole 14
Constable 83, 90
Cooper 70
Coqueau 62
Corbridge 70
Cotesworth 71
Crakanthorp 67
Crawshay 33
Crewe 46
Curdy 26

Daniel 18
Danny 112
Darby 39
Davenant 87
Davy 69
Devereux 101
Devonshire 68
Dewar 39
Dicker 36
Dixons 9
Dore 15
Doughty 78
Downshire 101
Drummond 114
Dudley 65, 101
Dunsdon 61
Dunsire 18, 97

Edington 107
Elam 34
Eldred 39
Ellis 17
Erineveine 117

Fairbank 116
Fardell 76
Fawkes 92
Fell 81
Fielden 29
Finch 101
Fisher 17
Fitch 30
Fleming 59, 80, 104
Flemyng 58
Fletcher 67, 99
Fothergill 91
Fowler 9
Fox 70
Fraunces 65
Freeman 9
Frend 67
Frewen 112
Fuller 85

Gastrell 67, 91
Gaunt 24
Gilbert 99
Gitton 47
Gladstone 63
Glasier 48
Gleniel 24
Glynne 63
Goddard 61
Goldney 73
Grant 39
Gravesend 58
Gray 58
Green 73
Greenfield 71
Grenville 66
Griffiths 25
Grimston 39
Grindal 113
Grinter 25

Haggerston 71
Hallum 59
Halton 58
Hamlyn 17
Hammond 67
Harveys 24
Hassall 73
Hastings 63
Hatfield 70

Hathorne 99
Hayton 66
Hearne 79
Hemingby 86
Hertford 86
Hethe 58
Hext 16
Hicks 77
Hill 78
Hines 18
Hobhouse 87
Holcroft 106
Holland 48
Holles 79
Howard 40
Hungerford 87
Hunt 87
Hurlock 10
Hutton 77

Irvin 117
Irvine 117
Irving 117

James 79
Jenkinson 68
Joseph 80
Josselin 51

Kirby 59
Kirbye 40
Kirkby 59
Knight 33

Lacy 58, 59
Langham 58
Langley 71
Leaman 16
Lear 16
Leslie 7, 40
L'Estrange 9
Leyburn 7
Liddell 71
Lindo 47
Londonderry 105
Longland 75
L'Oste 19
Low 94
Lowther 71
Lyttelton 25

139

Lytton 112

MacGibbon 34
Mackintosh 114
Mallory 40
Mann 16, 50
Manning 99
Marsden 25
Martival 58, 59
May 94
Mayett 66
Maynard 106
McAdam 94
McClellan 92
McLeish 7
Mead 17
Melton 59
Melvin 95
Mesquita 47
Mimms 9
Moffat 40
Montacute 88
Moor 14
Morton 59
Murray 40

Newark 70
Newcastle 85
Nicholson 34
Nicolson 34
Nisbit 40
Norfolk 40
Norris 77
Norrish 17

O'Neil 74
Orleton, de 58

Paiba 47
Parker 58
Parkhurst 78
Parsons 17

Passey 9
Pecham 59
Pedler 40
Peniston 87
Percy 91
Pilkington 71, 75
Plantagenet 23, 24
Plumpton 65
Pollexfen 17
Praty 85
Prideaux 40
Purkiss 41
Pyel 65

Radcliffe 79
Radnor 87
Raikes 40
Rede 80, 85
Redvers 69
Repingdon 76
Reynell 69
Reynolds 67
Richmond 85
Ridge 40
Roberts 85
Romeyn, le 70
Ross 59
Rotherham 59
Rowntree 46, 114
Russell 50, 102

Saint Leger 40
Salisbury 101
Salkeld 40
Scrope 113, 114
Secker 81
Senior 68
Shaftesbury 70
Sharp 52
Sitwell 33
Skayman 78
Slater 103

Smerdon 16
Smith 25, 99
Spedding 15
Spencer 33
Spiers 47
Stanley 36
Stannard 78
Stevens 81
Stewarts 27
Stockman 25
Stonor 65
Strathmore 105
Stratton 86
Stratton, de 86
Surtees 71
Sutton 75, 76
Swinfield 58
Sydenham 70

Talbot 101
Tallick 25
Tapper 17
Tate 90
Tellick 25
Thomas 98
Thynne 87
Tinley 48
Tison 91
Titford 40
Tooms 15
Toops 17
Tounson 87
Townshead 78
Treadgold 48
Treswell 77
Trumbull 101
Tudor 24
Tuke 46
Tunstall 71
Turner 50
Tyrell 40

Urquhart 94

Vining 7

Wagner 40
Wakefield 87
Waldby 113
Wallace 76
Walter 7
Waltham 59
Warne 70
Warneford 87
Welles, de 58
Wenlok 65
Wharton 116
Whichcot 76
Whitaker 87
Whitbread 65
Whitelocke 52
Whiteway 70
Whithed 107
Wigg 40
Wilberforce 66, 81
Willoughby 69
Wilton 40
Winchelsey 58
Windeat 17
Wise 69
Wood 69, 79
Woodforde 80
Woodleigh 17
Woodlock 58
Woodward 86
Woolway 15
Worthington 40
Wrey 17
Wright 14
Wyatt 84

Yelland 50
Young 71

Author Index

Abbott, P. 43
Ablitt, P. 115
Ackers, C. 7
Ackers, J. 7
Adam, F. 13
Adam, R. 94
Adams, B. 73
Adams, I. 94
Adams, R. 37, 81
Adams, S. 65
Adamson, D. 94
Addison, W. 37
Ainsworth, J. 56
Albert, W. 107
Alcock, E. 73
Alcock, N. 37
Alcock, S. 73
Alderson, B. 88, 89
Allen, C. 7
Allen, D. 105
Allen, M. 84, 99
Allen, N. 20
Altman, A. 101
Anderson, M. 39
Anderson, R. 99
Anderson, S. 101
Anderson, T. 43
Anderson, W. 26
Annesley, C. 114
Anstey, H. 80
Appleby, D. 105
Appleby, J. 105
Apted, M. 94
Archer, M. 76
Ashcroft, L. 104
Aspin, C. 75
Atkins, P. 32
Atkinson, J. 71
Austin, J. 9
Aveling, H. 80
Aveling, J. 60
Avery, S. 87
Axton, M. 63
Axton, R. 63
Ayres, J. 48
Ayton, C. 8

Baber, A. 87
Baggott, C. 57
Bagley, J. 74

Bagshaw, S. 26
Baildon, W. 91
Bailey, D. 82
Bailey, M. 84
Baker, C. 12
Baker, D. 65
Baker, G. 78
Baker, L. 32
Baker, W. 8, 30, 31
Ballard, A. 51
Banks, C. 22
Bannister, A. 58
Barber, H. 13, 99
Barclay, R. 94
Baring-Gould, S. 13
Barker, E. 59
Barlow, F. 51
Barlow, J. 72
Barnard, R. 115
Barnes, F. 67
Barnes, P. 64
Barnes, T. 100
Barnett, L. 47
Barnett, R. 47
Barnsley Archives and Local Studies Dept. 115
Barratt, D. 57, 58, 81
Barrett, J. 46, 47
Barriskill, D. 109
Barron, C. 25
Barrow, J. 51, 99
Barry, J. 72
Basing, P. 77
Battye, K. 68
Bayley, N. 42
Beardwood, A. 81
Bearman, R. 69
Beasley, J. 111
Beaton, E. 94
Beattie, A. 98
Beauchamp, P. 81
Beauroy, J. 52
Beckett, J. 52, 68
Beckett, R. 83
Beckinsale, R. 86
Beckwith, F. 92
Bedingfeld, A. 77
Beeson, F. 81
Bell, P. 8, 66
Bennett, J. 26

Bennett, M. 79
Bennett, N. 59
Bennison, B. 110
Beresford, M. 48
Berry, J. 112
Berryman, B. 84
Besse, J. 46
Bettey, J. 70
Bevan, A. 100
Beverly, S. 94
Beverly, W. 94
Bickley, F. 101
Bigland 72
Bird, C. 37
Bird, J. 33
Bird, Y. 37
Bishop, L. 11
Bisset, A. 115
Black, A. 103
Black, J. 77
Blagg, T. 55, 56
Blair, C. 70
Blaydes, F. 99
Blomefield, F. 78
Blundell, N. 74
Boase, C. 79
Boatwright, L. 67
Boersma, O. 62
Bolitho, W. 27
Bolton, J. 81
Bond, S. 88
Bonsey, C. 66
Booker, J. 112
Booth, P. 74
Boswell, G. 70
Boumphrey, R. 67
Bourgeois, E. 67
Bourn, J. 82
Bourne, J. 69
Bourne, S. 8
Boutflower, D. 70
Bowers, G. 28
Bowker, M. 76
Bowler, H. 60
Brace, H. 75, 76
Bradley, A. 47
Brander, M. 24
Brandow, J. 22
Brassley, P. 67
Brault, G. 8, 65

141

Brears, P. 90
Breckon, B. 15
Brent, A. 89, 91
Brent, J. 112
Bridgeman, I. 52
Bridger, C. 13
Briers, P. 81
Brinkworth, E. 82
Britton, T. 110
Broad, J. 67
Brockett, A. 68
Brocklesby, R. 59
Bromell, A. 41
Bromley, R. 73
Brooke-Little, J. 42
Brown, M. 15-17
Brown, N. 40
Brown, O. 40
Brown, P. 84
Brown, R. 64
Brown, S. 113
Brown, W. 70, 90
Browning, D. 9
Brunskill, E. 88
Buchanan, A. 115
Bullock-Anderson, J. 109
Bullock-Davies, C. 8
Bulmer, J. 74
Burch, B. 109
Burch, D. 10
Burg, J. 114
Burgess, C. 72
Burke, A. 13
Burke, B. 26
Burke, J. 13, 22
Burns, C. 94
Burton, E. 59
Burton, J. 113
Bury, M. 67
Bush, R. 111
Bushby, D. 65
Butler, D. 112
Butler, L. 67, 91

Cairns-Smith-Barth, J. 31
Cale, M. 100
Cameron, A. 93
Cameron, V. 13
Camp, A. 22
Campbell, A. 97
Campbell, R. 50
Capes, W. 58
Carlin, M. 12
Carpenter, C. 65
Carr, A. 74
Carr, D. 87
Carstairs, N. 92
Carstairs, S. 92

Carter, C. 43
Carter, J. 31
Carter, N. 43
Cash, M. 68
Catlett, E. 18
Chadwick, R. 18
Chambers, B. 12, 13
Chambers, J. 13
Chandler, J. 87
Chapman, C. 22, 30
Chapman, J. 107
Chapman, L. 46
Chapman, S. 69
Charlesworth, J. 89
Cheney, C. 51, 64
Chew, H. 77, 86
Chibnall, A. 66
Chibnall, M. 64
Child, H. 13
Child, K. 39
Childs, W. 91
Chinnery, A. 82
Christensen, P. 27
Christian, P. 25
Chuk, F. 36
Church, R. 19
Cirket, A. 57, 65, 101
Clanchy, M. 86
Clapinson, M. 81
Clark, A. 79
Clark, G. 66
Clark, J. 92, 109
Clark, P. 76
Clark, R. 68
Clarke, A. 28
Clay, C. 90, 91
Clay, J. 70, 90
Cleveland, D. 99
Clifford, F. 68
Clifford, H. 39
Clifford, J. 68
Clwyd Record Office 63
Cockburn, J. 65, 82
Cokayne, G. 54
Colby, F. 99
Coldham, P. 13, 22, 23, 99
Cole, C. 9, 14, 15
Cole, J. 15, 19
Coleman, M. 67
Collett-White, J. 66
Collins, F. 89, 90
Collins, R. 48
Colwell, S. 28, 48, 100
Conyers, A. 86
Cook, A. 43
Cook, F. 43
Cook, M. 68
Cooper, J. 81

Cooper, L. 70
Cooper, M. 88
Cordeaux, E. 80, 81
Corder, J. 61, 84
Cornwall, J. 82
Cory, K. 23
Cory, M. 61
Cory, V. 61
Costen, M. 82
Couth, B. 77
Cowan, M. 87
Cowper, A. 94
Cox, J. 39, 100
Cox, M. 61, 94
Craig, H. 95
Craster, E. 81
Craven, M. 68
Crawshay, G. 33
Creagh, O. 43
Creaton, H. 52, 62
Crellin, V. 18
Crisp, F. 26, 27
Crispin, M. 23
Crittall, E. 87
Crook, D. 100
Crook, J. 107
Cross, A. 109
Cross, C. 91, 114
Crossley, D. 85
Crossley, E. 26
Crouch, D. 33, 98
Crowder, N. 23
Crowe, E. 32
Crowley, D. 87
Crowther, J. 52
Crowther, P. 52
Crozier, W. 13
Culliford, M. 99
Currer-Briggs, N. 26, 37, 39, 40
Currie, C. 48
Curtis, M. 15

Dale, A. 40
Dale, C. 86
Daly, A. 84
Danbury, E. 37
Dance, E. 84
Darlington, I. 37, 77
Darlington, R. 64
Davenport, I. 103
Davey, C. 107
Davey, R. 85
Davidson, F. 94
Davies, J. 98
Davis, F. 58, 59
Deadman, H. 109
De Boer, G. 71

142

Deedes, C. 85
Dell, R. 85, 112
Dendy, F. 70
Denning, R. 98
Denny, A. 83
Dewar, P. 39
Diack, L. 95
Dale, A. 40
Dale, C. 86
Daly, A. 84
Danbury, E. 37
Dance, E. 84
Darlington, I. 37, 77
Darlington, R. 64
Davenport, I. 103
Davey, C. 107
Davey, R. 85
Davidson, F. 94
Davies, J. 98
Davis, F. 58, 59
Deadman, H. 109
De Boer, G. 71
Deedes, C. 85
Dell, R. 85, 112
Dendy, F. 70
Denning, R. 98
Denny, A. 83
Dewar, P. 39
Diack, L. 95
Dibben, A. 112
Dicker, G. 36
Dickinson, F. 67, 73
Dickinson, H. 71
Dickinson, R. 67, 73
Dobb, J. 17
Doble, C. 79
Dobson, D. 13, 17, 23, 92
Dobson, R. 71
Dodd, K. 83
Dodwell, B. 64
Doe, V. 68
Dollarhide, W. 27
Donald, J. 66
Doree, S. 73
Dorward, D. 25
Douglas, D. 51
Douie, D. 59
Dowler, G. 37
Draisey, J. 69
Drake, M. 11
Drennan, B. 37
Drucker, L. 56
Drury, C. 89, 90
Du Boulay, F. 58
Dudley-Higham, M. 18
Duncan, J. 19
Duncan, P. 18
Dunkin, E. 85

Dunkin, H. 85
Dunlop, A. 46, 94
Dunn, F. 103
Dunn, J. 41
Dunn, R. 78
Dunning, R. 38
Dunsire, A. 18, 97
Dunstan, G. 58, 59, 68
Durrant, P. 66
Dwelly, E. 19
Dymond, D. 52, 78

Easson, D. 93
Ebden, E. 64
Edmunds, M. 99
Edward, S. 72
Edwards, F. 38
Edwards, K. 58, 59
Edwards, P. 8
Eedle, M. 18
Eldred, N. 39
Eldrid, J. 39
Elliott, D. 38
Ellis, J. 71
Ellis, M. 100
Elrington, C. 58, 72, 86
Elvey, E. 66
Elvey, G. 66
Emery, A. 32
Emmison, F. 30, 38, 99, 105, 106
Emsley, C. 115
Emsley, K. 71, 91
English, B. 91
Erikson, C. 19
Erskine, A. 68, 69
Escott, A. 117
Eustace, J. 11
Evans, C. 33
Evans, E. 52
Evans, M. 79
Evans, N. 84, 99
Evans, P. 114
Ewen, C. 13
Exwood, E. 89

Fairbairn, J. 23
Faraday, M. 65, 67
Farie, J. 97
Faris, D. 23
Farr, B. 86, 87
Farr, M. 86
Farrar, M. 103
Farrell, J. 109
Farrow, M. 56
Fearn, J. 46
Felstead, A. 32
Fendley, J. 72

Fenwick, C. 52
Ferguson, J. 27, 116
Ferguson, K. 95
Fernie, E. 78
Filby, P. 99
Finch, H. 110
Finch, M. 76
Finlay, R. 62
Finnegan, R. 10, 11
Fisher, P. 19
Fitch, M. 57
Fitzhugh, T. 8
Fitzsimmons, L. 46
Fletcher, C. 90
Fletcher, D. 90
Fletcher, I. 67
Fletcher, J. 80, 81
Fletcher, S. 25
Flood, S. 73
Flynn, B. 71
Fonge, C. 114
Foot, W. 100
Ford, W. 85
Forster, A. 71
Foster, C. 54-58, 75
Foster, D. 52
Foster, I. 73
Foster, J. 13, 32
Fowkes, D. 68
Fowle, J. 86
Fowler, S. 100
Fox, H. 69
France, R. 108
Franklin, J. 32
Franklin, M. 51
Franklin, P. 19, 48
Fraser, C. 71, 91
Freeman, G. 9
Freeman, J. 47, 87
Freeth, S. 112
French, E. 23
Frere, M. 58
Friar, S. 8, 48
Frith, B. 72
Frostick, C. 78
Fry, E. 53-56
Fry, G. 53-55
Fyfe, J. 94

Galloway, J. 12
Gambier, R. 26, 37
Gandon, J. 62
Gandy, M. 15, 21, 22
Gardiner, D. 69
Gardner, N. 63
Garnett, E. 25
Garratt, H. 68
Garratt, J. 22

Garrett-Pegge, J. 27
Gatley, D. 83
Gerard, T. 82
Gerhold, D. 40
Gervers, M. 52
Gervis, J. 34
Gibbons, A. 27
Gibson, J. 23, 81, 82
Giese, L. 77
Gilchrist, G. 94
Gilkes, R. 82
Gilling, I. 68
Gillow, J. 59, 60
Gitton, G. 47
Glass, D. 77
Glencross, R. 56
Goddard, J. 61
Golby, J. 11
Goldie, D. 27
Goldschmidt-Lehmann, R. 62
Goode, A. 82
Goodison, J. 67
Goodman, A. 58
Goose, N. 49
Gore, D. 24
Goulden, R. 73
Graham, I. 14, 65
Graham, M. 81
Graham, R. 58
Grannum, G. 100
Gransden, A. 83
Grant, F. 14, 53, 54
Grant, J. 65
Grant, R. 33
Graves, A. 29
Gray, A. 97
Gray, I. 62
Gray, T. 17, 69
Gray, V. 52
Greatrex, J. 107
Greaves, R. 66
Greenhill, F. 75
Greenwell, W. 70
Grieve, H. 106
Griffiths, B. 25
Griffiths, R. 58
Grimwade, M. 57
Grinter, J. 25
Groves, J. 34, 35
Gurney, N. 89, 90
Guy, A. 105
Guy, J. 33, 98
Guy, S. 49
Gwynn, R. 62
Gwynne, R. 62
Gwynne-Jones, P. 61

Habberjam, M. 91

Haines, R. 88, 101
Haines, T. 78
Hains, G. 57
Hainsworth, D. 71
Hale, B. 91
Hall, C. 67
Hall, D. 38
Hall, T. 89, 90
Hall, W. 54
Hamilton-Edwards, G. 38
Hammond, P. 48
Hampson, G. 107
Hamshaw, R. 89
Hands, A. 62
Hanham, A. 69
Hanks, P. 35
Hanna, K. 107
Hannabuss, S. 94
Hansell, M. 89
Hansen, A. 35
Hansom, J. 59, 60
Hansom, S. 59
Harding, V. 77
Hardwick, N. 72
Hargreaves-Mawdesley, R. 14
Hargreaves-Mawdesley, W. 80
Harington, D. 7
Harley, J. 82
Harper-Bill, C. 51, 59, 84
Harris, A. 90
Harris, G. 77
Harris, P. 60
Harrison, H. 14
Harrot, J. 32
Hartopp, H. 54, 55
Harvey, B. 65
Harvey, J. 38
Harvey, P. 52, 107
Harvey, R. 63, 109
Harvey, W. 40
Hassall, W. 52, 64, 81
Hastings, R. 113
Hawgood, D. 25
Hawgood, P. 25
Hawkings, D. 20, 21, 48
Haydon, R. 32
Hayton, T. 66
Hearne, T. 79
Heath, J. 68
Heber, M. 48
Hembry, P. 87
Henderson, A. 47
Henderson, J. 26
Henly, H. 87
Henson, N. 117
Herber, M. 23
Heseltine, P. 103

Hewitt, L. 118
Hey, D. 35
Hicks, J. 88
Hill, J. 76, 78
Hill, R. 59, 75, 76
Hinde, G. 71
Hinds, A. 101
Hinton, R. 76
Hitchcock, T. 77
Hitching, F. 14
Hitching, S. 14
Hobbs, J. 67
Hobbs, S. 87
Hobson, C. 43
Hobson, M. 80
Hockey, S. 65, 107, 108
Hodges, F. 35
Hodgett, G. 76, 77
Hodgson, J. 70
Hodsdon, J. 72
Hoffman, M. 23
Holden, J. 61
Holdsworth, C. 79
Holles, J. 79
Holmes, C. 83
Holt, G. 60
Holt, J. 64
Holton, G. 48
Holworthy, R. 20
Homer, R. 38
Hook, P. 60
Hopkins, A. 33
Horn, J. 59
Horn, P. 81
Horrox, R. 91
Horwitz, B. 46
Horwitz, H. 63, 100
Hoskin, P. 51, 114
Hoskins, W. 26, 38, 68
Houghton, J. 15
Houlbrooke, R. 78
Howard, J. 27
Howard-Drake, J. 58, 81, 110
Howden, M. 70
Howells, C. 23
Hoyle, R. 72, 89, 91, 100
Hudleston, C. 67, 71
Hughes, E. 107
Hull, P. 68, 69
Humphery-Smith, C. 38
Humphrey, S. 111
Humphries, V. 9
Humphris, E. 43
Hunnisett, R. 52, 79, 85, 87, 100
Hunter, D. 94
Hurley, M. 21
Hurst, N. 28

Hutchinson, F. 81
Hyde, P. 7, 81

Ifans, D. 117
Imrie, J. 94
Imrie, M. 28
Ince, L. 33
Iredale, D. 38, 46, 47
Irvine, S. 7
Irving, J. 103

Jackson, A. 69
Jacob, E. 58
James, A. 92
James, J. 70
Jeffries, R. 61
Jelsma, A. 62
Jenkins, A. 81
Jenkins, C. 56
Jenkins, J. 66
Jenkinson, H. 62
Jewell, H. 91
John, T. 52
Johnson, A. 35
Johnson, C. 58
Johnson, G. 95
Johnson, H. 86
Johnson, M. 25
Johnston, J. 76
Johnstone, C. 14, 27
Jones, F. 61
Jones, J. 38, 99
Jones, N. 117
Joseph, R. 80
Josselin, R. 51
Jurkowski, M. 100

Keats-Rohan, K. 8
Keene, D. 77
Kellaway, W. 77
Kelly, B. 22
Kemp, B. 47, 65
Kemp, T. 46
Kenny, A. 60
Kerridge, E. 86
Kershaw, I. 90
Ketchell, C. 115
Kettle, P. 68
Kidd, R. 10
Kimball, E. 67, 76, 81
King, A. 73
King, H. 90
King, N. 39
Kingsbury, S. 27
Kingsford, C. 65
Kingsley, D. 85
Kirby, D. 71
Kirby, I. 112

Kirby, J. 40, 65, 87, 92
Kirk, J. 46, 52, 94
Kirkus, A. 76
Kitching, C. 38, 46, 71, 77
Klieforth, A. 40
Knight, F. 67
Knox, G. 20
Konrad, J. 50
Kowaleski, M. 69
Kreckeler, D. 67
Kussmaul, A. 66

Laffin, J. 48
Lamara, J. 108
Lambert, A. 67
Lambrick, G. 81
Lamming, D. 28
Lancaster, W. 91
Lang, R. 77
Lang, S. 72
Langston, B. 103
Langton, F. 60
La Rocca, J. 60
Lart, C. 14
Law, B. 29
Lawrance, N. 90, 91
Laws, D. 29
Lawson, J. 95
Lawton, G. 25
Lee, G. 39
Lee, J. 109
Lee, R. 65
Leech, R. 72
Lees, B. 51
Leese, T. 27
Leeson, F. 23, 40
Lehmann, R. 62
Leith, R. 95
Le Patourel, J. 92
Leslie, I. 7
Lewis, C. 48
Lewis, R. 27, 115
Lewis, S. 24
Liddell, B. 52
Lilly, D. 20
Lilly, J. 20
Lindsay, E. 93
Liquorice, M. 103
Litzenberger, C. 72
Llewellyn, H. 33
Lloyd, C. 76
Lobb, D. 30
Lock, R. 84
Lodge, E. 51
Loengard, J. 77
Loewe, C. 47
Lomas, R. 71
London, V. 68, 87

Longden, H. 57
Longley, K. 113
Loomes, B. 8
Lowe, J. 107
Lower, M. 27
Lumas, S. 8, 100
Lumb, G. 88, 92
Lutt, N. 66
Lynskey, M. 38

Mabbs, A. 8
Maber, R. 30
Macary, L. 23
Macfarlane, A. 51
Macgibbon, J. 34
Machin, R. 70
Macintyre, S. 94
Maclean, J. 14
Macray, W. 36
Madan, F. 36
Madge, N. 48
Madge, S. 54
Magrath, J. 80
Major, K. 75, 76
Malcolm, C. 93
Mallory-Smith, S. 40
Marcan, P. 32
Marcombe, D. 49
Marett, W. 87
Marmoy, C. 62
Marsh, J. 107
Marshall, G. 14
Marshall, L. 65
Martin, C. 14, 38
Martin, G. 83
Martin, J. 108
Martine, R. 32
Martins, S. 78
Maslen, M. 81
Mason, A. 106
Mason, E. 77
Mason, I. 112
Massil, S. 62
Masters, B. 77
Matthews, J. 59, 60
Maxted, I. 17, 32, 33
Mayett, T. 66
Mayr-Harting, H. 58
McAdam, J. 94
McBeth, S. 31
McCall, H. 89
McCann, A. 112
McCann, T. 85, 112
McCoog, T. 60
McDermid, R. 91
McDermott, P. 43
McDonald, A. 46
McDonnell, F. 14

145

McGregor, M. 65
McGurk, F. 94
McHardy, A. 76, 77
Mckenna, J. 113
McKinley, R. 30
McLane, B. 76
McLaren, M. 27
McLaughlin, E. 9, 10, 15, 31
Mcleish, N. 7
Mcleish, P. 7
Medlycott, M. 20, 23
Meekings, C. 84, 86, 88
Meeres, F. 110
Meredith, R. 116
Merry, D. 80, 81
Merson, D. 95
Message, C. 43
Metters, G. 78
Michelmore, D. 90
Midgley, L. 64
Milburn, G. 71
Millard, A. 41
Miller, S. 97
Millett, G. 27
Millett, S. 14
Millican, P. 57
Mills, A. 70
Mills, D. 62, 63
Mills, M. 84
Milne, A. 64
Milward, R. 33, 68
Mimms, P. 9
Mitchell, A. 93
Mitchell, W. 80, 81
Mitchinson, A. 63
Moffat, F. 40
Moir, J. 55
Moody, D. 24
Moore, J. 40
Moreton, C. 63, 78
Morgan, F. 51
Morgan, K. 72
Morgan, P. 49, 88
Morgan, R. 65
Morgan, T. 49
Morland, S. 82
Morris, J. 38
Morrison, J. 87
Mortimer, E. 95
Mortimer, I. 66, 101
Mortimer, J. 90
Mortimer, R. 84, 90
Morton, M. 89
Moulton, J. 25
Mulgrew, M. 90
Mullet, M. 52
Mullins, E. 64
Munby, L. 52

Munckton, T. 20
Muncton, T. 50
Munro, J. 94
Murphy, M. 12, 52, 60
Murphy, W. 86
Murray, J. 33, 34
Murray, M. 33, 34
Myhill, O. 12

Neill, N. 34
Neilson, N. 51
Neininger, F. 51
Nesbitt, R. 40
Neville, G. 77
Newsome, A. 34
Newsome, E. 114
Newsome, W. 114
Nicholls, Y. 65
Nicholson, G. 14
Nicholson, N. 34
Noble, C. 78
Noble, W. 55
Nolan, D. 68
Norden, J. 67
Northeast, P. 84
Norton, J. 64
Nussey, J. 88
Nuttal, G. 101

Oakley, A. 62
O'Byrne, W. 43
O'Connor, S. 65
Oestman, C. 9
Oliver, A. 70
O'Neil, J. 74
O'Regan, M. 91
Osborne, N. 112
Outhwaite, R. 25
Owen, A. 76-78, 103
Owen, D. 52, 59, 67, 76, 103
Owen, G. 101
Owen, W. 90
Owens, B. 117
Oxley, G. 115

Padel, O. 69
Pafford, J. 86
Page, M. 107
Pain, J. 12
Paley, R. 77
Pantin, W. 80, 81
Park, P. 36
Parker, J. 15
Parkhurst, J. 78
Parkinson, E. 98
Parrish, P. 20, 21
Parsons, K. 67
Pastoureau, M. 48

Patterson, R. 72
Paver 90
Payne, D. 32
Pearce, C. 62
Pearce, T. 111
Pedler, F. 40
Pelling, G. 15
Pellow, A. 98
Percy, J. 71
Perkins, J. 74
Perry, T. 9
Peskett, H. 69
Peyton, S. 75
Phillimore, W. 53, 54, 58
Phillipart, J. 43
Phillips, C. 71
Phillipson, L. 103
Pickles, J. 67
Pine, L. 26
Pinfield, L. 32
Pinkerton, J. 94
Piper, A. 71
Place, J. 92
Playne, E. 71
Plomer, H. 55
Pobst, P. 59
Pocock, S. 41
Pollen, J. 60
Pols, R. 8, 15
Ponsford, C. 69
Portass, V. 71
Porter, S. 88
Postles, D. 30
Potter, G. 68
Potts, R. 69
Pound, J. 84
Pounds, N. 69
Pracy, D. 34
Pratt, D. 46
Precious, J. 105
Preece, F. 19
Preece, P. 19
Preston, C. 89, 90
Price, F. 38, 81
Price, M. 33
Price, V. 9
Priddey, M. 58
Priddy, M. 81
Prideaux, R. 40
Priestley, U. 78
Pritchard, M. 40
Proudfoot, K. 39
Pryce, W. 10
Pryde, E. 64
Pugh, R. 66, 81, 86, 87
Purcell, M. 41
Purkiss, M. 41
Purkiss, T. 41

146

Purves, A. 43, 45
Purvis, J. 113

Quick, B. 9
Quick, K. 9, 10
Quick, P. 10
Quintrell. 106

Raikes, R. 40
Raine, J. 70
Ralph, E. 72
Ramsay, G. 86
Ramsey, F. 51
Ransford, R. 9
Ransome, M. 86, 87
Rathbone, M. 86
Ravendale, J. 67
Rawcliffe, C. 68
Readhead, M. 115
Readman, A. 112
Reakes, J. 7
Reaney, P. 35
Redmonds, G. 42, 99
Reed, M. 66, 67, 83
Reeves, M. 87
Reid, A. 52
Reid, J. 24
Reilly, L. 108, 111
Renold, P. 82
Reynolds, S. 58
Rhodes, J. 72
Rice, R. 85
Richards, G. 80
Richardson, D. 72
Richardson, H. 88, 90
Richardson, J. 28, 38
Richter, M. 59
Richwood, D. 77
Rickard, G. 42
Rickard, R. 86
Riden, P. 33, 68
Ridgard, J. 84
Ridge, C. 56, 57
Ridge, D. 40
Rigg, J. 62
Roberts, F. 115
Roberts, J. 115
Roberts, S. 88
Roberts, T. 14
Robinson, D. 59, 101, 113
Robinson, J. 35, 40
Robinson, L. 91
Robinson, O. 59
Rodger, N. 100
Rodrigues-Pereira, M. 47
Roebuck, P. 90
Rogers, C. 23, 27, 32, 73, 74
Rogers, J. 79

Rogers, K. 87
Romilly 67
Romney, P. 91
Rosenheim, J. 78
Rosie, A. 116
Ross, B. 85
Ross, J. 97
Round, J. 14
Rowe, D. 71
Rowe, M. 69
Rowlands, J. 24
Rowlands, S. 24
Rowley, P. 89
Roy, I. 81, 88
Rudd, E. 118
Ruddock, N. 90
Rumble, A. 70
Ruston, A. 42
Ruthven-Murray, P. 40, 92
Rutledge, P. 77
Ruvigny & Raineval, Marquis of 24
Rycraft, A. 114

Sachse, W. 77
Saint Leger 40
Sainty, J. 63
Sale, A. 72
Salinger, P. 62
Salter, H. 58, 80
Salter,H. 80
Salzmann, L. 85
Sandell, R. 86
Saul, P. 15
Saunders, P. 67
Saville, R. 85
Schafer, R. 88
Schofield, J. 77
Schürer, K. 63
Scott, M. 100
Scottish Record Office 116, 117
Scouloudi, I. 62
Searle, A. 65
Searle, E. 85
Secker, T. 81
Seddon, P. 79
Seeliger, S. 107
Serjeant, R. 57
Serjeant, W. 57
Sessions, E. 46
Sessions, W. 46
Sharp, R. 52
Sharpe, J. 106
Sharpe, R. 28
Sharples, M. 92
Sharratt, M. 60
Shaw, G. 32

Shaw, W. 14
Sheils, W. 113, 114
Sheldrick, G. 73
Sheppard, J. 32
Shorney, D. 100
Shorrocks, D. 111
Short, B. 85
Short, D. 76
Siddons, M. 61, 118
Sillem, R. 75
Silverthorne, E. 84
Simons, J. 47
Simpson, J. 74, 75
Sims, R. 14
Sinclair, C. 117
Singlehurst, K. 71
Siraut, M. 20
Sitwell, G. 33
Skeggs, J. 20, 21
Slack, P. 86
Slade, C. 64, 81
Slater, J. 103
Sleigh, A. 49
Slocombe, P. 113
Sludder, E. 109
Smith, A. 12, 78
Smith, C. 49, 50, 100
Smith, D. 64, 89, 113-115
Smith, F. 19, 24
Smith, H. 71
Smith, J. 32, 53
Smith, K. 100
Smith, M. 89, 90
Smith, R. 62
Smith, S. 95
Smith, V. 85
Snelling, S. 48
Somerset County Library Service 20
Somerville, R. 38
Southwick, M. 29
Spalding, R. 52
Spencer, E. 47
Spencer, J. 47
Spencer, W. 100
Spicer, A. 62
Spiers, R. 47
Spokes, P. 80
Spurrell, M. 76
Squibb, G. 41, 61
Squire, R. 25
Stafford, G. 9
Stagg, D. 107
Staines, E. 41
Stanes, R. 69
Stanewell, L. 115
Stanford, M. 72
Stanley, P. 36

147

Stapleton, B. 79
Steer, F. 30, 85, 112
Stembridge, P. 73
Stenton, D. 64
Stenton, F. 51
Stephens, R. 30
Stephens, W. 38, 52
Stevenson, D. 64
Stevenson, J. 87
Steward, A. 83
Stewart, A. 94
Stoate, G. 20
Stoate, T. 21
Stockdill, R. 48
Stoker, D. 78
Stokes, E. 55
Stone, E. 81
Stones, A. 74
Storey, R. 59
Strathspey, Lord 39
Stride, S. 69
Stuart, D. 38
Stuart, J. 57
Stuart, M. 24
Stuart, R. 24
Styles, L. 31
Summers, P. 38
Summerson, H. 69
Surry, N. 107
Susser, B. 49
Sutton, A. 25
Sutton, D. 90
Swanson, R. 59, 113, 114
Sweeney, P. 32

Tamblin, S. 20, 100
Tamplin, J. 43
Tanner, N. 65
Tanner, R. 46
Tarver, A. 39
Tate, W. 39, 49
Taylor, A. 97
Taylor, B. 12
Taylor, H. 88
Taylor, J. 24, 88
Taylor, K. 74
Tearle, J. 30
Tepper, M. 24
Thacker, A. 103
Thomas, G. 100
Thomas, H. 33
Thomas, J. 107
Thomas, W. 98
Thompson, A. 58, 71, 75
Thompson, E. 58
Thompson, J. 66
Thompson, W. 58
Thomson, R. 83

Thomson, W. 75
Thorne, R. 105
Thornton, D. 8
Thurley, C. 57
Thurley, D. 57, 67
Thwaite, H. 90
Tibbutt, H. 65
Tiller, K. 48
Tillott, P. 88
Timmins, T. 59, 87
Tinley, R. 48
Tipper, A. 32
Tippey, D. 25
Titford, J. 15, 40
Titterton, J. 38
Tittler, R. 85
Todd, A. 7
Todd, J. 67, 72
Tohill, M. 113
Torrance, D. 92
Torrie, E. 94
Toynbee, M. 81
Tranter, N. 94
Trappes-Lomax, R. 60
Travers, A. 66
Tremlett, T. 65
Trinder, B. 39
Tringham, N. 91
Tucker, G. 48
Turner, J. 51
Turton, W. 24
Twining, A. 49
Twining, S. 49
Tyrwhitt-Drake, B. 10

Unwin, R. 52
Upton, C. 81

Vage, J. 105
Venables, J. 112
Vickers, N. 91
Vincent, N. 51, 59
Vinogradoff, P. 51

Wade, J. 72
Wade-Matthews, M. 26
Wadsworth, F. 56
Wagner, A. 39, 40, 65
Walker, D. 72
Wall, A. 87
Wallace, M. 95
Wallace, N. 95
Walne, P. 118
Walton, M. 68, 90
Wanklyn, M. 47
Ward, J. 106
Ward, K. 102
Ward, W. 61, 85, 107

Warne, H. 112
Warne, J. 70
Warneford, F. 87
Warner, J. 49
Waters, H. 14, 99
Watkin, A. 77, 82
Watkinson, J. 42
Watkinson, W. 68
Watson, F. 95
Watts, C. 100
Watts, M. 100
Watts-Williams, J. 118
Way, G. 25
Wearing, J. 46
Weaver, J. 81
Webb, A. 20, 21
Webb, C. 57, 114
Webb, J. 83, 84
Webb, P. 35, 36
Webster, J. 49
Webster, W. 79
Weddall, G. 89
Weikel, A. 91
Weinbaum, M. 77
Weinstock, M. 69
Weir, N. 35, 36
Welch, E. 66, 68
Wells, P. 57
Wells, R. 42
Wenham, L. 115
Wenham, P. 90
West, J. 39
Westcott, B. 49
Whetter, J. 30
White, A. 9
White, P. 107
Whitehead, B. 90
Whitehill, G. 47
Whitelocke, B. 52
Whiteway, W. 70
Whittingham, A. 78
Whyte, D. 14, 99
Wigfield, W. 82
Wigram, S. 79
Wilberforce, S. 81
Wilkerson, J. 67
Wilkes, I. 26
Wilkinson, P. 112
Williams, B. 87
Williams, C. 70, 118
Williams, D. 112
Williams, J. 60
Williams, N. 86
Williams, S. 87
Williamson, T. 78
Willing, J. 97
Willis, A. 39, 107
Wills, M. 39, 78

Wills, V. 117
Wilshere, J. 26
Wilson, E. 25, 89, 92
Wilson, J. 12, 50, 66
Wilson, M. 95
Wilson, R. 35
Wilton, R. 40
Winch, J. 48
Winchester, A. 67
Withers, C. 50

Wood, A. 58, 79
Wood, H. 70
Woodcock, T. 35, 65
Woodward, G. 82
Wooldridge, J. 112
Worrall, E. 60
Worthington, J. 40
Wright, D. 59
Wright, G. 47
Wright, L. 77

Wright, P. 82
Wyatt, I. 72
Wyatt, P. 69

Yaxley, D. 78
Yelland, G. 50
Youings, J. 68
Young, M. 46
Youngs, F. 64

Place Name Index

Aberdeenshire 31, 96
  Aberdeen 18, 31, 95, 96
  Aberdeen. Frederick Street 95
  Aberdeen. John Knox Church 95
  Aberdeen. Old Town 96
  Aberdeen. Saint Clement 96
  Aberdour 95, 96
  Aboyne 95
  Alford 95
  Auchindoir 95
  Auchredie 96
  Belhelvie 95
  Birse 93
  Botarie 96
  Bourtie 95
  Braemar 93, 95
  Chapel of Garioch 95
  Cluny 95
  Crathie 93
  Crimond 95, 96
  Culsalmond 95
  Daviot 95
  Drumblade 95
  Drumoak 96
  Dumbennan 96
  Dyce 95, 96
  Echt 95
  Ellon 95
  Essie 96
  Fetterangus 95
  Fintray 96
  Fraserburgh 96
  Fyvie 95
  Gartly 96
  Glass 96
  Glenmuick 95
  Hatton of Fintray 95
  Keig 93
  Keithhall 95
  Keithhall & Kinkell 95
  Kincardine O'Neil 93, 95
  Kinellar 96
  King Edward 95
  Kinnoir 96
  Leslie 95
  Logie Durno 95
  Longside 96
  Lonmay 95, 96
  Millbrex 95
  Monymusk 95
  New Deer 95, 96
  Newhills 95, 96
  Old Deer 96
  Old Machar 96
  Old Meldrum 95
  Peathill 95
  Peterculter 95
  Peterhead 95, 96
  Pitsligo 96
  Rathen 96
  Rattray 95
  Rhynie 96
  Ruthven 96
  Skene 96
  Strathbogie 96
  Strathdon 93
  Strichen 96
  Tough 96
  Tyrie 96
  Udny 96
  Upper Deeside 93
  Upper Donside 93
  Woodhead 95

Anglesey 11

Angus 13, 17, 18, 92
  Arbroath 92
  Brechin 92
  Broughty Ferry 92
  Dundee 18, 92
  Forfar 92
  Kirriemuir 92
  Montrose 92
  Old Pert 98

Argyll 18, 45, 94, 97
  Inveraray 94
  Keil 93
  Kilmun 93
  Kinlochlaich 93
  Kintyre 94
  Loch Leven. Isla Munda 93

Ayrshire 97, 98
  Ayr 98
  Barnwell 98
  Carrick 93
  Coodham 98
  Coylton 98
  Craigie 98
  Crosbie 98
  Culzean 98
  Dundonald 98
  Fairfield 98
  Kilmarnock 93
  Kyle 98
  Largs 97
  Loudoun 93
  Monkton 98
  Newton Green 98
  Newton on Ayr 98
  Old Alloway 98
  Prestwick 98
  Saint Quivox 98
  Symington 98
  Troon 98
  Wallacetown 98

Ayrshire, North 97

Banffshire 18, 31, 95
  Alvah 95
  Banff 31, 95
  Boyndie 95
  Cullen 95
  Deskford 95
  Fordyce 95
  Forglen 95
  Gamrie 95
  Grange 95
  Inverkeithny 95
  Marnoch 95
  Ordiquhill 95
  Rathven 95
  Rothiemay 95

Bedfordshire 11, 30, 38, 39, 44, 47, 57, 65, 66, 76, 99, 102
  Ampthill 102
  Arlesey 102
  Aspley Guise 102
  Astwick 102
  Barton le Clay 102
  Battlesden 102

Bedford 65, 66, 102
Bedford. Saint Cuthbert 102
Bedford. Saint John 102
Bedford. Saint Mary 102
Bedford. Saint Paul 102
Bedford. Saint Peter 102
Biddenham 102
Biggleswade 102
Billington 102
Bletsoe 102
Blunham 66, 102
Brook End 65
Campton 102
Cardington 65
Carlton 65
Eaton Socon 102
Edworth 102
Eggington 102
Egginton 66
Elstow 102
Eversholt 102
Everton 102
Eyeworth 102
Farndish 102
Felmersham 102
Flitton 102
Flitwick 102
Goldington 102
Great Barford 102
Harlington 102
Harrold 102
Hatley Cockayne 102
Heath 102
Henlow 102
Higham Gobion 66
Highham Gobion 102
Hockcliffe 102
Houghton Conquest 102
Houghton Regis 102
Hulcote 102
Husborne Crawley 102
Kempston 102
Kensworth 65, 102
Keysoe 65, 102
Knotting 102
Langford 102
Leighton Buzzard 102
Lidlington 102
Little Barford 102
Little Staughton 102
Lower Gravenhurst 102
Luton 102
Marston Moretaine 102
Maulden 102
Melchbourne 102
Meppershall 102

Millbrook 102
Milton Bryan 102
Milton Ernest 102
Northill 102
Oakley 102
Odell 102
Old Warden 102
Pavenham 102
Pertenhall 102
Podington 102
Potsgrove 102
Potton 102
Pulloxhill 102
Ravensden 102
Reach 102
Renhold 102
Ridgmont 102
Riseley 102
Roxton 102
Salford 102
Sandy 102
Sharnbrook 102
Shefford 102
Shelton 102
Shillington 102
Souldrop 102
Southill 65, 102
Stagsden 102
Stanbridge 102
Steppingley 103
Stevington 65, 103
Stotfold 103
Streatley 66, 103
Studham 103
Sundon 103
Sutton 103
Swineshead 103
Tempsford 103
Thurleigh 103
Tilbrook 103
Tilsworth 103
Tingrith 103
Toddington 103
Tottenhoe 103
Turvey 66, 103
Upper Gravenhurst 103
Upper Stondon 103
Westoning 103
Whipsnade 103
Wilden 103
Willington 103
Wilshampstead 103
Woburn 102, 103
Wootton 103
Wrestlingworth 103
Wymington 103
Yelden 103

Berkshire 11, 38, 39, 44, 65, 66
  Abingdon Abbey 81
  Hidden 61
  Reading 66
  Reading Abbey 65

Berkshire Archdeaconry 53

Berkshire, North 81, 82

Berwickshire 71
  Birgham 96
  Eccles 96
  Fogo 96
  Greenlaw 96
  Leitholm 96
  Mertoun 96
  Polwarth 96

Breconshire 11
  Aberyscir 29
  Brecon Archdeaconry 117
  Llanapyddid 29
  Llandefailogfach 29
  Llandeilo'rfan 29
  Llanfihangel Fechan 29
  Llanfihangel Nantbran 29
  Llywel 29

Breconshire, South West 29

Buckinghamshire 9-11, 13, 38, 39, 44, 66, 67
  Amersham 10
  Aylesbury 10
  Aylesbury Hundred 10
  Beaconsfield 10
  Bledlow 9
  Boarstall 80
  Buckingham 10
  Buckingham Archdeaconry 66
  Buckingham Hundred 10
  Chalfont Saint Peter 10
  Chalfonts 10
  Chenies 10
  Chesham 10, 27
  Cottesloe Hundred 10
  Great Hampden 10
  High Wycombe 9, 66
  Horwoods 10
  Iver 10
  Latimer 10
  Long Crendon 66
  Luffield Priory 66
  Marlow 10
  Milton Keynes 10

Buckinghamshire (*cont.*)
Missenden Abbey 66
Missendens 10
Newport Hundred 10
Newport Pagnell 10
Princes Risborough 9, 10
Quainton 10, 66
Shenley 10
Stoke Poges 10
Stony Stratford 10
West Wycombe 9
Whaddon 10
Wycombe 10

Bute 92, 97
Arran 92
Cumbrae 92

Caernarvonshire 11
Bangor Diocese 117

Caithness 92
Bower 92
Canisbay 92
Dunnet 92
Halkirk 92
Latheron 92
Olrig 92
Reay 92
Thurso 92
Watten 92
Wick 92, 97

Cambridgeshire 38, 39, 67, 103
Cambridge 67
Cambridge. Christ's College 67
Cambridge. Clare College 67
Cambridge. Sidney Sussex College 67
Cambridge. West Fields 67
Crowland 103
Downham 67
Ely 67
Ely Diocese 57, 103
Fenstanton 67
Fowlmere 67
Isleham 67
Little Paxton 67
Wisbech 103

Cardiganshire 11

Carmarthenshire 11

Carmarthenshire, North East 29

Channel Islands 27, 45
Guernsey 67
Sark 63

Cheshire 11, 38, 39, 44, 74, 103
Chester 63, 74, 103
Chester Diocese 7, 74, 103
Macclesfield 75, 103
Malpas 74
Northwich Hundred 74
Saltney 103
Stockport 104

Cheshire, North East 35

Connaught 45

Cornwall 11, 25, 26, 38-40, 44, 50, 55, 56, 64, 68, 69, 104
Bodmin 41
Chasewater 24
Gulval 27
Jacobstow 18
Lanisley 27
Launceston Priory 69
Penhallym 18
Saint Buryan 56
Saint Michael's Mount 68

Cornwall, North 18

Cumberland 11, 38, 67, 70, 71
Carlisle 74
Carlisle Diocese 58, 59
Copeland 74
Lanercost 67, 72
Naworth 71
Underwood 67

Denbighshire 11, 51, 118
Llangollen 118

Derbyshire 11, 19, 38, 39, 44, 48, 61, 68
Buxworth 61
Calke Abbey 46
Chapel en le Frith 68
Chesterfield 68
Chinley 61
Derby 53
Dronfield 68
Eckington 22
Eyam 68
High Peak 61
Kniveton 101
Ockbrook 25

Renishaw 33
Scarsdale 68
Sutton cum Duckmanton 68

Devon 11, 16, 17, 19, 25, 30, 33, 38, 39, 44, 50, 55, 56, 68, 69, 99, 102, 104, 105
Ashburton 16, 17, 69
Ashreigney 9, 14
Beer Ferrers 16
Belstone 16
Bickleigh 16
Bishop's Nympton 14
Brentor 16
Buckfastleigh 16
Buckland 16
Buckland in the Moor 16, 17
Buckland Monachorum 16
Burrington 15
Canonsleigh Abbey 68
Chagford 16
Coldridge 14
Cornwood 16
Dartmoor 16, 17
Dartmoor, Western 17
Dean Prior 16
Drewsteignton 16
Dunsford 16
Exeter 38, 68, 69
Exeter. Cathedral 69
Exeter Diocese 51, 55, 58, 59, 68, 105
Forde 69
Gidleigh 16
Harford 16
Holne 16
Hooe 16
Horrabridge 16
Ilsington 16, 17
Ivybridge 16
Kelly 16
Kitley 17
Kitley House 17
Lamerton 16
Leusdon 16
Leyhill 69
Lustleigh 16
Lydford 16
Manaton 16
Maristow 17
Mary Tavy 16
Meavy 16
Meavy Chapel 16
Moretonhampstead 16
North Bovey 16
North Molton 14

152

Peter Tavy 16
Plymouth 16, 22, 68
Plympton Saint Mary 16
Plympton Saint Maurice 16
Postbridge 16
Princetown 16
Providence Place 16
River Exe 69
Saint Budeaux 16
Sampford 16
Scoritton 16
Shaugh Prior 16
Sheepstor 16, 17
Sourton 16
South Brent 16
South Molton 14
South Tawton 16
Stoke Damerel 16
Sydenham 69
Sydenham Damerel 16
Tavistock 16
Tawstock 17, 69
Throwleigh 16
Tiverton 15, 69
Topsham 69
Uffculme 69
Ugborough 16
Walkhampton 16
Whitchurch 16
Widecombe 16, 17
Widworthy 32
Woodbury 18
Zoar Down Chapel 16

Devon, West 16

Dorset 11, 20, 38, 39, 44, 54, 55, 61, 70, 105, 107
Beaminster 18
Bournemouth 107
Dorchester 70
Horn Hill 18
Knowle Court 18
Lulworth Castle 60
Lyme Regis 49
Mapperton 70
Melcombe Regis 69
Poole 70
Puddletown 70
Weymouth 69

Dumfriesshire 14, 27, 96, 117
Annan 94, 96

Dunbartonshire 93, 97

Durham 11, 38, 45, 71, 105
Benfieldside 50
Blackhill 50
Castleside 50
Consett 50
Conside 50
Darlington 71
Durham Diocese 70, 71
Durham. Cathedral 71
Gibside 39, 78, 105
Healeyfield 50
Knitsley 50
Medomsley 50
Muggleswick 50
Shotley Bridge 50
Streatlam 105
Sunderland 71

Essex 11, 30, 34, 37-39, 44, 52, 106
Colchester Archdeaconry 106
Crondon Park 60
Essex Archdeaconry 106
Nazeing 34
Nazeing Wood 34
Waltham Abbey 9

Essex, North 105

Fermanagh
Enniskillen 44

Fife 17, 18, 97
Cairneyhill 97
Dunfermline 94, 97
Dunfermline Abbey 93
Inchcolm 93
Inverkeithing 97
Kirkcaldy 18, 97
Saint Andrews 17, 18

Flintshire 11, 74, 118
Holywell 60

Forfarshire
Arbroath 94
Craig 95

Galloway 92, 96, 117

Glamorgan 11, 33, 98, 118
Cardiff 33
Cowbridge 33
Fonmon Castle 118
Ilston 117
Llandaff Diocese 33, 98
Margam 118

Merthyr Tydfil 33, 118
Neath 33
Pennard 99
Swansea 33

Gloucestershire & Bristol 11, 37-39, 44, 48, 53-55, 72, 106
Arlingham 15
Bibury 53
Bishop's Cleeve 53
Bristol 14, 22, 53, 60, 61, 72, 73, 106, 107
Bristol. All Saints 72
Bristol. Saint Augustine's Abbey 72
Bristol Diocese 54
Cheltenham 72
Chipping Campden 11, 61
Gloucester 72
Gloucester Diocese 53, 54, 72
Gloucester. Cathedral 72
Gloucester. Saint Peter's Abbey 72
Quinton 61
Stanway 61
Tewkesbury 72
Vale of Evesham 61

Gloucestershire, North 61

Hampshire 11, 13, 25, 34, 38, 39, 44, 61, 107, 108
Beaulieu Abbey 65
Carisbrooke Priory 108
Isle of Wight 25, 39, 41, 108
New Forest 107
Portsmouth 107
Quarr Abbey 108
Sheet 107
Southampton 62, 108
Southwick Priory 107
Winchester 59, 108
Winchester. Cathedral 107
Winchester. Saint Swithun's Priory 107
Winchester Diocese 39, 51, 58, 108

Herefordshire 11, 38, 39, 45, 65, 108
Hereford Diocese 58

Hertfordshire 11, 38, 39, 45
Amwell 73
Baldock 18

153

Barley 67
Berkhamstead 49
Bishops Stortford 73
Gorhambury 39
Hertford 73
Saint Albans 49, 73

Huntingdonshire 11, 38, 39, 45, 55, 103
  Hail Weston 65
  Kimbolton 65
  Saint Neots 65

Inverness-shire
  Abernethy 93
  Abertarff 93
  Alvie 93
  Andersier 93
  Boleskine 93
  Bone 93
  Chisholm 94
  Conwinth 93
  Croy 93
  Dalarossie 93
  Dalcross 93
  Devlot 93
  Dores 93
  Dunlichity 93
  Duthil 93
  Garten 93
  Glenormiston 93
  Insh 93
  Inverallan 93
  Inverness 54, 93
  Inverness. Old Hugh 97
  Kilmorack 93
  Kiltarlty 93
  Kincardine 93
  Kingussie 93
  Kirkhill 93
  Laggan 93
  Moy 93
  Petty 93
  Rothiemurchus 93
  Speyside 93
  Urquhart 93

Inverness-shire, West 93

Ireland 14, 17, 26, 39, 44, 45, 50

Isle of Man 27

Kent 8, 11, 34, 38, 39, 42, 45, 47, 51
  Aldington 12
  Ashford 12

Barming 12
Bearstead 12
Bethersden 12
Bexley 108
Bilsington 12, 51
Bircholt 12
Bonnington 12
Boughton Aluph 12
Boughton Malherbe 12
Boughton Monchelsea 12
Brabourne 12
Brook 12
Broomfield 12
Canterbury 39, 42
Canterbury Diocese 39, 42, 51, 55, 56
Canterbury. Saint Augustine's Abbey 51
Challock 12
Charing 12
Chart Sutton 12
Chilham 12
Crundale 12
Deptford 77
Dover 40
East Farleigh 12
East Sutton 12
Eastwell 12
Egerton 12
Faversham 73
Faversham Hundred 7
Godmersham 12
Great Chart 12
Harrietsham 12
Hastingleigh 12
Headcorn 12
Hinxhill 12
Hothfield 12
Hurst 12
Hurton 12
Kennington 12
Kingsnorth 12
Langley 12
Leeds 12
Lenham 12
Linton 12
Little Chart 12
Loose 12
Maidstone 12
Maidstone Union 12
Marden 12
Mersham 12
Molash 12
Nettlestead 12
Orlestone 12
Otham 12
Otterden 12
Pluckley 12

Rochester. 7
Rochester Diocese 42, 58
Ruckinge 12
Sevington 12
Shadoxhurst 12
Smarden 12
Smeeth 12
Staplehurst 12, 42
Sutton Valence 12
Tenterden 42
Teston 12
Ulcomb 12
Warehorne 12
West Farleigh 12
Westwell 12
Willesborough 12
Wychling 12
Wye 12
Yalding 12

Kent, East 42, 43

Kent, West 42

Kincardineshire 31, 93
  Dunnottar 95
  Durris 95
  Fettercairn 95
  Glenbervie 95
  Marykirk 95
  Portlethen 94
  Strachan 96

Kinrossshire 97

Kirkcudbrightshire 93, 97
  Applegarth 97
  Auchencairn 93
  Balmaclellan 93
  Balmaghie 93, 97
  Borgue 93
  Buittle 93, 97
  Canonbie 97
  Carsphairn 93, 97
  Colvend 93
  Corsock 93
  Creetown 93, 97
  Crossmichael 93, 97
  Cummertrees 97
  Dalbeattie 93
  Dalry 93, 97
  Dundrennan Abbey 93
  Dunrod 93
  Durisdeer 97
  Galtway 93
  Gatehouse of Fleet 93
  Gelston 93
  Girthon 93, 97

Kirkcudbrightshire
  (*continued*)
  Johnstone 97
  Kells 93
  Kelton 93
  Kirkandrews 93
  Kirkbean 97
  Kirkchrist 93
  Kirkcormack 93
  Kirkcudbright 92, 93, 97
  Kirkdale 93
  Kirkgunzeon 93, 97
  Kirkirkbean 93
  Kirkmabreck 93, 97
  Kirkpatrick Durham 93
  Kirkpatrick Irongray 93
  Lincluden College 93
  Lochrutton 93, 97
  Minnigaff 93, 97
  Newabbey 93
  Orr 93
  Parton 93, 97
  Perrick 93
  Sandgreen 93
  Senwick 93
  Southwick 93
  Stell 93
  Terregles 93, 97
  Tongland 93, 97
  Troqueer 93
  Twynholm 93

Lanarkshire 93, 97
  Glasgow 18, 97
  Hamilton 7, 54
  Upper Ward 93

Lancashire 7, 11, 30, 38, 43-45, 63, 74, 108
  Amounderness 74
  Ashton in Makerfield 74
  Ashton under Lyne 73
  Blackley 73
  Burnley 14
  Childwall 73
  Chorley 73
  Chorlton 73
  Clitheroe 74
  Colton 73
  Copp 74
  Copp Chapel 74
  Dolphinholme 74
  Eccles 73
  Egton 74
  Finsthwaite 75
  Furness Deanery 74
  Halton 73
  Heaton Norris 73
  Helmshore 75
  Hindley 74
  Hollinfare 73
  Hopcar 60
  Ireleth 73
  Lancaster 33, 38, 73
  Little Crosby 74
  Liverpool 14, 23, 44, 60, 75, 108
  Lonsdale 71
  Lonsdale Deanery 74
  Manchester 44, 73
  Merseyside 103
  Newland 74
  Prescot 73, 74
  Preston 41, 74
  Rivington 74
  Rusland 73
  Saint Michaels on Wyre 74
  Salford 109
  Southport 14
  Southport. Haweside 14
  Stockport 74
  Todmorden 74
  Towneley Hall 59
  Ulverston 67
  Urswick 73
  Warrington 73
  Wigan 109
  Woodplumpton 73

Lancashire, East 44

Lancashire, North 44, 67

Lancashire, South 44

Leicestershire 11, 19, 26, 38, 39, 44, 54, 55, 75, 76, 109
  Allexton 26
  Evington 26, 54
  Groby 54
  Leicester 26
  Leicester Archdeaconry 55
  Leicester. Saint Margaret 54, 55
  Leicester. Saint Martin 26
  Leicester. Saint Mary de Castro 26
  Market Harborough 15
  Ratby 26
  Rothley 55

Leinster 45

Lincolnshire 11, 17, 19, 27, 38, 39, 44, 48, 75, 76, 109
  Boston 76
  Fleet 51
  Gainsborough 75, 76
  Grantham 77
  Great Gonerby 48
  Harpswell 76
  Holland 76
  Kesteven 75, 76
  Lincoln 76
  Lincoln Archdeaconry 75
  Lincoln Diocese 54, 55, 57-59, 75-77
  Lincoln. Cathedral 75
  Lindsey 76
  Lindsey Marsh 77
  Revesby Abbey 76
  Spalding 76
  Stamford 76
  Stow in Lindsey Archdeaconry 56
  Stowe 76

London & Middlesex 10, 12, 22, 25, 27-29, 32, 33, 37-41, 43-47, 52, 53, 54, 55, 60, 62, 69, 77, 106, 109
  Alderney Road Cemetery 49
  Aldgate. Holy Trinity 77
  Bermondsey 8
  Bethnal Green 8
  Chelsea. Saint Luke 77
  Christ's Hospital 22
  City of London 109
  Clerkenwell 64, 77
  Enfield 61
  Foundling Hospital 66
  Hackney 77
  Haggerstone West 8
  Hillingdon 110
  London Archdeaconry 57
  London Bridge 77
  London Diocese 51, 56, 57, 77
  Poplar 8
  Regents Park 8
  Saint Botolph without Aldersgate 77
  Saint Pancras 8
  Shoreditch 8
  Spitalfields 61, 62
  Threadneedle Street 62
  Tower Hamlets 110
  Westminster 41, 65
  Westminster Abbey 77
  Westminster. Saint Margaret 61

Lothian 18, 43, 94

Merionethshire 11

Midlothian
Borthwick 98
Carrington 98
Cockpen 98
Colinton 98
Cranston 98
Edinburgh 46, 53, 92-94
Edinburgh. Canongate 92
Edinburgh. Dean Cemetery 93
Edinburgh. Duddingston 93
Edinburgh. New Town 92
Edinburgh. Old Town 92
Fala 98
Glencross 98
Heriot 98
Soutra 98
Tron 92

Monmouthshire 11, 39, 45, 60, 99
Llanarth 60
Llanthony Priory 72
Monmouth 60
Perthir 59
Tredegar 99
Welsh Bicknor. Courtfield 60

Montgomeryshire 11
Montgomery 86

Moray 18
Aberlour 93
Advie 93
Bellie 93
Cromdale 93
Elgin 31
Forres 31
Inverallan 93
Inveraven 93
Knockando 93
Rothes Speymouth 93
Speyside 93

Nairnshire 31
Geddes 97

Norfolk 11, 12, 19, 26, 34, 37, 38, 41, 44, 64, 78
Creake Abbey 77
East Raynham 78
Great Yarmouth 77
Holkham Hundred 52
Houghton Hall 78
Hunstanton 9
Kings Lynn 47
Norwich 37, 77, 78
Norwich. Cathedral 78, 110
Norwich Archdeaconry 77
Norwich Diocese 51, 56, 57, 59, 65, 78
Stiffkey 12, 78
Thetford Priory 52, 78
Wiggenhall 78
Wymondham 12

Northamptonshire 11, 19, 30, 38, 44
Northampton Archdeaconry 53, 56, 57, 75, 82
Rothwell 65

Northumberland 11, 38, 43, 70, 71
Callaly 60
Felton 78, 79
Morpeth 78
Newcastle upon Tyne 46, 70-72, 110

Nottinghamshire 11, 19, 38, 39, 44, 48, 56, 61, 70, 79
Nottingham Archdeaconry 71
Rufford 79
Southwell 56
Upton 79

Orkney 18, 94

Oxfordshire 11, 30, 38, 39, 44, 58, 61, 80-82
Bampton Hundred 81
Banbury 82
Begbroke 79
Benson 9
Charlbury 15
Eynsham 80
Hailey 15
Henley 81
Kidlington 79
Oseney Abbey 80
Oxford 35, 79-81
Oxford. All Souls College 81
Oxford. Balliol College 38, 80
Oxford. Bodleian Library 36
Oxford. Canterbury College 80, 81
Oxford. Exeter College 79
Oxford. Gloucester College 80
Oxford. Keble College 37
Oxford. Magdalen College 36
Oxford. Merton College 80, 81
Oxford. New College 30, 86
Oxford. Oriel College 80
Oxford. Queens College 79
Oxford. Saint Frideswide 79
Oxford. Saint Johns College 81
Oxford. University 79-81
Oxford Diocese 57, 58, 81
Sandford Saint Martin 15
Whitchurch 81
Wigginton 38, 81
Witney 81
Woodstock 81
Yarnton 79

Peebleshire 93, 94

Pembrokeshire 11
Pembroke 86
Saint Davids Diocese 99

Perthshire 18
Abernyte 98
Carse of Gowrie 93
Dunblane Diocese 94
Dunkeld 93
Inchture 98
Kinnoul 98
Longforgan 98
Perth 93, 98
Strathmore 93

Perthshire, East 93

Perthshire, North 93

Radnorshire 11

Renfrewshire 93, 97
Arthurlie 93
Bridge of Weir 93
Cathcart 93
Eaglesham 93
Eastwood 93
Erskine 93
Gourock 93
Greenock 93

Houston 93
Inchannan 93
Inverkipp 93
Johnstone 93
Kilbarchan 93
Kilellan 93
Kilmacolm 93
Lochwinnoch 93
Mearns 93
Neilston 93
Paisley 31, 33, 34, 93
Paisley Abbey 34
Pollokshaws 93
Port Glasgow 93
Renfrew 93

Ross & Cromarty 45
Ardgay 93
Avoch 97
Croick 97
Dingwall 97
Easter Suddie 97
Fearn 94
Fortrose 97
Killearnan 97
Killearnon 97
Kilmuir 97
Kiltearn 97
Kincardine 93, 97
Knockbain 97
Old Alness 97
Tain 97
Wester Ross 93

Roxburghshire
Bedrule 96
Crailing 96
Eckford 96
Edgerston 96
Ednam 96
Hounam 96
Hume 96
Kelso 96
Lempitlaw 96
Linton 96
Makerstoun 96
Maxton 96
Morebattle 96
Nisbet 96
Oxnam 96
Roxburgh 96
Rulewater 40
Smailholm 96
Sprouston 96
Stichill 96
Yetholm 96

Rutland 9, 19, 30, 38, 39, 53, 75, 76, 82

Caldecott 55
Liddington 55
Oakham 9, 82
Tixover 55

Scotland 7, 8, 13, 14, 17, 18, 22-27, 31, 32, 34, 38, 39, 44, 46, 48, 50, 64, 65, 92-95, 116-118

Scotland, Highlands 14, 18, 45

Scotland, North 95

Scotland, North East 18, 31, 95

Scotland, Southern 18

Scotland, West 18

Scottish Borders 27, 44

Shetland 18, 98

Shropshire 11, 26, 38, 39, 44, 110
Bridgnorth 47
Coalbrookdale 39
Dawley 39
Lilleshall 39
Telford 39
Wellington 39
Wrockwardine 39

Somerset 11, 19-21, 25, 38, 39, 41, 44, 48, 61, 82, 111
Abbots Leigh 20
Aisholt 21
Axbridge 20
Backwell 20, 82
Banwell 20
Barrow Gurney 20
Bath 60, 69, 82, 106
Bath & Wells Diocese 21, 51
Berrow 20
Blagdon 20
Bleadon 20
Brean 20
Brent Knoll 20
Bridgwater 20
Brockley 20
Burnham 20
Burrington 20
Butcombe 20
Carhampton 21
Charlinch 21
Charterhouse 20
Cheddar 20
Christon 20

Churchill 20
Clapton in Gordano 20
Clevedon 20
Compton Bishop 20
Congresbury 20
Creech Saint Michael 21
Dundry 20
East Brent 20
Easton in Gordano 20
Enmore 21
Exmoor 20
Failand 20
Flax Bourton 20
Glastonbury 82
Hewish 20
Highbridge 20
Hutton 20
Kenn 20
Kewstoke 20
Kingston Seymour 20
Locking 20
Long Ashton 20
Loxton 20
Luccombe 21
Luxborough 21
Lympsham 20
Martock 30
Nailsea 20, 82
North Petherton 20
Nyland cum Batcombe 20
Oake 21
Portbury 20
Portishead 20
Puxton 20
Ridgehill 20
Rowberrow 20
Selworthy 21
Shipham 20
Sidcot School 20
Stoke Pero 21
Taunton Archdeaconry 55
Tickenham 20
Timberscombe 21
Treborough 21
Uphill 20
Walton in Gordano 20
Wells 82
Weston Super Mare 20
Wick Saint Lawrence 20
Wilton 20, 21
Winford 20
Winscombe 20
Withycombe 21
Wootton Courtenay 20
Worle 20
Wraxall 20
Wrington 20
Yatton 20

157

Somerset, East 20

Somerset, North 20

Somerset, South 82

Staffordshire 11, 38, 39, 83, 111
  Alton 82
  Biddulph 83
  Black Country 111
  Bradeley 83
  Brierley Hill 83
  Burntwood 83
  Chase Terrace 83
  Chasetown 83
  Dudley 83
  Edial 83
  Hanley 111
  Keele 111
  Lichfield 53, 111
  Milwich 83
  Penn 83
  Stoke upon Trent 83
  Walsall 111
  Wednesbury 29
  Wolverhampton 9
  Woodhouses 83

Staffordshire, North 45

Staffordshire, South 44

Stirlingshire 97
  Airth 93
  Baldernock 93
  Balfron 93
  Bothkennar 93
  Buchanan 93
  Buchlyvie 93
  Callendar 94
  Cambuskenneth 93
  Campsie 54, 93
  Denny 93
  Dennyloanhead 93
  Drymen 93
  Dunipace 93
  Falkirk 93, 94
  Fintry 93
  Gargunnock 93
  Inchcaillench 93
  Killearn 93
  Kilsyth 93
  Kippen 93
  Kirk O'Muir 93
  Larbert 93
  Lennoxtown 93
  Logie 93

Muiravonside 93
Plean 93
Polmont 93
Saint Ninians 93
Slamannan 93
Stirling 93, 94, 96
Strathblane 93

Stirlingshire, East 93

Stirlingshire, West 93

Suffolk 8, 11, 26, 34, 38, 41, 44, 61, 83, 84
  Babergh Hundred 84
  Blythburgh Priory 84
  Boxford 84
  Bury Saint Edmunds 51, 83, 84
  Butley Priory 84
  Clare 84
  Dodnash Priory 84
  Dunwich 84
  East Bergholt 83
  Eye Priory 84
  Framlingham 84
  Great Waldingfield 28
  Hoo 83
  Ipswich 83, 84
  Leiston Abbey 84
  Sibton Abbey 83, 84
  Stoke by Clare 84
  Sudbury 84
  Sudbury Archdeaconry 57, 84
  Suffolk Archdeaconry 57, 84
  Walsham le Willows 83, 84

Surrey 12, 25, 34, 38, 39, 57, 84, 111
  Cheam 59
  Mitcham 84
  Nunhead 111
  Peckham 111
  Richmond 60
  Southwark 12, 111
  Sutton 111
  Wimbledon 33, 84

Surrey, East 44

Surrey, West 43

Sussex 12, 25, 30, 34-36, 38-40, 44, 47, 85, 100
  Arundel Castle 112, 116
  Ashdown Forest 85

Battle Abbey 85, 99, 112
Boarzell 85
Brighton 40
Burwash 35
Chichester Deanery 56
Chichester Diocese 55, 56, 58, 85, 112
Chichester. Cathedral 112
Chiddingley 35
Cowdray 59
East Dean 35
Eastbourne 35, 59
Edburton 54
Ewhurst 35
Goodwood 112
Greatham 112
Hailsham 35
Hartfield 35
Hastings 35, 36
Hickstead Place 112
Horsham 112
Lewes 35, 85
Lewes Archdeaconry 54, 85
Midhurst 59
Newhaven 35
Petworth House 112
Pevensey 35
Pevensey Rape 35
Rottingdean 35
Rye 85
Saint Leonards 36
Slindon 60
South Malling 54, 85
Ticehurst 35
Uckfield 35
Winchelsea 112
Withyham 35

Sussex, East 54, 85

Sussex, West 112

Sutherland 45, 93

Wales 14, 22, 24, 26, 27, 31, 32, 39, 44, 49, 61, 117, 118

Wales, South 44, 59, 118

Warwickshire 12, 19, 38, 43
  Birmingham 53, 113
  Coventry & Lichfield Diocese 51, 53, 59
  Kineton Hundred 52
  Merevale 9
  Stoneleigh 37
  Stoneleigh Hundred 52
  Wootton Wawen 59

West Lothian 93, 94
 Bathgate 92
Westmorland 12, 38, 67, 70, 71, 104
 Kendal Deanery 74
 Rydal 80
Wigtownshire
 Applegarth 117
 Balmadellan 117
 Canonbie 117
 Cummertrees 117
 Durisdeer 117
 Johnstone 117
 Portpatrick 94, 96
 Wigtown 117
Wiltshire 12, 13, 38, 39, 44, 54, 55, 60, 86, 87
 Aldbourne 61
 Alton Barnes 86
 Amesbury 86
 Berwick Bassett 61
 Bradenstoke Priory 87
 Bradford on Avon 87
 Bratton 87
 Bromham 87
 Calne 86
 Clatford 61
 Colerne 86
 Great Chalfield 86
 Highworth 86
 Highworth Hundred 86
 Lacock Abbey 87
 Longleat 87
 Malmesbury 86
 Mere 61
 Salisbury 86, 87
 Salisbury Diocese 58, 59, 86
 Sevenhampton 87
 Steeple Ashton 61
 Stert 86
 Trowbridge 86
 Vale of Pewsey 61
Wiltshire, North 61
Worcestershire 12, 38, 44, 113
 Bromsgrove 87
 Evesham 80, 88
 Kings Norton 87
 Stour Valley 88
 Tardebigge 9
 Worcester 88
 Worcester. Cathedral 64
 Worcester Diocese 51, 54, 55, 87, 88

Yorkshire 29, 38, 41, 44-46, 60, 70, 71, 90, 91, 113, 114
 Acomb 88, 90
 Ainsty 60
 Almondbury 88
 Alwoodley 28
 Askham Bryan 88
 Askham Richard 88
 Austerfield 88
 Baildon 28
 Bainbridge 115
 Batley 15
 Beverley 46, 91
 Bilsdale 115
 Birstall 88
 Bishopthorpe 88
 Blyth 88
 Bolton Priory 90
 Bowes 88
 Bracewell 28
 Bradford 28
 Bradford. Great Horton 28
 Bradford. Kirkgate Chapel 28
 Bradford. Sion Chapel 29
 Bradford. Toad Lane Chapel 29
 Braithwell 88
 Bramhope 28
 Brandsburton 88
 Bubwith 89
 Buckrose Deanery 91
 Burley 28
 Burton Agnes 28
 Calverley 28
 Carlton in Craven 28
 Castle Bolton 29
 Clayton 28
 Cleveland 113
 Cleveland Archdeaconry 71
 Clifton 28
 Collingham 89
 Craven 91, 115
 Craven Deanery 90
 Dent 74
 Dewsbury 15
 Dickering 90
 Doncaster 46
 Dunkeswick 28
 Easingwold 89
 East Keswick 28
 East Riding 12, 44, 113, 115
 East Riding Archdeaconry 71
 Eccleshill 28
 Elland 28
 Esholt 28

Everingham 60, 90
Farsley 28
Flamborough 91
Fountains Abbey 90
Fylingdales 115
Giggleswick 89
Goole 91
Great Horton 28
Greetland 28
Halifax 26, 46
Harewood 28
Hartshead 28
Hawksworth 28
Heckmondwike 28
Heslington 89
Holme on Spalding Moor 60
Hornby Castle 25
Howden 89
Hull 28, 41, 46, 91, 115
Hull. Westbourne Avenue 115
Hunsworth 28
Ilkley 28
Keighley 28
Kilburn 28
Kirk Deighton 89
Kirkstall 91
Leeds 28, 46, 90, 92
Leeming Bar 28
Lythe 89
Malton 115
Masham 89
Menston 28
Middleton 28
Myton upon Swale 89
Nidd 60
North Riding 12, 15, 113, 115, 116
Oswaldkirk 29, 89
Otley 28, 92
Owston 89
Pontefract 46, 92
Pool 28
Raskelf 89
Riccall 89
Richmond 91, 115
Richmond Archdeaconry 71
Riseborough 46
Rokeby 89
Scarborough 115
Scruton 89
Settle 116
Settrington 89, 90
Sheffield 46, 89, 90, 116
South Cave 52
South Otterington 28

Yorkshire (*continued*)
Spofforth 28
Stanningley 28
Stansfield 29
Swaledale 116
Swillington 28
Thirsk 29
Thornton 29
Thorpe Bassett 90
Thrybergh 28
Todmorden 28, 29
Tong 28, 29
Wadworth 90
Wakefield 28, 46, 91, 92
Walsden 28
Walton 90
Weardley 28
Weeton 28
Wensley 90
West Riding 12, 29, 44
Wetherby 28, 29
Wharfedale 92
Wigton 28
Wike 28
Yeadon 29
York 29, 46, 60, 71, 90, 91, 113-115
York. Minster 113, 114
York. Saint Giles 29
York. Saint Mary Bishophill Junior 90
York. Saint Mary Castlegate 90
York. Saint Maurice 29
York. Saint Michael Spurriergate 114
York Archdeaconry 71
York Diocese 59, 113, 114
York Province 46, 71

Overseas

Africa 72

America 17

Australasia 18

Australia 7, 10, 18, 41, 49, 67, 72, 97, 109
South Australia 50

Belgium
Bruges 60

Canada 18, 45, 50, 95

Europe 17

France
Avignon 94
Bec 64
Douai 60
Saint Omer 60

India
Bengal 43

Ireland
Dublin 45

Italy
Rome 46, 60, 93

New Zealand 34, 41, 97

North America 14

Portugal
Lisbon 60

Russia
Crimea 43

South Africa 43
Natal 43

Spain
Seville 60

United States 13, 14, 18, 22-24, 27, 34, 49, 50, 72
Carolinas 23
Maryland 23
Massachusetts. Boston 22
New England 22, 47, 99
Virginia 23, 37

West Indies 18, 100